Lecture Notes in Computer Science 15831

The series Lecture Notes in Computer Science (LNCS), including its subseries Lecture Notes in Artificial Intelligence (LNAI) and Lecture Notes in Bioinformatics (LNBI), has established itself as a medium for the publication of new developments in computer science and information technology research, teaching, and education.

LNCS enjoys close cooperation with the computer science R & D community, the series counts many renowned academics among its volume editors and paper authors, and collaborates with prestigious societies. Its mission is to serve this international community by providing an invaluable service, mainly focused on the publication of conference and workshop proceedings and postproceedings. LNCS commenced publication in 1973.

Sara Riva · Adrien Richard
Editors

Cellular Automata and Discrete Complex Systems

31st IFIP WG 1.5 International Workshop, AUTOMATA 2025
Lille, France, June 30 – July 2, 2025
Proceedings

Springer

Editors
Sara Riva
Université de Lille
Villeneuve d'Ascq, France

Adrien Richard
Université Côte d'Azur
Sophia Antipolis, France

ISSN 0302-9743 ISSN 1611-3349 (electronic)
Lecture Notes in Computer Science
ISBN 978-3-032-01569-3 ISBN 978-3-032-01570-9 (eBook)
https://doi.org/10.1007/978-3-032-01570-9

This Springer imprint is published by the registered company Springer Nature Switzerland AG
The registered company address is: Gewerbestrasse 11, 6330 Cham, Switzerland

Preface

This volume contains the full papers presented at the 31st International Workshop on Cellular Automata and Discrete Complex Systems, AUTOMATA 2025, which took place between June 30 and July 2, 2025, at the University of Lille, France, colocated with the Workshop on Automata Networks. These AUTOMATA workshops aim to establish and maintain a regular, international, multi-disciplinary forum for the collaboration of researchers in the field of Cellular Automata (CA) and Discrete Complex Systems (DCS) while providing a platform for presenting and discussing new ideas and results.

These workshops support the development of theory and applications of CA and DCS (e.g. parallel computing, physics, biology, social sciences, and others) and identification and study within an interdisciplinary and multidisciplinary context of the important fundamental aspects, concepts, notions, and problems concerning CA and DCS. The AUTOMATA series is the official annual event of IFIP WG 1.5, Working Group 5 (on Cellular Automata and Discrete Complex Systems) of Technical Committee 1 (on Foundations of Computer Science) of the International Federation for Information Processing (IFIP).

At AUTOMATA 2025, we had four invited talks given by Bastien Chopard, Stefan Haar, Irène Marcovici, and Barbara Wolnik, and this volume contains an invited paper submitted by each of these speakers. Moreover, we received nineteen submissions as full papers for the conference. Each submission was single-blindly reviewed by three members of the Program Committee. Based on these reviews and an open discussion, a total of eleven papers were accepted to be presented at the conference and to be included in the proceedings. We thank all authors for their contributions and hard work that made this event possible. The conference program also involved short presentations of exploratory papers and extended abstracts that are not included in these proceedings, and we wish to extend our thanks to the authors of these additional submissions. We are indebted to the Steering Committee and the Program Committee for their valuable help during the months before the conference. We are very grateful for the support of the local Organizing Committee in ensuring all aspects of the event went smoothly. Finally, we acknowledge the excellent cooperation from the Lecture Notes in Computer Science team of Springer for their help in producing this volume in time for the conference.

June 2025

Sara Riva
Adrien Richard

Organization

Steering Committee

Pedro Paulo Balbi	Universidade Presbiteriana Mackenzie, Brazil
Nazim Fatès	Inria Centre Université de Lorraine, France
Luca Manzoni	University of Trieste, Italy
Dipanwita Roy Chowdhury	IIT Kharagpur, India
Maximilien Gadouleau	Durham University, UK

Program Committee

Jan Baetens	Ghent University, Belgium
Pedro Paulo Balbi	Universidade Presbiteriana Mackenzie, Brazil
Kamalika Bhattacharjee	National Institute of Technology, Tiruchirappalli, India
Alonso Castillo-Ramirez	Universidad de Guadalajara, Mexico
Alberto Dennunzio	Università degli Studi di Milano-Bicocca, Italy
Nazim Fatès	Inria Centre Université de Lorraine, France
Paola Flocchini	University of Ottawa, Canada
Enrico Formenti	Université Côte d'Azur, France
Maximilien Gadouleau	Durham University, UK
Anahí Gajardo	Universidad de Concepción, Chile
Pierre Guillon	CNRS & Aix-Marseille Université, France
Katsunobu Imai	Fukuyama University, Japan
Jarkko Kari	University of Turku, Finland
Kutrib Martin	Universität Gießen, Germany
Jia Lee	Chongqing University, China
Malcher Andreas	Universität Gießen, Germany
Luca Manzoni	University of Trieste, Italy
Perdo Montealegre	Universidad Adolfo Ibáñez, Chile
Ollinger Nicolas	Université d'Orléans, France
Kévin Perrot	Université Aix-Marseille, France
Adrien Richard	CNRS & Université Côte d'Azur, France
Sara Riva	Université de Lille, France
Dipanwita Roy Chawdhury	IIT Kharagpur, India
Ville Salo	University of Turku, Finland
Guillaume Theyssier	CNRS & Université Aix-Marseille, France

Ilkka Törmä	University of Turku, Finland
Barbara Wolnik	University of Gdańsk, Poland

Organizing Committee

Maxime Folschette	Centrale Lille Institut, France
Clémence Prévost	Université de Lille, France
Adrien Richard	CNRS & Université Côte d'Azur, France
Sara Riva	Université de Lille, France
Cristian Versari	Université de Lille, France

Additional Reviewers

Martin Delacourt
Augusto Modanese
Gaétan Richard
Martín Ríos-Wilson
Michiel Rollier
Felipe Santos

Contents

Determination of Platelets Properties in Blood: Combining Discrete Numerical Models with Experiments

Bastien Chopard[1](✉), Ritabrata Dutta[2], Christos Kotsalos[1], Franck Raynaud[1], and Karim Zouaoui Boudjeltia[3]

[1] Computer Science Department, University of Geneva, Geneva, Switzerland
Bastien.Chopard@unige.ch
[2] Department of Statistics, University of Warwick, Warwick, UK
[3] Laboratory of Experimental Medicine (ULB222), Faculty of Medicine, Université Libre de Bruxelles & CHU-Charleroi, Charleroi, Belgium

Abstract. Platelets are small blood particles that play a fundamental role in various physiological processes such as, for instance, the formation of clots that prevent bleeding. Their successful action depends on their adhesion and aggregation capabilities, as well as their transport properties in blood, that is their presence at a vessel wall. Their movement being affected by the shape and deformability of red blood cells within the blood flow, an accurate description of platelets transport is very challenging. Currently, medical devices aimed at the determination of platelets function often fail to detect platelets disorder. Here, we combine discrete numerical models, high performance computing, Bayesian computation with in vitro experiments to infer platelets properties for healthy and unhealthy patients.

1 Introduction

Blood is a complex fluid in the sense that it is composed of many particles in suspension in the plasma fluid. Among these particles, we are interested in platelets (PLTs), which are small disks of about 2 μm in diameter, and which plays a central role in several physiological process, such as thrombus formation and hemostastis. Platelets are transported by blood, subject to the presence of red blood cells (RBCs), abundant and deformable particles of about 8 μm in diameter, whose main function is to carry oxygen throughout the body.

Platelets disorder may accompany several diseases. An important properties of PLTs is to adhere to an injured vessel, and aggregate to form a preliminary clot. Usually, PLTs diffuse towards the vessel wall, as the result of a process call *margination*, caused by the interaction between PLTs and RBCs in an non-uniform flow.

There are several reasons that cause PLTs to dysfunction. Their concentration might be insufficient, their transport affected by pathological RBCs (e.g.

Published by Springer Nature Switzerland AG 2026
S. Riva and A. Richard (Eds.): AUTOMATA 2025, LNCS 15831, pp. 1–14, 2026.
https://doi.org/10.1007/978-3-032-01570-9_1

with abnormal shapes and deformability) and, finally, their adhesion and aggregation capabilities may be modified by a pathology.

From a clinical perspective, it is important to quantify PLTs disorder. Unfortunately, current PLTs function analyzers are not reliable enough. A direct observation of PLTs behavior on whole blood is often impossible, so PLTs properties have to be inferred from indirect experiments, such as in vitro PLTs deposition on different coated surfaces.

However, deposition experiments usually involve several competing process that are difficult to disentangle. For instance, PLTs can deposit inefficiently due to a low flux towards the surface, or because of a low adhesion rate.

In the first part of this paper (Sects. 2 and 3), we present the results of a study aimed at the determination of PLTs function. It combines deposition images of in vitro PLTs deposition and a mathematical model of the process whose parameters are the PLTs properties we are looking for. Inference algorithms, or optimization methods, are used to calibrate these unknown parameters so as to match the experimental observations.

Whereas this approach turns out to be successful, it reveals an important inconsistency with respect to the current knowledge about how PLTs diffuse in blood. In an attempt to clarify this issue, we have also developed bloodflow simulations, with fully resolved deformable RBCs and PLTs in interaction in the plasma fluid. The results of these simulations are presented in the second part of this paper, in Sect. 4. They clearly indicate that our understanding of PLTs transport is insufficient and departs from literature knowledge.

From a mathematical point of view, our approach includes discrete numerical models inspired by cellular automata, lattice Boltzmann methods, Bayesian optimization techniques, and partial differential equations, in an integrated vision. We have combined these tools with in vitro experiments of PLTs deposition and High Performance Computations (HPC) to obtain a set of new results with both clinical and fundamental relevance. The use of discrete models, whose intuitive content is large, was instrumental to create a very positive synergy between the computational approach and the experimental work.

Interested readers can find a detailed version of our findings in [2–4,6,9,10].

2 Model and Experiments

The device used to perform the PLTs deposition experiments is known as *Impact-R* [15] and is illustrated in Fig. 1. It is made of a cylinder of 1.7 cm of diameter and 0.82 mm of height that can be filled in with whole blood from donors or patients. The upper part of the cylinder is a rotating lid that creates a shear flow. The bottom part is a deposition surface on which PLTs can adhere. An area of 1 mm by 1 mm of this surface can be observed with a microscope. As time goes on, more and more PLTs deposit and form clusters that will grow in size and number.

The right panel of Fig. 1 sketches the model we propose to describe this process. PLTs move towards the deposition surface due to the so-called shear induced diffusion [17] caused by the RBCs and the imposed shear flow. Blood always contains a fraction of so-called pre-activated PLTs, that are immediately functional. The non-activated ones need special conditions be activated. Pre-activated PLTs reaching the deposition surface will adhere with a given probability, and non-activated PLTs can aggregate next to or on top of existing deposition clusters. However, as discussed in [2], albumin should be taken into account in the process, as it also deposits and prevents platelets to do so. Albumin is a very small protein which is very abundant in blood.

Albumin, PLTs (activated or not) are transported to the bottom of the cylinder through a diffusion process, that is perpendicular to the lines of flow. In our model, each of these quantities are assumed to obey a diffusion equation $\partial_t \rho = D\partial_x^2 \rho$, where ρ represents the concentration of one of the species. The initial condition is a uniform distribution along the vertical axis. The upper boundary condition is a no-flux condition. The diffusion process is coupled at the bottom of the cylinder with a particles based deposition layer model. This layer is fed by the diffusion flow $-D\partial_x \rho$ and depleted by the deposition process illustrated in Fig. 2. In this boundary layer, the concentration is interpreted as individual particles that can deposit or rebound with some probabilities that represent the deposition rates. See [2] for details.

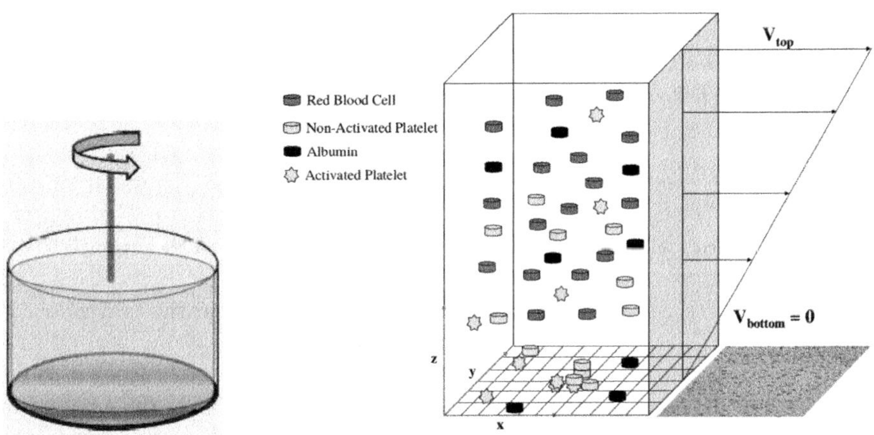

Fig. 1. Sketch of the Impact-R device and representation of the transport-deposition process.

As depicted in Fig. 2, the PLTs adhesion-aggregation process assumes that the deposition surface is discretized in square cells whose size is that of one platelet. The deposition is subject to several rules, corresponding to a stochastic cellular automata. The probability that a platelet is available for deposition is given by their number in the boundary layer, the amount of albumin already present in the cell, and the composition of the neighboring cells. While a cell

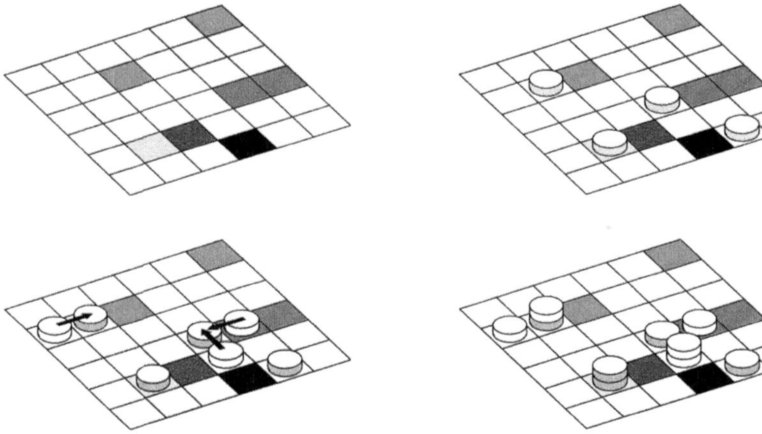

Fig. 2. These panels show the four steps of the deposition rules used in this model, at each time step dt. Activated PLTs are shown as white disks with a gray side, and non activated PLTs as plain white disks. Albumin is too small to be depicted here. Its effect is represented by the gray level of each cell. A white cell is free of albumin, a black one is saturated, and prevents further PLTs deposition. The upper-left panel shows the albumin deposition phase. Colors are exaggerated for the sake of illustration. At each time step, all cells are, on average, covered homogeneously and progressively. The upper-right panel illustrate the adhesion of activated platelets, with a higher probability on low albumin cells. The lower-left panel shows non-activated PLTs aggregating on a free cell, next to already deposited PLTs, whether activated or not. Finally, the last panel shows the fact that PLTs can aggregate on top of each other.

can received at most one platelet, it can accumulate a large number of albumin particles. Activated PLTs can adhere anywhere, but with a probability that decreases as more albumin has already populated the cell. Non-activated PLTs can deposit next to, or on top of an already deposited platelet, with also a probability that decreases with the amount of albumin stored in the corresponding cell.

The precise adhesion-aggregation rules can be found in [2]. They involve 5 unknown parameters, the adhesion rate p_{Ad} of activated PLTs, the aggregation rate p_{Ag} of non-activated PLTs, the deposition rate p_F of albumin particles, the rate p_T for a deposition on top of an existing platelet, and a factor a_T that described the exponential decay of PLTs deposition rate due to the increase of albumin in a cell.

Figure 3 shows the results of a numerical simulation of the above mathematical model, with carefully calibrated value of the 5 unknown parameters. The continuous lines are the model predictions, which are obtained every second over the 5-min duration of the experiment. Experimental observations are done at time $t = 0$, $t = 20$ s, $t = 60$ s, $t = 120$ s and $t = 300$ s. On the one hand, they concern the number of aggregates on the 1 mm $\times$ 1 mm observation window, the average size of the deposition clusters. On the other hand, measurements are also giving the number of activated and non-activated PLTs still in suspension in the cylinder cavity of the Impact-R. Note that these observations require to interrupt the experiment at each measurement time, and restart them from $t = 0$.

The right panels of Fig. 3 shows the 1 mm × 1 mm deposition surface, as obtained in the experiment (up) and the simulation (bottom). The parameters used to produce the simulation are $p_{Ad} = 110\ [s^{-1}]$, $p_{Ag} = 14.6\ [s^{-1}]$ $p_F = 1.7 \times 10^{-3}\ [s^{-1}]$, $p_T = 0.6\ [s^{-1}]$ and $a_T = 30\ [(\mu m)^2]$. For this figure, they have been tediously determined by a manual trial and error process.

Figure 3 clearly shows an excellent agreement between experiment and the prediction of our numerical model. This is even more convincing when considering Fig. 4 which shows a property of the deposition process that was not used

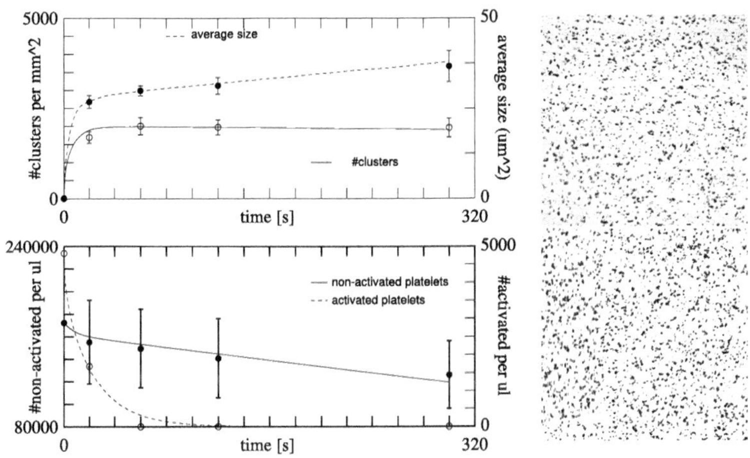

Fig. 3. left: Behavior of the model (lines) that best matches experimental data (dots) with error bars determined from the data of 7 donors. **Right:** Snapshot of the deposition surface after 5 min, as obtained in the experiment (up) and simulation (bottom).

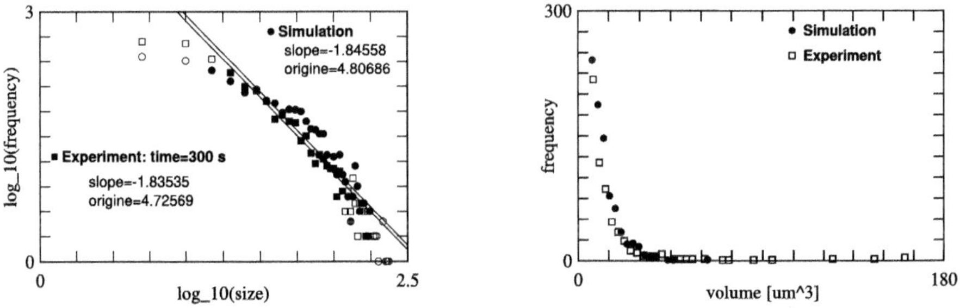

Fig. 4. Cross-validation with observations not used for the calibration of the five model parameters. The left panel shows the size distribution of the aggregation clusters and the right panel gives their volume distribution.

to determine the values of the five unknown parameters. They are the distribution of cluster sizes at $t = 300$ s, and the distribution of their volume (PLTs can aggregate on top of each other). We observe again a very good match between the model predictions and the in vitro measurements.

3 Parameters Inference

From a clinical perspective, the goal of this study is to analyze the deposition of PLTs of patients with different diseases and determine whether they suffer from platelets disorders. If yes, we want to know which function is affected, such as adhesion or aggregation rate, or transport properties.

A simulation of the model described in Sect. 2 lasts 5 min on a standard processor. Exploring the five-parameter space of our model for an optimal match with in vitro Impact-R blood test is therefore a challenging numerical task.

The manual approach used to obtain Fig. 3 must be replaced by Machine Learning techniques. Here, we used the so-called Approximate Bayesian Computation (ABC) to determine the values of our five parameters that characterize a given experiment.

In addition to obtain the parameter values that best explain the data, the ABC methods also provides a quantification of the uncertainty by computing

$$\text{Prob}(\theta|\text{Obs}) = \frac{\text{Prob}(\text{Obs}|\theta)\text{Prob}(\theta)}{\text{Prob}(\text{Obs})} \tag{1}$$

with

$$\theta = (p_{Ag}, p_{Ad}, p_T, p_F, \ldots)$$

the values of the unknown parameters. The quantity Obs denotes the experimental data.

Equation (1) is Bayes theorem. It indicated how to obtain Prob(θ|Obs), the uncertainty of the parameter values, from Prob(Obs|θ), the probability to obtain the data knowing the parameters. Prob(Obs|θ) is what the simulation of the numerical model provides. Prob(θ) is known as the *prior* and is determined by the range of possible values of the parameters. Prob(Obs) is a normalization value that is computed by summing all simulations output compatible with Obs.

The application of the ABC method requires High Performance Computing (HPC) capabilities to obtained the desired probabilities by an adequate sampling procedure. However, a detail description of this approach and the software that was used for this task is out of the scope of the present paper. Interested readers are referred to [3,4].

Here, we simply present the results obtained in [3,4]. Figure 5 shows the probability distribution of the various model parameters, for the case of COPD (Chronic Obstructive Pulmonary Disease) patients. The experimental observations are given by an average over 8 subjects.

Table 1 shows, for patents in different clinical states, what parameters is clinically relevant to discriminate the pathology with respect to a healthy person.

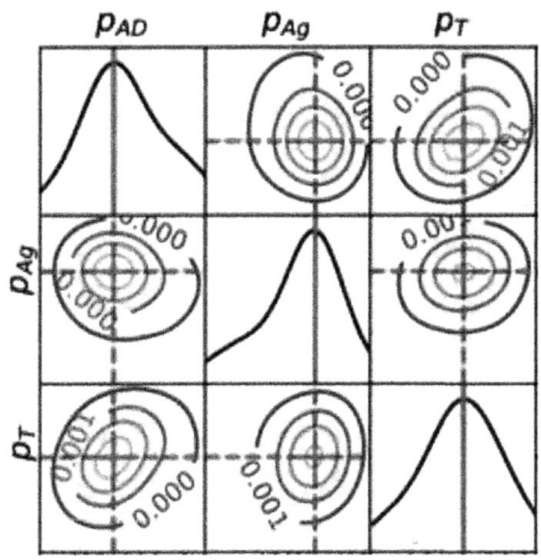

Fig. 5. Probability distribution of the model parameters for the case of COPD (Chronic Obstructive Pulmonary Disease).

This table actually contains additional parameters, namely v_y^{AP} and v_y^{NAP}. They belong to a variant of the model presented in Sect. 2, in which the diffusion of PLTs towards the deposition surface is implemented as an explicit random walk, characterized by random jumps at each time step dt of amplitude $v_y^{AP} \times dt$ and $v_y^{NAP} \times dt$, for activated an non-activated platelets, respectively. Thus, v_y^{AP} and v_y^{NAP} are replacing the diffusion coefficient and the random walk replaces the solution of the partial differential equation. See [3,4] for detailed explanations.

Table 1. Discriminatory properties for different situations: healthy donors, Dialyzed (treatment for a dysfunction kidney) and COPD (Chronic obstructive pulmonary disease) patients.

	Healthy	Dialysis	COPD
Healthy	–	p_{Ad}, p_{Ag}, v_y^{AP}, v_y^{NAP}	p_{Ag}
Dialysis	p_{Ad}, p_{Ag}, v_y^{AP}, v_y^{NAP}	–	p_T, v_y^{NAP}
COPD	p_{Ag}	p_T, v_y^{NAP}	–

4 Platelet Transport: Fully Resolved Flow Simulation

As discussed previously, PLTs in the bulk of the Impact-R diffuse towards the deposition surface. This phenomenon is known as *shear-induced* diffusion [16] as it results from the combined action of RBCs and a shear flow, produced by upper lid rotation in the Impact-R device. This mechanism is responsible for the *margination* of the PLTs [11], which is characterized by a high concentration of PLTs near the vessel walls.

In an experiment such as the Impact-R, the properties of the PLTs aggregates depend on their adhesion and aggregation rates, as well as their flux towards the deposition surface, that is their transport properties.

The diffusion constant D that describes the movement of PLTs in blood is found in the literature [1] as

$$D_{ZC}(\dot{\gamma}) = D_0 \times (1 - H) + 0.15\dot{\gamma}d_{RBC}^2\frac{H}{4}(1 - H)^{1.8} \tag{2}$$

where H is the hematrocrit (fraction of blood volume occupied by RBCs), $\dot{\gamma}$ the shear rate and D_0 the thermal diffusivity. This relation is often referred to as the Zydney-Colton (ZC) formula [18], hence the subscript ZC.

This formula, when applied for the healthy patients considered with the Impact-R, gives

$$D_{ZC} = 2.9 \times 10^{-11}\ \mathrm{m}^2/\mathrm{s} \tag{3}$$

However, the value of D_{ZC} is way to small to explain the number of PLTs that have reached the deposition surface within the first 20 s of the experiment and which can be counted within the experimental process. Analytically, the above value of D_{ZC} predicts a deposition of about 150 PLTs per mm^2, whereas the experiment measures around 3000 of them. Experimental observations require a much larger diffusion coefficient, estimated to [2]

$$D_{eff} = 1.32 \times 10^{-8}\ \mathrm{m}^2/\mathrm{s} \tag{4}$$

thus, showing a mismatch of about 3 orders of magnitude between theory and experiment

In an attempt to solve this discrepancy, we have developed a fully resolved blood flow simulation, as depicted in Fig. 6. This simulation implements the plasma fluid using the Lattice Boltzmann method and introduces RBCs as deformable particles in suspension, subject to a fluid-solid interaction (FSI) based on the immersed boundary method. Mutual interactions between RBCs are also introduced, as well as RBCs-PLTs collisions. A detailed account of this model is given in [9,10]. It is a major work, in terms of software development, data analysis and in terms of the huge amount of CPU required to study the system shown in Fig. 6, even for only 1 s of physical time. Several days on a supercomputer with multiple CPUs and multiple GPUs where necessary (see [7,9] for more details).

From such simulations, despite of the rather small spatial and temporal scales, the trajectory of PLTs perpendicular to the flow (i.e. in direction of the bottom of the system) can be recorded with high resolution. These trajectories can be analyzed to reveal the macroscopic behavior of PLTs subject to a pure shear flow with the given RBCs hematocrit.

A standard approach to analyze PLTs movement is to compute the so-called Mean-Square Displacement (MSD), defined as

$$\mathrm{MSD}(t) = \langle [y_i(t) - y_i(0)]^2 \rangle_i \tag{5}$$

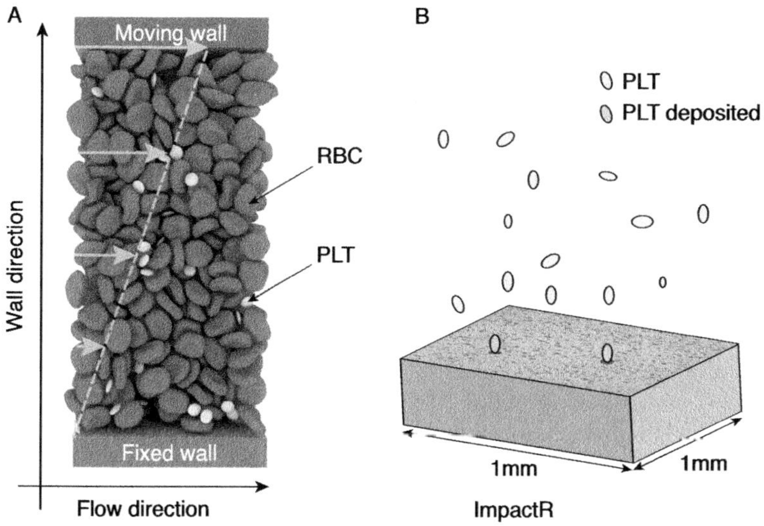

Fig. 6. Simulation setup: horizontal dimensions $L_x = L_z = 50$ μm, vertical dimension $L_y \in \{50, 100, 200, 500\}\mu m$. Periodic boundary conditions for the horizontal axis, zero flow velocity on the bottom plans and imposed horizontal velocity of the upper plan along the x-axis.

where $\langle . \rangle_i$ is an average over all platelets i and $y_i(t)$ is the vertical coordinate of platelet i at time t. It is well known that, in one-dimension, the mean-square displacement is related to diffusion as

$$D_{MSD} = \frac{\mathrm{MSD}(t)}{2t}. \tag{6}$$

This can be checked by expressing MSD(t) with the probability distribution $\rho(y,t)$ of finding the particle et location y at time t

$$\mathrm{MSD}(t) = \int_{\mathbb{R}} y^2 \rho(y,t)\, dy$$

where ρ obeys the diffusion equation along the y-axis

$$\partial_t \rho = D \partial_y^2 \rho.$$

Thus the time derivative of MSD(t) is

$$\frac{d}{dt}\mathrm{MSD}(t) = \int_{\mathbb{R}} y^2 \partial_t \rho(y,t)\, dy = D \int_{\mathbb{R}} y^2 \partial_y^2 \rho(y,t)\, dy$$

By integrating by part two times and assuming that ρ and $\partial_y \rho$ vanish at $\pm\infty$, we obtain $d\mathrm{MSD}/dt = 2D$, whose solution is Eq. (6). Interestingly, the hypothesis that ρ and its derivative are zero at the domain boundary is only valid at short time, before PLTs reach the system walls. The effect of a finite system will be illustrated below.

Figure 7 shows the results of this data analysis to obtain MSD(t) from the PLTs movements (see also [6]). The trajectory of two randomly selected platelets are shown in the left panel. We have excluded from the averaging procedure, PLTs that are too close to the wall, to avoid PLTs trapped in the so-called Cell-Free-Layer (CFL), a thin layer next to solid wall, were RBCs are mostly absent (see for instance [5,12,14]).

The right panel of Fig. 7 shows the mean-square displacement computed from the PLTs trajectories, for two family of PLTs. Those which have never penetrated the excluded region, and those that went in and out. As suggested by the plot and Eq. (6), MSD(t) is obtained by a straight line fit, whose slope gives us the corresponding diffusion coefficient. The fit suggests the value $D = 3 \times 10^{-10}$ m$^2/s$, compatible with results obtained by other researches [13]. This is not the value we derived indirectly for the Impact-R, but it is much larger than $D_{ZC} \sim 10^{-11}$ m$^2/s$. The significance of this difference is well illustrated by the MSD behavior shown in the figure for D_{ZC}. Such a diffusion value is way to small to explain the PLTs trajectories.

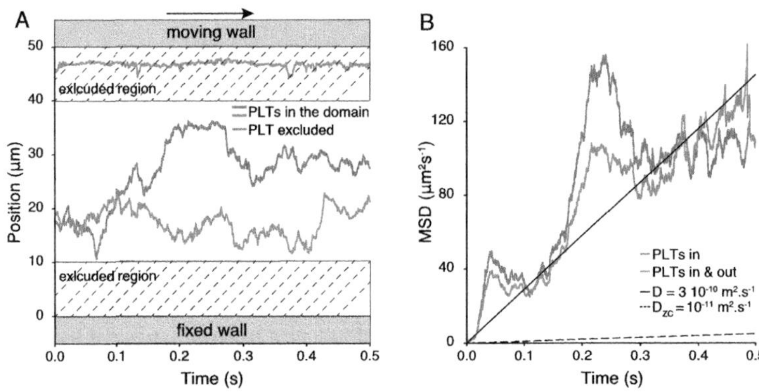

Fig. 7. Left: PLTs trajectories (wall to wall distance of $L_y = 50$ µm. **Right:** Mean-square displacement. In blue, the average is done with PLTs that never entered the excluded region. In red, the average also includes PLTs that entered and left the excluded region. The slope of the fit of MSD(t) gives the corresponding diffusion coefficient. The value of D_{ZC} is clearly too small to explain the data. (Color figure online)

The system we have analyzed here, with $L_y = 50$ µm, is significantly smaller than the 820 µm height of the impact-R device. A value of 50 µm is however more convenient due to the formidable CPU requirement necessary to reach a well established flow regime within in a fully resolved blood simulation that last only 1 s of physical time. However, simulations with larger L_y where also performed [8,9]. They indicate that the mean-square displacement tends to increase with the system size. This may be explained by the fact that large amplitude platelets jumps are prevented by walls in small systems, thus giving an smaller effective value of MSD(t).

It turns out that measuring the probability distribution of the PLTs velocity provides another way to determine the MSD and shows that, indeed, the system size impacts the inferred value of the diffusion coefficient when computed through Eq. (6).

Figure 8 illustrates our approach. From the $L_y = 50\,\mu$m simulation, we can determine the PLTs velocity distribution by sampling their jump size at time intervals $\delta t = 10^{-5} = 10^{-2}$ ms. The histogram of the resulting absolute velocities is shown as the blue line in the left panel of the figure. Note that the simulation time step is actually 10^{-7}s but taking δt smaller than 10^{-5} s does not change the velocity distribution. However, a larger value of δt may miss events and compute a different velocity distribution, as sketched with the orange color.

The PLTs velocity distribution $P(v)$ shown in blue in Fig. 8 can be fitted extremely well with Eq. (7).

$$P(v) = \begin{cases} p_0 \exp(-\lambda v) & \text{for } v \leq v_{min} \\ p_0 \exp(-\lambda v_{min}) \left(\frac{v}{v_{min}}\right)^{-1-\alpha} & \text{for } v \geq v_{min} \end{cases} \tag{7}$$

where p_0 is a normalization, and λ, v_{min} and α are parameters that are found to be

$$\alpha = 3.8 \qquad v_{min} = 5 \times 10^{-3}[m/s] \qquad v_{moy} = 10^{-3}[m/s] \tag{8}$$

This fit reveals that $P(v)$ is not a Gaussian distribution, as could have been assumed. Up to some velocity v_{min}, $P(v)$ follows an exponential distribution. Then, for larger velocities, it behaves as a power-law distribution with exponent α. The value of α may have some important consequences. If smaller than 2, it would imply that PLTs obey a so-called Lévy flight, a random walk with a non-zero probability of arbitrary large jumps, making the dependence in the systems size critical. Although some data with larger values of L_y support this hypothesis [8], the analysis performed at $L_y = 50\,\mu$m gives $\alpha = 3.8$, ensuring the locality of the random walk.

The distribution $P(V)$ can now be used to generate PLTs displacement without the need for a fully resolved and costly bloodflow simulation. The random walks obtained by sampling $P(v)$ produces a mean-square displacement MSD(t) can be considered in arbitrary large systems and for very long time spans, and a diffusion constant D valid at large spatial and temporal scales.

The asymptotic value of D is found to be [6]

$$D = 0.678 \times 10^{-9} \text{ m}^2/s$$

that is 65 times larger than D_{ZC}. It is also about 4 times larger than the value obtained from a direct measurement of MSD(t) for the PLTs in the simulation with $L_s = 50\,\mu$m.

The study of the PLTs trajectories also provides information on their velocity auto-correlation, defined as

$$\text{VACF}(\tau) = \langle v(t+\tau)v(t) \rangle. \tag{9}$$

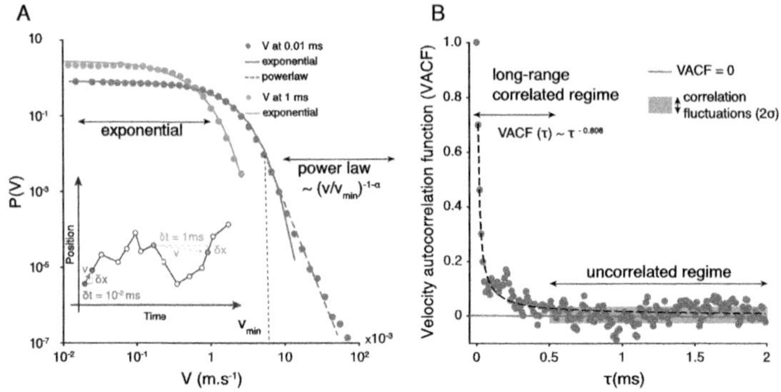

Fig. 8. Left: Platelets velocity probability distribution obtained by sampling the PLTs trajectories at two different time scales δt. The resolution $\delta t = 10^{-5}$ s $= 10^{-3}$ ms is appropriate to capture the correct distribution, which turns out to be composed of an exponential part, followed by a power-law distribution. **Right:** Velocity auto-correlation VACF(τ) as a function of τ. The data shows a power-law correlated regime that contrasts with a more standard exponential decay of the auto-correlation function. (Color figure online)

This quantity can be seen as a measure of how long a platelet remembers its velocity before getting a new one, sampled from $P(v)$ and due to RBCs and fluid interactions. As shown in the right panel of Fig. 8, the velocity auto-correlation behaves as a power-law

$$\mathrm{VACF}(\tau) = a\tau^{-b} \tag{10}$$

with $b = 0.808$, and $a = 0.017 \times 10^{-3}$ s when τ is expressed in ms. The data also shows that memory is lost after a decorrelation time $\Delta t = 0.5 \times 10^{-3}$ s. However, the power-law decay of the auto-correlation for short values of τ is remarkable as an exponential decay is to be expected in a random walk process.

5 Conclusions

In this paper we have studied the adhesion-aggregation and transport properties of platelets, by combining in vitro experimental data with mathematical models and numerical simulations. From a clinical perspective, our goal is the determination of platelets function and possible disorders due to some diseases that affect blood properties.

As a direct measurement of PLTs adhesion or aggregation rates in whole blood subject to flow, as well as their transport is extremely difficult experimentally, we considered indirect evidences provided by deposition experiments under selected wall shear rates.

Using microscope images of PLTs deposition, the parameters of a mathematical model of transport and deposition was possible, revealing for different classes of diseases, which properties is modified. The values of the model parameters could be inferred efficiently using the Approximate Bayesian Computation

(ABC) method, yet requiring super computing resources, but offering an important new clinical knowledge.

Our study has however shown a significant discrepancy between the usually accepted Zydney-Colton diffusion coefficient of PLTs in a sheared blood flow, and the value that we were able to infer from the experimental data. Thus, the characterization of the transport of PLTs perpendicular to the flow, that is in direction of the deposition walls, remains partially open. To help solving this issue, we have developed fully resolved blood simulations. They implement a Lattice Boltzmann fluid in interaction with deformable RBC and PLTs in suspension. From the PLTs trajectories, we have determined their diffusion properties along the vertical direction, in order to estimate the flow of PLTs to the deposition surface.

An important finding of our investigations is that the diffusion coefficient D cannot be reliably measured in small systems, as the walls are likely to affect the behavior of the PLTs mean-square displacement. Thus, a value of D inferred in a 50 μm high system may be significantly wrong when considering a larger system. The value D_{ZC} computed from Eq. (2) is then restricted to system even smaller than 50 μm high.

Another remarkable results is that, $P(v)$, the velocity distribution of PLTs moving perpendicular to the flow is clearly non-Gaussian. Its tail is a power-law, indicating the possibility of movements of large amplitude. Finally, we showed evidence that the PLTs velocity auto-correlation function does not decay exponentially but with a power-low τ^{-b} of exponent $b = 0.8$ and decorrelation time $\Delta t = 0.5$ ms. Note that these values are expected to depend on the RBC and PLTS concentrations and the imposed shear rate.

References

1. Affeld, K., Goubergrits, L., Watanabe, N., Kertzscher, U.: Numerical and experimental evaluation of platelet deposition to collagen coated surface at low shear rates. J. Biomech. **46**(2), 430–436 (2013)
2. Chopard, B., et al.: A physical description of the adhesion and aggregation of platelets. Royal Soc. Open Sci. **4**(4), 170219 (2017)
3. Dutta, R., Chopard, B., Lätt, J., Dubois, F., Zouaoui Boudjeltia, K., Mira, A.: Parameter estimation of platelets deposition: approximate Bayesian computation with high performance computing. Front. Physiol. **9**, 1128 (2018)
4. Dutta, R., et al.: Personalized pathology test for cardio-vascular disease: approximate bayesian computation with discriminative summary statistics learning. PLoS Comput. Biol., e1009910 (2022)
5. Fedosov, D.A., Caswell, B., Popel, A.S., Karniadakis, G.E.: Blood flow and cell-free layer in microvessels. Microcirculation **17**(8), 615–628 (2010)
6. Kotsalos, C., et al.: Shear induced diffusion of platelets revisited. Front. Physiol. **13**(985905) (2022)
7. Kotsalos, C.: Digital blood. Ph.D. thesis, University of Geneva (2020)
8. Kotsalos, C., Zouaoui Boudjeltia, K., Dutta, R., Latt, J., Chopard, B.: Anomalous platelet transport & fat-tailed distributions. https://arxiv.org/abs/2006.11755 (2020)

9. Kotsalos, C., Latt, J., Beny, J., Chopard, B.: Digital blood in massively parallel CPU/GPU systems for the study of platelet transport. Interface Focus **20190116**(11) (2021)
10. Kotsalos, C., Latt, J., Chopard, B.: Bridging the computational gap between mesoscopic and continuum modeling of red blood cells for fully resolved blood flow. J. Comput. Phys. **398** (2019)
11. Kumar, A., Graham, M.D.: Margination and segregation in confined flows of blood and other multicomponent suspensions. Soft Matter **8**(41), 10536–10548 (2012)
12. Mehrabadi, M., Ku, D.N., Aidun, C.K.: Effects of shear rate, confinement, and particle parameters on margination in blood flow. Phys. Rev. E **93**(2), 023109 (2016)
13. Reasor, D.A., Mehrabadi, M., Ku, D.N., Aidun, C.K.: Determination of critical parameters in platelet margination. Ann. Biomed. Eng. **41**(2), 238–249 (2013)
14. Kim, S., Ong, P.K., Yalcin, O., Intaglietta, M., Johnson, P.C.: The cell-free layer in microvascular blood flow. Biorheology **46**(3), 181–189 (2009)
15. Shenkman, B., Savion, N., Dardik, R., Tamarin, I., Varon, D.: Testing of platelet deposition on polystyrene surfaces under flow conditions by the cone and plate(let) analyzer: role of platelet activation, fibrinogen, and von willebrand factor. Thromb. Res. **99**, 353–361 (2000)
16. Zhao, H., Shaqfeh, E.S.G.: Shear-induced platelet margination in a microchannel. Phys. Rev. E Stat. Nonl. Soft Matter Phys. **83**(6), 061924 (2011)
17. Zhao, H., Shaqfeh, E.S.G., Narsimhan, V.: Shear-induced particle migration and margination in a cellular suspension. Phys. Fluids **24**(1), 011902 (2012)
18. Zydney, A.L., Colton, C.K.: Augmented solute transport in the shear flow of a concentrated suspension. PCH PhysicoChem. Hydrodyn **10**, 77 (1988)

Searching for Attractors: To Infinity and Beyond

Stefan Haar(✉)

INRIA, Paris, France
stefan.haar@inria.fr

Abstract. Discrete and nondeterministic modelling of regulatory and signalling networks allows to characterize many of their crucial dynamical properties, with a reasonable computational effort. A dynamical feature of particular interest in its own right, as well as in terms of biological relevance, is the landscape of attractors and their attraction basins. In recent years, we have developped new approaches to discovery and global cartography of this basin landscape. We enlarge the set of models used, by moving to Petri nets on the one hand and an opening to continuous dynamics on the other. Surprisingly, these openings are rewarded not only by a sharpening of the analysis, but also the emergence of compact and readable data structures, and fast search algorithms. The talk will advocate the cross-fertilization between discrete and continuous approaches, and to not be afraid of pushing limits.

1 Boolean Networks and Their Attractors

Discrete models, and in particular *Boolean Networks (BNs)*, are a rich and fertile object of study in their own right, with a powerful theory. A driving force in the development of this field lies in the massive and successful application of BNs as dynamical systems models for interaction systems in engineering and live sciences, especially in the area of gene regulation [5,7,12,14].

While this application is not our main focus here, we highlight two desiderata that seem crucial to us in this context:

- The capacity of identifying the *attractors* of the system under study, that is, the absorbing strongly connected subspaces of the systems state space; these constitute the stable regimes of the network, and most notably the *phenotypes* of a cell whose regulatory network is captured by the BN model; and
- best possible coverage of the state space, i.e. a full account of the states reachable and pathways available in the network.

It is a well-known fact that the choice of *update mode* for applying the boolean function that constitutes the BN has a very strong impact on the way the systems dynamics are discovered. The following are the fundamental modes studied in the literature:

Published by Springer Nature Switzerland AG 2026
S. Riva and A. Richard (Eds.): AUTOMATA 2025, LNCS 15831, pp. 15–26, 2026.
https://doi.org/10.1007/978-3-032-01570-9_2

- asynchronous mode: in every round only one variable, chosen nondeterministically, updates its value according to its component function;
- synchronous: all variables update value simultaneously; and
- generalised asynchronous: any nondeterministically chosen subset of variables updates value simultaneously.

Further variants in the literature are obtained by e.g. imposing, for the asynchronous semantics, an order in which individual variables are considered in successive rounds, etc.; we will not dwell on those variants here since they allow *fewer* actions than their counterpart in the above, and will not improve the coverage we are striving to achieve.

Note here that these semantics allow - with suitable adaptations according to the update mode chosen - to benefit from translation into other formal models, in particular into Petri nets. We have detailed some aspects of this transfer in [2]; the two-way translation allows to retrieve theoretical results from one domain into the other, and to benefit e.g. from the powerful *unfolding* method for Petri net to conduct efficient and exhaustive searches for attractors [1]. In continuation of the work in [2], we will advocate below to study *continuous* Petri nets and to move back and forth between continuous and discrete representations, obtaining better coverage of the dynamics and access to attractors, as in our desiderata above.

Returning to BNs, it had long been assumed that the generalised asynchronous semantics is the all-en-compassing updating mode of BNs and capable of expressing all possible behaviours. Doubts arose when, in particular, the authors of [11] present an element of gene regulation that exhibits behaviours that cannot be explained with the classical, generalized asynchronous BNs. One may think of it as a *pulse generator*, visualised below by the interaction graph and an approximate experimental expression profile of specie 3.

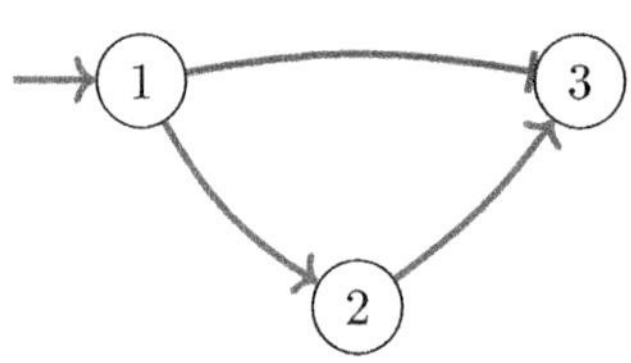

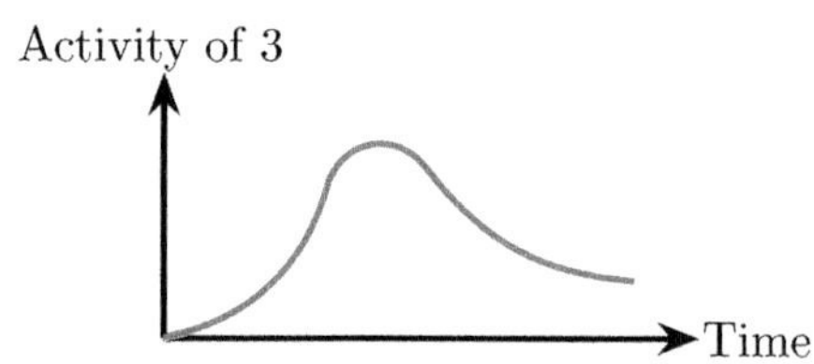

Here, an incoming signal activating 1 causes a short term spike in activity of 3, thus generating a pulse. Note that in a continuous dynamical model, such as ODE, such a behaviour can be captured using precise timing parameters that reflect speed differences between the processes involved; or equivalently, in terms of activation or exhibition *thresholds*, admitting gradual continuous increases in variable values.

The issue touches upon the very essence and justification of using discrete models, who are hoped to provide sound *overapproximations* of the behaviour of the underlying natural systems. In fact, the above semantics are all grounded in abstracting away from such activation thresholds. The only behaviours possible with asynchronous BNs are those where 3 never activates due to the inhibition from 1, or 2 activates 3 in spite of that inhibition, resulting in a continuous activation, rather than a pulse.

In this context of growing evidence that discrete BNs may not be sufficient for coverage, our development of *Most permissive (MP) semantics* [2,4,13] can be seen to address this challenge, while remaining rooted in the discrete approach, with only a moderate increase of the size of the model. The development had been inspired by previous discoveries in the domain of Petri nets [3], showing how a weakening of synchronization limitations in the semantics allows for opening new behaviours which can in turn be captured by a suitable discrete refinement. In Boolean networks, the *most permissive* semantics we will detail below works in a similar way, adding nondeterministic choices in a slightly refined discrete structure. The keystone in this series of development will then be, further below, the connection with *continuous Petri nets*, capturing the rich behaviour of most permissive boolean networks, while eventually giving a compact and discrete picture of it. The following sections will discuss in greater depth, in this order,

- most permissive Boolean networks,
- Petri nets, both discrete and continuous, and finally
- the emerging picture of a connection between those models.

2 Beyond Limitations: Most Permissive Semantics for Boolean Networks

Recall that a BN of dimension $n \in \mathbb{N}$ (on n variables) is a function $f\colon \mathbb{B}^n \to \mathbb{B}^n$, typically given component-wise as local Boolean functions $f_i\colon \mathbb{B}^n \to \mathbb{B}$ describing the evolution of the variables $i \in \{1, \ldots, n\}$, $f = (f_1, \ldots, f_n)$. An n-ary Boolean vector $\mathbf{x} \in \mathbb{B}^n$ is a *configuration* for f. The interaction graph of f has the n variables as vertex set, and links variable i to j by an oriented arc iff i participates in the update function of j; a positive influence (promotion) is indicated by coloring the arc green, a negative one by red. An example BN network and its associated interaction graph are given in Fig. 1.

$$\begin{aligned} f_1(\mathbf{x}) &= \neg\mathbf{x}_2 \\ f_2(\mathbf{x}) &= \neg\mathbf{x}_1 \\ f_3(\mathbf{x}) &= \neg\mathbf{x}_1 \wedge \mathbf{x}_2. \end{aligned}$$

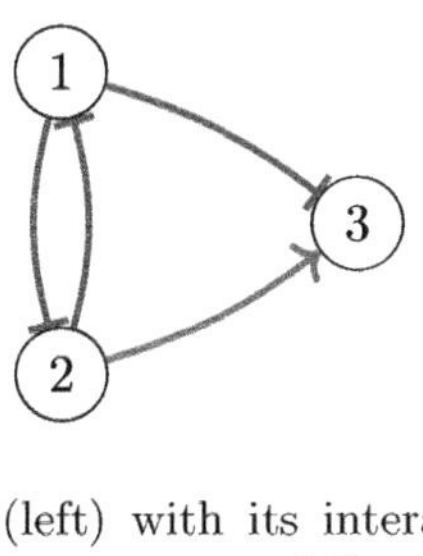

Fig. 1. A running example BN on three variables (left) with its interaction graph (right). Positive interactions are depicted by pointed green arrows while negative interactions are depicted by flat red arrows. (Color figure online)

For a BN f of dimension n and any two configurations $\mathbf{x}, \mathbf{y} \in \mathbb{B}^n$, let $\Delta(\mathbf{x}, \mathbf{y}) = \{i \in \{1, \ldots, n\} \mid \mathbf{x}_i \neq \mathbf{y}_i\}$ be the set of all variables whose value differs between $\mathbf{x}$ and $\mathbf{y}$. Then the fully asynchronous semantics of f, $fa(f)$, synchronous semantics of f, $syn(f)$, and asynchronous semantics of f, $ga(f)$ are defined as follows for any pair of configurations $\mathbf{x}, \mathbf{y} \in \mathbb{B}^n$:

$$(\mathbf{x}, \mathbf{y}) \in fa(f) \iff \exists i \in \{1, \ldots, n\}, \Delta(\mathbf{x}, \mathbf{y}) = \{i\} \wedge f_i(\mathbf{x}) = y_i$$
$$(\mathbf{x}, \mathbf{y}) \in syn(f) \iff \forall i \in \{1, \ldots, n\}, f_i(\mathbf{x}) = y_i$$
$$(\mathbf{x}, \mathbf{y}) \in ga(f) \iff \forall i \in \Delta(\mathbf{x}, \mathbf{y}), f_i(\mathbf{x}) = y_i$$

It follows immediately that $fa(f) \subseteq ga(f)$ as well as $syn(f) \subseteq ga(f)$.

With the natural infix notation for the semantics relations we write, e.g., $\mathbf{x} \xrightarrow[f]{fa} \mathbf{y}$. The associated reachability relations are obtained as the reflexive and transitive closures of the semantics relations, $\mathbf{x} \xrightarrow[f]{fa}{}^{*} \mathbf{y}$, etc.

Configurations of the example BN from Fig. 1 reachable from $(0,0,0)$ under fully asynchronous or asynchronous semantics are visualised in Fig. 2. Synchronous semantics are omitted, as the only reachable configurations are $(1,1,0)$ and $(0,0,0)$ itself (the cycle in asynchronous reachability).

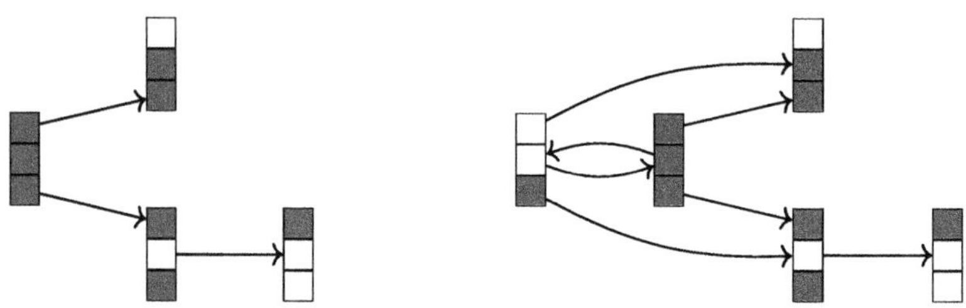

Fig. 2. [9] All configurations of the example BN (Fig. 1) reachable from $(0,0,0)$ under fully asynchronous semantics (left) and asynchronous semantics (right). The variables are ordered from top to bottom and dark tiles represent value 0 while light tiles represent value 1. Self-loops are omitted.

Variants of definitions for MP semantics can be found in [4,13]; to remain conceptually close to state updates of PNs, we use here the original definition from [13]. MP differs from other semantics by the introduction of two transient (or intermediate) values, namely $\nearrow$ to signify that a variable is increasing from 0 to 1, and $\searrow$ when the variable is decreasing from 1 to 0.

For a BN f of dimension n and any MP configuration $\hat{\mathbf{x}} \in \{0, 1, \nearrow, \searrow\}^n$, let $\beta(\hat{\mathbf{x}}) = \{\mathbf{x} \in \mathbb{B}^n \mid \forall i \in \{1, \ldots, n\}, \hat{\mathbf{x}}_i \in \mathbb{B} \implies \mathbf{x}_i = \hat{\mathbf{x}}_i\}$ be the set of compatible binarisations expressed as Boolean configurations. Then, the MP semantics of a BN f, $\hat{mp}(f)$, is defined as follows for any pair of MP configurations $\hat{\mathbf{x}}, \hat{\mathbf{y}} \in$

$\{0, 1, \nearrow, \searrow\}^n$:

$$\begin{aligned}(\hat{\mathbf{x}}, \hat{\mathbf{y}}) \in \hat{mp}(f) \iff \exists i \in \{1, \ldots, n\}, \Delta(\hat{\mathbf{x}}, \hat{\mathbf{y}}) = \{i\} \wedge [(\hat{\mathbf{x}}_i = \nearrow \wedge \hat{\mathbf{y}}_i = 1) \vee \\ (\hat{\mathbf{x}}_i = \searrow \wedge \hat{\mathbf{y}}_i = 0) \vee \\ (\hat{\mathbf{x}}_i \neq 1 \wedge \hat{\mathbf{y}}_i = \nearrow \wedge \exists \mathbf{x} \in \beta(\hat{\mathbf{x}}), f_i(\mathbf{x}) = 1) \vee \\ (\hat{\mathbf{x}}_i \neq 0 \wedge \hat{\mathbf{y}}_i = \searrow \wedge \exists \mathbf{x} \in \beta(\hat{\mathbf{x}}), f_i(\mathbf{x}) = 0)]\end{aligned}$$

The top two lines of the disjunction enable a variable in a transient value to collapse into the target Boolean value at any time, allowing a nondeterministic choice between this 'unguarded' transition and idling in the intermediate state. The bottom two lines dictate that for a variable to change to a transient value, a binarisation must exist for which the local function returns the target Boolean value of said transient value.

Since Boolean configurations are the objects we are interested in, we will often only keep the induced reachability relations between such 'pure states', abstracting away the intermediate states that allowed MP semantics to obtain those paths in the first place, and note this relation as $(\mathbf{x}, \mathbf{y}) \in mp(f)$.

We have $ga(f) \subseteq mp(f)$, since any asynchronous update can be reproduced in MP by first putting all relevant variables into transient value and subsequently collapsing them. The inclusion is strict in general, as shown in Fig. 3 of all Boolean configurations of the example BN from Fig. 1 reachable under MP semantics.

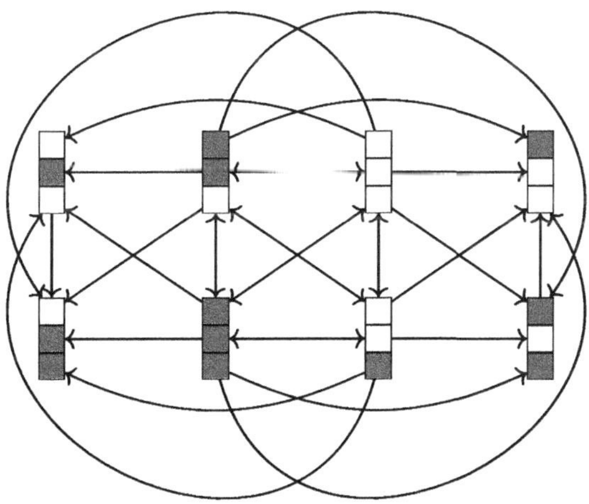

Fig. 3. [9] All Boolean configurations of the example BN (Fig. 1) reachable from $(0, 0, 0)$ under MP semantics. While the fixed points are preserved, all other configurations become transiently reachable, as opposed to asynchronous semantics.

MP BNs are known to have very favorable algorithmic properties [4,13]:

- for any $(\mathbf{x}, \mathbf{y}) \in mp(f)^*$, there is a path of at most $3n$ transitions connecting $\mathbf{x}$ to $\mathbf{y}$;
- all attractors are hypercubes; in fact, minimal trap spaces and attractors coincide.

The question now is whether there are fast and compact ways of representing and analysing the semantics of MP, allowing to treat larger systems efficiently. The following will develop the lead along which this can be done

3 Beyond Infinity: Petri Nets, Discrete and Continuous

Nets are bipartite directed graphs with two sets of nodes, *places* and *transitions*. Places model resource types available in the system, and can hold a certain amount of *tokens* or *token mass* representing availability of said resource; once token mass has been assigned to places, the marked net is called a *Petri net*. Transitions allow removing (reducing) or adding tokens (token mass), according to the *arcs* connecting them to places.

Formally, a *net* is a tuple $\mathsf{N} = (P, T, \mathbf{W})$, where P is a finite set of places, T is a finite set of transitions and $\mathbf{W}\colon (P \times T) \cup (T \times P) \to \mathbb{N}_0$ is a weight function assigning each transition the amount of resources consumed or produced in each place. For $x, y \in P \cup T$, we say there is an arc from x to y if $\mathbf{W}(x, y) > 0$. A simple example net is visualised in Fig. 4; it also shows a case of discrete transition firing.

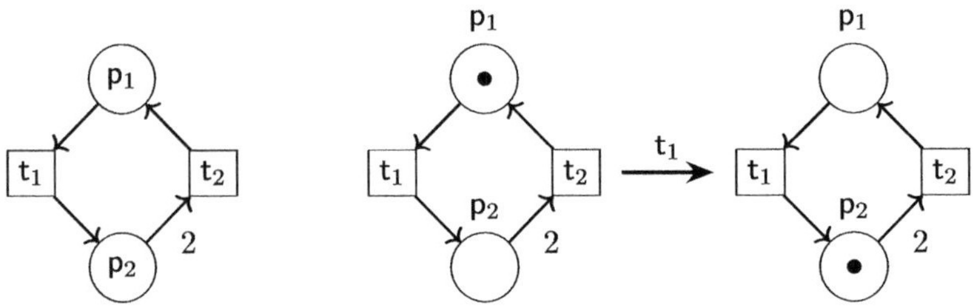

Fig. 4. Left: An example net with two places (depicted as circles) and two transitions (depicted as squares). The arc weights are given as labels on the arrows. As per convention, arc weights equal to 1 are omitted. Right: An example of a transition firing in a DPN with the same net structure. The tokens assigned by the markings are depicted as black dots inside the places.

For each place or transition $x \in P \cup T$, we call ${}^\bullet x = \{y \in P \cup T \mid \mathbf{W}(y, x) > 0\}$ the *pre-set* of x. Similarly, $x^\bullet = \{y \in P \cup T \mid \mathbf{W}(x, y) > 0\}$ is the *post-set* of x.

Discrete Petri Nets. A DPN $\mathcal{N} = (\mathsf{N}, M_0)$ is a net $\mathsf{N} = (P, T, \mathbf{W})$, with $\mathbf{W}$ taking values in $\mathbb{Z}$, together with a (discrete) *marking* $M_0\colon P \to \mathbb{N}_0$, called the *initial marking*. A discrete marking models the resource allocation in the system by assigning a natural number of tokens to each place. A transition $t \in T$ is *enabled* at a marking M, denoted $M \xrightarrow{t}$, if and only if $\forall p \in {}^\bullet t, M(p) \geq \mathbf{W}(p,t)$. An enabled transition can fire, $M \xrightarrow{t} M'$, leading to a new marking M' defined for each $p \in P$ as follows:

$$M'(p) \triangleq M(p) - \mathbf{W}(p,t) + \mathbf{W}(t,p)$$

Let us consider the example net from Fig. 4 with the initial marking $M_0 = \{(p_1, 1), (p_2, 0)\}$. Transition t_1 is enabled at M_0, leading to marking $M_1 = \{(p_1, 0), (p_2, 1)\}$ as illustrated in Fig. 4 on the right hand side. M_1, however, is a *deadlock*, i.e. a marking at which no transition is enabled.

A *(finite) firing sequence* is a word $w = (t_i)_{i<n\in\mathbb{N}_0}$ over T for which there exists a sequence of markings $(M_i)_{i<n+1}$ such that $M_i \xrightarrow{t_i} M_{i+1}$ for all $i < n$. We denote the set of markings reachable from some marking M in $\mathcal{N}$ by $\mathbf{RS}_{\mathcal{N}}(M) = \{M' \mid \exists w \in T^*, M \xrightarrow{w} M'\}$, or simply $\mathbf{RS}(M)$ when there is no ambiguity about $\mathcal{N}$.

A DPN all of whose reachable markings have at most one token per place, $\forall M \in \mathbf{RS}(M_0), \forall p \in P, M(p) \leq 1$, is *safe* (also 1-bounded). The PNs that encode BNs are necessarily safe; therefore we will focus on bounded nets throughout.

We only describe discrete PNs in passing here, to prepare the discussion of continuous Petri nets; however, DPNs and their connection to BNs with classical asynchronous semantics are interesting in their own right, witness the results and discussion in [2] and the effective attractor search developed in [1].

Beyond Infinity: Continuous Petri Nets. A CPN $\mathcal{N} = (\mathsf{N}, \mathbf{m}_0)$ is a net $\mathsf{N} = (P, T, \mathbf{W})$ with a (continuous) marking $\mathbf{m}_0 \colon P \to \mathbb{R}_0^+$, called the initial marking. Similarly to the discrete case, continuous markings also model resource allocation, but assign $\mathbb{R}_0^+$-valued token mass instead of discrete tokens. A transition $t \in T$ has an *enabling degree* at marking $\mathbf{m}$ given by $\mathsf{enab}(t, \mathbf{m}) = \min_{p\in {}^\bullet t} \frac{\mathbf{m}(p)}{\mathbf{W}(p,t)}$ when ${}^\bullet t \neq \emptyset$, and equal to ∞ otherwise. A transition with $\mathsf{enab}(t, \mathbf{m}) > 0$ is enabled at $\mathbf{m}$ and can α-fire for any $\alpha \in [0, \mathsf{enab}(t, \mathbf{m})] \cap \mathbb{R}$, $\mathbf{m} \xrightarrow{\alpha t} \mathbf{m}'$, leading to a new marking $\mathbf{m}'$ defined for each $p \in P$ as follows:

$$\mathbf{m}'(p) \triangleq \mathbf{m}(p) - \alpha\mathbf{W}(p,t) + \alpha\mathbf{W}(t,p)$$

Again, a finite firing sequence is a finite word, but this time of the form $\sigma = (\alpha_i t_i)_{i<n\in\mathbb{N}_0}$ over $\mathbb{R}_0^+ \times T$ for which there exists a finite sequence of markings $(\mathbf{m}_i)_{i<n+1}$ such that $\mathbf{m}_i \xrightarrow{\alpha_i t_i} \mathbf{m}_{i+1}$ for all $i < n$. An infinite firing sequence is an infinite word $\sigma = (\alpha_i t_i)_{n\in\mathbb{N}_0}$ over $\mathbb{R}_0^+ \times T$ for which there exists an infinite family of markings $(\mathbf{m}_i)_{i\leq\omega}$ such that $\mathbf{m}_i \xrightarrow{\alpha_i t_i} \mathbf{m}_{i+1}$ for all $i \in \mathbb{N}_0$ and $\lim_{i\to\infty} \mathbf{m}_i = \mathbf{m}_\omega$.

We denote the set of markings reachable from some marking $\mathbf{m}$ in $\mathcal{N}$ by $\mathbf{RS}_{\mathcal{N}}(\mathbf{m}) = \{\mathbf{m}' \mid \exists \sigma \in (\mathbb{R}_0^+ \times T)^*, \mathbf{m} \xrightarrow{\sigma} \mathbf{m}'\}$. We further denote the set of markings reachable in the limit (lim-reachable) from some marking $\mathbf{m}$ in $\mathcal{N}$ by lim$-\mathbf{RS}_{\mathcal{N}}(\mathbf{m}) = \{\mathbf{m}' \mid \exists \sigma \in (\mathbb{R}_0^+ \times T)^\omega, \mathbf{m} \xrightarrow{\sigma} \mathbf{m}'\}$. Since an infinite firing sequence can include null firings ($\alpha = 0$), we have $\mathbf{RS}_{\mathcal{N}}(\mathbf{m}) \subseteq$ lim$-\mathbf{RS}_{\mathcal{N}}(\mathbf{m})$. We write simply $\mathbf{RS}(\mathbf{m})$ and lim$-\mathbf{RS}(\mathbf{m})$ when $\mathcal{N}$ is obvious.

Similar to DPNs, a CPN all of whose reachable markings have token mass at most 1 per place, $\forall \mathbf{m} \in \mathbf{RS}(\mathbf{m}_0), \forall p \in P, \mathbf{m}(p) \leq 1$, is safe. The notions of safeness and lim-safeness coincide [10].

The ability to fire a transition by varying degree means that there are infinitely many possible firings in any marking at which at least one transition is enabled. We therefore cannot visualise all the possible transition firings of a CPN in the same fashion as Fig. 4 does for a DPN. Symbolic analysis methods have therefore been introduced for CPN dynamics, namely abstract reachability graphs (ARG) and symbolic reachability trees (SRT) [8].

The ARG constitutes an abstraction of the state space, in which markings that have the same *support*, i.e. the set of places which have non-zero token mass, $[[\mathbf{m}]] \triangleq \{p \in P \mid \mathbf{m}(p) > 0\}$, are grouped into equivalence classes. Supports are linked between one another by two types of edges, *anonymous* and *border*, both representing the possibility of the system evolving into a marking with different support. Anonymous edges indicate reversible changes; Border edges are of special interest, as they represent occurrences that *permanently disable* one or more transitions, thus shaping the reachability landscape.

The SRT provides a refined view at such a landscape in the form of a directed tree linked by border edges. The nodes of the tree are aggregations of markings by their *mode*, i.e. the set of transitions eventually fireable from the given marking: $T_{\mathbf{m}} \triangleq \{t \in T \mid \exists \mathbf{m} \xrightarrow{\sigma}, t \in [[\sigma]]\}$, where $[[\sigma]]$ is the set of all transitions occurring along σ with $\alpha > 0$. The branches of the tree then indicate refinements of those modes, as less and less transitions remain available. The depth of the SRT is naturally bounded by $|T|$.

We omit the formal definition of ARG and SRT due to space constraints. The reader is instead referred to [8]. Both the ARG and SRT of the example net are illustrated in Fig. 5.

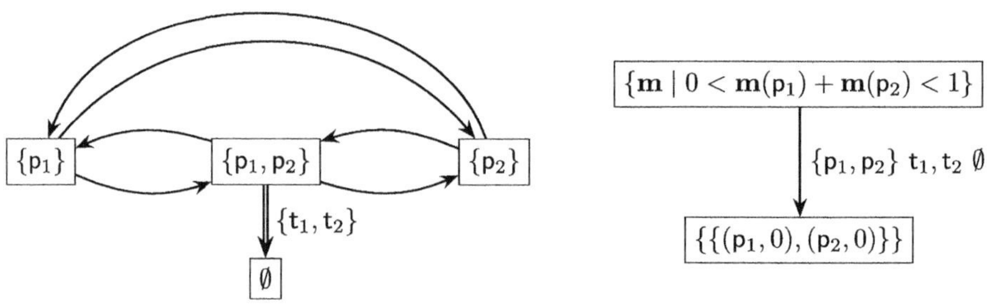

Fig. 5. [8,9] The ARG (left) and the SRT (right) of the example net from Fig. 4. The border edges are given as double line arrows in the ARG. The SRT for this example is trivial, as there is only one border edge leading from a marking whose support (set of places with positive token mass) is $\{p_1, p_2\}$, and which uses an infinite firing sequence of instances of t_1 and t_2 to reach the empty marking.

Observe that as opposed to the DPN (Fig. 4), t_2 can be fired in a CPN with the same initial marking $\mathbf{m}_0 = M_0$. Firing of t_2 halfs the token mass, every *loop* around the net thus results in a marking with less total token mass. This phenomenon is illustrative, as the two places of the net are a trap, that is $\{p_1, p_2\}^\bullet \subseteq {}^\bullet\{p_1, p_2\}$. It is a well known result for DPNs that an initially marked trap cannot be emptied [6]. This result extends to reachability in CPNs, indeed after any finite number of transition firings, there will always be some token mass left, however, the empty marking is lim-reachable.

Transfinite Sequences. Classical reachability, i.e. underwritten by some finite firing sequences, has been seen to be an insufficient measure of the CPN dynamics; the natural semantics here is indeed lim-reachability, as argued above. However, to capture the dynamics that sets in *from* some lim −reached state $\mathbf{m}$, one would like to concatenate the new sequence of actions *after* the infinite sequence that led into $\mathbf{m}$: it becomes thus natural to look at *transfinite* sequences $(\alpha_n t_n)_{n<\kappa}$ for κ some transfinite ordinal. In fact, even small examples suffice to see that the exploration of CPN dynamics requires the passage to such transfinite sequences. In the CPN of Fig. 6, consider the following transfinite firing sequence whose (countable) ordinal is $\omega + 1$:

$$\sigma = (2^{-n}t_1)_{n\geq 1} \cdot 1t_3$$

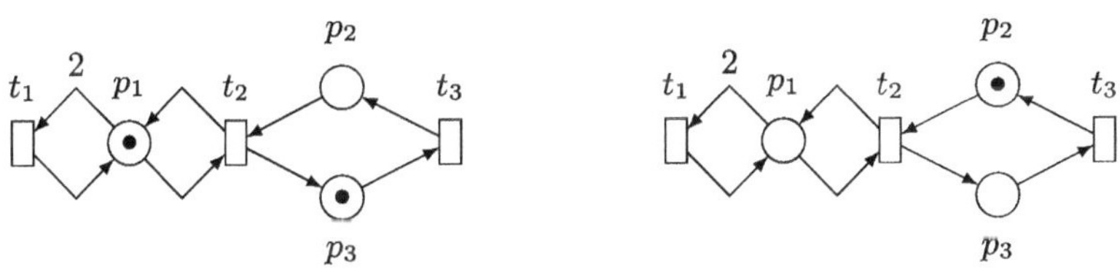

Fig. 6. An example CPN exhibiting the necessity of studying transfinite sequences.

The trajectory generated by σ is: $T \cdot \{t_3\} \cdot \emptyset$; *it cannot be generated by an infinite firing sequence.* This means that in order to fully apprehend the state space and pathways in a CPN, transfinite sequences have to be systematically explored; note that results from [8] show that no sequences longer than ω^2 are relevant.

4 Why CPNs Are Worth the Effort

We will now state the main reasons why the use of CPNs is relevant, in our opinion, for the attractor search in boolean systems.

4.1 The SRT Gives All Attractors

Indeed:

Theorem 1 ([8]). *Let* $(\mathcal{N}, \mathbf{m}_0)$ *be a bounded marked CPN such that for all* $\mathbf{m} \in \lim\!-\mathbf{RS}(\mathcal{N}, \mathbf{m}_0)$, $T_{\mathbf{m}} = T_{\mathbf{m}_0}$. *Then for all* $\mathbf{m} \in \lim\!-\mathbf{RS}(\mathcal{N}, \mathbf{m}_0)$, $\lim\!-\mathbf{RS}(\mathcal{N}, \mathbf{m}) = \lim\!-\mathbf{RS}(\mathcal{N}, \mathbf{m}_0)$.

In fact, this result implies that the leaves of the SRT (those are the modes from which no other mode is reachable) all correspond (in general not 1-1) to an attractor of the underlying continuous Petri net; conversely, every attractor is represented by one or more of those leaves.

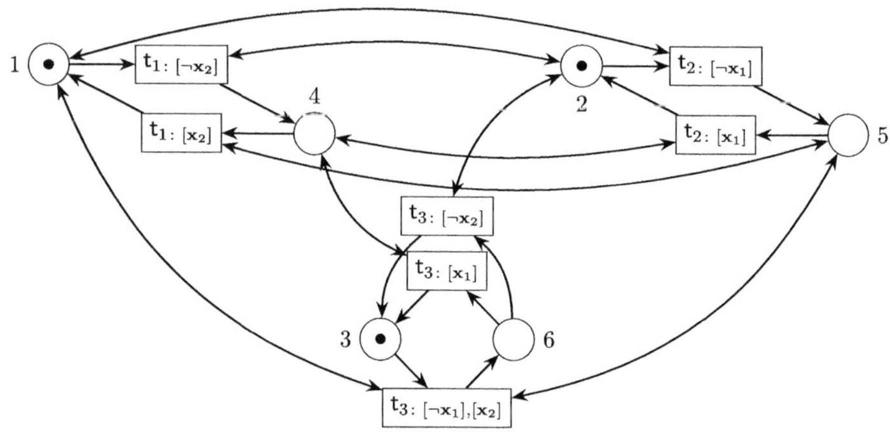

Fig. 7. [9] The PN encoding of the example BN given in Fig. 1. The loops are depicted as double headed arrows to avoid clutter.

4.2 Encoding a BN as a CPN Faithfully Translates Reachability, both Ways

While we will not detail the construction that takes as input a BN and produces a CPN (those elements can be found in [9]), a comparison of Fig. 7 with Fig. 1 may suffice here: for every variable we create two Petri net places, whose token mass will always add up to 1 and represent the increase or decrease in value of the variable concerned. Transitions are created for all cases of increase or decrease that the boolean function imposes, depending on the marking of influencing variables that are connected by arc loops. If we denote the Petri net that is associated to boolean network f by $\mathsf{N}(f)$, we obtain the following result (not yet reviewed):

Theorem 2 ([9]**Continuous Petri Nets Simulate MP Boolean Networks**). *Let* f *be a Boolean network of dimension* n. *Then, for any configurations* $\mathbf{x}, \mathbf{y} \in \mathbb{B}^n$, $\mathbf{x} \xrightarrow[f]{mp}{}^{*}\, \mathbf{y} \iff \langle \mathbf{y} \rangle \in \lim\!-\mathbf{RS}_{\mathsf{N}(f)}(\langle \mathbf{x} \rangle)$.

5 Conclusion

It had been known that the power of Boolean network can be enhanced by MP semantics for improved coverage and attractor detection, while completely preserving the discrete nature of the model and accepting only a mild increase in the size of the data structure. Recent results have now shown that MP semantics can be given a compagnon representation in the form of continuous Petri nets, where the MP dynamics is faithfully reflected. While the admission of *infinite* state spaces and *transfinite* transition sequences may seem an inacceptable price to pay, the consistent use of adequate abstraction and purely structural methods for Petri nets actually allows to obtain discrete behavioural representations of bounded size and at a reasonable computational cost. We hope these arguments motivate our colleagues from the AUTOMATA community to join our journey - *to infinity and beyond*.

References

1. Chatain, T., Haar, S., Jezequel, L., Paulevé, L., Schwoon, S.: Characterization of reachable attractors using Petri net unfoldings. Comput. Methods Syst. Biol. **8859**, 129–142 (2014)
2. Chatain, T., Haar, S., Kolčák, J., Paulevé, L., Thakkar, A.: Concurrency in boolean networks. Nat. Comput. **19**, 91–109 (2020)
3. Chatain, T., Haar, S., Koutny, M., Schwoon, S.: Non-atomic transition firing in contextual nets. In: Devillers, R., Valmari, A. (eds.) PETRI NETS 2015. LNCS, vol. 9115, pp. 117–136. Springer, Cham (2015). https://doi.org/10.1007/978-3-319-19488-2_6
4. Chatain, T., Haar, S., Paulevé, L.: Boolean networks: beyond generalized asynchronicity. In: Baetens, J.M., Kutrib, M. (eds.) AUTOMATA 2018. LNCS, vol. 10875, pp. 29–42. Springer, Cham (2018). https://doi.org/10.1007/978-3-319-92675-9_3
5. de Jong, H.: Modeling and simulation of genetic regulatory systems: a literature review. J. Comput. Biol. **9**(1), 67–103 (2002)
6. Desel, J., Esparza, J.: Free Choice Petri Nets. Cambridge University Press, Cambridge (1995)
7. Faure, A., Naldi, A., Chaouiya, C., Thieffry, D.: Dynamical analysis of a generic Boolean model for the control of the mammalian cell cycle. Bioinformatics **22**(14), 124–131 (2006)
8. Haar, S., Haddad, S.: On the expressive power of transfinite sequences for continuous Petri nets. In: Kristensen, L.M., van der Werf, J.M. (eds.) PETRI NETS 2024. LNCS, vol. 14628, pp. 109–131. Springer, Cham (2024). https://doi.org/10.1007/978-3-031-61433-0_6
9. Haar, S., Kolčák, J.: Continuous petri nets faithfully fluidify most permissive boolean networks (2025). arXiv:2505.16683 [cs.DM]
10. Júlvez, J., Recalde, L., Silva, M.: On reachability in autonomous continuous Petri net systems. In: van der Aalst, W.M.P., Best, E. (eds.) ICATPN 2003. LNCS, vol. 2679, pp. 221–240. Springer, Heidelberg (2003). https://doi.org/10.1007/3-540-44919-1_16

11. Mangan, S., Alon, U.: Structure and function of the feed-forward loop network motif. Proc. Natl. Acad. Sci. **100**(21), 11980–11985 (2003)
12. Martínez-Sosa, P., Mendoza, L.: The regulatory network that controls the differentiation of t lymphocytes. Biosystems **113**(2), 96–103 (2013)
13. Paulevé, L., Kolčák, J., Chatain, T., Haar, S.: Reconciling qualitative, abstract, and scalable modeling of biological networks. Nat. Commun. **11**(4256), 5 (2020)
14. Wang, R.-S., Saadatpour, A., Albert, R.: Boolean modeling in systems biology: an overview of methodology and applications. Phys. Biol. **9**(5), 055001 (2012)

Cellular Automata and Percolation: an Overview of Selected Connections

Irène Marcovici(✉)

Univ Rouen Normandie, CNRS, Normandie Univ, LMRS UMR 6085, 76000 Rouen, France
irene.marcovici@univ-rouen.fr

Abstract. Cellular automata and percolation theory have been mutually enriching for some time now. Percolation theory studies the connectivity properties of random subgraphs of a regular network, and provides tools for studying probabilistic cellular automata. In some cases, it is also a great help for analysing the evolution of deterministic cellular automata which evolve from random configurations. Conversely, the theory of cellular automata provides new insights into some percolation properties, and raises many questions. In the present survey article, we recall some well-known connections between cellular automata and percolation, together with a more recent development, the study of a percolation game.

Keywords: cellular automata · percolation

In the last decades, various works have highlighted some connections between cellular automata and percolation [12,20–22]. The aim of this article is to give a few examples illustrating the different forms these connections can take. To begin with, let us introduce cellular automata and percolation in a few words.

A cellular automaton (CA) is a dynamical system defined on the set $S^{\mathbb{Z}^d}$, for some finite set S of *symbols* (or *states*). It is obtained by iterating a local update rule simultaneously at every site of the lattice. Formally, for $n_1, \dots, n_m \in \mathbb{Z}^d$, the *cellular automaton* (CA) of *neighbourhood* $\mathcal{N} = \{n_1, \dots, n_m\}$ and local rule $f : S^m \to S$ is the function: $F : S^{\mathbb{Z}^d} \to S^{\mathbb{Z}^d}$ defined by:

$$\forall x \in S^{\mathbb{Z}^d},\ \forall k \in \mathbb{Z}^d,\ F(x)_k = f(x_{k+n_1}, \dots, x_{k+n_m}).$$

For probabilistic cellular automata (PCA), all the cells are still updated simultaneously in discrete time, but the local rule is now a function $\varphi : S^m \to \mathcal{M}(S)$, where $\mathcal{M}(S)$ denotes the set of probability distributions on S. From a configuration $x \in S^{\mathbb{Z}^d}$, cell $k \in \mathbb{Z}^d$ is updated by a symbol chosen according to the distribution $\varphi(x_{k+n_1}, \dots, x_{k+n_m})$, independently for different cells. The local function φ allows one to define a global map $\Phi : \mathcal{M}(S^{\mathbb{Z}^d}) \to \mathcal{M}(S^{\mathbb{Z}^d})$, describing the action of the PCA on a configuration drawn according to a certain probability distribution.

Published by Springer Nature Switzerland AG 2026
S. Riva and A. Richard (Eds.): AUTOMATA 2025, LNCS 15831, pp. 27–42, 2026.
https://doi.org/10.1007/978-3-032-01570-9_3

As an example, let us fix a value $\varepsilon \in [0,1]$, and consider the one-dimensional binary CA of neighbourhood $\mathcal{N} = \{-1, 0, 1\}$, defined by the local rule:

$$\varphi(x, y, z) = (1-\varepsilon)\,\delta_{x+z} + \varepsilon\,\delta_{x+z+1} = \begin{cases} x+z \text{ with probability } 1-\varepsilon \\ x+z+1 \text{ with probability } \varepsilon \end{cases},$$

where the sums $x + z$ and $x + z + 1$ are computed modulo 2. The local rule thus consists in computing the sum (modulo 2) of the left neighbour and of the right neighbour, but with a probability ε of making a mistake, independently for different cells. For $\varepsilon = 0$, we recover a deterministic CA (rule 90 in Wolfram's notation), whose space-time diagram reveals a Sierpiński triangle when the initial configuration contains a single 1. Figure 1 shows two examples of space-time diagrams for the parameter $\varepsilon = 0.001$, from different initial configurations. Observe that if we erase the first few lines of the space-time diagram, it is quite difficult to have an idea of what the initial configuration was. The *noisy sum PCA* can indeed be shown to be ergodic for any $\varepsilon \in (0,1)$, see Sect. 2 for a formal definition. Moreover, its unique invariant measure is the uniform distribution [22].

Initial config. with a single 1

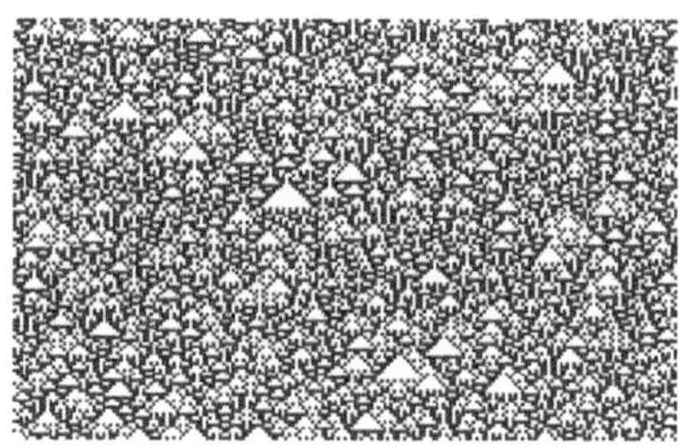

Initial config. distributed unif. at random

Fig. 1. Two space-time diagrams of the noisy sum PCA of parameter $\varepsilon = 0.001$, from different initial configurations (time goes up).

Percolation theory studies the properties of connected clusters in a random subgraph of a lattice. Let us label each cell of the grid $\mathbb{Z}^d$ independently by a 1 with probability p, and by a 0 with probability $1-p$, for some parameter $p \in (0,1)$. For p sufficiently large, the random configurations obtained contain almost surely an infinite path of cells labeled by 1, while for p small, the islands of cells in state 1 are almost surely all finite, see Fig. 2 for an illustration with $d = 2$. Among other questions, percolation theory is interested in investigating the critical value of the parameter p above which there exists almost surely such an infinite cluster.

Given a neighbourhood $\mathcal{N} = \{n_1, \ldots, n_m\}$, one can also consider the directed graph with set of vertices $\mathbb{Z}^d \times \mathbb{N}$, and bonds from (k,t) to $(k - n_i, t+1)$, for $k \in \mathbb{Z}^d, t \in \mathbb{N}$ and $n_i \in \mathcal{N}$. Again, we can label each vertex of $\mathbb{Z}^d \times \mathbb{N}$

independently by a 1 with probability p, and ask whether there exist infinite directed paths of vertices in state 1 in this directed percolation model, see Fig. 3 for an illustration with $d = 1$ and $\mathcal{N} = \{-1, 0, 1\}$.

$p = 0.4$ $p = 0.5$ $p = 0.6$

Fig. 2. Undirected site percolation on $\mathbb{Z}^2$: connected component of the origin for random configurations with different parameters.

$p = 0.4$ $p = 0.5$ $p = 0.6$

Fig. 3. Directed site percolation of neighbourhood $\mathcal{N} = \{-1, 0, 1\}$: connected component of the origin for random configurations with different parameters.

In Sect. 1, we study the evolution of some specific two-dimensional binary deterministic CA from random initial configurations. The first one is the *bootstrap CA*, which can be seen as a dynamical model of percolation. The second one is *Toom majority CA*, and exhibits a bifurcation behaviour, depending on whether the density of the initial configuration is greater or smaller than 1/2. The proof strongly relies on the fact that on the triangular lattice, the site percolation threshold is equal to 1/2.

In Sect. 2, we study the asymptotic behaviour of PCA, and show that properties of directed percolation on $\mathbb{Z}^d \times \mathbb{N}$ can be used to prove the ergodicity of a PCA on $\mathbb{Z}^d$.

Finally, in Sect. 3, we introduce and study a specific PCA that is related to the *hardcore model*, a model of lattice gas systems which has received much attention in statistical physics. We show that this PCA plays an unexpected role in the enumeration of *directed animals*, which are the possible shapes that directed percolation clusters can take, and that it is also involved in the study of a combinatorial game on percolation configurations.

We will sketch the strategies of the proofs without writing the proofs in detail. For further precision, the interested readers can consult the references that are provided all along the article. We shall generally refer to the book by Kůrka [16] and the survey by Kari [15] for background on deterministic cellular automata and to the surveys by Toom et al. [22] and Mairesse and Marcovici [18] for background on probabilistic cellular automata. The authoritative reference on percolation is the book by Grimmett [11].

1 Two Well-Known Examples of CA Related to Percolation

In the following, we denote by $e_1 = (1,0)$ and $e_2 = (0,1)$ the two vectors of the standard basis of $\mathbb{R}^2$.

1.1 Bootstrap Cellular Automaton

Let us consider a binary CA whose local rule satisfies the following property: a cell in state 1 remains in state 1, and a cell in state 0 changes to a 1 if it has at least ℓ neighbours in state 1, for some fixed value ℓ. Such a CA can be seen as a simple model of infection spreading, where a cell becomes "infected" by contact with ℓ or more already infected neighbours, without possible remission. The two-dimensional case with $\ell = 2$ has attracted much attention. Precisely, let us define the *bootstrap CA* as the CA $F_B : \{0,1\}^{\mathbb{Z}^2} \to \{0,1\}^{\mathbb{Z}^2}$ defined on von Neumann neighbourhood $\mathcal{N} = \{0, \pm e_1, \pm e_2\}$ by the local rule

$$f_B((x_i)_{i\in\mathcal{N}}) = \begin{cases} 1 & \text{if} \quad x_0 = 1 \quad \text{or} \quad \text{Card}\,\{i \in \mathcal{N} : x_i = 1\} \geq 2, \\ 0 & \text{otherwise.} \end{cases}$$

Experimentally, when iterating this CA from an initial configuration where cells are in state 1 with probability p, independently for different cells, the state 1 invades the grid very quickly if p is large, while for p very small, we observe a stabilisation on a configuration made of disjoint rectangles of occupied cells. However, the following result was proved by van Enter [7].

Theorem 1. *For any $p > 0$, the bootstrap CA on the infinite lattice $\mathbb{Z}^2$ converges almost surely to the configuration "all 1", when iterated from an initial configuration where cells are in state 1 with probability p, independently for different cells.*

Sketch of the Proof. The proof is based on the following observation: if there is somewhere in the configuration an occupied square (that is, a square whose cells are all in state 1) that is not surrounded by any empty rectangular contour (that is, a closed path of cells having a regular shape, whose cells are all in state 0), then we are sure that the state 1 will invade the grid. Even if p is very small, whatever the value of N, the probability of a square with side N being occupied is strictly positive, so that there exists almost surely such an occupied square in the configuration, as we work with infinite configurations. If N is sufficiently large, it is very likely that this occupied square has at least one cell in state 1 on its edge, and so on, resulting in the entire grid being invaded. □

More recent work by Holroyd has led to a better understanding of what happens on finite grids [13]. In a nutshell, on a large $N \times N$ grid, if $p > \pi^2/(18 \log N)$, convergence to total occupancy occurs with high probability, while if $p < \pi^2/(18 \log N)$, it is not the case. However, one would need to do simulations on grids with a side of the order of 10^{20} to observe this threshold experimentally, as explained by Gravner and Holroyd [10].

1.2 Toom's Majority CA

Another class of interesting binary CA consists in majority CA, for which the local rule is such that a cell changes to a 0 (resp. 1) if it has a strict majority of neighbours in state 0 (resp. 1). As a particular case, let us introduce Toom's majority CA: it is the binary CA $F_T : \{0,1\}^{\mathbb{Z}^2} \to \{0,1\}^{\mathbb{Z}^2}$ of neighbourhood $\mathcal{N} = \{0, e_1, e_2\}$ defined by the local rule

$$f_T(x_0, x_{e_1}, x_{e_2}) = \begin{cases} 1 & \text{if} \quad x_0 + x_{e_1} + x_{e_2} \geq 2, \\ 0 & \text{otherwise.} \end{cases}$$

Unlike the bootstrap CA presented above, it presents a bifurcation phenomenon, according to the initial density of 1's [2].

Theorem 2. *Let us consider an initial configuration where cells are in state* 1 *with probability* p*, independently for different cells. If* $p < 1/2$*, Toom's majority CA converges almost surely to the configuration "all* 0*", while if* $p > 1/2$*, it converges almost surely to the configuration "all* 1*".*

Sketch of the Proof. The proof of this result strongly relies on the fact that on the triangular lattice, the value of the site percolation threshold is exactly 1/2. By symmetry, it is sufficient to prove the result for $p < 1/2$. Let us consider the (undirected) graph whose set of vertices is $\mathbb{Z}^2$, with the usual horizontal and vertical edges $\{x, x + e_1\}$ and $\{x, x + e_2\}$, for $x \in \mathbb{Z}^2$, together with NW-SE diagonal edges $\{x, x + e_2 - e_1\}$. We thus obtain a triangular lattice, and it is known that for $p < 1/2$, there exists almost surely no infinite 1-cluster in the initial configuration. Thus, the set of initially occupied cells consists almost surely of a countable union of finite 1-clusters. Toom's rule does not break up or connect different 1-clusters, and it is an *eroder*, which implies that any finite 1-cluster disappears in finite time. These ingredients allow one to demonstrate the desired result. □

For a given $\varepsilon > 0$, let us consider the PCA that applies Toom's rule with probability $1 - \varepsilon$, and do the contrary with probability ε, independently for different cells. For ε small enough, this PCA is known to have several invariant distributions. More precisely, it has at least one invariant distribution close to the configuration "all 0" and one close to "all 1". It thus provides a simple example of two-dimensional non-ergodic *positive-rate* PCA (all the probability transitions are strictly between 0 and 1). In dimension 1, it is much harder to exhibit positive-rate PCA that are non-ergodic: the only known example is due to Gács [9], and is very complicated. Also, it is on open problem to know whether there exists a one-dimensional CA that presents the same bifurcation phenomenon as Toom's CA. This is related to the density classification problem [2].

2 Ergodicity of PCA and Directed Percolation

A PCA is said to be *ergodic* if it asymptotically "forgets" its initial condition, meaning that the trajectories always converge to the same distribution regardless of the initial configuration. Formally, a PCA Φ is ergodic if it has a unique invariant probability distribution π that attracts every initial distribution, in the sense that for any distribution μ of $\mathcal{M}(S^{\mathbb{Z}^d})$, $\mu\Phi^t \to \pi$ weakly as $t \to +\infty$.

We will see that a comparison with directed percolation of same neighbourhood provides a sufficient condition for the ergodicity of PCA. First, let us come back to the directed percolation model, and show that this process can be interpreted as a PCA.

2.1 The Percolation PCA

Let $\mathcal{N} = \{n_1, \ldots, n_m\}$ be a given subset of $\mathbb{Z}^d$, and consider the PCA Φ_p on $\{0,1\}^{\mathbb{Z}^d}$ defined by the local function:

$$\varphi_p(a_1, \ldots, a_m) = p\, \delta_{\max\{a_1,\ldots,a_m\}} + (1-p)\, \delta_0,$$

meaning that if a cell has at least a 1 in its neighbourhood, it becomes a 1 with probability p, and otherwise, it takes state 0. This PCA, which is also referred to as *Stavskaya PCA* for $d = 1$ and $\mathcal{N} = \{0, 1\}$, can be seen as a dynamical version of directed percolation of neighbourhood $\mathcal{N}$. Assume that all sites are in state 1 in the initial configuration of the PCA. We can then couple the space-time diagram of Stavskaya PCA with a directed percolation process, in such a way that cell k is in state 1 at time t for the PCA if and only if in the percolation process, there is a directed path from some site $(l, 0)$ to the site (k, t), along which all sites are in state 1. As a consequence, the PCA has two possible behaviour depending on whether p is smaller or larger than the percolation threshold $p_c(\mathcal{N})$ of the directed percolation model of neighbourhood $\mathcal{N}$. If $p < p_c(\mathcal{N})$, then whatever the initial configuration is, the state 1 dies out and the PCA converges to the configuration containing only the state 0, while if $p > p_c(\mathcal{N})$, from an initial configuration that contains cells in state 1, the state 1 has a positive survival probability.

2.2 Ergodicity Criterion

We will now present a criterion of ergodicity that is based on a coupling of the trajectories from all the possible initial configurations, and on a comparison with directed percolation. Intuitively, a PCA is ergodic if it "forgets" its initial condition. In some cases, it is possible to prove the ergodicity in a constructive way, by making evolve simultaneously the trajectories from different initial conditions, using a common source of randomness, and showing that the evolutions of all these trajectories are asymptotically the same.

The *envelope PCA* allows one to systematize this idea of *coupling*. Instead of running the PCA from different initial configurations, we define a new PCA on an extended alphabet, containing a symbol ? representing sites whose values are not known (i.e. which may differ between the different copies) and we run it from a single initial configuration containing only the symbol ?. Each time we are able to make the different copies match on a cell, the symbol ? is replaced by the state $q \in S$ on which the different copies agree. An evolution of the envelope PCA thus encodes a coupling of different copies of the original PCA, with a symbol ? denoting sites where the copies disagree. If the density of symbols ? converges to 0 when time goes to infinity, it means that the PCA is ergodic.

The envelope PCA was introduced in [3] as a tool to prove the ergodicity of a PCA and to generate perfect samples from its unique invariant distribution. The idea of the envelope PCA is reminiscent of the minorant PCA introduced by Toom et al. [22, Chap. 3], which can be used in a more or less similar fashion to prove ergodicity in the high-noise regime, and similar ideas have been pursued by others [8].

To simplify the presentation, let us assume that Φ is a PCA defined on a binary symbol set $S = \{0, 1\}$, and let $\tilde{S} = \{0, 1, ?\}$. We define a partial order on $\tilde{S}$ by $0 \prec ? \succ 1$. The *envelope PCA* $\tilde{\Phi}$ of Φ is the PCA of neighbourhood $\mathcal{N}$ and local function $\tilde{\varphi} : \tilde{S}^m \to \mathcal{M}(\tilde{S})$, defined for $q \in S$ by:

$$\tilde{\varphi}(y_1, \ldots, y_m)(q) = \min\{\varphi(x_1, \ldots, x_m)(q) : x_1 \preceq y_1, \ldots, x_m \preceq y_m\},$$

where in the expression above, $x_1, \ldots, x_m$ are taken in S. The probability of a transition to the symbol ? is then given by:

$$\tilde{\varphi}(y_1, \ldots, y_m)(?) = 1 - \tilde{\varphi}(y_1, \ldots, y_m)(0) - \tilde{\varphi}(y_1, \ldots, y_m)(1).$$

From a configuration $y \in \tilde{S}^{\mathbb{Z}^d}$, cell k is thus updated by the symbol $q \in S$ with the minimum of the probabilities of transition to the symbol q for Φ, taken over all the values of the neighbourhood of cell k that are compatible with the unknown cells of y. With the remaining probability, the cell is updated by a ?.

In particular, in the evolution of the envelope PCA, at each time step, a cell is updated by the symbol ? only if it has at least one neighbour in state ?, and in that case, it becomes a ? with probability at most:

$$p_? = 1 - \min_{x_1, \ldots, x_m \in S} \varphi(x_1, \ldots, x_m)(0) - \min_{x_1, \ldots, x_m \in S} \varphi(x_1, \ldots, x_m)(1).$$

This quantity measures how much the probability transitions depend on the value of the neighbourhood, and we have the following result [3].

Theorem 3. *Let* $p_c(\mathcal{N})$ *be the critical value of the two-dimensional directed site percolation of neighbourhood* $\mathcal{N}$. *If* $p_? < p_c(\mathcal{N})$, *then* $\tilde{\Phi}^t \delta_{?^{\mathbb{Z}^d}}[?] \xrightarrow[t \to +\infty]{} 0$, *so that the PCA* Φ *is ergodic.*

Sketch of the Proof. Let us consider the directed graph describing the dependences between cells in the space-time diagram of the PCA. It is exactly the graph of set of vertices $\mathbb{Z}^d \times \mathbb{N}$, and bonds:

$$\vec{E} = \{((k,t),(k-n_i,t+1)) : k \in \mathbb{Z}^d, t \in \mathbb{Z}, n_i \in \mathcal{N}\}.$$

By dominating the process of symbols ? in the space-time diagram of the envelope PCA by Stavskaya PCA of parameter $p_?$, one proves that if $p_? < p_c(\mathcal{N})$, then the symbols ? die out. The result follows. □

2.3 The General Ergodicity Problem

As already noted, Theorem 3 only provides a sufficient condition for ergodicity. First, there exist simple examples of PCA that can be proved to be ergodic, but for which the envelope PCA is not ergodic. It is the case for example of the noisy sum PCA, when the noise ε is small [3]. Second, there are PCA for which the envelope PCA is ergodic, but with $p_? > p_c(\mathcal{N})$, so that the criterion of Theorem 3 is of no help for proving the ergodicity, see Sect. 3.2. In fact, Theorem 3 proves the ergodicity in the *high-noise regime*, when the local rule of the PCA depends sufficiently weakly on the value of the neighbourhood. Outside this regime, ergodicity is often difficult to prove, even in cases where it appears clear from heuristics or simulations. In Ref. [19], the authors gather different techniques for proving the ergodicity of PCA that are the perturbation of a deterministic CA by a small (positive) noise, but apart from specific families of CA (nilpotent, permutive, gliders, CA with a spreading symbol, surjective, algebraic), the problem is still largely open.

3 The Hardcore PCA: A Combinatorial Excursion on Percolation

In this section, we study from different points of view the binary one-dimensional PCA of neighbourhood $\mathcal{N} = \{0,1\}$ that is presented in Fig. 4. We first present the close relationship between this PCA and the *hardcore model* from statistical physics. Then, we show that this PCA is related to percolation in at least two ways: it has an invariant distribution that is related to the counting series of directed percolation clusters, and it also appears in the study of a combinatorial game on percolation configurations.

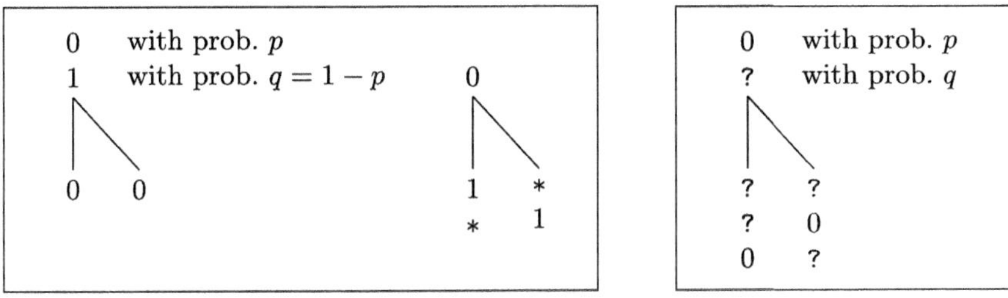

Fig. 4. Probability transitions of the hardcore PCA (left) and additional transitions of its envelope PCA (right). The symbol $*$ denotes an arbitrary symbol.

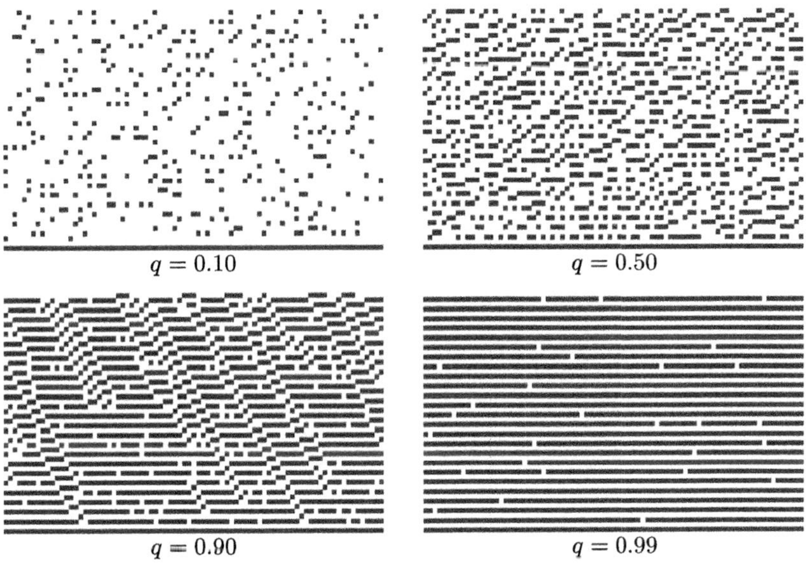

Fig. 5. Space-time diagrams of the hardcore PCA for the parameters $q = 0.10$, $q = 0.50$, $q = 0.90$ and $q = 0.99$, from the initial configuration "all 1" (time is going up).

3.1 The Hardcore Model

The hardcore model is a model of statistical mechanics in which particles are allowed to be on the vertices of a graph, but with the constraint that no two particles may be adjacent. Formally, let $G = (V, E)$ be a finite graph. A configuration $\omega \in \{0,1\}^V$ is said to be a *hardcore configuration* (or an *independent set*) if for any $i, j \in V$ such that $\{i, j\} \in E$, $(\omega_i, \omega_j) \neq (1, 1)$. We denote by $\mathcal{H}$ the set of hardcore configurations. Let $\lambda > 0$. The *hardcore measure on G with activity λ* is the probability distribution μ on $\{0,1\}^V$ defined by:

$$\forall \omega \in \{0,1\}^V, \quad \mu(\omega) = \frac{\lambda^{\sum_{i \in V} \omega_i}}{Z_\lambda} \mathbf{1}_{\omega \in \mathcal{H}},$$

where Z_λ is the *normalizing constant* (or *partition function*), defined by $Z_\lambda = \sum_{\omega \in \mathcal{H}} \lambda^{\sum_{i \in V} \omega_i}$. The distribution μ can also be characterized as follows: it is the probability measure under which the labels ω_i, for $i \in V$, are independent Bernoulli random variables of parameter $\lambda/(1+\lambda)$, conditioned on "having no adjacent 1's".

For an infinite graph G (countable, and locally finite), we can extend this definition by saying that a probability measure μ on $\{0,1\}^V$ is a hardcore measure on G with activity λ if the conditional distribution on a finite set A, given the configuration outside A, is just the distribution under which the vertices of A that are adjacent to a vertice of $V \setminus A$ in state 1 take value 0, and the distribution on the remaining set follows the (finite-case) hardcore measure with activity λ. It follows from standard argument of Gibbs measure theory that at least one such measure always exists. In the case of the lattice graph $(\mathbb{Z}^d, E_d)$, it is known that for $d = 1$, for any activity $\lambda > 0$, there exists a unique hardcore measure, while a *phase transition* phenomenon occurs for $d \geq 2$: the hardcore measure is unique if λ is sufficiently small, but not for larger values of λ. In particular, when λ goes to infinity, there are two extremal Gibbs measure that concentrate asymptotically on the two odd and even "checkerboard" configurations.

Let us focus on the case of the one-dimensional lattice $\mathbb{Z}$. It can be seen that the (unique) hardcore measure μ of activity λ corresponds to the stationary Markov chain of transition matrix:

$$P_\lambda = \begin{pmatrix} p_{0,0} & p_{0,1} \\ p_{1,0} & p_{1,1} \end{pmatrix} = \begin{pmatrix} 1 - x_\lambda & x_\lambda \\ 1 & 0 \end{pmatrix},$$

$$\text{with:} \qquad \frac{p_{0,1}p_{1,0}}{p_{0,1}p_{1,0} + p_{0,0}p_{0,0}} = \frac{x_\lambda}{x_\lambda + (1 - x_\lambda)^2} = \frac{\lambda}{1+\lambda}.$$

Let X be a configuration distributed according to μ, and consider now the subfamily $X_{\text{even}} = (X_{2i})_{i \in \mathbb{Z}}$ of even cells, and the subfamily $X_{\text{odd}} = (X_{2i+1})_{i \in \mathbb{Z}}$ of odd cells. Then, X_{even} and X_{odd} are both distributed according to a same distribution μ_{half}, which is the stationary measure of the Markov chain of transition matrix P_λ^2. By definition of μ, if we update the state of a cell of X by a 1 with probability $\lambda/(1+\lambda)$ if it two neighbours are in state 0, and by a 0 otherwise, the resulting configuration still has distribution μ. This is also true if we update simultaneously all even (resp. odd) sites. As a consequence, the measure μ_{half}, seen as a measure on $\{0,1\}^{\mathbb{Z}}$, is an invariant distribution of the hardcore PCA of parameter $q = \lambda/(1+\lambda)$. This invariant distribution is *reversible*: if we first draw X_{even} according to μ_{half} and then update X_{odd} as above, the resulting configuration, which encodes the two consecutive configurations in the evolution of the PCA, has the same distribution as if we first draw the odd cells according to μ_{half} and then update the even cells using the PCA rule.

3.2 Ergodicity of the Hardcore PCA

We have exhibited an invariant distribution of the one-dimensional hardcore PCA, having a Markovian structure. With the notations of Sect. 2.2, we have

$p_? = q$. Thus, the criterion of Theorem 3 provides the ergodicity of the PCA only for small enough values of q. Furthermore, for large values of q, simulations can cast doubts on the asymptotic behaviour of the hardcore PCA, since starting from the configuration "all 1", we observe for a very long time an alternance between configurations with a very large majority of 1's and configurations with a very large majority of 0's (see Fig. 5), meaning that the system still remembers some information about the initial configuration. Nevertheless, one can prove the following.

Theorem 4. *For any $p \in (0, 1)$, the hardcore PCA of parameter p is ergodic.*

There exist at least three ways to prove this result, each of them having some advantages and disavantages.

(i) **Connection with the hardcore PCA.** Thanks to a monotonicity argument, one can deduce the ergodicity of the PCA from the uniqueness of the Gibbs measure for the corresponding hardcore model, see the proof of Theorem 2 (ii) in Ref. [14].
(ii) **Weight system.** One can prove the ergodicity of the envelope PCA by introducing a suitable weight system that plays the role of a Lyapunov function, in order to prove that the density of the symbol ? goes to zero, see Sect. 2.2. of Ref. [14].
(iii) **Decorrelated islands.** A proof of the ergodicity of the envelope PCA can also be made by studying the boundaries of islands of symbols ? where the PCA is totally decorrelated from its initial condition [4].

The first proof strongly relies on the connection with the hardcore model, and allows one to recover the expression of the unique invariant measure of the hardcore PCA as the measure μ_{half} of "one in every two" cells of the Gibbs measure. It can be extended to other bipartite graphs for which the hardcore Gibbs measure is unique. In contrast, proofs (*i*) and (*ii*) do not require any knowledge about the hardcore model, but does not give any information about the expression of the unique invariant distribution of the hardcore PCA. However, even though the weighting system is quite specific to the local rule of this PCA, proof (*ii*) is still valid for a larger family of PCA [14]. The strategy of proof (*iii*) also allows us to handle hardcore PCA with two parameters, or defined on a neighbourhood of size 3, even if it is at the cost of many computations [5].

Actually, the ergodicity of the envelope PCA can also be seen as a consequence of the ergodicity of the hardcore PCA, using the monotonicity of the envelope PCA with respect to the order on configurations induced by the order on symbols defined by $0 \preceq ? \preceq 1$.

3.3 Directed Animals

Directed animals are combinatorial objects related to directed percolation models. As shown by Dhar [6], enumerating directed animals according to the area on certain graphs is equivalent to solving a hard particle model on another graph.

We will see that when the graph is the two-dimensional lattice, the counting series is then closely related to the unique invariant distribution of the hardcore PCA.

Consider the directed graph of set of vertices $\mathbb{Z} \times \mathbb{N}$, and edges $\vec{E} = \{((k,t),(k+v_i,t+1)) : k \in \mathbb{Z}, t \in \mathbb{N}, v_i \in \{0,1\}\}$. Let B be a non-empty finite subset of $\mathbb{Z}$. A *directed animal of base* B is a finite subset $\mathcal{A}$ of $\mathbb{Z} \times \mathbb{N}$ such that:

- $\mathcal{A} \cap (\mathbb{Z} \times \{0\}) = B \times \{0\}$,
- $\forall x \in \mathcal{A}, \exists n \in \mathbb{N}, \exists x_0 \dots, x_n \in \mathcal{A}, \begin{cases} x_0 \in B \times \{0\}, & x_n = x, \\ \forall i \in \{0, \dots, n-1\}, (x_i, x_{i+1}) \in \vec{E} \end{cases}.$

A *directed animal* is a directed animal of base $\{0\}$, see Fig. 6.

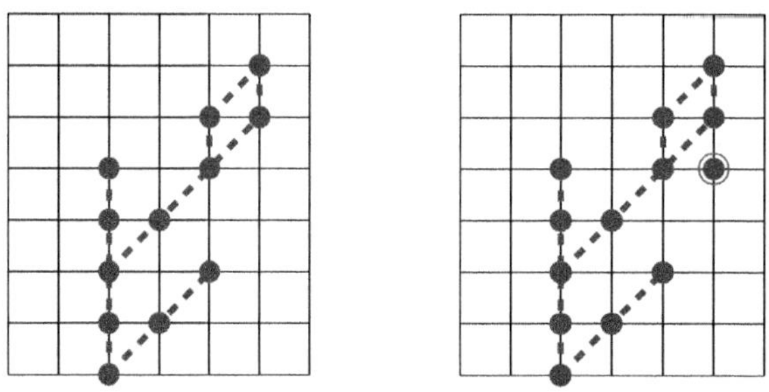

Fig. 6. A directed animal (left) and a set which is not a directed animal (right).

The *counting series* of directed animals of base B, respectively of directed animals, is the formal series defined by:

$$S_B(x) = \sum_{\mathcal{A}\text{: directed animal of base } B} x^{|\mathcal{A}|} \qquad (\text{resp. } S(x) = S_{\{0\}}(x)).$$

The coefficient of x^n in $S(x)$ thus gives the number of directed animals of size n. Removing the bottom line of a directed animal provides either the empty set or a new animal on the lines $\{1, 2, \dots\}$. This simple observation provides a recurrence relation on counting series:

$$S_B(x) = x^{|B|} \Big(\sum_{C \subset B + \mathcal{N}} S_C(x) \Big),$$

where $\mathcal{N} = \{0, 1\}$, and with the convention $S_\emptyset(x) = 1$.

Consider now a sequence of random variables $X = (X_i)_{i \in \mathbb{Z}}$ with values in $\{0, 1\}$, and let $Y = (Y_i)_{i \in \mathbb{Z}}$ be a realization of the image of $(X_i)_{i \in \mathbb{Z}}$ by the hardcore PCA of parameter q. By definition of the PCA, for a finite set $B \subset \mathbb{Z}$, we have:

$$\mathbb{P}\big(\forall i \in B, Y_i = 1\big) = \mathbb{P}\big(\forall i \in B + \mathcal{N}, X_i = 0\big) q^{|B|}.$$

It then follows from the inclusion-exclusion principle that:

$$\mathbb{P}(\forall i \in B+\mathcal{N}, X_i = 0) = \sum_{C \subset B+\mathcal{N}} (-1)^{|C|} \mathbb{P}(\forall i \in C,\ X_i = 1).$$

Assume that X is distributed according to an invariant distribution π of the PCA, and for $C \subset \mathbb{Z}$, let $T_C = \pi(\{\omega \in S^{\mathbb{Z}} : \forall i \in C, \omega_i = 1\})$.
Then, Y is also distributed according to π, and we obtain:

$$T_B = q^{|B|} \sum_{C \subset B+\mathcal{N}} (-1)^{|C|} T_C.$$

It follows that the family $(-1)^{|B|} T_B$, for finite subsets B of $\mathbb{Z}$, satisfies the same recursion as the family $S_B(-q)$. This provides an unexpected relation between these two models. Furthermore, since μ_{half} is one explicit invariant distribution of the hardcore PCA, it provides a candidate for the counting series of directed animals. The last step consists in arguing that the counting series indeed satisfies:

$$S_B(-q) = (-1)^{|B|} \mu_{\text{half}}(\{\omega \in S^{\mathbb{Z}} : \forall i \in B, \omega_i = 1\}).$$

This requires an argument since the recurrence relations may admit several families of solutions, with only one of them defining the counting series. The idea is to proceed in reverse direction: from the actual counting series, one can define a probability distribution π, that can be proved to be an invariant distribution of the hardcore PCA, and it is thus equal to μ_{half}, see Ref. [1,6,17] for details and extensions.

3.4 Playing with Percolation

We now show that the hardcore PCA is also related to the study of a combinatorial game on percolation configurations. Let each cell of the square lattice $\mathbb{Z}^2$ be independently assigned one of the state *trap* with probability p, and *open* with probability $q = 1-p$, where $p \in [0,1]$. Consider the following game: a token starts at the origin, and two players take turns to move, where a move consists of moving the token from its current cell x to either $x + (0,1)$ or $x + (1,0)$. A player who moves the token to a trap loses the game immediately. Otherwise (i.e. if the destination cell is open), the game continues with the other player's turn. The entire random assignment of traps and open cells to $\mathbb{Z}^2$ (which we call the *percolation configuration*) is known to both players at all times. We call this game the *percolation game* on $\mathbb{Z}^2$.

If $q \leq p_c$, where p_c is the critical probability for directed site percolation with neighbourhood $\mathcal{N} = \{0,1\}$, then, with probability 1, only finitely many cells can be reached from the origin along directed paths of open cells, and so the game must end in finite time. In particular, one or other player must have a winning strategy, where a *strategy* for one or other player is a map that assigns a legal move (where one exists), to each cell, and a *winning* strategy is one that results in a win for that player, whatever strategy the other player uses. Suppose on the other hand that $q > p_c$, is there now a positive probability that neither player has a winning strategy? In that case, we say that the game is a *draw*, with the interpretation that it continues forever with the best play. Note that when $p = 0$, the game is clearly always a draw.

As we will see, the outcome (first-player win, first-player loss, draw) of the game started from each cell can be interpreted in terms of the evolution of the hardcore PCA, where the state of the PCA at a given time relates to the outcomes associated to the cells on a given Northwest-Southeast diagonal of $\mathbb{Z}^2$. Using the ergodicity of the hardcore PCA, one can prove that as soon as $p > 0$, the probability that the game is a draw is equal to 0, and the Markovian description of the invariant distribution then permits an explicit description of the distribution of game outcomes along a diagonal [14].

Theorem 5. *For any $p \in (0,1)$, there is almost surely no draws, and the probability that the first player wins the game (conditional on the origin being open), is equal to:*

$$\frac{1 - 2p + \sqrt{\frac{p}{4-3p}}}{2(1-p)}. \tag{1}$$

This probability is greater than 1/2 if and only if $p \in (0, 1/3)$, and its maximum value is $4 - 2\sqrt{3} = 0.5358...$, attained at $p = (2 - \sqrt{3})/3 = 0.0893....$

Sketch of the Proof. Suppose x is an open site of $\mathbb{Z}^2$. Let $\eta(x)$ be W, L or D according to whether the game started with the token at x is a win for the first player, a loss for the first player, or a draw, respectively (recall that we assume optimal play, with the players able to see entire percolation configuration when deciding on their strategies). If x is a trap, it is convenient to set $\eta(x) = \mathrm{W}$ (we adopt the convention that if the game starts at a trap, then it is a win for the first player).

Let $\mathrm{Out}(x) = \{x + e_1, x + e_2\}$ be the set of cells to which the token can move from x. By considering the first move, we have the following recursion for the status of the cells:

$$\begin{aligned} x \text{ a trap } &\Rightarrow \ \eta(x) = \mathrm{W}, \\ x \text{ open } &\Rightarrow \ \eta(x) = \begin{cases} \mathrm{L} & \text{if } \eta(y) = \mathrm{W} \text{ for all } y \in \mathrm{Out}(x), \\ \mathrm{W} & \text{if } \eta(y) = \mathrm{L} \text{ for some } y \in \mathrm{Out}(x), \\ \mathrm{D} & \text{otherwise.} \end{cases} \end{aligned} \tag{2}$$

For $k \in \mathbb{Z}$, let S_k be the set $\{x = (x_1, x_2) \in \mathbb{Z}^2 : x_1 + x_2 = k\}$, a NW-SE diagonal of $\mathbb{Z}^2$. The recursion (2) gives us the values $(\eta(x))_{x \in S_k}$ in terms of the values $(\eta(x))_{x \in S_{k+1}}$ together with the information about which sites in S_k are traps. Via this recursion, we can regard the configurations on successive diagonals S_k, as k decreases, as successive states of a one-dimensional PCA. Let us introduce the following recoding:

$$\mathrm{W} = 0, \quad \mathrm{L} = 1, \quad \mathrm{D} = ?.$$

Then, one can check that the PCA evolves as follows: given the values for cells in S_{k+1}, each value $\eta(x)$ for $x \in S_k$ is derived independently using the values $\eta(x+e_1)$ and $\eta(x+e_2)$, according to a local rule which is exactly the same as for the envelope of the hardcore PCA, see Fig. 4.

Let us fix some integer $N \geq 0$, and assume that on S_N, the configuration η is such that $\forall x \in S_k, \eta(x) = ?$. Then, if we iterate the PCA starting from this configuration, from diagonal S_N to S_0, the probability that the origin $O = (0,0)$ is in state 0 (resp. 1) can be interpreted as the probability that the first (respectively second) player can force a win within at most N moves of the game. In particular, if the probability that the origin is in state ? goes to 0 when N goes to infinity, it means that the game is almost surely not a draw. But as shown in Sect. 3.2, we already know that starting from the configuration $\delta_{?^{\mathbb{Z}}}$, the density of symbols ? goes to 0. This concludes the proof that there are no draws, and the description of the unique invariant measure of the hardcore PCA provides the expression of the winning probability. □

References

1. Bousquet-Mélou, M.: New enumerative results on two-dimensional directed animals. In: Proceedings of the 7th Conference on Formal Power Series and Algebraic Combinatorics (Noisy-le-Grand, 1995), vol. 180, pp. 73–106 (1998)
2. Bušić, A., Fatès, N., Mairesse, J., Marcovici, I.: Density classification on infinite lattices and trees. Electron. J. Probab. **18**(51), 22 (2013)
3. Bušić, A., Mairesse, J., Marcovici, I.: Probabilistic cellular automata, invariant measures, and perfect sampling. Adv. Appl. Probab. **45**(4), 960–980 (2013)
4. Casse, J.: Ergodicity of some probabilistic cellular automata with binary alphabet via random walks. Electron. J. Probab. **28**, 17 (2023)
5. Casse, J., Marcovici, I., Poutrel, M.: Ergodicity of the hard-core PCA with a random walk method. In: Riva, S., Richard, A. (eds.) AUTOMATA 2025. LNCS, vol. 15831, pp. xx–yy. Springer, Cham (2025)
6. Dhar, D.: Exact solution of a directed-site animals-enumeration problem in three dimensions. Phys. Rev. Lett. **51**(10), 853–856 (1983)
7. van Enter, A.: Proof of Straley's argument for bootstrap percolation. J. Stat. Phys. **48**(3–4), 943–945 (1987)
8. Ferrari, P.A.: Ergodicity for a class of probabilistic cellular automata. Rev. Mat. Apl. **12**(2), 93–102 (1991)
9. Gács, P.: Reliable cellular automata with self-organization. J. Stat. Phys. **103**(1), 45–267 (2001)
10. Gravner, J., Holroyd, A.E.: Slow convergence in bootstrap percolation. Ann. Appl. Probab. **18**(3), 909–928 (2008)
11. Grimmett, G.: Percolation, Grundlehren Der Mathematischen Wissenschaften [Fundamental Principles of Mathematical Sciences], vol. 321, 2nd edn. Springer, Berlin (1999)
12. Hartarsky, I.: Bootstrap percolation, probabilistic cellular automata and sharpness. J. Stat. Phys. **187**(3), 17 (2022)
13. Holroyd, A.E.: Sharp metastability threshold for two-dimensional bootstrap percolation. Probab. Theory Relat. Fields **125**(2), 195–224 (2003)

14. Holroyd, A.E., Marcovici, I., Martin, J.B.: Percolation games, probabilistic cellular automata, and the hard-core model. Probab. Theory Relat. Fields **174**(3–4), 1187–1217 (2019)
15. Kari, J.: Theory of cellular automata: a survey. Theoret. Comput. Sci. **334**, 3–33 (2005)
16. Kůrka, P.: Topological and Symbolic Dynamics, Cours Spécialisés, vol. 11. Société Mathématique de France (2003)
17. Le Borgne, Y., Marckert, J.F.: Directed animals and gas models revisited. Electron. J. Combin. **14**(1), 36 (2007)
18. Mairesse, J., Marcovici, I.: Around probabilistic cellular automata. Theoret. Comput. Sci. **559**, 42–72 (2014)
19. Marcovici, I., Sablik, M., Taati, S.: Ergodicity of some classes of cellular automata subject to noise. Electron. J. Probab. **24**, 44 (2019)
20. Schonmann, R.H.: On the behavior of some cellular automata related to bootstrap percolation. Ann. Probab. **20**(1), 174–193 (1992)
21. Steif, J.E.: Two applications of percolation to cellular automata. J. Stat. Phys. **78**(5–6), 1325–1335 (1995)
22. Toom, A.L., Vasilyev, N.B., Stavskaya, O.N., Mityushin, L.G., Kurdyumov, G.L., Pirogov, S.A.: Discrete local Markov systems. In: Dobrushin, R.L., Kryukov, V.I., Toom, A.L. (eds.) Stochastic Cellular Systems: Ergodicity, Memory, Morphogenesis. Manchester University Press (1990)

In Search of Cellular Automata that Preserve Numbers: Advances, Limitations, and Open Problems

Barbara Wolnik[1,3], Witold Bołt[2(✉)], and Bernard De Baets[3]

[1] Institute of Mathematics, Faculty of Mathematics, Physics and Informatics, University of Gdańsk, Wita Stwosza 57, 80-308 Gdańsk, Poland
barbara.wolnik@ug.edu.pl

[2] Jit Team, Łużycka 8C, 81-537 Gdynia, Poland
witold.bolt@jit.team

[3] KERMIT, Department of Data Analysis and Mathematical Modelling, Faculty of Bioscience Engineering, Ghent University, Coupure links 653, 9000 Gent, Belgium
bernard.debaets@ugent.be

Abstract. This paper provides a brief summary of recent results on the number-conserving capabilities of cellular automata. We focus on studies that resulted in establishing complete lists of such CAs for a given dimension, state set, and neighborhood type. Moreover, we outline key, new questions arising from these results and point to obstacles hampering further progress.

Keywords: cellular automata · number conservation · state conservation · reversibility

1 Introduction

Number-conserving cellular automata (NCCAs), also called *conservative cellular automata*, constitute a particularly interesting class of cellular automata (CAs), in which the states are numbers, and the global rule has the special feature of preserving the sum of the states upon every update. This property can be related to the natural behavior of many physical systems that are governed by traditional conservation laws (*e.g.*, conservation of mass or energy).

Historically, when CAs were first introduced in the early works of Ulam and von Neumann [35,36], number conservation was not considered. The initial focus was mainly on reversibility and related properties. Yet, in the 80s and 90s of the last century, pioneering works on *conservation laws* in CAs were published by multiple authors, most notably Fredkin and Toffoli [11], Nagel and Schreckenberger [28], Tamotsu Kohyama [21], and Kotze and Steeb [22]. The most important contribution among these early studies on NCCAs has been authored by Hattori and Takesue [15]. Later works by Takesue [32], Pivato [30], Taati [31] and the lesser known, yet important paper by Baird and Fagin [1], continued the

Published by Springer Nature Switzerland AG 2026
S. Riva and A. Richard (Eds.): AUTOMATA 2025, LNCS 15831, pp. 43–58, 2026.
https://doi.org/10.1007/978-3-032-01570-9_4

exploration and study of conservation laws for CAs, clearly showing their importance and rich, non-trivial properties. Over the years, many different views on and definitions of conservation laws for CAs (in some sense different or broader than the one given for NCCAs) have been proposed. Yet, the number conservation property considered here is the one still gaining the most attention and thus we limit our consideration to it. The motivation for it is purely practical, as number conservation is implicitly assumed in a broad range of modeling tasks.

In this paper, we focus only on a selection of recent and highly important results regarding NCCAs, more explicitly, on those studies employing tools that made it possible to find complete lists of NCCAs for a given dimension, state set and neighborhood type. Thus, our goal is not to provide an exhaustive coverage of all NCCA topics. Even more, the choice of problems covered here is determined by our personal area of expertise. Note that there is also a number of important issues in the study of NCCAs that are absent from our review, *e.g.*, motion representation, computational complexity, relations with specific laws from theoretical physics, results from theoretical computer science and universality. Notably, following the results in [24], where it is shown that NCCAs can simulate an arbitrary CA, the topic of universality of NCCAs is of significant importance. Interested reader is advised to examine [11,16,27] for some of the important results.

Aside from summarizing the main findings, we also formulate and briefly discuss some of the key open problems in the field. We hope that this survey will instigate further research in this direction and will help to uncover new properties of NCCAs.

2 Basic Definitions of NCCAs

Roughly speaking, a CA is a discrete dynamical system that consists of a regular grid of cells that update their states in consecutive time steps, depending on the states of their neighbors, and according to some local rule.

More formally, a d-dimensional CA is a quadruple $(\mathcal{C}, Q, V, f)$, where

- $\mathcal{C} \subseteq \mathbb{Z}^d$ is the cellular space;
- Q is the set of states and for our purpose we will assume that Q is represented by numbers (*i.e.*, $Q \subset \mathbb{R}$) and that $0 \in Q$;
- $V = (\overrightarrow{\mathbf{v}_1}, \overrightarrow{\mathbf{v}_2}, \ldots, \overrightarrow{\mathbf{v}_m})$ is the neighborhood vector, which means that, for a cell $\mathbf{i} \in \mathcal{C}$, the cells $\mathbf{i} + \overrightarrow{\mathbf{v}_1}, \mathbf{i} + \overrightarrow{\mathbf{v}_2}, \ldots, \mathbf{i} + \overrightarrow{\mathbf{v}_m}$ are its neighbors (it is usually assumed that the zero vector belongs to V, *i.e.*, that the cell itself belongs to its neighborhood);
- $f : Q^m \to Q$ is the local rule: the state of a cell $\mathbf{i}$ in the next time step is given by $f(x_1, x_2, \ldots, x_m)$, where $x_1, x_2, \ldots, x_m$ are the current states of the cells $\mathbf{i} + \overrightarrow{\mathbf{v}_1}, \mathbf{i} + \overrightarrow{\mathbf{v}_2}, \ldots, \mathbf{i} + \overrightarrow{\mathbf{v}_m}$, respectively. Such a local rule is referred to as an "m-input local rule" when emphasizing that the neighborhood size is important.

Usually, the cellular space is infinite and corresponds to the entire space $\mathbb{Z}^d$ or is finite and corresponds to some d-dimensional cuboid of size $\mathbf{N} = (n_1, n_2, \ldots, n_d)$ with periodic boundary conditions, *i.e.*,

$$\begin{aligned}\mathcal{C} &= \mathcal{C}_{\mathbf{N}} = (\mathbb{Z}/n_1\mathbb{Z}) \times (\mathbb{Z}/n_2\mathbb{Z}) \times \cdots \times (\mathbb{Z}/n_d\mathbb{Z}) \\ &= \{0, 1, \ldots, n_1 - 1\} \times \{0, 1, \ldots, n_2 - 1\} \times \cdots \times \{0, 1, \ldots, n_d - 1\}.\end{aligned}$$

The most commonly used set of states is $\{0, 1, \ldots, k-1\}$, for some integer $k \geq 2$, and in this case the CA is called "k-ary" (binary, ternary, quaternary, quinary, senary, septenary and so on). It should be noted that, unlike most properties studied for CAs, the notion of number conservation is strongly affected by state renaming, so the choice of Q is important.

As for the neighborhood, among the many different ones that could be adopted (see, *e.g.*, [45]), the two most popular ones are the Moore neighborhood and the von Neumann neighborhood. They differ in terms of the metric considered in $\mathbb{Z}^d$: the Moore neighborhood is defined by the Chebyshev distance

$$\mathrm{dist}_{\mathrm{Ch}}(\mathbf{i}, \mathbf{j}) = \max_{1 \leq k \leq d} |i_k - j_k| \,, \tag{1}$$

whereas the von Neumann neighborhood is defined by the Manhattan distance:

$$\mathrm{dist}_{\mathrm{M}}(\mathbf{i}, \mathbf{j}) = \sum_{k=1}^{d} |i_k - j_k| \,, \tag{2}$$

where $\mathbf{i} = (i_1, i_2, \ldots, i_d) \in \mathcal{C}$ and $\mathbf{j} = (j_1, j_2, \ldots, j_d) \in \mathcal{C}$. From this point of view, these neighborhoods of a cell $\mathbf{i}$ can be seen as closed balls centered at $\mathbf{i}$, *i.e.*, consisting of those cells whose distance (Chebyshev or Manhattan) to $\mathbf{i}$ does not exceed the radius r ($r = 1$ being the most popular choice). While the Moore neighborhood has a very simple structure (each ball is a d-dimensional cube), the von Neumann neighborhood is a much more interesting and difficult object to study, since is not a Cartesian product of one-dimensional neighborhoods. In the rest of the paper, in the case of the von Neumann neighborhood, we will only consider radius $r = 1$, even if this is not explicitly stated.

A *configuration* is any mapping from the grid $\mathcal{C}$ to Q; the set of all configurations is denoted by X. When considering finite grids, often not just one specific grid is considered, but all finite grids together and then the set of configurations has a slightly more complicated structure than $X_{\mathbf{N}} = Q^{\mathcal{C}_{\mathbf{N}}}$, namely:

$$X^* = \bigcup_{\mathbf{N} \in \mathbb{N}^d} X_{\mathbf{N}} \,.$$

The latter case is equivalent to considering all spatially periodic configurations on the entire grid $\mathbb{Z}^d$ (see, *i.e.*, [20] for more information). Unless this leads to confusion, we will simply write X to denote the set of configurations under consideration. The state of a cell $\mathbf{i} \in \mathcal{C}$ in a configuration $\mathbf{x} \in X$ is denoted by $x_{\mathbf{i}}$. A configuration $\mathbf{x} \in X$ is called *finite* if at most finitely many cells are assigned a non-zero state, *i.e.*, the set $\{\mathbf{i} \in \mathcal{C} \mid x_{\mathbf{i}} \neq 0\}$ is finite.

A given local rule f induces a *global rule* $F : X \to X$ defined for any $\mathbf{x} \in X$ and $\mathbf{i} \in \mathcal{C}$ as follows

$$F(\mathbf{x})_{\mathbf{i}} = f(x_{\mathbf{i}+\overrightarrow{\mathbf{v}_1}}, x_{\mathbf{i}+\overrightarrow{\mathbf{v}_2}}, \ldots, x_{\mathbf{i}+\overrightarrow{\mathbf{v}_m}})$$

(we recall that for finite grids the addition '+' is, in fact, the addition modulo). Usually, the global rule F is identified with the cellular automaton.

Number conservation, the main property of CAs investigated in this paper is usually defined in one of the following ways.

Definition 1. (Finite NC) *A local rule f is* finite number-conserving *if for every finite configuration $\mathbf{x} \in X$ it holds that $\sum_{\mathbf{i} \in \mathcal{C}} F(\mathbf{x})_{\mathbf{i}} = \sum_{\mathbf{i} \in \mathcal{C}} \mathbf{x}_{\mathbf{i}}$.*

Definition 2. (Periodic NC) *A local rule f is* periodic number-conserving *if for every configuration $\mathbf{x} \in X^*$ it holds that $\sum_{\mathbf{i} \in \mathcal{C}} F(\mathbf{x})_{\mathbf{i}} = \sum_{\mathbf{i} \in \mathcal{C}} \mathbf{x}_{\mathbf{i}}$.*

Definition 3. (NC on a given finite grid) *A local rule f is* number-conserving *on a given grid $\mathcal{C}_{\mathbf{N}}$ if for every configuration $\mathbf{x} \in X_{\mathbf{N}}$ it holds that $\sum_{\mathbf{i} \in \mathcal{C}} F(\mathbf{x})_{\mathbf{i}} = \sum_{\mathbf{i} \in \mathcal{C}} \mathbf{x}_{\mathbf{i}}$.*

One can also consider all configurations, not necessarily finite ones only, and extend the definition of number conservation. Durand *et al.* [5] discuss different ways of obtaining such extension. However, as it turns out, all these definitions can be shown to be equivalent, with the proviso that, as for Definition 3, $\mathbf{N}$ must be sufficiently large compared to the size of the neighborhood of the local rule f (see, *e.g.*, [4,5]).

In later discussions, we will often limit the study to certain subclasses of NCCAs, the most important ones being *state-conserving* CAs (SCCAs) and *reversible* NCCAs.

Definition 4. *A global rule $F : X^* \to X^*$ is state-conserving if for every state $q \in Q$ it holds that $\delta_q(F(\mathbf{x})) = \delta_q(\mathbf{x})$ for each configuration $\mathbf{x} \in X^*$, where $\delta_q : X^* \to \mathbb{N}$, with $\mathbb{N} = \{0, 1, 2, \ldots\}$ is the function that counts the number of appearances of the state q in $\mathbf{x}$.*

Roughly speaking, being state-conserving simply means that for each initial configuration the number of cells in each state is constant throughout the entire evolution of the system.

Definition 5. *A global rule $F : X^* \to X^*$ is reversible if F is a bijection, i.e., for any $\mathbf{x}_1, \mathbf{x}_2 \in X^*$ such that $\mathbf{x}_1 \neq \mathbf{x}_2$, it holds that $F(\mathbf{x}_1) \neq F(\mathbf{x}_2)$.*

The simplest examples of CAs that are both number-conserving and state-conserving are the so-called *shifts*, *i.e.*, CAs induced by local rules of the form: $f(x_1, x_2, \ldots, x_m) = x_k$, for a given $k \in \{1, 2, \ldots, m\}$ (provided that $\overrightarrow{\mathbf{v}_k}$ is not a null vector, because then such a local rule induces a CA that is simply the identity).

3 One-Dimensional NCCAs

Both the property of being number-conserving and the property of being state-conserving are decidable for CA. This is due to the existence of necessary and sufficient conditions formulated for CA to be number- or state-conserving in terms of its local rule. This positive information encourages researchers to try to find the full list of NCCAs (or SCCAs, at least) for a given state set and a size of the neighborhood.

However, as one might expect, even in the one-dimensional case the cardinality of the set of all NCCAs grows very quickly with a growing state set and/or increasing neighborhood size. Hence, it is natural to narrow down the search to SCCAs or to reversible NCCAs. For convenience, let us denote the number of one-dimensional m-input k-ary NCCAs (resp. SCCAs and reversible NCCAs) by $\Lambda_{m,k}$ (resp. $\Upsilon_{m,k}$ and $\Phi_{m,k}$).

When it comes to one-dimensional 2-input k-ary NCCAs, we can say with no hesitation that we know everything on this subject. First of all, the formula for the sequence $\Lambda_{2,k}$ is known:

$$\Lambda_{2,k} = \begin{cases} 2\sum\limits_{j=1}^{k/2}(j!)^2 j^{k-2j} & \text{, if } k \text{ is even,} \\ 2\sum\limits_{j=1}^{(k-1)/2}(j!)^2 j^{k-2j} + \left(\frac{k+1}{2}\right)!\left(\frac{k-1}{2}\right)! & \text{, if } k \text{ is odd.} \end{cases}$$

(see, [12], for more details).

The formula for $\Upsilon_{2,k}$ is also known, but it is not a great result, since regardless of k, $\Upsilon_{2,k} = 2$. Indeed, it is easy to see that when the neighborhood size is two, there are only two state-conserving one-dimensional CAs with a given state set: the identity and shift rules [40].

Moreover, it has been possible to characterize all reversible one-dimensional 2-input NCCAs and it turns out that all such CAs are relatively simple: each of them is a shift-identity product CA (see, [14], for more information). One of the more surprising conclusions of this characterization is the following.

Theorem 1. *For any prime number k there are only two reversible one-dimensional 2-input k-ary NCCAs: the identity and shift rule.*

The case of one-dimensional 3-input NCCAs is definitely the one most of the papers are devoted to.

Necessary and sufficient conditions for a one-dimensional CA to be number-conserving are stated in [3] for the binary state set and more generally in [4] for k-ary CAs. These conditions are derived from the results of Hattori and Takesue [15] or Takesue [32] regarding general conserved additive quantities. One can also obtain such conditions from the theory presented in [39]. Finally, one can apply the decomposition theorem to obtain necessary and sufficient conditions written in terms of split functions and perturbations (see [43] for details).

Unfortunately, despite this plethora of tools, no general formula for $\Lambda_{3,k}$ is known, and only a few particular values of this sequence have been obtained through a computer-assisted search. The same applies to the number of those one-dimensional 3-input k-ary NCCAs that are reversible. Table 1 presents the current state-of-the-art (to the best of our knowledge).

Table 1. Numbers of one-dimensional 3-input k-ary NCCAs: $\Lambda_{3,k}$ – all of them, $\Phi_{3,k}$ – only reversible ones.

k	2	3	4	5	6	7
$\Lambda_{3,k}$	**5**	**144**	**89 585**	**1 876 088 314**	?	?
$\Phi_{3,k}$	**3**	**3**	**21**	**21**	**471**	**1 669**

All the results presented in the middle row of Table 1 can be found in the literature (see [3,4,13,23,25]). The exception is the number $\Lambda_{3,5} = 1\,876\,088\,314$, which has been obtained by M. Dziemiańczuk using the decomposition theorem and a computer-assisted search, but this result is still unpublished. The results of the last row can be found in [18,41]. Moreover, the complete lists of one-dimensional 3-input k-ary NCCAs for $k \leq 7$ are available online [10].

Having established complete lists of reversible one-dimensional 3-input k-ary NCCAs up to $k = 7$, it was possible to initiate the study of their dynamics. This investigation revealed, for example, that for $k = 7$ all reversible k-ary NCCAs (septenary NCCAs), except for shifts, have a finite order. Moreover, each of them repeats every configuration in a 60-cycle [41]. Hence, their dynamics is definitely simpler than that of reversible k-ary NCCAs for $k = 6$ (senary NCCAs), as most of the latter (306 out of 471) do not have a finite order. For example, this means that in a particle interpretation of a reversible septenary NCCA, each particle moves in a restricted space, while for reversible senary NCCAs the particles can move arbitrarily far (see Fig. 1 for a visual comparison of the dynamics of reversible senary and septenary NCCAs).

It is not known why reversible 3-input septenary NCCAs are so simple, but intuition says that it has to do with the fact that 7 is a prime number. Indeed, if k is a composite number, then there exist methods (see, *e.g.*, [41]) that allow to construct reversible k-ary NCCAs with neighborhood size three having infinite order (other than shifts). Hence, such a simple dynamics can happen only for prime k. But does it happen for every prime k? An affirmative answer to this question will yield a result that is a generalization of Theorem 1.

Quite recently, it turned out that it is possible to characterize all one-dimensional 3-input k-ary SCCAc and this characterization allows to obtain a general formula for $\Upsilon_{3,k}$:

$$\Upsilon_{3,k} = 2 + \sum_{i=0}^{k} \binom{k}{i} \left(2^{k-i} - 1\right)^{i}.$$

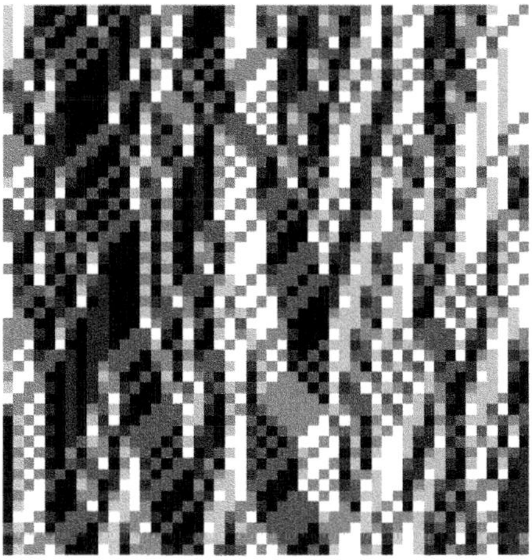
(a) $k = 6$

(b) $k = 7$

Fig. 1. Space-time diagrams of reversible NCCAs with (a) six and (b) seven states.

From the aforementioned characterization, it is also easy to deduce that among all one-dimensional 3-input k-ary SCCAs there are only three reversible ones: the identity and shift rules [40].

When it comes to neighborhoods of size greater than three, there are only a few results. Even when considering binary CAs, only the first six terms of the sequence $(\Lambda_{m,2})_{m=2}^{\infty}$ are known so far: 2, 5, 22, 428, 843, 133 184, 1 571 814 309 (see [23]). There is also no idea of a general formula for this sequence. As for larger values of k, on the other hand, apart from $\Lambda_{3,4} = 5\,448\,642$, there are no results at all (see [25]).

4 Two-Dimensional NCCAs

Necessary and sufficient conditions for a two-dimensional CA to be number-conserving are stated in [5,24].[1] They are expressed in terms of the local rule and can be use for any kind of a rectangular neighborhood, and therefore, for any type of neighborhood. However, they are best suited for the Moore neighborhood. Unfortunately, even in the simplest case (binary), it is not possible to answer the question of how all NCCAs with the Moore neighborhood look like. The only results known to the authors can be found in [19], where an algorithm is proposed that allows to generate all two-dimensional binary "motion-representable" NCCAs defined on $n \times m$ neighborhoods (see [19] for the definition and details).

[1] As we see the property of being number-conserving is decidable in all dimensions, which is quite surprising since almost all non-trivial properties of CAs are rather undecidable. Moreover, it is known that the property of being number-decreasing (the sum of states does not increase during the evolution) is decidable in dimension one and undecidable in dimension two or greater [2].

It turns out that in the cases 2×2 and 2×3 this algorithm effectively searches for all binary NCCAs for the neighborhood under consideration, but it has never been shown that this is also the case for the Moore neighborhood or a larger one. For this reason, research has focused on smaller neighborhoods that are not necessarily rectangular in shape.

In [26] the author studies the problem of number conservation of binary CAs for arbitrary two-dimensional neighborhoods containing at most five cells and derives necessary and sufficient conditions for NCCAs for all these cases. However, the best studied two-dimensional neighborhood is the von Neumann neighborhood.

The family of necessary and sufficient conditions dedicated specifically to the von Neumann neighborhood can be found in [39], where the results are stated in a way similar to [26], and also in [33], where the results are stated in terms of some flow functions (in the vertical, horizontal, and diagonal direction).

So far, the most useful tool when considering NCCAs with the von Neumann neighborhood turns out to be the decomposition theorem presented in [43]. This theorem states that the local rule of any two-dimensional NCCA with the von Neumann neighborhood can be decomposed into two parts: *a split function* and *a perturbation*. In applications, it suffices to find all possible split functions h and for each of them to find all perturbations g that are compatible with h in the sense that $h+g$ takes values in the considered set of states. This is easy enough, since the set of perturbations forms a linear space of fairly small dimension.

For example, to find all two-dimensional binary NCCAs with the von Neumann neighborhood, we do not need to consider all 2^{32} local rules and check which of them are number-conserving by means of some necessary and sufficient conditions. The theory presented in [43] allows us to find very quickly all five split functions: the identity (h_0), right-shift (h_1), left-shift (h_2), up-shift (h_3) and down-shift (h_4) rules. In this case the space of perturbations has dimension four, and we know the basis $\{g_1, g_2, g_3, g_4\}$ of this space (see Table 2). Thus, according to the decomposition theorem, every number-conserving local rule can be represented as $h_i + ag_1 + bg_2 + cg_3 + dg_4$, where $i \in \{0, 1, 2, 3, 4\}$ and $a, b, c, d \in \mathbb{R}$. As h_2, h_3, h_4 are equivalent to h_1 by rotation, we can restrict our search to h_0 and h_1. The LUTs of the local functions $h_0 + ag_1 + bg_2 + cg_3 + dg_4$ and $h_1 + ag_1 + bg_2 + cg_3 + dg_4$ are shown in Tables 2 and 3, respectively.

Now it suffices to choose the values of the coefficients a, b, c and d so that all the values in column f are equal to 0 or 1. As can be easily seen, in the case of h_0 we get only one possibility: $(a, b, c, d) = (0, 0, 0, 0)$, whereas in the case of h_1 we get only two possibilities: $(a, b, c, d) = (0, 0, 0, 0)$ and $(a, b, c, d) = (-1, 0, 0, 0)$. Thus, finally, we get nine two-dimensional binary NCCAs with the von Neumann neighborhood: the identity rule, four shift rules, and four traffic rules (in each of the four possible directions).

An analogous procedure can be repeated for a ternary state set ($k = 3$) (here, of course, a computer must already be used) to obtain the complete list of 1327 two-dimensional ternary NCCAs with the von Neumann neighborhood (see [8], and the list is available online [6]).

Table 2. The LUTs of the split functions h_0, basic perturbations and local functions $f = h_0 + ag_1 + bg_2 + cg_3 + dg_4$, for two-dimensional binary CAs with the von Neumann neighborhood.

	h_0	g_1	g_2	g_3	g_4	f		h_0	g_1	g_2	g_3	g_4	f
$\begin{array}{c}0\\000\\0\end{array}$	0						$\begin{array}{c}1\\000\\0\end{array}$	0					
$\begin{array}{c}0\\000\\1\end{array}$	0						$\begin{array}{c}1\\000\\1\end{array}$	0					
$\begin{array}{c}0\\001\\0\end{array}$	0						$\begin{array}{c}1\\001\\0\end{array}$	0			1		c
$\begin{array}{c}0\\001\\1\end{array}$	0				1	d	$\begin{array}{c}1\\001\\1\end{array}$	0			1	1	$c+d$
$\begin{array}{c}0\\010\\0\end{array}$	1					1	$\begin{array}{c}1\\010\\0\end{array}$	1		1			$1+b$
$\begin{array}{c}0\\010\\1\end{array}$	1		-1			$1-b$	$\begin{array}{c}1\\010\\1\end{array}$	1					1
$\begin{array}{c}0\\011\\0\end{array}$	1	1				$1+a$	$\begin{array}{c}1\\011\\0\end{array}$	1	1	1	1		$1+a+b+c$
$\begin{array}{c}0\\011\\1\end{array}$	1	1	-1		1	$1+a-b+d$	$\begin{array}{c}1\\011\\1\end{array}$	1	1		1	1	$1+a+c+d$
$\begin{array}{c}0\\100\\0\end{array}$	0						$\begin{array}{c}1\\100\\0\end{array}$	0				-1	$-d$
$\begin{array}{c}0\\100\\1\end{array}$	0			-1		$-c$	$\begin{array}{c}1\\100\\1\end{array}$	0			-1	-1	$-c-d$
$\begin{array}{c}0\\101\\0\end{array}$	0						$\begin{array}{c}1\\101\\0\end{array}$	0			1	-1	$c-d$
$\begin{array}{c}0\\101\\1\end{array}$	0			-1	1	$-c+d$	$\begin{array}{c}1\\101\\1\end{array}$	0					
$\begin{array}{c}0\\110\\0\end{array}$	1	-1				$1-a$	$\begin{array}{c}1\\110\\0\end{array}$	1	-1	1		-1	$1-a+b-d$
$\begin{array}{c}0\\110\\1\end{array}$	1	-1	-1	-1		$1-a-b-c$	$\begin{array}{c}1\\110\\1\end{array}$	1	-1		-1	-1	$1-a-c-d$
$\begin{array}{c}0\\111\\0\end{array}$	1					1	$\begin{array}{c}1\\111\\0\end{array}$	1		1	1	-1	$1+b+c-d$
$\begin{array}{c}0\\111\\1\end{array}$	1		-1	-1	1	$1-b-c+d$	$\begin{array}{c}1\\111\\1\end{array}$	1					1

Similarly to the one-dimensional case, it is clear that a further increase of k will lead to infeasibly high numbers, which makes further exploration not that interesting. Therefore, additional assumptions are again considered to limit the rule space.

Firstly, the case of reversible two-dimensional NCCAs with the von Neumann neighborhood has been considered. In the ternary case ($k = 3$), it has been shown that only the identity and shift rules are reversible. The case $k = 4$ has been solved in [7] and there are 65 two-dimensional quaternary NCCAs with the von Neumann neighborhood. Each such CA turns out to amount to two interconnected one-dimensional binary NCCAs and an important role is played here by the fact that k can be decomposed as $4 = 2 \cdot 2$. For this reason, the case of $k = 5$ seems very interesting, as 5 is a prime number. Do quinary NCCAs have

Table 3. The LUTs of the split functions h_1, basic perturbations and local functions $f = h_1 + ag_1 + bg_2 + cg_3 + dg_4$, for two-dimensional binary CAs with the von Neumann neighborhood.

	h_1	g_1	g_2	g_3	g_4	f
0 000 0	0					
0 000 1	0					
0 001 0	1					1
0 001 1	1				1	$1+d$
0 010 0	0				1	
0 010 1	0		-1			$-b$
0 011 0	1	1				$1+a$
0 011 1	1	1	-1		1	$1+a-b+d$
0 100 0	0					
0 100 1	0			-1		$-c$
0 101 0	1					1
0 101 1	1			-1	1	$1-c+d$
0 110 0	0	-1				$-a$
0 110 1	0	-1	-1	-1		$-a-b-c$
0 111 0	1					1
0 111 1	1		-1	-1	1	$1-b-c+d$

	h_1	g_1	g_2	g_3	g_4	f
1 000 0	0					
1 000 1	0					
1 001 0	1			1		$1+c$
1 001 1	1			1	1	$1+c+d$
1 010 0	0		1			b
1 010 1	0				1	
1 011 0	1	1	1	1		$1+a+b+c$
1 011 1	1	1		1	1	$1+a+c+d$
1 100 0	0				-1	$-d$
1 100 1	0			-1	-1	$-c-d$
1 101 0	1			1	-1	$1+c-d$
1 101 1	1					1
1 110 0	0	-1	1		-1	$-a+b-d$
1 110 1	0	-1		-1	-1	$-a-c-d$
1 111 0	1		1	1	-1	$1+b+c-d$
1 111 1	1					1

dynamics at least as complex as quaternary ones, or does a theorem analogous to Theorem 1 exist? Unfortunately, to date, a complete list of two-dimensional quinary NCCAs with the von Neumann neighborhood has not yet been found.

Secondly, rotation-symmetric two-dimensional NCCAs with the von Neumann neighborhood have been studied. The known numbers are listed in Table 4 (the results can be found in [9,17,29]). Unfortunately, despite finding the first six terms of this sequence, it was not possible to prove, or even propose, any general formula.

During the study of rotation-symmetric two-dimensional NCCAs with the von Neumann neighborhood, another issue arose, which can certainly be called surprising. Namely, it turned out that when considering CAs with a k-element

Table 4. Number of rotation-symmetric two-dimensional k-ary NCCAs with the von Neumann neighborhood.

k	2	3	4	5	6	7
	1	**1**	**1**	**4**	**116**	**30 144**

set of states, it is not always possible to treat the set $\{0, 1, 2, \ldots, k-1\}$ as "sufficient for consideration".

For example, when we consider six-state rotation-symmetric NCCAs with the von Neumann neighborhood, then, as proved in [9], no matter what six elements the considered set of states $\widetilde{Q} \subset \mathbb{R}$ consists of, each such CA is isomorphic to some senary rotation-symmetric NCCA with the von Neumann neighborhood. Here, by saying that a two-dimensional CA with the von Neumann neighborhood with a local rule $\widetilde{f}$ and a state set $\widetilde{Q}$ is isomorphic to another one with a local rule f and a state set Q, we mean that there is a bijection $\phi : Q \to \widetilde{Q}$ such that for any $u, l, c, r, d, x \in Q$

$$f\begin{pmatrix} u \\ l\,c\,r \\ d \end{pmatrix} = x \quad \Longleftrightarrow \quad \widetilde{f}\begin{pmatrix} \phi(u) \\ \phi(l)\;\phi(c)\;\phi(r) \\ \phi(d) \end{pmatrix} = \phi(x)\,. \tag{3}$$

Thus, the mentioned result states that any six-state rotation-symmetric NCCAs with the von Neumann neighborhood is isomorphic to some of 116 senary rotation-symmetric NCCAs with the von Neumann neighborhood (see Table 4). Therefore, knowing the dynamics of those 116 senary NCCAs, we know the dynamics of any six-state rotation-symmetric NCCAs with the von Neumann neighborhood. Analogous results for $k \le 5$ were proved in [17,34].

Surprisingly, it was shown in [44] that the situation is different for $k = 7$. By a careful selection of a seven-state $\widetilde{Q}$, one can obtain new NCCAs that are not isomorphic to any of the NCCAs found for $Q = \{0, 1, 2, 3, 4, 5, 6\}$. We suspect that for the number of states greater than 7, this will also be the case.

5 Multi-dimensional NCCAs

Although the necessary and sufficient conditions for a CA to be number-conserving presented in [15,32] can be formulated for any dimension, they have never been used to find a complete list of NCCAs for any dimension $d \ge 3$ and any set of states, due to their complexity. For this reason, nothing is known about d-dimensional NCCAs with the Moore neighborhood.

As for the von Neumann neighborhood, the situation is much better. The necessary and sufficient conditions presented in [39] work for any dimension d. Moreover, they can be formulated in $(2d+1)2^{d^2}$ different ways. Hence, considering NCCAs with some additional properties, one can choose the version that suits best.

In addition, the decomposition theorem holds for any dimension d and the main result of [43] reads as follows.

Theorem 2. *Let f be the local rule of a d-dimensional CA with the von Neumann neighborhood. This CA is number-conserving if and only if there exist a split function h and a perturbation g such that $f = h + g$. Moreover, for a given local rule f, the functions h and g are uniquely determined.*

Thus, as mentioned earlier, to enumerate all d-dimensional NCCAs with the von Neumann neighborhood and with a given state set Q, it suffices to consider each split function h separately and find all perturbations g that are compatible with h in the sense that $h + g$ takes values in Q. Moreover, the set $\mathcal{S}$ of all split functions has a very simple structure, since it can be identified with a Cartesian product, whereas the set $\mathcal{P}$ of all perturbations is a linear space.

For example, it is not hard to shown that in case of $Q = \{0, 1, 2, \ldots, k-1\}$, the cardinality of the set $\mathcal{S}$ equals

$$|\mathcal{S}| = \binom{2d+1}{1}\binom{2d+2}{2}\cdots\binom{2d+k-1}{k-1},$$

whereas the cardinality of a basis of $\mathcal{P}$ equals $d^2(k-1)^2$. Table 5 lists the sizes of $\mathcal{S}$ and $\mathcal{P}$ in relation to the number of all possible k-ary CAs with the von Neumann neighborhood for dimensions $d = 3$ and $d = 4$.

Table 5. The number of all split functions and the dimension of the space of perturbations (as a linear space) versus the number of all d-dimensional k-ary CAs with the von Neumann neighborhood.

	$d=3$			$d=4$		
	$k=2$	$k=3$	$k=4$	$k=2$	$k=3$	$k=4$
all k-ary CAs	2^{128}	$3^{2\,187}$	$4^{16\,384}$	2^{512}	$3^{19\,683}$	$4^{262\,144}$
the cardinality of $\mathcal{S}$	7	196	16 464	9	405	66 825
the dimension of $\mathcal{P}$	9	36	81	16	64	144

To convince the reader that the decomposition theorem is useful, we show how it allows us to reduce the computational complexity of finding all three-dimensional ternary NCCAs with the von Neumann neighborhood. Of course, it is difficult to imagine checking all $3^{3^7} \approx 2.9 \cdot 10^{1043}$ three-dimensional ternary CAs with the von Neumann neighborhood by testing them for number conservation. Instead, by using a computer, one can consider all 196 split functions one by one and find matching perturbations for each of them. This way, we ca see that there are 5 302 NCCAs in this setting.

Using the decomposition theorem also allowed us to answer some theoretical questions in the field. For example, it can be proven that in the binary case, increasing the dimension of the cell space does not result in the appearance of a new kind of number-conserving CAs (see [37]).

Theorem 3. *There are exactly $4d + 1$ d-dimensional binary NCCAs with the von Neumann neighborhood: the identity rule, the shift rules and the traffic rules in each of the $2d$ directions.*

It also made it possible to characterize all reversible d-dimensional ternary NCCAs with the von Neumann neighborhood (see [38]).

Theorem 4. *Any reversible d-dimensional ternary NCCA with the von Neumann neighborhood is a shift in one of the $2d$ directions.*

The following conjecture has also been put forward (see [7]), but remained unproven so far.

Conjecture 1. There are exactly $(2d + 1)(6d + 1)$ d-dimensional reversible quaternary NCCAs with the von Neumann neighborhood.

Rotation-symmetric three-dimensional k-ary NCCAs with the von Neumann neighborhood have been studied in [42], learning us that the number of such CAs for $2 \leq k \leq 7$ are 1, 1, 1, 1, 1, 2. Unfortunately, higher values of k have not been considered so far.

The decomposition theorem applies only to the von Neumann neighborhood. The natural question arises whether similar characterizations can be obtained for neighborhoods of a different kind, such as those defined in [45].

6 Conclusions

The aim of this survey paper was to summarize the recent results on finding complete lists of NCCAs with certain properties. The journey toward the presented results followed two complementary paths. Initially, extensive efforts involved computer simulations and exhaustive explorations of large rule spaces in search of meaningful insights. This computational approach yielded valuable observations and allowed the formulation of initial hypotheses. However, these efforts inevitably reached computational limitations. It became clear that further progress required the application of rigorous mathematical reasoning to overcome these barriers. We advocate for the continuation of this integrated approach, which combines computational experiments with analytical methods, as it holds promise for resolving the open problems outlined in this paper.

References

1. Baird, L., Fagin, B.: Conservation functions for 1-D automata: efficient algorithms, new results, and a partial taxonomy. J. Cell. Autom. **3**(4), 271–288 (2008)
2. Bernardi, V., Durand, B., Formenti, E., Kari, J.: A new dimension sensitive property for cellular automata. Theoret. Comput. Sci. **345**(2), 235–247 (2005). https://doi.org/10.1016/j.tcs.2005.07.009

3. Boccara, N., Fukś, H.: Cellular automaton rules conserving the number of active sites. J. Phys. A: Math. Gen. **31**(28), 6007–6018 (1998). https://doi.org/10.1088/0305-4470/31/28/014
4. Boccara, N., Fukś, H.: Number-conserving cellular automaton rules. Fund. Inform. **52**(1–3), 1–13 (2002)
5. Durand, B., Formenti, E., Róka, Z.: Number-conserving cellular automata I: decidability. Theoret. Comput. Sci. **299**(1), 523–535 (2003). https://doi.org/10.1016/S0304-3975(02)00534-0
6. Dzedzej, A., Dziemiańczuk, M., Nenca, A., Wardyn, A., Wolnik, B.: The complete list of two-dimensional number-conserving ternary cellular automata [dataset] (2020). https://doi.org/10.34808/phjp-ah07
7. Dzedzej, A., Wolnik, B., Dziemiańczuk, M., Nenca, A., Baetens, J.M., De Baets, B.: A two-layer representation of four-state reversible number-conserving 2D cellular automata. J. Stat. Mech: Theory Exp. **2019**(7), 073202 (2019). https://doi.org/10.1088/1742-5468/ab25df
8. Dzedzej, A., Wolnik, B., Nenca, A., Baetens, J., De Baets, B.: Efficient enumeration of three-state two-dimensional number-conserving cellular automata. Inf. Comput. **274**, 14 (2020). https://doi.org/10.1016/j.ic.2020.104534
9. Dzedzej, A., Wolnik, B., Nenca, A., Baetens, J.M., De Baets, B.: Two-dimensional rotation-symmetric number-conserving cellular automata. Inf. Sci. **577**, 599–621 (2021). https://doi.org/10.1016/j.ins.2021.06.041
10. Dziemiańczuk, M., Wolnik, B., Dzedzej, A.: The complete lists of 1D reversible number-conserving cellular automata with radius one of up to 7 states [dataset] (2020). https://doi.org/10.34808/b8pn-1523
11. Fredkin, E., Toffoli, T.: Conservative logic. Int. J. Theor. Phys. **21**(3), 219–253 (1982). https://doi.org/10.1007/BF01857727
12. Fukś, H., Sullivan, K.: Enumeration of number-conserving cellular automata rules with two inputs. J. Cell. Autom. **2**, 141–148 (2007)
13. Fukś, H., Sullivan, K.: Enumeration of number-conserving cellular automata rules with two inputs. J. Cell. Autom. **2**(2), 141–148 (2007)
14. García-Ramos, F.: Product decomposition for surjective 2-block NCCA. Discret. Math. Theoret. Comput. Sci. 147–158 (2011). https://doi.org/10.46298/dmtcs.2971
15. Hattori, T., Takesue, S.: Additive conserved quantities in discrete-time lattice dynamical systems. Physica D **49**(3), 295–322 (1991). https://doi.org/10.1016/0167-2789(91)90150-8
16. Imai, K., Fujita, K., Iwamoto, C., Morita, K.: Embedding a logically universal model and a self-reproducing model into number-conserving cellular automata. In: Calude, C.S., Dinneen, M.J., Peper, F. (eds.) UMC 2002. LNCS, vol. 2509, pp. 164–175. Springer, Heidelberg (2002). https://doi.org/10.1007/3-540-45833-6_14
17. Imai, K., Ishizaka, H., Poupet, V.: 5-state rotation-symmetric number-conserving cellular automata are not strongly universal. In: Isokawa, T., Imai, K., Matsui, N., Peper, F., Umeo, H. (eds.) AUTOMATA 2014. LNCS, vol. 8996, pp. 31–43. Springer, Cham (2015). https://doi.org/10.1007/978-3-319-18812-6_3
18. Imai, K., Martin, B., Saito, R.: On radius 1 nontrivial reversible and number-conserving cellular automata. In: Adamatzky, A. (ed.) Reversibility and Universality. ECC, vol. 30, pp. 269–277. Springer, Cham (2018). https://doi.org/10.1007/978-3-319-73216-9_12
19. Ishizaka, H., Takemura, Y., Imai, K.: On enumeration of motion representable two-dimensional two-state number-conserving cellular automata. In: 2015 Third

International Symposium on Computing and Networking (CANDAR), pp. 412–417 (2015). https://doi.org/10.1109/CANDAR.2015.52
20. Kari, J.: Theory of cellular automata: a survey. Theoret. Comput. Sci. **334**, 3–33 (2005). https://doi.org/10.1016/j.tcs.2004.11.021
21. Kohyama, T.: Cellular automata with particle conservation. Progr. Theoret. Phys. **81**(1), 47–59 (1989). https://doi.org/10.1143/PTP.81.47
22. Kotze, L., Steeb, W.H.: Conservation laws in cellular automata. In: Finite Dimensional Integrable Nonlinear Dynamical Systems, pp. 333–346. World Scientific (1988)
23. Miquey, É.: State-conserving cellular automata (2011). https://www.i2m.univ-amu.fr/perso/etienne.miquey/stage/utu.pdf
24. Moreira, A.: Universality and decidability of number-conserving cellular automata. Theoret. Comput. Sci. **292**(3), 711–721 (2003). https://doi.org/10.1016/S0304-3975(02)00065-8
25. Moreira, A.: NCCA – some of my work (2003). http://www.dim.uchile.cl/~anmoreir/ncca/mywork.html. Accessed 31 Oct 2023
26. Moreira, A.: Two-dimensional number-conserving cellular automata (2003). http://www.dim.uchile.cl/~anmoreir/ncca/res_2d.pdf. Unpublished report available online
27. Morita, K.: Universality of one-dimensional reversible and number-conserving cellular automata. In: Proceedings 18th International Workshop on Cellular Automata and Discrete Complex Systems and 3rd International Symposium Journées Automates Cellulaires, AUTOMATA and JAC 2012, La Marana, Corsica, 19–21 September 2012. EPTCS, vol. 90, pp. 142–150 (2012). https://doi.org/10.4204/EPTCS.90.12
28. Nagel, K., Schreckenberg, M.: A cellular automaton model for freeway traffic. J. Phys. I **2**(12), 2221–2229 (1992). https://doi.org/10.1051/jp1:1992277
29. Nenca, A., Dzedzej, A., Wolnik, B.: The complete list of two-dimensional rotation-symmetric number-conserving septenary cellular automata [dataset] (2022). https://doi.org/10.34808/jr67-r637
30. Pivato, M.: Conservation laws in cellular automata. Nonlinearity **15**(6), 1781–1793 (2002). https://doi.org/10.1088/0951-7715/15/6/305
31. Taati, S.: Conservation laws in cellular automata. In: Rozenberg, G., Bäck, T., Kok, J.N. (eds.) Handbook of Natural Computing, pp. 259–286. Springer, Heidelberg (2012). https://doi.org/10.1007/978-3-540-92910-9_8
32. Takesue, S.: Staggered invariants in cellular automata. Complex Syst. **9**(2), 149–168 (1995)
33. Tanimoto, N., Imai, K.: A characterization of von Neumann neighbor number-conserving cellular automata. J. Cell. Autom. **4**, 39–54 (2009)
34. Tanimoto, N., Imai, K., Iwamoto, C., Morita, K.: On the non-existance of rotation-symmetric von Neumann neighbor number-conserving cellular automata of which the state number is less than four. IEICE Trans. Inf. Syst. **92-D**, 255–257 (2009)
35. Ulam, S.: On some mathematical problems connected with patterns of growth of figures. In: Proceedings of Symposia in Applied Mathematics, vol. 14, pp. 215–224 (1962)
36. von Neumann, J.: Theory of Self-Reproducing Automata. University of Illinois Press, Champaign, IL, USA (1966)
37. Wolnik, B., De Baets, B.: All binary number-conserving cellular automata based on adjacent cells are intrinsically one-dimensional. Phys. Rev. E **100**, 022126 (2019). https://doi.org/10.1103/PhysRevE.100.022126

38. Wolnik, B., De Baets, B.: Ternary reversible number-conserving cellular automata are trivial. Inf. Sci. **513**, 180–189 (2020). https://doi.org/10.1016/j.ins.2019.10.068
39. Wolnik, B., Dzedzej, A., Baetens, J.M., De Baets, B.: Number-conserving cellular automata with a von Neumann neighborhood of range one. J. Phys. A: Math. Theor. **50**(43), 435101 (2017). https://doi.org/10.1088/1751-8121/aa89cf
40. Wolnik, B., Dziemiańczuk, M., De Baets, B.: State-conserving one-dimensional cellular automata with radius one. Nonlinear Dyn. (2025). https://doi.org/10.1007/s11071-025-10896-9
41. Wolnik, B., Dziemiańczuk, M., Dzedzej, A., De Baets, B.: Reversibility of number-conserving 1D cellular automata: unlocking insights into the dynamics for larger state sets. Physica D **429**, 133075 (2022). https://doi.org/10.1016/j.physd.2021.133075
42. Wolnik, B., Mrożek, N., Dzedzej, A., De Baets, B.: Three-dimensional rotation-symmetric number-conserving cellular automata. J. Cell. Autom. **15**(4), 243–259 (2020)
43. Wolnik, B., Nenca, A., Baetens, J.M., De Baets, B.: A split-and-perturb decomposition of number-conserving cellular automata. Physica D **413**, 132645 (2020). https://doi.org/10.1016/j.physd.2020.132645
44. Wolnik, B., Nenca, A., Dzedzej, A., De Baets, B.: Seven-state rotation-symmetric number-conserving cellular automaton that is not isomorphic to any septenary one. Phys. Rev. E **107**, 024211 (2023). https://doi.org/10.1103/PhysRevE.107.024211
45. Zaitsev, D.A.: A generalized neighborhood for cellular automata. Theoret. Comput. Sci. **666**, 21–35 (2017). https://doi.org/10.1016/j.tcs.2016.11.002

Categorical Products of Cellular Automata

Alonso Castillo-Ramirez[(✉)], Alejandro Vazquez-Aceves, and Angel Zaldivar-Corichi

Centro Universitario de Ciencias Exactas e Ingenierías, Universidad de Guadalajara, Guadalajara, Mexico
alonso.castillor@academicos.udg.mx

Abstract. We study two categories of cellular automata. First, for any group G, we consider the category $\mathcal{CA}(G)$ whose objects are configuration spaces of the form A^G, where A is a set, and whose morphisms are cellular automata of the form $\tau : A_1^G \to A_2^G$. We prove that the categorical product of two configuration spaces A_1^G and A_2^G in $\mathcal{CA}(G)$ is the configuration space $(A_1 \times A_2)^G$. Then, we consider the category of generalized cellular automata $\mathcal{GCA}$, whose objects are configuration spaces of the form A^G, where A is a set and G is a group, and whose morphisms are ϕ-cellular automata of the form $\mathcal{T} : A_1^{G_1} \to A_2^{G_2}$, where $\phi : G_2 \to G_1$ is a group homomorphism. We prove that a categorical weak product of two configuration spaces $A_1^{G_1}$ and $A_2^{G_2}$ in $\mathcal{GCA}$ is the configuration space $(A_1 \times A_2)^{G_1 * G_2}$, where $G_1 * G_2$ is the free product of G_1 and G_2. The previous results allow us to naturally define the product of two cellular automata in $\mathcal{CA}(G)$ and a weak product of two generalized cellular automata in $\mathcal{GCA}$.

Keywords: Cellular automata · Generalized cellular automata · Category theory · Categorical product

1 Introduction

Category theory is a powerful foundation of mathematics that provides a unifying framework to describe and analyze different structures and their relationships. Many constructions and concepts that appear in different contexts throughout mathematics, such as quotient spaces, direct products, adjoints, and duality, are unified with a precise definition in category theory. In particular, a *categorical product*, or simply a *product*, of two objects in a category is a generalization of the Cartesian product of two sets, the direct product of two groups, and the product topology of two topological spaces. This captures the idea of combining two objects to produce a new object, while preserving in some way its relationship with the original objects.

In this paper, we study products in categories of cellular automata (CA). Recall that a *cellular automaton* over a group G, known as the *universe*, and a set A, known as the *alphabet*, is a transformation $\tau : A^G \to A^G$ of the configuration

Published by Springer Nature Switzerland AG 2026
S. Riva and A. Richard (Eds.): AUTOMATA 2025, LNCS 15831, pp. 59–71, 2026.
https://doi.org/10.1007/978-3-032-01570-9_5

space $A^G := \{x : G \to A\}$ such that there exists a finite subset $S \subseteq G$ and a local function $\mu : A^S \to A$ that determines the behavior of τ (see Definition 3). Traditionally, CA have been studied when $G = \mathbb{Z}^d$, but interest in the more general setting of an arbitrary group has recently grown (e.g., see [7]).

Before reviewing our work with more detail, we shall mention a few previous studies on cellular automata from a categorical point of view. In [3], Silvio Capobianco and Tarmo Uustalu explore various properties of CA, such as the Curtis-Hedlund-Lyndon theorem and the reversibility principle, using category theory. In [6], Tullio Ceccherini-Silberstein and Michel Coornaert considered cellular automata $\tau : A^G \to B^G$ where G is a fixed group, and A and B are objects in a concrete category. They prove analogous to various important results in the theory of CA, including theorems of surjunctivity and reversibility. In [14], Ville Salo and Ilkka Törmä examined various categories whose objects are subshifts of $A^{\mathbb{Z}}$ and whose morphisms are cellular automata, or block maps, between subshifts. Finally, in [9,10], A. Fernandez, L. Maignan, and A. Spicher, use the categorical notion of a Kan extension to formalize how a cellular automaton is a natural extension of its local defining map, which among other things, provides a new point of view of the well-known Curtis-Hedlund-Lyndon theorem.

Our work concerns two distinct categories of cellular automata. The first one is the category $\mathcal{CA}(G)$ of all cellular automata over a fixed group G, whose objects are configuration spaces of the form A^G, where A is any set, and whose morphisms are cellular automata $\tau : A_1^G \to A_2^G$ as defined in Definition 3. The second one is the category $\mathcal{GCA}$ of *generalized cellular automata*, whose objects are configuration spaces of the form A^G, where A is a set and G is a group, and whose morphisms are ϕ-cellular automata $\mathcal{T} : A_1^{G_1} \to A_2^{G_2}$, where $\phi : G_2 \to G_1$ is a group homomorphism, as defined in [5].

We show the categorical product of two configuration spaces A_1^G and A_2^G in the category $\mathcal{CA}(G)$ is the configuration space $(A_1 \times A_2)^G$ together with the projections

$$\pi_i^G : (A_1 \times A_2)^G \to A_i^G, \quad \pi_i^G := \pi_i \circ x, \forall x \in (A_1 \times A_2)^G,$$

where $\pi_i : A_1 \times A_2 \to A_i$ are the natural projections of the Cartesian product of sets. This allows us to define the categorical product for a pair of cellular automata $\tau_1 : A_1^G \to B_1^G$ and $\tau_2 : A_2^G \to B_2^G$ to be the cellular automaton $\tau_1 \times \tau_2 : (A_1 \times A_2)^G \to (B_1 \times B_2)^G$ such that

$$(\tau_1 \times \tau_2)(x)(g) = (\tau_1(\pi_{A_1}^G(x)(g)), \tau_2(\pi_{A_2}^G(x)(g)), \quad \forall x \in (A_1 \times A_2)^G, g \in G;$$

this coincides with what is usually considered to be the product of two CA (see [8, Ex. 1.17]).

On the other hand, we show that a *weak product* of two configuration spaces $A_1^{G_1}$ and $A_2^{G_2}$ in the category $\mathcal{GCA}$ is the configuration space $(A_1 \times A_2)^{G_1 * G_2}$, where $G_1 * G_2$ denotes the free product of G_1 and G_2, together with projections induced by π_i and the canonical embeddings $\iota_i : G_i \to G_1 * G_2$ (see Theorem 3). The definition of a weak product in a category is analogous to a product, except that the morphism that satisfies the universal property is only required to exist but not to be unique. The reason behind why this weak product in $\mathcal{GCA}$ fails to be a product is because generalized CA may fail to have the *unique homomorphisms property* as introduced in [4]; this means that there are generalized CA $\mathcal{T} : A_1^{G_1} \to A_2^{G_2}$ that are ϕ- and ψ-cellular automata for $\phi \neq \psi$.

The structure of this paper is as follows. In Sect. 2 we review some basic notions of category theory, including the product and coproduct, as well as some examples. In Sect. 3 we show that the category of cellular automata has products, while in Sect. 4 we show review some basic theory of generalized cellular automata and show that their category has a weak product.

2 Category Theory

In this section we shall review some basic notions of category theory; for a broader treatment see [2,11,12,16].

A *category* $\mathcal{C}$ consists of a class of *objects*, denoted by $\mathrm{Obj}(\mathcal{C})$, and a class of *morphisms*, or *arrows*, denoted by $\mathrm{Mor}(\mathcal{C})$. Each morphism $f \in \mathrm{Mor}(\mathcal{C})$ has a source object $\mathrm{Dom}(f) \in \mathrm{Obj}(\mathcal{C})$, which we call the *domain* of f, and an *arrival* object $\mathrm{Cod}(f) \in \mathrm{Obj}(\mathcal{C})$, which we call the *codomain* of f. All the information that a morphism carries is condensed in the notation

$$f : \mathrm{Dom}(f) \to \mathrm{Cod}(f).$$

The class of morphisms with domain A and codomain B is denoted by $\mathrm{Hom}_{\mathcal{C}}(A, B)$. Part of the essence of category theory is that objects are treated as if they are not necessarily sets, and morphisms are treated as if they are not necessarily functions.

The morphisms in a category must satisfy some additional axioms. For each pair of morphisms $f, g \in \mathrm{Mor}(\mathcal{C})$, such that $\mathrm{Cod}(f) = \mathrm{Dom}(g)$, there exists a morphism $g \circ f : \mathrm{Dom}(f) \to \mathrm{Cod}(g)$, called a *composition* of g with f, which satisfies the following properties:

1. For any objects $A, B, C, D \in \mathrm{Obj}(\mathcal{C})$, and morphisms $f : A \to B, g : B \to C$ and $h : C \to D$, we have
$$h \circ (g \circ f) = (h \circ g) \circ f.$$
2. For every object $A \in \mathrm{Obj}(\mathcal{C})$, there exists a morphism $\mathrm{id}_A \in \mathrm{Hom}_{\mathcal{C}}(A, A)$ that satisfies the following: for every $B \in \mathrm{Obj}(\mathcal{C})$ and $g \in \mathrm{Hom}_{\mathcal{C}}(A, B)$, $h \in \mathrm{Hom}_{\mathcal{C}}(B, A)$,
$$g \circ \mathrm{id}_A = g \text{ and } \mathrm{id}_A \circ h = h.$$

To simplify the notation, when referring to an object or a morphism of a category $\mathcal{C}$, we will write $A \in \mathcal{C}$ or $f \in \mathcal{C}$, instead of $A \in \mathrm{Obj}(\mathcal{C})$ or $f \in \mathrm{Mor}(\mathcal{C})$. Moreover, when there is no doubt about the category in question, we will denote the collection $\mathrm{Hom}_{\mathcal{C}}(A, B)$ simply by $\mathrm{Hom}(A, B)$. Morphisms in $\mathrm{Hom}(A, A)$ are called *endomorphisms*, so we will denote such a collection as $\mathrm{End}(A)$.

Example 1. We introduce some examples of categories.

1. The class of sets, together with the class of all functions between sets, form the *category of sets*, which we denote as **Set**.
2. The class of all groups, together with the class of all group homomorphisms, form the *category of groups*, which we denote as **Grp**.
3. The class of all topological spaces, together with the class of all continuous functions, form the *category of topological spaces*, which we denote as **Top**.
4. Given a field $\mathbb{K}$, the class of vector spaces over $\mathbb{K}$, together with the class of linear transformations, form the *category of vector spaces* over $\mathbb{K}$, which we denote by $\mathbf{Vec}_{\mathbb{K}}$.
5. Let M be a monoid, that is, a set with an associative binary operation and with identity $1 \in M$. We can view M as a category with one object, i.e., $\text{Obj}(M) = \{\bullet\}$, and each element in M is a morphism in the category, i.e., $\text{Mor}(M) = M$, with the monoid operation as composition of morphisms. All morphisms in this category are endomorphisms of the single object, i.e., $M = \text{End}(\bullet)$.
6. Let $(P, \leq)$ be a partially ordered set, we can view P as a category, where $\text{Obj}(P) = P$, and given $a, b \in P$, there is a unique morphism from a to b if and only if $a \leq b$. By the properties of the order relation it is clear that all the category axioms are satisfied.

In the first four examples, the objects of the categories are sets with additional structure, and the morphisms are functions that preserve these structures. These categories are called *concrete categories*. On the other hand, the last two examples seek to point out that morphisms do not necessarily have to be functions between sets.

Now we introduce the definition of the product in an arbitrary category.

Definition 1 (product). *Let $\mathcal{C}$ be a category. A* product *of two objects A and B in $\mathcal{C}$ is an object $A \times B \in \mathcal{C}$ together with morphisms $\pi_1 : A \times B \to A$ and $\pi_2 : A \times B \to B$ satisfying the following universal property: for any object X and any morphisms $f : X \to A$ and $g : X \to B$, there exists a unique morphism $h : X \to A \times B$ such that $\pi_1 \circ h = f$ and $\pi_2 \circ h = g$; this is equivalent of saying that the diagram in Fig. 1 commutes.*

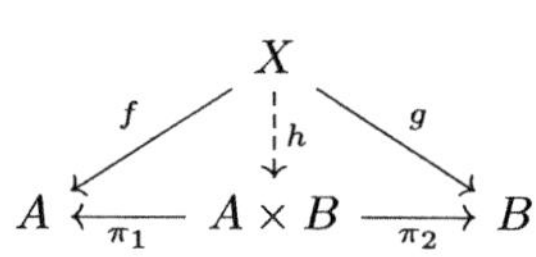

Fig. 1. Definition of the product of two objects in a category.

It turns out that if a product of two objects exists, then it is unique up to isomorphism. The morphisms $\pi_1 : A \times B \to A$ and $\pi_2 : A \times B \to B$ are called the *projections* to A and B, respectively. We say that the category $\mathcal{C}$ itself has *finite products* if any two objects in $\mathcal{C}$ have a product.

A *weak product* of two objects $A \times B \in \mathcal{C}$ is defined analogously as the product in Definition 1, except that the morphism $h : X \to A \times B$ is not required to be unique (see [11, Sec. X.2]).

Example 2. We introduce a few examples of products in categories.

1. In the concrete categories described above, the product of two objects A and B is the Cartesian product of sets $A \times B$ equipped with the corresponding structure so that the projections $\pi_1 : A \times B \to A$ and $\pi_2 : A \times B \to B$, defined as $\pi_1(a, b) = a$ and $\pi_2(a, b) = b$, are morphisms in the corresponding categories (**Set**, **Grp**, **Top**, $\mathbf{Vec}_{\mathbb{K}}$, etc.). However, there exist concrete categories where the product is not the Cartesian product together with the projections described above. When it does coincide, we say that the concrete category has *concrete products* (see [1, Ex. 10.55]).
2. Consider a set A and the partially ordered set $(2^A, \subseteq)$, where 2^A is the power set of A. Considering 2^A as a category as in Example 1.6., the product of two objects $X, Y \in 2^A$ is the set $X \cap Y$ together with the unique arrows $X \cap Y \to X$ and $X \cap Y \to Y$ satisfying that $X \cap Y \subseteq X$ and $XapY \subseteq Y$.
3. Consider as a category the partially ordered set $(\mathbb{N}, |)$, where $\mathbb{N}$ is the set of natural numbers and $|$ is the divisibility relation. The product of two objects $m, n \in \mathbb{N}$ is the greatest common divisor of m and n together with the unique morphisms given by being divisors of m and n.

When a category $\mathcal{C}$ has finite products we may define the *product of two morphisms* of $\mathcal{C}$.

Theorem 1. *Let $\mathcal{C}$ be a category with finite products, and let $f_1 : A_1 \to B_1$ and $f_2 : A_2 \to B_2$ be two morphisms. Then there exists a unique morphism $f_1 \times f_2 : A_1 \times A_2 \to B_1 \times B_2$ such that*

$$\pi_{B_1} \circ (f_1 \times f_2) = f_1 \circ \pi_{A_1} \text{ and } \pi_{B_1} \circ (f_1 \times f_2) = f_2 \circ \pi_{A_2},$$

where $\pi_{A_i} : A_1 \times A_2 \to A_i$ and $\pi_{B_i} : B_1 \times B_2 \to B_i$ are the projection morphisms; this is equivalent of saying that the diagram in Fig. 2 commutes.

$$\begin{array}{ccccc} A_1 & \xleftarrow{\pi_{A_1}} & A_1 \times A_2 & \xrightarrow{\pi_{A_2}} & A_2 \\ {\scriptstyle f_1}\downarrow & & \downarrow{\scriptstyle f_1 \times f_2} & & {\scriptstyle f_2}\downarrow \\ B_1 & \xleftarrow[\pi_{B_1}]{} & B_1 \times B_2 & \xrightarrow[\pi_{B_2}]{} & B_2 \end{array}$$

Fig. 2. Product to two morphisms in a category.

Proof. This follows from the universal property of the product with $X = A_1 \times A_2$, $f = f_1 \circ \pi_{A_1}$ and $g = f_2 \circ \pi_{A_2}$ (c.f [12, p. 30]). $\square$

Example 3. In the category **Set**, the product of two functions $f_1 : A_1 \to B_1$ and $f_2 : A_2 \to B_2$ is the function $f_1 \times f_2 : A_1 \times A_2 \to B_1 \times B_2$ defined by

$$(f_1 \times f_2)(a_1, a_2) := (f_1(a_1), f_2(a_2)), \quad \forall (a_1, a_2) \in A_1 \times A_2.$$

The dual notion of a product in a category, called a *coproduct*, is defined by reversing the direction of the morphisms in the definition of a product. Despite this simple change in the definition, products and coproducts may behave dramatically different in a category.

Definition 2 (coproduct). *Let $\mathcal{C}$ be a category, and $A, B \in \mathcal{C}$ be objects of the category. A* coproduct *of objects A and B in $\mathcal{C}$ is an object $A + B \in \mathcal{C}$ together with morphisms $\iota_1 : A \to A + B$ and $\iota_2 : B \to A + B$ satisfying the following universal property: for any object X and morphisms $f : A \to X$ and $g : B \to X$ there exists a unique morphism $h : A+B \to X$ such that $h \circ \iota_1 = f$ and $h \circ \iota_2 = g$; this is equivalent of saying that the diagram in Fig. 3 commutes.*

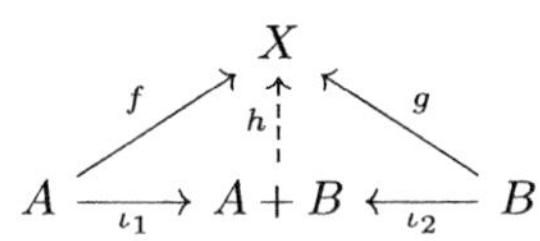

Fig. 3. Definition of the coproduct of two objects in a category.

Example 4. We introduce some examples of coproducts in categories.

1. In the category of sets **Set**, the coproduct of A and B corresponds to the disjoint union $A + B = (A \times \{A\}) \cup (B \times \{B\})$ together with the inclusions $\iota_1 : A \to A + B$ and $\iota_2 : B \to A + B$, defined as $\iota_1(a) = (a, A)$ and $\iota_2(b) = (b, B)$.
2. In the category of groups **Grp**, the coproduct of G and H corresponds to the *free product* of groups $G * H$ together with the canonical embeddings $\iota_1 : G \to G * H$ and $\iota_2 : H \to G * H$ (see [12, Ex. 88] or [11, Sec. III.3]). Explicitly, if G and H are given by the following presentations

$$G = \langle S_G \mid R_G \rangle \quad \text{and} \quad H = \langle S_H \mid R_H \rangle,$$

then the free product $G * H$ has presentation

$$G * H = \langle S_G + S_H \mid R_G + R_H \rangle,$$

where $+$ denotes the coproduct (disjoint union) in the category of sets (see [13, Theorem 11.53]). It is then clear that the canonical embeddings $\iota_1 : G \to G*H$ and $\iota_2 : H \to G * H$ are defined by mapping the generators S_G and S_H to $S_G + S_H$, respectively.
3. Consider as a category the partially ordered set $(\mathbb{N}, |)$. The coproduct of two objects $m, n \in \mathbb{N}$ is the least common multiple of m and n together with the unique morphism given by being a multiple of m and n.

3 Product of Cellular Automata

The category of cellular automata over a group G, denoted by $\mathcal{CA}(G)$, consists of objects that are *configuration spaces* over G; this is, sets of $A^G := \{x : G \to A\}$ where A is a set, usually called an *alphabet*. The morphisms of $\mathcal{CA}(G)$ are *cellular automata*, as given in the following definition, which is a slightly more general than Definition 1.4.1 in [7], as it involves two arbitrary alphabets A and B (see [8, Sec. 1.1.4]).

Definition 3. *Let A^G and B^G be two configuration spaces. We say that a function $\tau : A^G \to B^G$ is a* cellular automaton *if there exists a finite subset $S \subseteq G$ (called a* memory set*) and a function $\mu : A^S \to B$ (called a* local function*) such that:*

$$\tau(x)(g) = \mu((g \cdot x)|_S), \quad \forall x \in A^G, g \in G,$$

where $\cdot$ is the shift action *of G on A^G given by*

$$(g \cdot x)(h) = x(hg), \quad \forall x \in A^G, g, h \in G.$$

and $x|_S$ is the restriction of $x \in A^G$ to S.

Remark 1. Alternatively as introduced in Definition 3, we may consider the shift action of G on A^G to be

$$(g \star x)(h) = x(g^{-1}h), \quad \forall x \in A^G, g, h \in G.$$

However, we may check that $\cdot$ and $\star$ are *equivalent actions* in a formal sense: there exists a bijection $\beta : A^G \to A^G$ given by $\beta(x)(g) := x(g^{-1})$, for all $x \in A^G$, $g \in G$, such that

$$\beta(g \cdot x) = g \star \beta(x), \quad \forall x \in A^G, g \in G.$$

Since the composition of two cellular automata is a cellular automaton by [7, Prop. 1.4.9] and the identity function of A^G is a cellular automaton, then $\mathcal{CA}(G)$ is a category.

Example 5. For any function $f : A \to B$ between sets we may define a cellular automaton $f^G : A^G \to B^G$ by

$$f^G(x) := f \circ x, \quad \forall x \in A^G.$$

It is clear that f^G has memory set $\{e\}$ and local function $f : A^{\{e\}} \to B$.

Example 6. With the notation of Example 5, let $f : A \to B$ be a constant function with $f(a) = b \in B$, for all $a \in A$. Then $f^G : A^G \to B^G$ is the constant cellular automaton given by

$$f^G(x) = b^G, \quad \forall x \in A^G, \qquad \text{where } b^G(g) := b, \quad \forall g \in G.$$

The next result shows that the category $\mathcal{CA}(G)$ has concrete finite products.

Theorem 2. *Let G be a group, and let A_1^G and A_2^G be two configuration spaces in $\mathcal{CA}(G)$. The product of A_1^G and A_2^G in the category $\mathcal{CA}(G)$ is the configuration space $(A_1 \times A_2)^G$ together with the cellular automata $\pi_i^G : (A_1 \times A_2)^G \to A_i^G$ induced, as in Example 5, by the usual projections $\pi_i : A_1 \times A_2 \to A_i$ in the category of sets.*

Proof. Let $B^G \in \mathcal{CA}(G)$ be a configuration space, and consider two cellular automata $\tau_1 : B^G \to A_1^G$ and $\tau_2 : B^G \to A_2^G$. Let $S_1, S_2 \subseteq G$ be memory sets, and let $\mu_1 : B^{S_1} \to A_1$ and $\mu_2 : B^{S_2} \to A_2$ be local functions for τ_1 and τ_2, respectively. Define a finite set $S := S_1 \cup S_2 \subseteq G$ and local functions

$$\hat{\mu}_1 : B^S \to A_1 \text{ and } \hat{\mu}_2 : B^S \to A_2,$$

by $\hat{\mu}_1(x) := \mu_1(x|_{S_1})$ and $\hat{\mu}_2(x) := \mu_2(x|_{S_2})$, for all $x \in B^S$. The universal property of the product in the category of sets tells us that there exists a unique function

$$\mu : B^S \to A_1 \times A_2 \text{ such that } \pi_i \circ \mu = \hat{\mu}_i, \quad i \in \{1, 2\}. \tag{1}$$

Now let $\tau : B^G \to (A_1 \times A_2)^G$ be the cellular automaton defined by the local function μ. We shall check that the diagram given in Fig. 4 commutes. Indeed, for any $x \in B^G$ and $g \in G$, we have

$$\begin{aligned}
(\pi_i^G \circ \tau)(x)(g) &= \pi_i(\tau(x)(g)) \\
&= \pi_i(\mu((g \cdot x)|_S)) \\
&= \hat{\mu}_i((g \cdot x)|_S) \qquad \text{(by eq. (1))} \\
&= \mu_i((g \cdot x)|_{S_i}) \\
&= \tau_i(x)(g).
\end{aligned}$$

Therefore, $\pi_i^G \circ \tau = \tau_i$, for $i \in \{1, 2\}$.

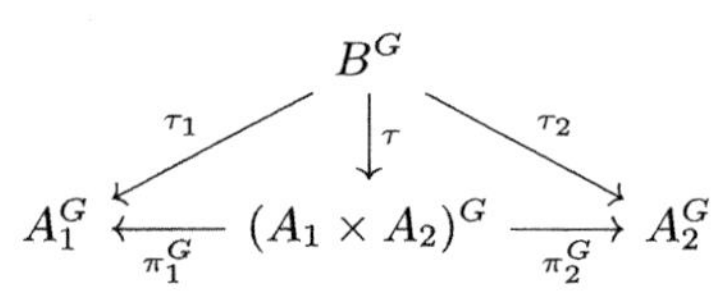

Fig. 4. Product of two configuration spaces in $\mathcal{CA}(G)$.

Finally, to prove that τ is unique, suppose there exists another cellular automaton $\sigma : B^G \to (A_1 \times A_2)^G$ such that $\tau_i = \pi_i^G \circ \sigma$. Then, for all $x \in B^G$ and $g \in G$ we have:

$$\pi_i(\sigma(x)(g)) = \pi_i^G(\sigma(x))(g) = \pi_i^G(\tau(x))(g) = \pi_i(\tau(x)(g))$$

for $i \in \{1, 2\}$. Hence $\sigma(x)(g) = \tau(x)(g)$ for all $x \in B^G$ and $g \in G$, which implies that $\sigma = \tau$. □

Corollary 1. *For any cellular automata $\tau_1 : A_1^G \to B_1^G$ and $\tau_2 : A_2^G \to B_2^G$ in $\mathcal{CA}(G)$ there is a unique cellular automaton $\tau_1 \times \tau_2 : (A_1 \times A_2)^G \to (B_1 \times B_2)^G$ such that*

$$\pi_{B_1}^G \circ (\tau_1 \times \tau_2) = \tau_1 \circ \pi_{A_1}^G \text{ and } \pi_{B_2}^G \circ (\tau_1 \times \tau_2) = \tau_2 \circ \pi_{A_2}^G,$$

With the notation of the previous corollary, we may identify $x \in (A_1 \times A_2)^G$ with a pair $(x_1, x_2) \in A_1^G \times A_2^G$ such that $x_i = \pi_{A_i} \circ x \in A_i^G$. Then $\tau_1 \times \tau_2 : (A_1 \times A_2)^G \to (B_1 \times B_2)^G$ satisfies

$$(\tau_1 \times \tau_2)(x_1, x_2)(g) = (\tau_1(x_1)(g), \tau_2(x_2)(g)), \quad \forall (x_1, x_2) \in A_1^G \times A_2^G, g \in G.$$

4 Weak Product of Generalized Cellular Automata

The main idea in the definition of *generalized cellular automata* is to consider CA between configuration spaces over different groups. The following is a slightly generalized version of the definition introduced in [5], as it also involves two different alphabets.

Definition 4. *Let $\phi : H \to G$ be a group homomorphism, and let A and B be sets. A* ϕ-cellular automaton *is a function $\mathcal{T} : A^G \to B^H$ such that there is a finite subset $S \subseteq G$ and a local function $\mu : A^S \to B$ satisfying*

$$\mathcal{T}(x)(h) = \mu((\phi(h) \cdot x)|_S), \quad \forall x \in A^G, h \in H.$$

We say that $\mathcal{T} : A^G \to B^H$ is a *generalized cellular automaton* if it is a ϕ-cellular automaton for some group homomorphism $\phi : H \to G$. Note that when $G = H$, an id-cellular automaton is the same as a cellular automaton over G.

Example 7. Consider the group of integers $\mathbb{Z}$ and the direct product $\mathbb{Z}^2$. Define a homomorphism $\phi : \mathbb{Z}^2 \to \mathbb{Z}$ by $\phi(n, m) := n + m$, for all $(n, m) \in \mathbb{Z}^2$. Let $S := \{-1, 0, 1\} \subseteq \mathbb{Z}$. Then, any local function $\mu : A^S \to B$ defines a ϕ-cellular automaton $\mathcal{T} : A^{\mathbb{Z}} \to B^{\mathbb{Z}^2}$ by

$$\tau(x)(n, m) = \mu(x(n + m - 1), x(n + m), x(n + m + 1)), \quad \forall x \in A^{\mathbb{Z}}, (n, m) \in \mathbb{Z}^2.$$

As shown in [4, Lemma 4]), for every ϕ-cellular automaton $\mathcal{T} : A^G \to B^H$ there exists a unique cellular automaton $\tau : A^G \to B^G$ such that

$$\mathcal{T} = \phi_B^* \circ \tau, \tag{2}$$

where $\phi_B^* : B^G \to B^H$ is the ϕ-cellular automaton defined by

$$\phi_B^*(x) = x \circ \phi, \quad \forall x \in B^G.$$

It is easy to check that for every pair of homomorphisms $\phi : H \to G$ and $\psi : K \to H$, we have

$$(\phi \circ \psi)_B^* = \psi_B^* \circ \phi_B^*. \tag{3}$$

It follows from [5, Theorem 2] that the composition of a ϕ-cellular automaton $\mathcal{T} : A^G \to B^H$ with a ψ-cellular automaton $\mathcal{S} : B^H \to C^K$ is a $(\psi \circ \phi)$-cellular automaton. Hence, we shall consider the category $\mathcal{GCA}$ whose objects are configuration spaces of the form A^G, where A is a set and G is a group, and whose morphisms are ϕ-cellular automata $\mathcal{T} : A_1^{G_1} \to A_2^{G_2}$, where $\phi : G_2 \to G_1$ is a group homomorphism.

For two groups G_1 and G_2, let $G_1 * G_2$ be their free product. The canonical embeddings $\iota_i : G_i \to G_1 * G_2$ induce corresponding ι_i-cellular automata

$$(\iota_i)^*_C : C^{G_1 * G_2} \to C^{G_i},$$

for any alphabet C.

Theorem 3. *A weak product of two configuration spaces $A_1^{G_1}$ and $A_2^{G_2}$ in $\mathcal{GCA}$ is the configuration space $(A_1 \times A_2)^{G_1 * G_2}$ together with the projections*

$$\gamma_i : (A_1 \times A_2)^{G_1 * G_2} \to A_i^{G_i} \quad \textit{given by} \quad \gamma_i := (\iota_i)^*_{A_i} \circ \pi_i^{G_1 * G_2},$$

where $\pi_i^{G_1 * G_2}$ are the cellular automata projections considered in Theorem 2.

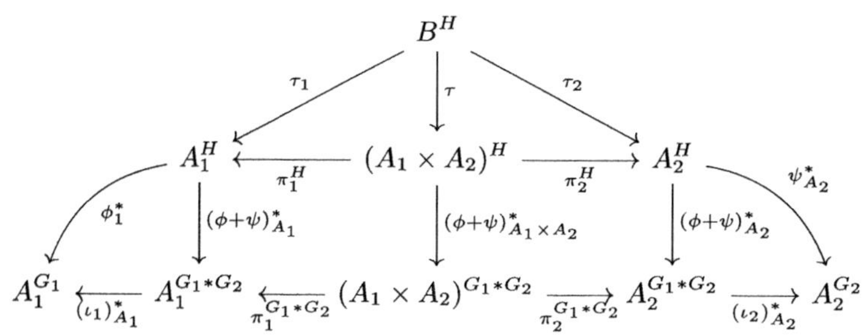

Fig. 5. Proof of the existence of a weak product in $\mathcal{GCA}$.

Proof. Let $\phi^*_{A_1} \circ \tau_1 : B^H \to A_1^{G_1}$ and $\psi^*_{A_2} \circ \tau_2 : B^H \to A_2^{G_2}$ be two generalized CA, where $\phi : G_1 \to H$ and $\psi : G_2 \to H$ are group homomorphisms and $\tau_i : B^H \to A_i^H$ are cellular automata. By the universal property of the coproduct in the category of groups, there exists a unique group homomorphism $\phi + \psi : G_1 * G_2 \to H$ such that the following diagram commutes:

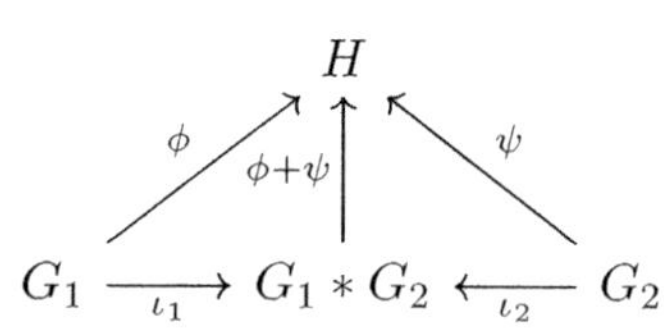

Equation (3) implies that the following diagram commutes for every alphabet C:

$$\begin{array}{ccccc} & {}^{\phi^*_C}\swarrow & C^H & \searrow^{\psi^*_C} & \\ & & \downarrow{\scriptstyle (\phi+\psi)^*_C} & & \\ C^{G_1} & \xleftarrow[(\iota_1)^*_C]{} & C^{G_1*G_2} & \xrightarrow[(\iota_2)^*_C]{} & C^{G_2} \end{array} \tag{4}$$

Our goal is to show that the diagram in Fig. 5 commutes, where the cellular automaton $\tau : B^H \to (A_1 \times A_2)^H$ is given by the universal property of the product of two cellular automata in $\mathcal{CA}(H)$ (Theorem 2). Clearly, the top triangle of diagram 5 commutes because of Theorem 2. Note that diagram (4) with $C = A_1$ and $C = A_2$ gives us the commutativity of the leftmost and rightmost lower triangles of diagram 5, respectively. Finally, we will show that the left and right squares of diagram 5 commute. For example, for the right square, note that for all $x \in (A_1 \times A_2)^H$, we have

$$(\phi+\psi)^*_{A_2} \circ \pi_2^H(x) = (\pi_2 \circ x) \circ (\phi+\psi) = \pi_2 \circ (x \circ (\phi+\psi)) = \pi_2^{G_1*G_2} \circ (\phi+\psi)^*_{A_1\times A_2}(x).$$

Similarly, the left square commutes. □

The problem with showing that the weak product given in Theorem 3 is unique, and hence a product, is that the factorization (2) of generalized CA is not unique in general. We say that $\mathcal{T}$ has the *unique homomorphism property* (UHP) if $\mathcal{T} = \phi^*_B \circ \tau = \psi^*_B \circ \tau$ implies $\phi = \psi$. It was shown in [4, Corollary 1], that if G is a torsion-free abelian group, then every non-constant $\mathcal{T}$ has the UHP; this result was generalized in [15] by removing the hypothesis of G being abelian. However, note that constant generalized CA never have the UHP: if $\mathcal{T} : A^G \to B^H$ is constant, then $\mathcal{T} = \phi^*_B \circ \tau = \psi^*_B \circ \tau$ for every pair of homomorphisms ϕ and ψ. This implies that the weak product given in Theorem 3 is not a product in $\mathcal{GCA}$, but it is an open question if a product actually exists in $\mathcal{GCA}$.

The coproduct in the category of groups gives us a coproduct of group homomorphisms: for any group homomorphisms $\phi : H_1 \to G_1$ and $\psi : H_2 \to G_2$ there exists a unique group homomorphisms $\phi * \psi : H_1 * H_2 \to G_1 * G_2$ such that the dual of the diagram in Fig. 2 commutes. Our last result shows the existence of a weak product of morphisms in $\mathcal{GCA}$.

Corollary 2. *For any ϕ-cellular automaton $\mathcal{T} : A_1^{G_1} \to B_1^{H_1}$ and a ψ-cellular automaton $\mathcal{S} : A_2^{G_2} \to B_2^{H_2}$ there exists $(\phi * \psi)$-cellular automaton*

$$\mathcal{T} * \mathcal{S} : (A_1 \times A_2)^{G_1 * G_2} \to (B_1 \times B_2)^{H_1 * H_2},$$

such that the diagram in Fig. 6 commutes.

Example 8. The free product if $\mathbb{Z} * \mathbb{Z}$ is isomorphic to the free group on two generators $F_2 = \langle X_1, X_2 \rangle$, where the canonical embedding $\iota_i : \mathbb{Z} \to F_2$ is given by $\iota_i(k) = X_i^k$, for all $k \in \mathbb{Z}$.

$$
\begin{array}{ccccccccc}
A_1^{G_1} & \xleftarrow[(\iota_1)^*_{A_1}]{} & A_1^{G_1*G_2} & \xleftarrow{\pi_{A_1}^{G_1*G_2}} & (A_1 \times A_2)^{G_1*G_2} & \xrightarrow{\pi_{A_2}^{G_1*G_2}} & A_2^{G_1*G_2} & \xrightarrow{(\iota_2)^*_{A_2}} & A_2^{G_2} \\
\downarrow{\scriptstyle \mathcal{T}} & & & & \downarrow{\scriptstyle \mathcal{T}*\mathcal{S}} & & & & \downarrow{\scriptstyle \mathcal{S}} \\
B_1^{H_1} & \xleftarrow[(\iota_1)^*_{B_1}]{} & B_1^{H_1*H_2} & \xleftarrow[\pi_{B_1}^{H_1*H_2}]{} & (B_1 \times B_2)^{H_1*H_2} & \xrightarrow[\pi_{B_2}^{H_1*H_2}]{} & B_2^{H_1*H_2} & \xrightarrow{(\iota_2)^*_{B_2}} & B_2^{H_2}
\end{array}
$$

Fig. 6. Weak product to two generalized cellular automata.

For any fixed alphabet A, we have a ι_i-cellular automaton $\iota_i^* : A^{F_2} \to A^{\mathbb{Z}}$ given by

$$\iota_i^*(x)(k) = x(\iota_i(k)) = x(X_i^k), \quad \forall x \in A^{F_2}.$$

Consider a one-dimensional cellular automaton $\tau : A^{\mathbb{Z}} \to A^{\mathbb{Z}}$ as an id-cellular automaton in the category $\mathcal{GCA}$. Then, a weak product given in Corollary 2 of τ with itself is an id-cellular automaton

$$\tau * \tau : (A \times A)^{F_2} \to (A \times A)^{F_2}$$

that satisfies

$$(\tau * \tau)(x_1, x_2) = (y_1, y_2),$$

where $x_i, y_i \in A^{F_2}$, as we are using the isomorphism $A^{F_2} \times A^{F_2} \cong (A \times A)^{F_2}$, and

$$\tau(\iota_i^*(x_i)) = \iota_i^*(y_i), \qquad \text{for } i = 1, 2.$$

In other words, for each $i = 1, 2$, $y_i \in A^{F_2}$ must be a preimage under $\iota_i^* : A^{F_2} \to A^{\mathbb{Z}}$ of $\tau(\iota_i^*(x_i)) \in A^{\mathbb{Z}}$; note that there is not a unique choice for y_i, so the weak product $\tau * \tau$ is not unique.

Acknowledgments. The second author was supported by a CONAHCYT *Becas nacionales para estudios de posgrado.* The third author was supported by a CONAHCYT grant No. CBF-2023-2024-2630.

Disclosure of Interests. The authors have no competing interests to declare that are relevant to the content of this article.

References

1. Adámek, J., Herrlich, H., Strecker, G.E.: Abstract and concrete categories: the joy of cats. Online Edition (2004). http://katmat.math.uni-bremen.de/acc/
2. Borceux, F.: Handbook of Categorical Algebra 1: Basic Category Theory. Cambridge University Press, Cambridge (1994)
3. Capobianco, S., Uustalu, T.: A categorical outlook on cellular automata. Journées Automates Cellulaires, 88–99 (2010). https://hal.science/hal-00542015v1
4. Castillo-Ramirez, A., de los Santos Baños, L.: Further results on generalized cellular automata. Comm. Algebra **52**(6), 2475–2488 (2024). https://doi.org/10.1080/00927872.2023.2301538

5. Castillo-Ramirez, A., Sanchez-Alvarez, M., Vazquez-Aceves, A., Zaldivar-Corichi, A.: A generalization of cellular automata over groups. Comm. Algebra **51**(7), 3114–3123 (2023). https://doi.org/10.1080/00927872.2023.2177663
6. Ceccherini-Silberstein, T., Coornaert, M.: Surjunctivity and reversibility of cellular automata over concrete categories. In: Picardello, M. (eds.) Trends in Harmonic Analysis. Springer INdAM Series, vol. 3, pp. 91–133. Springer, Milano (2013). https://doi.org/10.1007/978-88-470-2853-1_6
7. Ceccherini-Silberstein, T., Coornaert, M.: Cellular Automata and Groups. Springer Monographs in Mathematics, 2nd edn. Springer, Cham (2023). https://doi.org/10.1007/978-3-642-14034-1
8. Ceccherini-Silberstein, T., Coornaert, M.: Exercises in Cellular Automata and Groups. Springer Monographs in Mathematics, Springer, Cham (2023). https://doi.org/10.1007/978-3-031-10391-9
9. Fernandez, A., Maignan, L., Spicher, A.: Cellular Automata and KAN Extensions. In: Castillo-Ramirez, A., Guillon, P., Perrot, K. (eds.) 27th IFIP WG 1.5 International Workshop on Cellular Automata and Discrete Complex Systems (AUTOMATA 2021). Open Access Series in Informatics (OASIcs), vol. 90, pp. 7:1–7:12, Schloss Dagstuhl – Leibniz-Zentrum für Informatik (2021). https://doi.org/10.4230/OASIcs.AUTOMATA.2021.7
10. Maignan, L., Spicher, A.: Causal graph dynamics and KAN extensions. In: Harmer, R., Kosiol, J. (eds.) Graph Transformation. ICGT 2024. LNCS, vol. 14774, pp. 77–96. Springer, Cham (2024). https://doi.org/10.1007/978-3-031-64285-2_5
11. Mac Lane, S.: Categories for the Working Mathematician. Graduate Texts in Mathematics, 2nd edn. Springer, New York (2010). https://doi.org/10.1007/978-1-4757-4721-8
12. Roman, S.: An Introduction to the Language of Category Theory. Compact Textbooks in Mathematics. Birkhäuser Cham, Switzerland (2017)
13. Rotman, J.: An Introduction to the Theory of Groups. Graduate Texts in Mathematics, 4th edn. Springer-Verlag, New York (1995). https://doi.org/10.1007/978-1-4612-4176-8
14. Salo, V., Törmä, T.: Category theory of symbolic dynamics. Theoret. Comput. Sci. **567**, 21–45 (2015). https://doi.org/10.1016/j.tcs.2014.10.023
15. Salo, V.: About last weeks (2/n): a group-theoretic take on generalized cellular automata, Shift Happens (blog) (2024). https://symbolicdynamicsandotherthings.wordpress.com/2024/03/12/about-last-weeks-2-n-a-group-theoretic-take-on-generalized-cellular-automata/. Accessed 10 May 2025
16. Simmons, H.: An Introduction to Category Theory. Cambridge University Press, Cambridge (2011)

On Gottschalk's Surjunctivity Conjecture for Non-uniform Cellular Automata

Xuan Kien Phung[1,2(✉)]

[1] Département de Mathématiques et de Statistique, Université de Montréal, Montréal, Québec H3T 1J4, Canada

[2] Département d'informatique et de recherche opérationnelle, Université de Montréal, Montréal, Québec H3T 1J4, Canada

phungxuankien1@gmail.com, xuan.kien.phung@umontreal.ca

Abstract. Gottschalk's surjunctivity conjecture for a group G states that it is impossible for cellular automata (CA) over the universe G with finite alphabet to produce strict embeddings of the full shift into itself. A group universe G satisfying Gottschalk's surjunctivity conjecture is called a surjunctive group. The surjunctivity theorem of Gromov and Weiss shows that every sofic group is surjunctive. In this paper, we study the surjunctivity of local perturbations of CA and more generally of non-uniform cellular automata (NUCA) with finite memory and uniformly bounded singularity over surjunctive group universes. In particular, we show that such a NUCA must be invertible whenever it is reversible. We also obtain similar results which extend to the class of NUCA a certain dual surjunctivity theorem of Capobianco, Kari, and Taati for CA.

Keywords: Gottschalk's conjecture · surjunctivity · sofic group · cellular automata · non-uniform cellular automata · asynchronous cellular automata · reversibility

1 Introduction

In computational science and engineering, cellular automata (CA), especially reversible CA, arise as a fundamental and powerful model of simulation for various physical and biological systems [41] whose global evolution is described by spatially uniform local transition rules. In computer science, it is well-known that the CA called Game of Life of Conway [15] is Turing complete. Some notable recent mathematical theory of CA achieves a dynamical characterization of amenable groups by the Garden of Eden theorem for CA (pre-injectivity $\iff$ surjectivity, see Sect. 1.1 below) [1,11,23,24] and establishes the equivalence between Kaplansky's stable finiteness conjecture [19] for group rings and Gottschalk's surjunctivity conjecture (injectivity $\implies$ surjectivity) [17] for linear CA [10,31,32,35]. In this paper, we first explore Gottschalk's surjunctivity conjecture (see Sect. 1.2) over surjunctive group universes (see Definition 2), e.g. sofic groups such as amenable or residually finite groups, for non-uniform

Published by Springer Nature Switzerland AG 2026
S. Riva and A. Richard (Eds.): AUTOMATA 2025, LNCS 15831, pp. 72–87, 2026.
https://doi.org/10.1007/978-3-032-01570-9_6

CA (NUCA) with finite memory. We then obtain an extension of a well-known dual version of Gottschalk's surjunctivity conjecture due to Capobianco, Kari, and Taati [7] (see Sect. 1.2) over the class of post-injunctive groups (see Definition 3), e.g. sofic groups, also for NUCA with finite memory. Our main results cover NUCA which are local perturbations of CA in which a finite number of cells can follow local transition rules different from the local transition rule of the underlying CA. Among applications, such NUCA have close connections with asynchronous CA. For example, if F is an asynchronous CA in which only a finite number of cells are allowed to update at each (discrete) time, e.g. fully asynchronous CA [14] and skew-asynchronous CA [39], then F can be identified with a sequence $(F_n)_{n\in\mathbb{N}}$ of local perturbations of the identity CA: the system F at time $n \in \mathbb{N}$ is exactly the NUCA $F_n \circ F_{n-1} \circ \cdots \circ F_0$.

We generalize our results to a certain class of global perturbations of CA with uniformly bounded singularity. Essentially by definition and basic properties of CA, every reversible CA with finite memory over a surjunctive group universe must be invertible (see Sect. 1.1 for the exact definitions). Gottschalk's surjunctivity conjecture amounts to saying that every group is surjunctive. Hence, our results extend Gottschalk's surjunctivity conjecture by showing that over surjunctive group universes, reversible NUCA with finite memory and uniformly bounded singularity must be invertible (see Theorem A and Theorem C).

1.1 Basic Definitions

We recall notions of symbolic dynamics. Given a discrete set A and a group G, a *configuration* $x \in A^G$ is a map $x\colon G \to A$. Two configurations $x, y \in A^G$ are *asymptotic* if $x|_{G\setminus E} = y|_{G\setminus E}$ for some finite subset $E \subset G$. We say that $x \in A^G$ is *asymptotically constant* if x is asymptotic to some constant configuration $y \in A^G$. The *Bernoulli shift* action $G \times A^G \to A^G$ is defined by $(g, x) \mapsto gx$, where $(gx)(h) = x(g^{-1}h)$ for $g, h \in G$, $x \in A^G$. The *full shift* A^G is equipped with the prodiscrete topology. For each $x \in A^G$, we define $\Sigma(x) = \overline{\{gx\colon g \in G\}} \subset A^G$ as the smallest closed subshift containing x. For every subset $X \subset A^G$, we denote the restriction of X to a subset $F \subset G$ by $X_F = \{x|_F \colon \in X\}$.

Generalizing the first construction of a CA over $\mathbb{Z}^2$ by von Neumann [25] (see also [5]), a CA over the group G (the *universe*) and the set A (the *alphabet*) is a G-equivariant and uniformly continuous self-map $A^G \circlearrowleft$ [8,18]. One usually refers to each element $g \in G$ as a cell of the universe. Then every CA is uniform in the sense that all the cells follow the same local transition map. More generally, when different cells can evolve according to different local transition maps to break down the above uniformity, we obtain NUCA [12,13], [30, Definition 1.1]:

Definition 1. *Given a group G and an alphabet A, let $M \subset G$ and let $S = A^{A^M}$ be the set of all maps $A^M \to A$. For $s \in S^G$, we define the NUCA $\sigma_s\colon A^G \to A^G$ by $\sigma_s(x)(g) = s(g)((g^{-1}x)|_M)$ for all $x \in A^G$ and $g \in G$.*

The set M is called a *memory* and $s \in S^G$ the *configuration of local transition maps or local defining maps* of σ_s. Every CA is thus a NUCA with finite memory and constant configuration of local defining maps. Conversely, we regard NUCA as *global perturbations* of CA. When $s, t \in S^G$ are asymptotic, σ_s and σ_t are mutually *local perturbations* of each other. We also observe that NUCA with finite memory as defined in this paper form a proper subset of the set of uniformly continuous selfmaps of the full shift (see also [38][Proposition 14]), e.g. the map $F\colon A^G \to A^G$ given by $F(x)(g) = x(1_G)$ for all $x \in A^G$ and $g \in G$ is uniformly continuous but it is not a NUCA with finite memory. As for CA, NUCA with finite memory satisfy the closed image property [30, Theorem 4.4], several decidable and undecidable properties [12,20,36] and variants of the Garden of Eden theorem [26,33].

In this paper we analyze the relations between the following dynamic properties of σ_s. We say that σ_s is *pre-injective* if $\sigma_s(x) = \sigma_s(y)$ implies $x = y$ whenever $x, y \in A^G$ are asymptotic. Similarly, σ_s is *post-surjective* if for all $x, y \in A^G$ with y asymptotic to $\sigma_s(x)$, then $y = \sigma_s(z)$ for some $z \in A^G$ asymptotic to x. By the closed image property, it is known that post-surjectivity implies surjectivity for NUCA with finite memory. We say that σ_s is *stably injective*, resp. *stably post-surjective*, if σ_p is injective, resp. post-surjective, for every $p \in \Sigma(s)$.

The NUCA σ_s is said to be *reversible* or *left-invertible* if there exists a NUCA with finite memory $\tau\colon A^G \to A^G$ such that $\tau \circ \sigma_s = \mathrm{Id}_{A^G}$. A NUCA with finite memory is reversible if and only if it is stably injective (see [30, Theorem A]). We say that σ_s is *invertible* if it is bijective and the inverse map σ_s^{-1} is a NUCA with finite memory [30]. We define also *stable invertibility* which is in general stronger than invertibility, namely, σ_s is stably invertible if there exist $N \subset G$ finite and $t \in T^G$ where $T = A^{A^N}$ such that for every $p \in \Sigma(s)$, we have $\sigma_p \circ \sigma_q = \sigma_q \circ \sigma_p = \mathrm{Id}$ for some $q \in \Sigma(t)$. In fact, we will show (see Lemma 1) that every invertible NUCA with finite memory over a finite alphabet and a countable group universe is automatically stably invertible.

Remark 1. For CA, note that stable invertibility, resp. stable injectivity, resp. stable post-surjectivity, is equivalent to invertibility, resp. injectivity, resp. post-surjectivity since $\Sigma(s) = \{s\}$ if the configuration $s \in S^G$ is constant.

Remark 2. Suppose that the universe G is a countably infinite group and $s \in S^G$ is asymptotic to a constant configuration $c \in S^G$. By [30][Lemma 8.1] (which holds more generally for a countably infinite group G by a similar proof), we have $\Sigma(s) = \{c\} \cup \{gs \colon g \in G\}$. Consequently, a dynamic property is stable for σ_s simply means that the NUCA σ_s and the CA σ_c satisfy the same property.

1.2 Main Results

Gottschalk's surjunctivity conjecture [17] asserts that over any group universe, every CA with finite alphabet must be *surjunctive* (injectivity $\Longrightarrow$ surjectivity). In other words, it is impossible for CA to produce strict embeddings of the full shift into itself.

Definition 2. *A group G is said to be surjunctive if for every finite alphabet A, every injective CA $\tau\colon A^G \to A^G$ must be surjective.*

Every CA with finite memory is injective if and only if it is reversible. Therefore, a group G is surjunctive if and only if for every finite alphabet A, every reversible CA $\tau\colon A^G \to A^G$ must be invertible. Over the wide class of sofic group universes, the surjunctivity conjecture was famously shown by Gromov and Weiss in [16,40].

Theorem 1 (Gromov-Weiss). *Every sofic group is surjunctive.*

The class of sofic groups was first introduced by Gromov [16] and includes all amenable groups and all residually finite groups. The question of whether there exists a non-sofic group is still open.

The situation for the surjunctivity of NUCA admits some complications. While injective and even reversible NUCA with finite memory may fail to be surjective (see [30, Example 14.3]), results in [30] show that reversible local perturbations of CA with finite memory over an amenable group or a residually finite group universe must be surjective. More generally, we obtain an extension (Theorem A) to cover all reversible, or equivalently stably injective, local perturbations of CA over surjunctive group universes. We also strengthen the conclusion by showing that such NUCA must be stably invertible (see Sect. 4).

Theorem A. *Let M be a finite subset of a countable surjunctive group G. Let A be a finite alphabet and $S = A^{A^M}$. Suppose that σ_s is stably injective for some asymptotically constant $s \in S^G$. Then σ_s is stably invertible.*

Combining with Theorem 1 and the result in [30, Theorem B] where we can replace the stable injectivity by the weaker injectivity condition whenever G is an amenable group, we obtain the following general surjunctivity and invertibility result for NUCA which are local perturbations of CA.

Corollary 1. *Let M be a finite subset of a countable group G. Let A be a finite alphabet and $S = A^{A^M}$. Let $s \in S^G$ be an asymptotically constant configuration. Then σ_s is stably invertible in each of the following cases:*

(i) *G is an amenable group and σ_s is injective;*
(ii) *G is a sofic group and σ_s is reversible.*

Our next results concern a certain dual surjunctivity version of Gottschalk's conjecture introduced by Capobianco, Kari, and Taati in [7] which states that every post-surjective CA over a group universe and a finite alphabet is also pre-injective. The authors settled in the same paper [7] the case of sofic group universes. See also [29] for some extensions.

Theorem 2 (Capobianco-Kari-Taati). *Let G be a sofic group and let A be a finite alphabet. Then every post-surjective CA $\tau\colon A^G \to A^G$ is pre-injective.*

The above result motivates the following notion of *post-injunctive* groups.

Definition 3. *A group G is post-injunctive if for every finite alphabet A, every post-surjective CA $\tau\colon A^G \to A^G$ must be pre-injective.*

By a similar technique as in the proof of Theorem A, we establish (see Sect. 5) the following extension of the above result of Capobianco, Kari, and Taati to cover the class of stably post-surjective local perturbations of CA over post-injunctive group universes.

Theorem B. *Let G be a countable post-injunctive group and let A be a finite alphabet. Let $M \subset G$ be finite and $S = A^{A^M}$. Let $s \in S^G$ be asymptotically constant such that σ_s is stably post-surjective. Then σ_s is stably invertible.*

Our main results also hold for global perturbations of CA with *uniformly bounded singularity.* A NUCA $\sigma_s \colon A^G \to A^G$ has uniformly bounded singularity if for every finite subset $E \subset G$ with $1_G \in E = E^{-1}$, we can find a finite subset $F \subset G$ containing E such that the restriction $s|_{FE \backslash F}$ is constant. Note that in this paper, group operations are to be performed before boolean set operations. In particular, $FE \backslash F = (FE) \backslash F$. It is clear that σ_s has uniformly bounded singularity if s is asymptotically constant. When the universe G is a residually finite group, our notion of uniformly bounded singularity is closely related but not equivalent to the notion of (periodically) bounded singularity for NUCA defined in [30, Definition 10.1]. We obtain the following generalizations of Theorem A and Theorem B (see Sect. 6 and Sect. 7).

Theorem C. *Let M be a finite subset of a finitely generated surjunctive group G. Let A be a finite alphabet and let $S = A^{A^M}$. Suppose that $\sigma_s \colon A^G \to A^G$ is stably injective for some $s \in S^G$ with uniformly bounded singularity. Then σ_s is stably invertible.*

Theorem D. *Let G be a finitely generated post-injunctive group and let A be a finite alphabet. Let $M \subset G$ be finite and let $S = A^{A^M}$. Suppose that $\sigma_s \colon A^G \to A^G$ is stably post-surjective for some $s \in S^G$ with uniformly bounded singularity. Then σ_s is stably invertible.*

1.3 Perspectives

Our main results motivate the following natural questions which have an affirmative answer for surjunctive group universes and post-injunctive group universes respectively.

Question 1. Let G be a group universe and let A be a finite alphabet. Let $M \subset G$ be finite and let $S = A^{A^M}$. Suppose that $\sigma_s \colon A^G \to A^G$ is stably injective for some asymptotically constant $s \in S^G$. Is σ_s stably invertible?

Question 2. Let G be a group universe and let A be a finite alphabet. Let $M \subset G$ be finite and let $S = A^{A^M}$. Suppose that $\sigma_s \colon A^G \to A^G$ is stably post-surjective for some asymptotically constant $s \in S^G$. Is σ_s stably invertible?

We can actually show (see Proposition 1 below) that Question 1 and Question 2 are equivalent when restricted to the class of linear NUCA with finite memory. Given a possibly infinite vector space V, then V^G is a vector space with component-wise operations and a NUCA $\tau\colon V^G \to V^G$ is said to be *linear* if it is also a linear ap of vector spaces or equivalently, if its local transition maps are linear.

Proposition 1. *Let G be a countable group and let A be a finite vector space alphabet. Question 1 has an affirmative answer for all linear* NUCA $\tau\colon A^G \to A^G$ *with finite memory and uniformly bounded singularity if and only if so does Question 2.*

Proof. Let $M \subset G$ be a finite subset and let $s \in S^G$ where $S = \mathcal{L}(A^M, A)$. By linearity, we define $s(g,m) \in \mathrm{End}(A)$ for all $m \in M$ and $g \in G$ by $s(g)(v) = \sum_{m \in M} s(g,m)v(m)$ for all $v \in A^M$. By setting $s(g,m) = 0$ for $m \in G \backslash M$, we obtain for every $v \in A^G$ that $s(g)(v) = \sum_{h \in G} s(g,h)v(h)$. Let $T = \mathcal{L}(A^{*M^{-1}}, A^*)$ where A^* is the dual space of A. We use the right superscript $^\mathsf{T}$ to denote the transpose of linear maps. The dual configuration of local defining maps $s^* \in T^G$ is given by $s^*(g,m) := s(gm, m^{-1})^\mathsf{T}$ for all $g, m \in G$. We define $\sigma_s^* := \sigma_{s^*}$ to be the dual linear NUCA of σ_s. It is immediate from the definition that s has uniformly bounded singularity if and only if so does s^*. By [34, Lemma 5.2], note that $s^{**} = s$ and $\sigma_s^{**} = \sigma_s$ for all $s \in S^G$. We infer from the main results in [34] that

(i) σ_s is invertible $\iff$ σ_{s^*} is invertible,
(ii) σ_s is stably injective $\iff$ σ_{s^*} is stably post surjective,
(iii) σ_s is stably post-surjective $\iff$ σ_{s^*} is stably injective.

Note that every invertible NUCA with finite memory over a finite alphabet and a countable group universe is automatically stably invertible (see Lemma 1). By identifying A with its dual vector space A^*, we can now conclude that Question 1 has a positive answer for all linear NUCA $A^G \to A^G$ of finite memory with uniformly bounded singularity if and only if so does Question 2. □

Linear NUCA with finite memory enjoy similar properties as linear CA such as the shadowing property [2–4,6,9,21,22,27,28,34]. The recent result [34, Theorem D.(ii)] states that every stably post-surjective linear NUCA with finite vector space alphabet over a residually finite group universe is invertible whenever it is a local perturbation of a linear CA. When specialized to the class of linear NUCA, Theorem B thus generalizes [34, Theorem D.(ii)] because every residually finite group is sofic and thus post-injunctive by Theorem 2. To this end, we postulate another seemingly interesting question.

Question 3. Does an affirmative answer to Question 1 imply an affirmative answer to Question 2? Conversely, does an affirmative answer to Question 2 imply an affirmative answer to Question 1?

It is also natural to explore similar questions for the more general class of NUCA with uniformly bounded singularity.

1.4 Organization of the Paper

In Sect. 2, we prove that the notions of invertibility and stable invertibility are equivalent for NUCA with finite memory (Lemma 1). As a consequence, we relate the surjectivity, the invertibility, and the stable invertibility of a stably injective NUCA in Corollary 2. As another application, we show that pre-injective stably post-surjective NUCA with finite memory must be stably invertible. We then fix in Sect. 3 the notations and recall the construction of induced local maps of NUCA in Sect. 3. The proofs of Theorem A, Theorem B, Theorem C, and Theorem D are given respectively in the subsequent Sects. 4, 5, 6, and 7.

2 Invertibility Vs Stable Invertibility

Lemma 1. *Let M be a finite subset of a countable group G. Let A be a finite alphabet and let $s \in S^G$ where $S = A^{A^M}$. Suppose that σ_s is invertible. Then σ_s is stably invertible.*

Proof. Since σ_s is invertible, there exist $N \subset G$ finite and $t \in T^G$ where $T = A^{A^N}$ such that $\sigma_s \circ \sigma_t = \sigma_t \circ \sigma_s = \mathrm{Id}_{A^G}$. For every $p \in \Sigma(s)$, we obtain from the relation $\sigma_s \circ \sigma_t = \mathrm{Id}_{A^G}$ and [30, Theorem 11.1] some $q \in \Sigma(t)$ such that $\sigma_p \circ \sigma_q = \mathrm{Id}_{A^G}$. Since $q \in \Sigma(t)$ and $\sigma_t \circ \sigma_s = \mathrm{Id}_{A^G}$, another application of [30, Theorem 11.1] shows that there exists $r \in \Sigma(s)$ such that $\sigma_q \circ \sigma_r = \mathrm{Id}_{A^G}$. It follows that σ_q is invertible and thus $\sigma_p \circ \sigma_q = \sigma_q \circ \sigma_p = \mathrm{Id}_{A^G}$. Hence, σ_s is stably invertible. □

Corollary 2. *Let G be a countable group and let A be a finite alphabet. Let $\tau\colon A^G \to A^G$ be a stably injective NUCA with finite memory. Then the following are equivalent:*

(i) *τ is surjective,*
(ii) *τ is invertible,*
(iii) *τ is stably invertible.*

Proof. It is trivial that (iii) $\Longrightarrow$ (i). The implication (i) $\Longrightarrow$ (ii) results from the definition of invertibility and [30, Theorem A]. Lemma 1 states that (ii) $\Longrightarrow$ (iii) and the proof is thus complete. □

Corollary 3. *Let G be a countable group and let A be a finite alphabet. Let $\tau\colon A^G \to A^G$ be a pre-injective stably post-surjective NUCA with finite memory. Then τ is stably invertible.*

Proof. The fact that τ is invertible follows from [30, Theorem 13.4] (see also [7]). We can thus conclude from Lemma 1 that τ is stably invertible. □

3 Induced Local Maps of NUCA

Let G be a group and let A be an alphabet. For every subset $E \subset G$ and $x \in A^E$ we define $gx \in A^{gE}$ by $gx(gh) = x(h)$ for all $h \in E$. In particular, $gA^E = A^{gE}$. Let $M \subset G$ and let $S = A^{A^M}$ be the collection of all maps $A^M \to A$. For every finite subset $E \subset G$ and $w \in S^E$, we define a map $f_{E,w}^{+M} \colon A^{EM} \to A^E$ as follows. For every $x \in A^{EM}$ and $g \in E$, we set:

$$f_{E,w}^{+M}(x)(g) = w(g)((g^{-1}x)|_M). \tag{3.1}$$

In the above formula, note that $g^{-1}x \in A^{g^{-1}EM}$ and $M \subset g^{-1}EM$ since $1_G \in g^{-1}E$ for $g \in E$. Therefore, the map $f_{E,w}^{+M} \colon A^{EM} \to A^E$ is well defined. Consequently, for every $s \in S^G$, we have a well-defined induced local map $f_{E,s|_E}^{+M} \colon A^{EM} \to A^E$ for every finite subset $E \subset G$ which satisfies:

$$\sigma_s(x)(g) = f_{E,s|_E}^{+M}(x|_{EM})(g) \tag{3.2}$$

for every $x \in A^G$ and $g \in E$. Equivalently, we have for all $x \in A^G$ that:

$$\sigma_s(x)|_E = f_{E,s|_E}^{+M}(x|_{EM}). \tag{3.3}$$

For every $g \in G$, we have a canonical bijection $\gamma_g \colon G \mapsto G$ induced by the translation $a \mapsto g^{-1}a$. For each subset $K \subset G$, we denote by $\gamma_{g,K} \colon gK \to K$ the restriction to gK of γ_g. Now let $N \subset G$ and $T = A^{A^N}$. Let $t \in T^G$. With the above notations, we have the following auxiliary lemma.

Lemma 2. *Suppose that $1_G \in M \cap N$. Then for every $g \in G$, the condition $\sigma_t(\sigma_s(x))(g) = x(g)$ for all $x \in A^G$ is equivalent to the condition*

$$t(g) \circ \gamma_{g,N} \circ f_{gN,s|_{gN}}^{+M} \circ \gamma_{g,NM}^{-1} = \pi,$$

where $\pi \colon A^{NM} \to A$ is the projection $z \mapsto z(1_G)$.

Proof. For every $g \in G$ and $x \in A^G$, we deduce from Definition 1 and the relation (3.3) that

$$\begin{aligned}
\sigma_t(\sigma_s(x))(g) &= t(g)\left((g^{-1}\sigma_s(x))|_N\right) \\
&= t(g)\left(\gamma_{g,N}\left((\sigma_s(x))|_{gN}\right)\right) \\
&= t(g)\left(\gamma_{g,N} \circ f_{gN,o|_{gN}}^{+M}(x|_{gNM})\right) \\
&= t(g) \circ \gamma_{g,N} \circ f_{gN,s|_{gN}}^{+M}(x|_{gNM}) \\
&= t(g) \circ \gamma_{g,N} \circ f_{gN,s|_{gN}}^{+M} \circ \gamma_{g,NM}^{-1}\left((g^{-1}x)|_{NM}\right)
\end{aligned}$$

from which the conclusion follows as $x(g) = (g^{-1}x)(1_G)$. □

4 Proof of Theorem A

We give below the proof of the stable invertibility of stably injective NUCA which are local perturbations of CA over a surjunctive group universe.

Proof. Theorem A is trivial if G is finite since every injective selfmap of a finite set is also surjective. Thus, without loss of generality we can suppose that G is infinite. Up to enlarging M if necessary, we can also assume that $1_G \in M$. As $s \in S^G$ is asymptotically constant, we can find a constant configuration $c \in S^G$ and a finite subset $F \subset G$ such that $s|_{G\backslash F} = c|_{G\backslash F}$. Note that as G is infinite, we have $c \in \Sigma(s)$. Since σ_s is stably injective, we deduce that $\sigma_c \colon A^G \to A^G$ is an injective CA. We infer from the surjunctivity of the group G that σ_c is also surjective. By Corollary 2 and Remark 1, it follows that σ_c is invertible. Therefore, there exist a nonempty finite subset $N \subset G$ and a constant configuration $d \in T^G$, where $T = A^{A^N}$, such that $1_G \in N$ and

$$\sigma_c \circ \sigma_d = \sigma_d \circ \sigma_c = \mathrm{Id}_{A^G} . \tag{4.1}$$

The set of NUCA with finite memory over the universe G and the alphabet A forms a monoid with respect to the composition operation and we obtain from [30, Theorem 6.2] a configuration $q \in Q^G$, where $Q = A^{A^{MN}}$, such that $\sigma_s \circ \sigma_d = \sigma_q$. Note that MN is a memory set of σ_q. As both σ_s and σ_d are injective, $\sigma_q = \sigma_s \circ \sigma_d$ is also injective. Since $\sigma_c \circ \sigma_d = \mathrm{Id}_{A^G}$ and $\sigma_s \circ \sigma_d = \sigma_q$ and s is asymptotic to c, we deduce that the configuration $q \in Q^G$ is asymptotic to the constant configuration π^G where $\pi \colon A^{MN} \to A^{\{1_G\}}$ is the canonical projection $x \mapsto x(1_G)$. More precisely, $q|_{G\backslash F} = \pi^{G\backslash F}$ since $s|_{G\backslash F} = c|_{G\backslash F}$ so that for every $g \in G\backslash F$ (see 3 and the proof of [30, Theorem 6.2]):

$$q(g) = s(g) \circ f^{+N}_{M, g^{-1}d|_M} = c(g) \circ f^{+N}_{M, g^{-1}d|_M} = \pi \tag{4.2}$$

where the last equality results from (4.1).

Let $E = FMN \subset G$ then E is finite and $F \subset E$ as $1_G \in M \cap N$. It follows that $q|_{G\backslash E} = \pi^{G\backslash E}$. Consider the map $\Phi \colon A^E \to A^E$ induced by the restriction of σ_p to A^E. More specifically, for every $x \in A^E$, we define

$$\Phi(x) = \sigma_q(y)|_E \tag{4.3}$$

for any configuration $y \in A^G$ extending x, that is, $y|_E = x$. To check that Φ is well-defined, let $z \in A^G$ be another configuration such that $z|_E = x$. Let $g \in E\backslash F$ then we have $q(g) = \pi$ and thus

$$\begin{aligned} \sigma_q(z)(g) &= q(g)((g^{-1}z)|_{MN}) = \pi((g^{-1}z)|_{MN}) \\ &= z(g) = x(g) = y(g) \\ &= \pi((g^{-1}y)|_{MN}) = q(g)((g^{-1}y)|_{MN}) \\ &= \sigma_q(y)(g). \end{aligned}$$

Now let $g \in F$. Then $(g^{-1}z)|_{MN} = (g^{-1}y)|_{MN}$ since $(g^{-1}z)(h) = z(gh) = x(gh) = y(gh) = (g^{-1}y)(h)$ for all $h \in MN$. Therefore,

$$\sigma_q(z)(g) = q(g)((g^{-1}z)|_{MN}) = q(g)((g^{-1}z)|_{MN}) = q(g)((g^{-1}u)|_{MN}) = \sigma_q(z)(g).$$

We conclude that $\sigma_q(z)|_E = \sigma_q(y)|_E$ and thus Φ is well-defined.

As MN is a memory set of σ_q, we infer from (4.2) and the relation $E = FMN$ that $\sigma_q(x)|_{G\setminus E} = x|_{G\setminus E}$ for every $x \in A^G$. Combining with (4.3), we obtain

$$\sigma_q = \Phi \times \mathrm{Id}_{A^{G\setminus E}} : A^E \times A^{G\setminus E} \to A^E \times A^{G\setminus E}$$

because for every $x = (y, z) \in A^E \times A^{G\setminus E} = A^G$ where $y = x|_E$ and $z = x|_{G\setminus E}$, we have $\sigma_q(x) = (\sigma_q(x)|_E, \sigma_q(x)|_{G\setminus E}) = (\Phi(y), z) \in A^G$. We note here that such a map σ_q is related to the notion of a *gate* on a subshift [37][Lemma 15].

Since σ_q and $\mathrm{Id}_{A^{G\setminus E}}$ are injective, we deduce that Φ is also injective. Consequently, Φ must be surjective as A^E is finite. It follows that $\sigma_q = \Phi \times \mathrm{Id}_{A^{G\setminus E}}$ is surjective. Combining with (4.1) and the surjectivity of σ_c, we find that $\sigma_s = \sigma_q \circ (\sigma_d)^{-1} = \sigma_q \circ \sigma_c$ is also surjective. Since σ_s is stably injective by hypothesis, we can thus conclude from Corollary 2 that σ_s is stably invertible and the proof is complete. □

5 Proof of Theorem B

By following the same lines, *mutatis mutandis*, as in the proof of Theorem A, we obtain below the proof of Theorem B on the stable invertibility of stably post-surjective NUCA which are local perturbations of CA over post-injunctive group universes.

Proof. We can suppose without loss of generality that G is infinite since every surjective selfmap of a finite set is also injective. Up to enlarging M, we can also assume that $1_G \in M$. By hypothesis, there exist a constant configuration $c \in S^G$ and a finite subset $F \subset G$ with $s|_{G\setminus F} = c|_{G\setminus F}$. Note again that $c \in \Sigma(s)$ as G is infinite. We infer from the stable post-surjectivity of σ_s that the CA $\sigma_c : A^G \to A^G$ is post-surjective. Since G is post-injunctive, σ_c is pre-injective and thus invertible by Corollary 3 and Remark 1. Hence, we can find finite subset $N \subset G$ and a constant configuration $d \in T^G$, where $T = A^{A^N}$, such that $1_G \in N$ and

$$\sigma_c \circ \sigma_d = \sigma_d \circ \sigma_c = \mathrm{Id}_{A^G}. \tag{5.1}$$

By [30, Theorem 6.2], there exists a configuration $q \in Q^G$, where $Q = A^{A^{MN}}$, such that $\sigma_s \circ \sigma_d = \sigma_q$. As σ_s and σ_d are surjective, so is $\sigma_q = \sigma_s \circ \sigma_d$. Let $\pi : A^{MN} \to A^{\{1_G\}}$ be the canonical projection $x \mapsto x(1_G)$. As $s|_{G\setminus F} = c|_{G\setminus F}$, we have $q|_{G\setminus F} = \pi^{G\setminus F}$ since for every $g \in G\setminus F$ (see the proof of [30, Theorem 6.2]):

$$q(g) = s(g) \circ f^{+N}_{M, g^{-1}d|_M} = c(g) \circ f^{+N}_{M, g^{-1}d|_M} = \pi$$

where the last equality follows from (5.1). Let $E = FMN \subset G$ then $F \subset E$ as $1_G \in M \cap N$. It follows that $q|_{G\backslash E} = \pi^{G\backslash E}$. As in the proof of Theorem A, we can write $\sigma_q = \Phi \times \mathrm{Id}_{A^{G\backslash E}}$ where $\Phi\colon A^E \to A^E$ is the map given by $\Phi(x) = \sigma_q(y)|_E$ for every $x \in A^E$ and any $y \in A^G$ such that $y|_E = x$. Then Φ is surjective because σ_q and $\mathrm{Id}_{A^{G\backslash E}}$ are both surjective. It follows that Φ must be injective as A^E is finite. Consequently, $\sigma_q = \Phi \times \mathrm{Id}_{A^{G\backslash E}}$ is injective. Thus by (5.1), we have $\sigma_s = \sigma_q \circ (\sigma_d)^{-1} = \sigma_q \circ \sigma_c$ is injective and thus pre-injective. By the stable post-surjectivity of σ_s and Corollary 3, we conclude that σ_s is stably invertible and the proof is thus complete. □

6 Proof of Theorem C

The goal of this section is to establish Theorem C which states that over surjunctive group universes, every stably injective NUCA with finite memory and uniformly bounded singularity must be stably invertible. We first prove the following useful technical lemma which will enable a reduction of Theorem C to Theorem A.

Lemma 3. *Let A be an alphabet and let G be a finitely generated group. Let $M \subset G$ be a finite subset and $S = A^{A^M}$. Suppose that $\sigma_t \circ \sigma_s = \mathrm{Id}_{A^G}$ for some $s, t \in S^G$ and s has uniformly bounded singularity. Then for each $E \subset G$ finite, there exist asymptotically constant configurations $p, q \in S^G$ such that $p|_E = s|_E$, $q|_E = t|_E$, and $\sigma_q \circ \sigma_p = \mathrm{Id}_{A^G}$.*

Proof. Up to enlarging M, we can assume that $1_G \in M = M^{-1}$. Let $E \subset G$ be a finite subset. Up to enlarging E, we can suppose without loss of generality that $M \subset E = E^{-1}$ and E is a finite generating set of G. As s has uniformly bounded singularity, there exist a constant configuration $c \in S^G$ and a finite subset $F \subset G$ containing E^3 such that $s|_{FE^3\backslash F} = c|_{FE^3\backslash F}$. We define an asymptotically constant configuration $p \in S^G$ by setting $p|_{FE} = s|_{FE}$ and $p|_{G\backslash FE} = c|_{G\backslash FE}$. Note that $FE^2\backslash FE \neq \varnothing$. Indeed, if $FE^2 \subset FE$ then by induction $FE^n \subset FE$ for every integer $n \geqslant 1$ and thus $G = \bigcup_{n\geqslant 1} E^n \subset \bigcup_{n\geqslant 1} FE^n \subset FE$ which is a contradiction since G is infinite. Therefore, we can fix $g_0 \in FE^2\backslash FE$ and define $q \in S^G$ by $q(g) = t(g_0)$ if $g \in G\backslash FE$ and $q(g) = t(g)$ if $g \in FE$. Then q is asymptotic to the constant configuration $d \in S^G$ defined by $d(g) = t(g_0)$ for all $g \in G$. Since $1_G \in M$, we have a projection $\pi\colon A^{M^2} \to A$ given by $x \mapsto x(1_G)$. Since $E \subset E^3 \subset F \subset FE$, we deduce from our construction that $p|_E = s|_E$ and $q|_E = t|_E$. To conclude, we only need to check that $\sigma_q \circ \sigma_p = \mathrm{Id}_{A^G}$.

Let $g \in FE^2\backslash FE$. Then $gE \subset FE^3\backslash F$ since $E = E^{-1}$. Consequently, $s|_{gE} = c|_{gE} = p|_{gE}$ and thus $s|_{gM} = c|_{gM} = p|_{gM}$ since $M \subset E$. Hence, the condition $\sigma_t(\sigma_s(x))(g) = x(g)$ for all $x \in A^G$ is equivalent to $t(g) \circ f^{+M}_{M,c|_M} = \pi$ by Lemma 2. Similarly, the condition $\sigma_q(\sigma_p(x))(g) = x(g)$ for all $x \in A^G$ amounts to $q(g) \circ f^{+M}_{M,c|_M} = \pi$. Since $q(g) = t(g_0)$ and $\sigma_t \circ \sigma_s = \mathrm{Id}_{A^G}$, we conclude from the above discussion that $\sigma_q(\sigma_p(x))(g) = x(g)$ for all $x \in A^G$.

Let $g \in FE$. Since $s|_{FE^3\backslash F} = c|_{FE^3\backslash F}$, $p|_{FE} = s|_{FE}$, and $p|_{G\backslash FE} = c|_{G\backslash FE}$ by construction, we have $p|_{FE^3} = s|_{FE^3}$. In particular, $p|_{gM} = s|_{gM}$ since $gM \subset$

$(FE)E = FE^2 \subset FE^3$. Therefore, we can infer from the relations $\sigma_t \circ \sigma_s = \mathrm{Id}_{A^G}$ and $q(g) = t(g)$ that $\sigma_q(\sigma_p(x))(g) = x(g)$ for all $x \in A^G$.

Finally, let $g \in G \backslash FE^2$. Since $p|_{G\backslash FE} = c|_{G\backslash FE}$, $q|_{G\backslash FE} = d|_{G\backslash FE}$, and since c, d are constant, we deduce that $q(g) = d(g_0) = t(g_0)$ and $p|_{gM} = c|_{gM}$. The condition $\sigma_q(\sigma_p(x))(g) = x(g)$ for all $x \in A^G$ is thus equivalent to $t(g_0) \circ f^{+M}_{M,c|_M} = \pi$ by Lemma 2. But since $\sigma_t \circ \sigma_s = \mathrm{Id}_{A^G}$ and $s|_{g_0M} = c|_{g_0M}$, another application of Lemma 2 shows that $t(g_0) \circ f^{+M}_{M,c|_M} = \pi$. Thus, $\sigma_t(\sigma_s(x))(g) = x(g)$ for all $x \in A^G$. Therefore, we conclude that $\sigma_q \circ \sigma_p = \mathrm{Id}_{A^G}$. The proof is complete. □

We are now in position to prove Theorem C.

Proof of Theorem C. Since σ_s is stably injective by hypothesis, we deduce from [30, Theorem A] that there exist a finite subset $N \subset G$ and $t \in T^G$, where $T = A^{A^N}$, such that $\sigma_t \circ \sigma_s = \mathrm{Id}_{A^G}$. Up to enlarging M and N, we can assume that $1_G \in M = N$ and thus $S = T$. By Corollary 2, it suffices to show that σ_s is surjective to conclude that σ_s is stably invertible. We suppose on the contrary that σ_s is not surjective. Since $\Gamma = \sigma_s(A^G)$ is closed in A^G with respect to the prodiscrete topology by [30, Theorem 4.4], there must exist a nonempty finite subset $E \subset G$ such that $\Gamma_E \subsetneq A^E$. Since s has uniformly bounded singularity, we infer from Lemma 3 that there exist asymptotically constant configurations $p, q \in S^G$ such that $p|_E = s|_E$, $q|_E = t|_E$, and $\sigma_q \circ \sigma_p = \mathrm{Id}_{A^G}$. Let $\Lambda = \sigma_p(A^G)$. Then it follows from $p|_E = s|_E$ that $\Lambda_E = \Gamma_E \subsetneq A^E$. We deduce that σ_p is not surjective. In particular, σ_p is not invertible. On the other hand, the condition $\sigma_q \circ \sigma_p = \mathrm{Id}_{A^G}$ shows that σ_p is stably injective by [30, Theorem A]. We can thus apply Theorem A to deduce that σ_p is invertible and thus surjective. Therefore, we obtain a contradiction and the proof is complete. □

7 Proof of Theorem D

In this section, we prove that stably post-surjective NUCA with finite memory and uniformly bounded singularity is stably invertible whenever the group universe is post-injunctive. The following proof of Theorem D generalizes the proof of Theorem A and Theorem B.

Proof. We will show that σ_s is injective. Suppose on the contrary that there exist an element $h \in G$ and configurations $u, v \in A^G$ such that $\sigma_s(u) = \sigma_s(v)$ but $u(h) \neq v(h)$. Up to enlarging M, we can suppose without loss of generality that $M = M^{-1}$ (that is, M is symmetric) and $1_G, h \in M$. When G is finite, σ_s is trivially invertible as a surjective selfmap of a finite set. Hence, we assume in what follows that the group G is infinite.

Let $c_1, ..., c_n \in S^G$ be all the constant configurations in S^G where $n = |S|$. Let $\Delta \subset G$ be a finite generating set of G such that $1_G \in \Delta = \Delta^{-1}$ (that is, Δ is symmetric) and $M \subset \Delta$. Up to enlarging M, we can suppose that $M = \Delta$. For each $k \geqslant 1$, let $E_k = \Delta^k$ then E_k is a finite symmetric subset of G containing 1_G and we have an exhaustion $G = \bigcup_{k=1}^{\infty} E_k$. Since s has uniformly bounded singularity, we can find a finite subset $F_k \subset G$ such that $E_k^5 \subset F_k$ and

$s|_{F_k E_k^5 \setminus F_k} \in S^{F_k E_k^5 \setminus F_k}$ is constant for every $k \geqslant 1$. Since S is finite, there exist $m \in \{1, 2, ..., n\}$ and an infinite sequence $1 \leqslant k_1 < k_2 < k_3 < \ldots$ of integers such that for $c = c_m$, we have $E_{k_i}^5 \subset F_{k_i}$ for every $i \geqslant 1$ and

$$s|_{F_{k_i} E_{k_i}^5 \setminus F_{k_i}} = c|_{F_{k_i} E_{k_i}^5 \setminus F_{k_i}}. \tag{7.1}$$

For every $i \geqslant 1$, we claim that $F_{k_i} E_{k_i}^2 \setminus F_{k_i} E_{k_i} \neq \varnothing$. Indeed, we would have otherwise $F_{k_i} E_{k_i}^2 \subset F_{k_i} E_{k_i}$. Hence, $F_{k_i} E_{k_i}^r \subset F_{k_i} E_{k_i}$ by induction on $r \geqslant 2$ and

$$G = F_{k_i} G = F_{k_i} \bigcup_{r \geqslant 2} E_{k_i}^r = \bigcup_{r \geqslant 2} F_{k_i} E_{k_i}^r \subset F_{k_i} E_{k_i}$$

which is a contradiction since G is infinite. Therefore, for every $i \geqslant 1$, we can fix some $g_i \in F_{k_i} E_{k_i}^2 \setminus F_{k_i} E_{k_i}$. As $1_G \in E_{k_i}$ and E_{k_i} is symmetric, it follows that

$$g_i E_{k_i} \subset F_{k_i} E_{k_i}^3 \setminus F_{k_i}. \tag{7.2}$$

It follows from (7.1) and (7.2) that $c|_{g_i E_{k_i}} = s|_{g_i E_{k_i}}$. Since $G = \bigcup_{i=1}^{\infty} E_{k_i}$ and $\Sigma(s) = \overline{\{gs \colon g \in G\}} \subset S^G$, we deduce that $c \in \Sigma(s)$. We thus infer from the stable post-surjectivity of σ_s that $\sigma_c \colon A^G \to A^G$ is a post-surjective CA. Hence, σ_c is pre-injective by the post-injunctivity of the group universe G. Theorem C then implies that σ_s is an invertible CA. Therefore, there exists a CA $\tau \colon A^G \to A^G$ such that

$$\tau \circ \sigma_c = \sigma_c \circ \tau = \mathrm{Id}_{A^G}. \tag{7.3}$$

Without loss of generality, we can assume that M is also a memory set of τ up to enlarging M. Thus $\tau = \sigma_d$ for some constant configuration $d \in S^G$.

From [30, Theorem 6.2] we obtain a configuration $q \in Q^G$, where $Q = A^{A^{M^2}}$, such that $\sigma_d \circ \sigma_s = \sigma_q$. Let $\pi \colon A^{M^2} \to A^{\{1_G\}}$ denote the canonical projection $z \mapsto z(1_G)$ and fix $j \geqslant 1$ large enough such that $M^2 \subset E_{k_j}$. We claim that

$$q|_{F_{k_j} E_{k_j}^4 \setminus F_{k_j} E_{k_j}} = \pi^{F_{k_j} E_{k_j}^4 \setminus F_{k_j} E_{k_j}}. \tag{7.4}$$

Indeed, let $g \in F_{k_j} E_{k_j}^4 \setminus F_{k_j} E_{k_j}$. Then $g E_{k_j} \subset F_{k_j} E_{k_j}^5 \setminus F_{k_j}$ as E_{k_j} is symmetric. Hence, $gM \subset g E_{k_j} \subset F_{k_j} E_{k_j}^5 \setminus F_{k_j}$. It follows that $s|_{gM} = c|_{gM}$ by (7.1) and thus $g^{-1} s|_M = g^{-1} c|_M$. Since $\sigma_d \circ \sigma_c = \mathrm{Id}_{A^G}$ by (7.3), the claim (7.4) follows since (see the proof of [30, Theorem 6.2]):

$$q(g) = d(g) \circ f^{+M}_{M, g^{-1} s|_M} = d(g) \circ f^{+M}_{M, g^{-1} c|_M} = \pi.$$

Therefore, as in the proof of Theorem A, we deduce from (7.4) that

$$\sigma_q = \Phi \times \left(\mathrm{Id}_{A^{F_{k_j} E_{k_j}^3 \setminus F_{k_j} E_{k_j}^2}} \right) \times \Psi \tag{7.5}$$

where $\Phi \colon A^{F_{k_j} E_{k_j}^2} \to A^{F_{k_j} E_{k_j}^2}$ and $\Psi \colon A^{G \setminus F_{k_j} E_{k_j}^3} \to A^{G \setminus F_{k_j} E_{k_j}^3}$ are well-defined maps given by the following formula:

(i) $\Phi(x) = \sigma_q(y)|_{F_{k_j}E^2_{k_j}}$ for $x \in A^{F_{k_j}E^2_{k_j}}$ and $y \in A^G$ with $y|_{F_{k_j}E^2_{k_j}} = x$,

(ii) $\Psi(x) = \sigma_q(y)|_{G\setminus F_{k_j}E^3_{k_j}}$ for $x \in A^{G\setminus F_{k_j}E^3_{k_j}}$ and $y \in A^G$ with $y|_{G\setminus F_{k_j}E^3_{k_j}} = x$.

Recall the choice of the configurations $u, v \in A^G$ in the first paragraph of the proof with $u(h) \neq v(h)$ and $\sigma_s(u) = \sigma_s(v)$ for some $h \in M \subset F_{k_j}E^2_{k_j}$. It follows that $u|_{F_{k_j}E^2_{k_j}} \neq v|_{F_{k_j}E^2_{k_j}}$ and

$$\begin{aligned}\Phi\left(u|_{F_{k_j}E^2_{k_j}}\right) = \sigma_q(u)|_{F_{k_j}E^2_{k_j}} &= \sigma_d\left(\sigma_s(u)\right)|_{F_{k_j}E^2_{k_j}} \\ &= \sigma_d\left(\sigma_s(v)\right)|_{F_{k_j}E^2_{k_j}} = \sigma_q(v)|_{F_{k_j}E^2_{k_j}} = \Phi\left(v|_{F_{k_j}E^2_{k_j}}\right).\end{aligned}$$

We deduce that Φ is not injective and thus it is not surjective as a selfmap of the finite set $A^{F_{k_j}E^2_{k_j}}$. Consequently, (7.5) implies that σ_q is not surjective. We arrive at a contradiction since $\sigma_q = \sigma_d \circ \sigma_s$ is surjective as a composition of surjective maps. Hence, σ_s must be injective. By Corollary 3, we conclude that σ_s is stably invertible and the proof is complete. □

Disclosure of Interests. The authors have no competing interests to declare that are relevant to the content of this article.

References

1. Bartholdi, L.: Amenability of groups is characterized by Myhill's Theorem. J. Eur. Math. Soc. **21**(10), 3191–3197 (2019)
2. Birkhoff, G.D.: An extension of Poincaré's last geometric theorem. Acta Math. **47**, 297–311 (1926)
3. Blanchard, F., Maass, A.: Dynamical properties of expansive one-sided cellular automata. Israel J. Math. **99**, 149–174 (1997)
4. Bowen, R.E.R., Chazottes, J.-R., Ruelle, D.: Equilibrium States and the Ergodic Theory of Anosov Diffeomorphisms. LNM, vol. 470. Springer, Heidelberg (2008). https://doi.org/10.1007/978-3-540-77695-6
5. Burks, A.W.: von Neumann's self-reproducing automata. In: Burks, A.W. (ed.) Essays on Cellular Automata, pp. 3–64. University of Illinois Press, Champaign (1971)
6. Chung, N.P., Lee, K.: Topological stability and pseudo-orbit tracing property of group actions. Proc. Am. Math. Soc. **146**, 1047–1057 (2018)
7. Capobianco, S., Kari, J., Taati, S.: An "almost dual" to Gottschalk's Conjecture. In: 22th International Workshop on Cellular Automata and Discrete Complex Systems (AUTOMATA), Jun 2016, Zurich, Switzerland, pp.77–89 (2016)
8. Ceccherini-Silberstein, T., Coornaert, M.: A generalization of the Curtis-Hedlund theorem. Theoret. Comput. Sci. **400**, 225–229 (2008)
9. Ceccherini-Silberstein, T., Coornaert, M., Phung, X.K.: On linear shifts of finite type and their endomorphisms. J. Pure App. Algebra **226**(6), 106692 (2022)

10. Ceccherini-Silberstein, T., Coornaert, M., Phung, X.K.: First-order model theory and Kaplansky's stable finiteness conjecture, Groups, Geometry, and Dynamics (to appear)
11. Ceccherini-Silberstein, T., Machì, A., Scarabotti, F.: Amenable groups and cellular automata. Ann. Inst. Fourier (Grenoble) **49**, 673–685 (1999)
12. Dennunzio, A., Formenti, E., Provillard, J.: Non-uniform cellular automata: classes, dynamics, and decidability. Inf. Comput. **215**, 32–46 (2012)
13. Dennunzio, A., Formenti, E., Provillard, J.: Local rule distributions, language complexity and non-uniform cellular automata. Theoret. Comput. Sci. **504**, 38–51 (2013)
14. Fatès, N., Thierry, E., Morvan, M., Schabanel, N.: Fully asynchronous behavior of double-quiescent elementary cellular automata. Theoret. Comput. Sci. **362**(1), 1–16 (2006)
15. Gardner, M.: Mathematical games: the fantastic combinations of John Conway's new solitaire game "Life". Sci. Am. **223**(4), 120–123 (1970)
16. Gromov, M.: Endomorphisms of symbolic algebraic varieties. J. Eur. Math. Soc. (JEMS) **1**, 109–197 (1999)
17. Gottschalk, W.H.: Some general dynamical notions. In: Beck, A. (ed.) Recent Advances in Topological Dynamics. LNM, vol. 318, pp. 120–125. Springer, Heidelberg (1973). https://doi.org/10.1007/BFb0061728
18. Hedlund, G.A.: Endomorphisms and automorphisms of the shift dynamical system. Math. Syst. Theory **3**, 320–375 (1969)
19. Kaplansky, I.: Fields and Rings, Chicago Lectures in Mathematics, University of Chicago Press, Chicago (1969)
20. Kamilya, S., Kari, J.: Nilpotency and periodic points in non-uniform cellular automata. Acta Informatica **58**, 319–333 (2021)
21. Kurka, P.: Languages, equicontinuity and attractors in cellular automata. Ergod. Theory Dynam. Syst. **17**, 417–433 (1997)
22. Meyerovitch, T.: Pseudo-orbit tracing and algebraic actions of countable amenable groups. Ergod. Theory Dyn. Syst. **39**, 2570–2591 (2019)
23. Moore, E.F.: Machine models of self-reproduction. Proc. Symp. Appl. Math. Am. Math. Soc. Provid. **14**, 17–34 (1963)
24. Myhill, J.: The converse of Moore's Garden-of-Eden theorem. Proc. Am. Math. Soc. **14**, 685–686 (1963)
25. von Neumann, J.: Burks, A.W. (ed.) The Theory of Self-reproducing Automata. University of Illinois Press, Urbana (1966)
26. Paturi, P.: On the surjunctivity and the garden of Eden theorem for non-uniform cellular automata. In: Manzoni, L., Mariot, L., Roy Chowdhury, D. (eds.) Cellular Automata and Discrete Complex Systems. AUTOMATA 2023. LNCS, vol. 14152, pp. 19–32. Springer, Cham (2023). https://doi.org/10.1007/978-3-031-42250-8_2
27. Phung, X.K.: Shadowing for families of endomorphisms of generalized group shifts. Discrete Contin. Dyn. Syst. Ser. A **42**(1), 285–299 (2022)
28. Phung, X.K.: On dynamical finiteness properties of algebraic group shifts. Israel J. Math. **252**, 355–398 (2022). https://doi.org/10.1007/s11856-022-2351-1
29. Phung, X.K.: On symbolic group varieties and dual surjunctivity. Groups Geom. Dyn. **18**(1), 213–234 (2024). https://doi.org/10.4171/GGD/749
30. Phung, X.K.: On invertible and stably reversible non-uniform cellular automata. Theoret. Comput. Sci. **940**, 43–59 (2023)
31. Phung, X.K.: A geometric generalization of Kaplansky's direct finiteness conjecture. Proc. Am. Math. Soc. **151**, 2863–2871 (2023). https://doi.org/10.1090/proc/16333

32. Phung, X.K.: Stable finiteness of twisted group rings and noisy linear cellular automata. Can. J. Math. **76**(4), 1089–1108 (2024). https://doi.org/10.4153/S0008414X23000329
33. Phung, X.K.: On the Garden of Eden theorem for non-uniform cellular automata. Nonlinearity **37**, 065012 (2024). https://doi.org/10.1088/1361-6544/ad3ffa
34. Phung, X.K.: On linear non-uniform cellular automata: duality and dynamics. Linear Algebra Appl. **699**, 78–103 (2024)
35. Phung, X.K.: Weakly surjunctive groups and symbolic group varieties, Israel J. Math. arXiv:2111.13607. (to appear)
36. Phung, X.K.: Some pointwise and decidable properties of non-uniform cellular automata. arXiv:2210.00676. (preprint)
37. Salo, V.: Gate lattices and the stabilized automorphism group. J. Mod. Dyn. **19**, 717–749 (2023). https://doi.org/10.3934/jmd.2023018
38. Salo, V.: Realization problems for nonuniform cellular automata. Theoret. Comput. Sci. **559**, 91–107 (2014)
39. Roy, S., Gautam, V.K., Das, S.: A note on skew-asynchronous cellular automata. In: Gadouleau, M., Castillo-Ramirez, A. (eds) Cellular Automata and Discrete Complex Systems. AUTOMATA 2024. LNCS, vol. 14782, 146–158. Springer, Cham (2024). https://doi.org/10.1007/978-3-031-65887-7_10
40. Weiss, B.: Sofic groups and dynamical systems. Sankhyā Ser. A **62**(3), 350–359 (2000)
41. Wolfram, S.: A New Kind of Science. Champaign, IL, Wolfram Media (2002)

Ternary Cellular Automata Induced by Semigroups of Order 3 are Solvable

Henryk Fukś(✉)

Brock University, Department of Mathematics and Statistics, St. Catharines, Canada
hfuks@brocku.ca

Abstract. The minimal number of inputs in the local function of a non-trivial cellular automaton is two. Such a function can be viewed as as a kind of binary operation. If this operation is associative, it forms, together with the set of states, a semigroup. There are 18 semigroups of order 3 up to equivalence, and they define 18 cellular automata rules with three states. We investigate these rules with respect to solvability and show that all of them are solvable, meaning that the state of a given cell after n iterations can be expressed by an explicit formula. We derive the relevant formulae for all 18 rules using some additional properties possessed by particular semigroups of order 3, such as commutativity and idempotence.

Keywords: ternary cellular automata · semigroups · solvability

1 Introduction

Cellular automata (CA) are characterized by two crucial parameters, the number of states of the alphabet and the number of inputs of the local function. It is a well known fact that in the case of one-dimensional CA these two are not completely independent. The number of states of a cellular automaton can be decreased at the expense of increased neighbourhood size [6,7], and conversely, the number of inputs can be decreased at the expense of enlarging the alphabet [6]. The smallest possible non-trivial alphabet has two elements, and for this reason a significant part of research on CA is devoted to binary rules. If one wishes to study the binary rules in a systematic way, a natural strategy would be to look at rules with increasing neighbourhood size n, starting from $n = 1, 2, 3 \ldots$. Binary CA with one or two inputs are not very interesting, yet those with three inputs (called *elementary rules*) already exhibit a rich variety of dynamical behaviour, and they have been extensively studied. In particular, it has been recently demonstrated [3] that about 65% of all elementary rules are *solvable*, meaning that one can construct an explicit formula for the state of a given cell after a given number of iterations if the initial configuration is provided.

Given the aforementioned trade-off between the number of states n and the number of inputs k one could equally well consider CA with the minimal non-trivial neighbourhood size, which obviously means $n = 2$. Systematic study of

Published by Springer Nature Switzerland AG 2026
S. Riva and A. Richard (Eds.): AUTOMATA 2025, LNCS 15831, pp. 88–106, 2026.
https://doi.org/10.1007/978-3-032-01570-9_7

two-input rules would then involve investigating those with increasing number of states k, starting with $k = 1, 2, 3, \ldots$. The $k = 1$ case is not interesting, and $k = 2$ (binary) case is already well known. There are namely $2^4 = 16$ binary two-input rules, and all of them are equivalent to elementary CA with "effective" dependence on only two inputs. For example, for the elementary rule 34 the local function $f(x_1, x_2, x_3) = x_3 - x_2 x_3$ depends only on x_2 and x_3, thus it is effectively two-input. Since all elementary rules have been extensively studied, we will not discuss two-input binary rules here.

The next case, namely 3-state (or *ternary*) two-input rules, are much more interesting. In general, ternary CA rules have not received much attention in the literature, although some results regarding their solvability in the probabilistic sense [4,5] and existence of rules with conservation laws [9] are known. There are $3^9 = 19683$ two-input ternary rules, definitely too large a number to investigate systematically on one-by-one basis. We will, therefore, in this paper look only at a particular class of those rules, with much smaller number of members. Their solvability will be our main focus.

2 Definitions

In order to define a CA rule we need the set of states or alphabet $\mathcal{A}$ and the local function f. In the case of two-input rules the local function is a function $f : \mathcal{A}^2 \to \mathcal{A}$. A bi-infinite sequence $x \in \mathcal{A}^{\mathbb{Z}}$ of symbols of the alphabet will be called a *configuration*. With the local function f we associate a global function $F : \mathcal{A}^{\mathbb{Z}} \to \mathcal{A}^{\mathbb{Z}}$, such that

$$[F(x)]_i = f(x_i, x_{i+1})$$

for all $i \in \mathbb{Z}$. Multiple iterates of F will be denoted by F^n. Using the traditional nomenclature of cellular automata, $[F^n(x)]_i$ represents the state of the cell i after n iterations of rule F (with local function f).

We will also define a family of functions $f^n : \mathcal{A}^{n+1} \to \mathcal{A}$, such that

$$\begin{aligned} f^2(x_0, x_1, x_2) &= f\big(f(x_1, x_2), f(x_2, x_3)\big) \\ f^3(x_0, x_1, x_2, x_3) &= f^2\big(f(x_0, x_1), f(x_1, x_2), f(x_2, x_3)\big), \\ &\ldots \end{aligned}$$

and by induction

$$f^n(x_0, x_1, \ldots, x_n) = f^{n-1}\big(f(x_0, x_1), f(x_1, x_2), \ldots, f(x_{n-1}, x_n)\big).$$

It is not hard to see that

$$[F^n(x)]_i = f^n(x_i, x_{i+1}, \ldots, x_n).$$

This means that if we find an explicit formula for $f^n(x_0, x_1, \ldots, x_n)$ in terms of its n arguments, we will automatically have the formula for the state of cell i after n iterations.

Given a local function with two inputs $f(x_1, x_2)$ one can think of it as a kind of binary operation $\odot$,

$$x_1 \odot x_2 = f(x_1, x_2).$$

If $\mathcal{A}$ is the alphabet of the CA, then obviously $x_1 \odot x_2 \in \mathcal{A}$ for $x_1, x_2 \in \mathcal{A}$, meaning that the operation $\odot$ is closed. If no further conditions are imposed, the pair $(\mathcal{A}, \odot)$ is called *magma*. The set of local functions of ternary CA with two inputs is, therefore, equivalent to the set of magmas with three elements.

If for all $x_1, x_2, x_3 \in \mathcal{A}$

$$(x_1 \odot x_2) \odot x_3 = x_1 \odot (x_2 \odot x_3),$$

then $\odot$ is called *associative*. Associative magmas are called *semigroups*.

A semigroup with k elements is called a semigroup of order k. For small k's, semigroups of order k have been enumerated, most recently up to $k = 10$ [2]. The list of semigroups of order 3 is know since 1940's, and it is known that there are 113 of them. If we count semigroups related by isomorphism or anti-isomorphism as equivalent, then their number reduces to only 18 non-equivalent ones [1]. Assuming that the semigroup elements are $\{x, y, z\}$, the "multiplication tables" of the corresponding operation $\odot$ are shown in Table 1. Each of these multiplication tables define one ternary 2-input CA rule. We will denote the local function corresponding to G_i by f_i. Let us consider, for example, the semigroup G_4. Its multiplication table given in Table 1 with $x = 0, y = 1, z = 2$ becomes

	0	1	2
0	2	1	0
1	1	1	1
2	0	1	2

The corresponding local function is given by

$$f_4(u, v) = \begin{cases} 2 & \text{if } (u, v) = (0, 0) \text{ or } (2, 2), \\ 1 & \text{if } u = 1 \text{ or } v = 1, \\ 0 & \text{otherwise.} \end{cases} \tag{1}$$

Note that instead of the representation $x = 0, y = 1, z = 2$, we could have used other permutation of symbols, for instance, $x = 2, y = 1, z = 0$ etc. This would result in an equivalent rule but with differently named symbols.

We will now construct the so-called *polynomial representation* for each of the 18 rules, using the method outlined in [3]. This will be a polynomial with two variables u, v returning the same values as $f(u, v) = u \odot v$ for all $u, v \in \mathcal{A}$. Define indicator function

$$I_n(x) = \begin{cases} 1 & \text{if } x = n, \\ 0 & \text{otherwise.} \end{cases}$$

The following equation is obviously true

$$f(u, v) = \sum_{i,j \in \mathcal{A}} f(i, j) I_i(u) I_j(v). \tag{2}$$

Table 1. List of multiplication tables of 18 semigroups of order 3 (up to equivalence).

G_1 :

	x	y	z
x	x	y	z
y	y	z	x
z	z	x	y

G_2 :

	x	y	z
x	y	z	y
y	z	y	z
z	y	z	y

G_3 :

	x	y	z
x	y	z	z
y	z	z	z
z	z	z	z

G_4 :

	x	y	z
x	z	y	x
y	y	y	y
z	x	y	z

G_5 :

	x	y	z
x	z	x	x
y	x	y	z
z	x	z	z

G_6 :

	x	y	z
x	z	x	x
y	x	z	z
z	x	z	z

G_7 :

	x	y	z
x	z	z	z
y	z	z	z
z	z	z	z

G_8 :

	x	y	z
x	z	z	z
y	z	y	z
z	z	z	z

G_9 :

	x	y	z
x	z	y	z
y	y	y	y
z	z	y	z

G_{10} :

	x	y	z
x	z	x	z
y	x	y	z
z	z	z	z

G_{11} :

	x	y	z
x	z	z	z
y	y	y	y
z	z	z	z

G_{12} :

	x	y	z
x	z	z	z
y	x	y	z
z	z	z	z

G_{13} :

	x	y	z
x	x	y	z
y	y	y	z
z	z	z	z

G_{14} :

	x	y	z
x	x	z	z
y	z	y	z
z	z	z	z

G_{15} :

	x	y	z
x	x	x	x
y	y	y	y
z	x	x	z

G_{16} :

	x	y	z
x	x	x	z
y	y	y	z
z	z	z	z

G_{17} :

	x	y	z
x	x	x	x
y	y	y	y
z	z	z	z

G_{18} :

	x	y	z
x	x	x	x
y	y	y	y
z	x	y	z

For the ternary alphabet $\mathcal{A} = \{0, 1, 2\}$, the following polynomial forms of indicator functions can be used if $x \in \mathcal{A}$,

$$
\begin{aligned}
I_0(x) &= \frac{1}{2}(x-1)(x-2), \\
I_1(x) &= x(2-x), \\
I_2(x) &= \frac{1}{2}x(x-1).
\end{aligned} \tag{3}
$$

These have been obtained by direct fitting. For example, for I_0 we have three values needed, $I_0(0) = 1$, $I_0(1) = 0$ and $I_0(2) = 0$, thus we need a polynomial with three coefficients, i.e., the quadratic function. Taking $I_0(x) = ax^2 + bx + c$ we have three free constants and three conditions, so we can determine a, b and c, resulting in $I_0(x) = \frac{1}{2}x^2 - \frac{3}{2}x + 1$. This factorizes to $I_0(x) = \frac{1}{2}(x-1)(x-2)$, as listed above. Using expressions given in eq. (3) to replace indicator functions on the right hand side of eq. (2), one obtains a polynomial in two variables representing a given CA. For example, for G_4 the local function f_4 given by eq. (1) returns 2 if (u,v) is $(0,0)$ or $(2,2)$, and it returns 1 if at least one of (u,v) is 1, therefore

$$\begin{aligned} f_4(u,v) = {} & 2I_0(u)I_0(v) + 2I_2(u)I_2(v) \\ & + I_1(u)I_0(v) + I_1(u)I_1(v) + I_1(u)I_2(v) + I_0(u)I_1(v) + I_2(u)I_1(v). \end{aligned}$$

This simplifies to

$$f_4(u,v) = 2I_0(u)I_0(v) + 2I_2(u)I_2(v) + I_1(u) + I_1(v) - I_1(u)I_1(v),$$

where we used the fact that $I_0(x) + I_1(x) + I_2(x) = 1$. Using the expressions for indicator functions this yields

$$\begin{aligned} f_4(u,v) = {} & \frac{1}{2}(u-1)(u-2)(v-1)(v-2) + \frac{1}{2}u(u-1)v(v-1) \\ & + u(2-u) + v(2-v) - u(2-u)v(2-v), \end{aligned}$$

and, after simplification,

$$f_4(u,v) = 1 + (v-1)(u-1).$$

Table 2 shows polynomial representations of all 18 rules defined by semigroups of order 3, obtained in a similar way as above. As mentioned, when constructing the rule corresponding to a given semigroup, one can choose among $3! = 6$ permutations of symbols $\{0,1,2\}$ to represent $\{x,y,z\}$. This will produce six different polynomial representations. In Table 2 for each semigroup we listed the shortest and simplest polynomial among the six, giving in the second column the corresponding choice of $\{x,y,z\}$. In cases of G_1 and G_{13}, in addition of the polynomial representation, we also listed alternative expressions.

It is imperative to stress here that the polynomial expressions defining local functions in the last column of Table 2 use regular arithmetic addition and multiplication in the field of rational numbers. Although the set $\{0,1,2\}$ with addition and multiplication modulo 3 forms a finite field, we are *not* using this fact in subsequent considerations (except to provide an alternative definition of G_1 and the corresponding solution formula). Polynomials in Table 2 are simply integer-valued polynomials which take values in $\mathcal{A}$ if their arguments belong to $\mathcal{A}$.

In order for the reader to get some idea regarding dynamical behaviour of our 18 CA rules, Fig. 1 show examples of spatiotemporal patterns generated by them, starting from "random" initial conditions with periodic boundaries. We can see that these patterns range in complexity from very simple to rather complicated ones, the latter exhibiting triangular regions of varying sizes with fractal-like scaling often found in many other cellular automata. Using informal Wolfram classification [8], rules 1, 2, 5 and 6 are class 3, rules 11, 15, 17 and 18 are class 2, ad the remaining ones are class 1.

Table 2. Local function of CA defined by semigroups of order 3.

semigr.	representation	local function
G_1	$x=0, y=1, z=2$	$f_1(u,v)=u+v+\frac{3}{4}uv(3uv-5u-5v+7)$
		$f_1(u,v)=(u+v) \mod 3$
G_2	$x=1, y=2, z=0$	$f_2(u,v)=1+(v^2-v-1)(u^2-u-1)$
G_3	$x=1, y=2, z=0$	$f_3(u,v)=2u(u-2)v(v-2)$
G_4	$x=0, y=1, z=2$	$f_4(u,v)=1+(v-1)(u-1)$
G_5	$x=0, y=1, z=2$	$f_5(u,v)=2-(u+v-3)(uv-u-v)$
G_6	$x=0, y=1, z=2$	$f_6(u,v)=1+(v^2-3v+1)(u^2-3u+1)$
G_7	$x=0, y=1, z=2$	$f_7(u,v)=2$
G_8	$x=2, y=1, z=0$	$f_8(u,v)=u(u-2)v(v-2)$
G_9	$x=0, y=1, z=2$	$f_9(u,v)=\frac{1}{4}uv(v-3)(u-3)$
G_{10}	$x=2, y=1, z=0$	$f_{10}(u,v)=uv(u+v-uv)$
G_{11}	$x=0, y=1, z=2$	$f_{11}(u,v)=1+(u-1)^2$
G_{12}	$x=2, y=1, z=0$	$f_{12}(u,v)=uv(2-u)$
G_{13}	$x=0, y=1, z=2$	$f_{13}(u,v)=u+v-\frac{1}{2}uv(uv-2u-2v+5)$
		$f_{13}(u,v)=\max(u,v)$
G_{14}	$x=2, y=1, z=0$	$f_{14}(u,v)=\frac{1}{2}uv(3uv-5u-5v+9)$
G_{15}	$x=0, y=1, z=2$	$f_{15}(u,v)=\frac{1}{2}u(uv^2-uv-v^2-2u+v+4)$
G_{16}	$x=2, y=1, z=0$	$f_{16}(u,v)=1+(v-1)^2(u-1)$
G_{17}	$x=0, y=1, z=2$	$f_{17}(u,v)=u$
G_{18}	$x=0, y=1, z=2$	$f_{18}(u,v)=\frac{1}{2}u(uv-2u-v+4)$

3 Basic Results

Some semigroups listed in Table 1 have additional properties which will be useful in what follows. Some are *commutative*, meaning that $u \odot v = v \odot u$ for all $u, v \in \mathcal{A}$. Others are *idempotent*, meaning that $u \odot u = u$ for all $u \in \mathcal{A}$. Commutative semigroups are $G_1, G_2, \ldots, G_{10}$, as well as G_{13} and G_{14}. Semigroups $G_{13}, G_{14} \ldots, G_{18}$ are idempotent. Semigroups G_{11} and G_{12} are neither commutative nor idempotent.

The simplest to deal with are idempotent semigroups. For them it is very straightforward to construct an explicit formula for f^n.

Proposition 1. *If the semigroup* $(\mathcal{A}, \odot)$ *is idempotent and* $f(x_0, x_1) = x_0 \odot x_1$, *then*

$$f^n(x_0, x_1, \ldots, x_n) = x_0 \odot x_1 \odot \ldots \odot x_n.$$

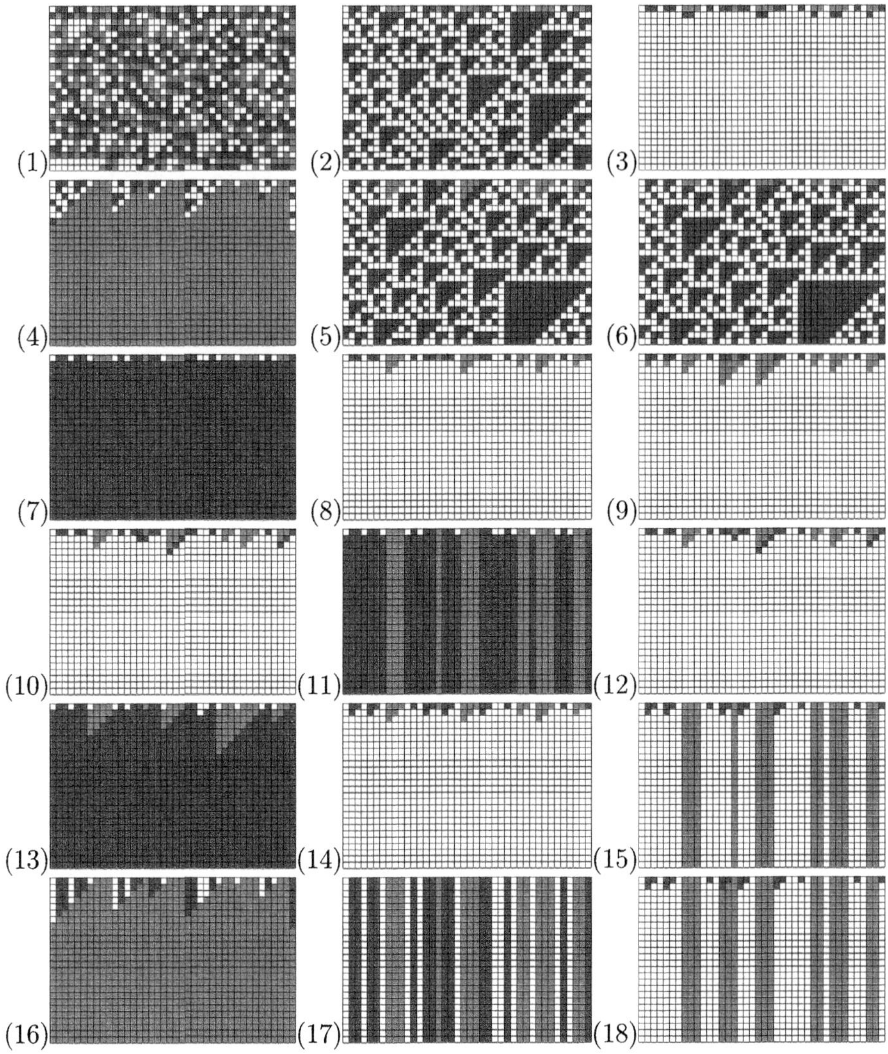

Fig. 1. Spatiotemporal patterns of all 18 semi-group rules generated from random initial condition of 40 sites with periodic boundary conditions, iterated 25 times. Color scheme: 0 =white, 1 =gray and 2 =blue. (Color figure online)

Proof. We will prove this by induction. For $n = 1$ there is nothing to prove. Assuming formula's validity for n and defining $y_i = x_i \odot x_{i+1}$, we obtain

$$
\begin{aligned}
f^{n+1}(x_0, x_1, \ldots, x_{n+1}) &= f^n(y_0, y_1, \ldots, y_n) \\
&= (x_0 \odot x_1) \odot (x_1 \odot x_2) \odot \ldots \odot (x_n \odot x_{n+1}) = \\
x_0 \odot (x_1 \odot x_1) &\odot (x_2 \odot x_2) \odot \ldots \odot (x_n \odot x_n) \odot x_{n+1} \\
&= x_0 \odot x_1 \odot \ldots \odot x_{n+1},
\end{aligned}
$$

where we used idempotency and associativity. This proves validity of the formula for $n+1$, as required. □

For commutative semigroups one can obtain a similar result. We will use the following notation,

$$x^{\cdot n} = \underbrace{x \odot x \odot \ldots \odot x}_{n}.$$

This is to distinguish $x^{\cdot n}$ from regular arithmetic powers x^n, as both will be used in the next section of this paper.

Proposition 2. *If the semigroup* $(\mathcal{A}, \odot)$ *is commutative and* $f(x_0, x_1) = x_0 \odot x_1$, *then*

$$f^n(x_0, x_1, \ldots, x_n) = x_0^{\cdot\binom{n}{0}} \odot x_1^{\cdot\binom{n}{1}} \odot \ldots \odot x_n^{\cdot\binom{n}{n}}.$$

Proof. We will again use induction. The $n=1$ case is obvious. Assume that the formula is true for n and consider

$$f^{n+1}(x_0, x_1, \ldots, x_{n+1}) = f^n(y_0, y_1, \ldots, y_n),$$

where $y_i = x_i \odot x_{i+1}$. Using the formula for n we have

$$\begin{aligned} f^n(y_0, y_1, \ldots, y_n) &= (x_0 \odot x_1)^{\cdot\binom{n}{0}} \odot (x_1 \odot x_2)^{\cdot\binom{n}{1}} \odot \ldots \odot (x_{n-1} \odot x_n)^{\cdot\binom{n}{n}} \\ &= x_0^{\cdot\binom{n}{0}} \odot x_1^{\cdot\binom{n}{0}+\binom{n}{1}} \odot x_2^{\cdot\binom{n}{1}+\binom{n}{2}} \ldots \odot x_{n-1}^{\cdot\binom{n}{n-1}+\binom{n}{n}} \odot x_n^{\cdot\binom{n}{n}}. \end{aligned}$$

Note that we used $(x \odot y)^{\cdot m} = x^{\cdot m} \odot y^{\cdot m}$ which is valid assuming commutativity. Now, since

$$\binom{n}{i} + \binom{n}{i+1} = \binom{n+1}{i+1} \quad \text{and} \quad \binom{n}{0} = \binom{n+1}{0} = \binom{n}{n} = \binom{n+1}{n+1} = 1,$$

we obtain

$$f^{n+1}(x_0, x_1, \ldots, x_{n+1}) = x_0^{\cdot\binom{n+1}{0}} \odot x_1^{\cdot\binom{n+1}{1}} \odot x_2^{\cdot\binom{n+1}{2}} \ldots \odot x_{n-1}^{\cdot\binom{n+1}{n}} \odot x_n^{\cdot\binom{n+1}{n+1}},$$

proving validity of our formula for $n+1$, as required. □

Note that the commutativity is not assumed in Proposition 1, thus Proposition 1 is *not* a special case of Proposition 2.

4 Solutions

Having the results of the previous section, we can now construct solution formulae for all 18 two-input ternary rules. We will start with the simplest ones.

4.1 Trivial Rules

Let us consider two trivial semigroups first, namely G_7 and G_{17}. For G_7 we have $f_j(u,v) = 2$, hence $f_7^n(x_0, x_1, \ldots, x_n) = 2$. For G_{17}, $f_{17}(u,v) = u$, so $f_{17}^n(x_0, x_1, \ldots, x_n) = x_0$. Therefore,

$$[F_7^n(x)]_i = 2 \quad \text{and} \quad [F_{17}^n(x)]_i = x_i.$$

Another rather simple case is G_3 for which $f_3(u,v) = 2u(u-2)v(v-2)$. This is a commutative rule, thus we can use Proposition 2. It is easy to verify that $x^{\cdot m} = 0$ for $x \in \{0,2\}$ when $m > 1$. When $x = 1$, we have $1 \odot 1 = 2$. Since $2 \odot y = 0$ for any y, this implies that $x^{\cdot m} = 0$ for $x = 1$ and $m > 2$. This yields

$$f_3^n(x_0, x_1, \ldots, x_n) = x_0^{\cdot\binom{n}{0}} \odot x_1^{\cdot\binom{n}{1}} \odot \ldots \odot x_n^{\cdot\binom{n}{n}} = \begin{cases} x_0 \odot 0 \odot x_n & n > 2, \\ x_0 \odot x_1^{\cdot 2} \odot x_2 & n = 2, \\ x_0 \odot x_1 & n = 1. \end{cases}$$

Obviously $x_0 \odot 0 \odot x_n = 0$. Furthermore, $x_0 \odot x_1^{\cdot 2} \odot x_2 = 0$ because $x_1^{\cdot 2}$ is either 0 or 2 and $f(0,y) = 0$, $f(2,y) = 0$ for any y. We also have $x_0 \odot x_1 = 2x_0(x_0-2)x_1(x_1-2)$, therefore

$$f_3^n(x_0, x_1, \ldots, x_n) = \begin{cases} 2x_0(x_0-2)x_1(x_1-2) & n = 1, \\ 0 & n > 1, \end{cases}$$

and finally

$$[F_3^n(x)]_i = \begin{cases} 2x_i(x_i-2)x_{i+1}(x_{i+1}-2) & n = 1, \\ 0 & n > 1. \end{cases}$$

For G_{11}, the local function depends only on the first variable, $f_{11}(u,v) = 1 + (u-1)^2$. We will define $g(u) = 1 + (u-1)^2$. Note that $g(u) = g(g(u))$ for $u \in \{0,1,2\}$. Since the semigroup is not commutative and it is not idempotent, we cannot use any of our propositions. We can, however, iterate functions f^n directly,

$$\begin{aligned} f_{11}^n(x_0, x_1, \ldots, x_n) &= f_{11}^{n-1}(g(x_0), g(x_1), \ldots, g(x_{n-1})) \\ = f_{11}^{n-2}(g(g(x_0)), g(g(x_1)), \ldots, g(g(x_{n-2}))) &= f_{11}^{n-2}(g(x_0), g(x_1), \ldots, g(x_{n-2})) \\ = \ldots = f_{11}(g(x_0), g(x_1)) &= g(x_0) = 1 + (x_0-1)^2, \end{aligned}$$

and finally

$$[F_{11}^n(x)]_i = 1 + (x_i - 1)^2.$$

4.2 Rules with Solutions Involving Binomial Coefficient

A more interesting case are semigroups inducing CA rules solvable by direct application of Proposition 2. The first one is G_1, for which $u \odot v = (u+v)$

mod 3, so Proposition 2 immediately yields

$$[F_1^n(x)]_i = \sum_{j=0}^{n} \binom{n}{j} x_{i+j} \mod 3.$$

Another one is G_4, with multiplication operation given by $u \odot v = 1+(u-1)(v-1)$. It will be convenient to change variables to $\tilde{u} = u - 1$ and $\tilde{v} = v - 1$. This transforms the set of states to $\{-1, 0, 1\}$ with semigroup multiplication defined as $\tilde{u} \odot \tilde{v} = \tilde{u}\tilde{v}$. The semigroup multiplication in new variables is thus a regular arithmetic multiplication, and we obtain

$$\tilde{x}_0^{\cdot\binom{n}{0}} \odot \tilde{x}_1^{\cdot\binom{n}{1}} \odot \ldots \odot \tilde{x}_n^{\cdot\binom{n}{n}} = \prod_{j=0}^{n} \tilde{x}_j^{\binom{n}{j}}.$$

Coming back to the original variables the solution formula follows immediately,

$$[F_4^n(x)]_i = 1 + \prod_{j=0}^{n} (x_{i+j} - 1)^{\binom{n}{j}}.$$

The same method can be used for G_2, with slight modification. For this case we have $f_2(u, v) = 1 + (v^2 - v - 1)(u^2 - u - 1)$ and recall that $f_4(u, v) = 1 + (v - 1)(u - 1)$. It is easy to see that $f_2(u, v) = f_4(g(u), g(v))$ where $g(x) = x^2 - x$. Denoting by $g(x)$ a bi-infinite configuration such that $[g(x)]_i = g(x_i)$, this implies

$$F_2(x) = F_4(g(x)).$$

Now let us note that $g(x) = x^2 - x$ takes values in $\{0, 2\}$ for any $x \in \{0, 1, 2\}$, hence $F_4(g(x))$ only contains 0's or 2's. Furthermore, one can easily verify that

$$f_4(u, v) = f_2(u, v) \quad \text{for } u, v \in \{0, 2\}.$$

For all further iterations, therefore, it does not matter if we apply F_2 or F_4, meaning that

$$[F_2^n(x)]_i = [F_2^{n-1} F_4(g(x))]_i = [F_4^n(g(x))]_i = 1 + \prod_{j=0}^{n} \left(g(x_{i+j}) - 1\right)^{\binom{n}{j}},$$

and finally

$$[F_2^n(x)]_i = 1 + \prod_{j=0}^{n} (x_{i+j}^2 - x_{i+j} - 1)^{\binom{n}{j}}.$$

For G_6 the derivation is the same, except that the function g is given by $g(x) = x^2 - 3x + 2$, and we have

$$\begin{aligned} f_6(u, v) &= 1 + (v^2 - 3v + 1)(u^2 - 3u + 1) \\ &= 1 + \big(g(u) - 1\big)\big(g(v) - 1\big) = f_4(g(u), g(u)). \end{aligned}$$

Identical procedure as for G_2 above yields the final result

$$[F_6^n(x)]_i = 1 + \prod_{j=0}^{n} (x_{i+j}^2 - 3x_{i+j} + 1)^{\binom{n}{j}}.$$

Closely related to G_6 is another commutative semigroup G_5. Using the formulas for f_5 and f_6 from Table 2 one can easily demonstrate that

$$f_5(u,v) = f_6(u,v) - u(2-u)v(2-v),$$

meaning that f_5 and f_6 differ only when $u = v = 1$. Furthermore, $f_5(1,u) = f_5(u,1) = u$, which means that the pair 11 cannot appear in iterations of rule f_5 if it was not present in the initial configuration. Therefore, if the sequence $x_0, x_1, \ldots, n_1$ does not contain any 1's, we have

$$f_5^n(x_0, x_1, \ldots, x_n) = f_6^n(x_0, x_1, \ldots, x_n).$$

What happens if $x_0, x_1, \ldots, x_n$ contains some 1's (but not all)? Due to commutativity we can freely permute x_i's and thus assume that $x_0 = 1$ and $x_1 \neq 1$. Note that $f_5(1,v) = f_6(2,v)$ if $v \neq 1$, and therefore

$$f_5^n(1, x_1, \ldots, x_n) = f_6^n(2, x_1, \ldots, x_n).$$

If there is more than a single 1, we can repeat this process again, bringing this 1 to the first position and replacing it by 2. This can be repeated for all 1's – as long as there exist at least one entry different from 1. Note that in the absence of 1's, both f_5 and f_6 agree, meaning that

$$f_5^n(x_0, x_1, \ldots, x_n) = f_6^n(x_0, x_1, \ldots, x_n),$$

as long as there is at least one i for which $x_i \neq 1$. When $x_i = 1$ for all i's, we have $f_5(1,1,\ldots,1) = 1$ and $f_6(1,1,\ldots,1) = 2$, thus we can write

$$f_5^n(1, x_1, \ldots, x_n) = \begin{cases} f_6^n(2, x_1, \ldots, x_n) - 1 & \text{if } x_1 = x_2 = \ldots = x_n = 1, \\ f_6^n(2, x_1, \ldots, x_n) & \text{otherwise.} \end{cases}$$

All we need to do now is to construct indicator function for $11\ldots1$, which is

$$1 - \prod_{j=0}^{n} x_j(2-x_j) = \begin{cases} 1 & \text{if } x_1 = x_2 = \ldots = x_n = 1, \\ 0 & \text{otherwise.} \end{cases}$$

Subtracting this indicator function from the expression for F_6^n yields

$$[F_5^n(x)]_i = 1 + \prod_{j=0}^{n} (x_{i+j}^2 - 3x_{i+j} + 1)^{\binom{n}{j}} - \prod_{j=0}^{n} x_{i+j}(2 - x_{i+j}).$$

4.3 Rules 8 and 9

For G_8, $f_8(u,v) = u(2-u)v(2-v) = g(u)g(v)$, where $g(u) = u(2-u)$. When $u,v \in \{0,1\}$, $f_8(u,v) = uv$. Furthermore, $g(u) \in \{0,1\}$ for any $u \in \{0,1,2\}$ and $g(0) = 0$, $g(1) = 1$. This means that

$$x \odot x = (g(x))^2 = g(x),$$

$$x \odot x \odot x = x \odot g(x) = g(x)g(g(x)) = g(g(x))^2 = g(x),$$

and by induction

$$x^{\cdot m} = g(x).$$

This yields

$$\begin{aligned} f^n(x_0, x_1, \ldots, x_n) &= x_0^{\cdot\binom{n}{0}} \odot x_1^{\cdot\binom{n}{1}} \odot \ldots \odot x_n^{\cdot\binom{n}{n}} = g(x_0) \odot g(x_1) \odot \ldots \odot g(x_n) \\ &= \prod_{j=0}^{n} g(x_j) = \prod_{j=0}^{n} x_j(2-x_j), \end{aligned}$$

and finally

$$[F_8^n(x)]_i = \prod_{j=0}^{n} x_{i+j}(2 - x_{i+j}).$$

For G_9, $f_9(u,v) = \frac{1}{4}uv(3-v)(3-u) = g(u)g(v)$, where $g(u) = \frac{1}{2}u(3-u)$. The function g has the same properties as in the case of G_8, thus we will not repeat the derivation, writing just the final answer,

$$[F_9^n(x)]_i = \prod_{j=0}^{n} \frac{1}{2} x_{i+j}(3 - x_{i+j}).$$

4.4 Rule 10

Rule 10 has the local function $f_{10}(u,v) = uv(u+v-uv)$. We first note that

$$f_{10}(u,u) = u^3(2-u) = \begin{cases} 0 & u = 0, \\ 1 & u = 1, \\ 0 & u = 2. \end{cases}$$

This implies that, for $n > 1$, $x^{\cdot n} = 0$ if $x \in \{0,2\}$ and $x^{\cdot n} = 1$ if $x = 1$. Using the indicator function for 1 we can write

$$x^{\cdot n} = \begin{cases} x(2-x) & \text{if } n > 1, \\ x & \text{if } n = 1. \end{cases}$$

Since G_{10} is commutative, we have

$$\begin{aligned} f_{10}^n(x_0, x_1, \ldots, x_n) &= x_0^{\cdot\binom{n}{0}} \odot x_1^{\cdot\binom{n}{1}} \odot \ldots \odot x_n^{\cdot\binom{n}{n}}. \\ &= x_0 \odot x_1(2-x_1) \odot x_2(2-x_2) \odot \ldots \odot x_{n-1}(2-x_{n-1}) \odot x_n. \end{aligned}$$

Note that $x(2-x)$ takes only values 0 or 1, and if $u, v \in \{0, 1\}$ then $f_{10}(u, v) = uv$, i.e., the semigroup multiplication becomes just the normal arithmetic multiplication. For this reason,

$$f_{10}^n(x_0, x_1, \ldots, x_n) = x_0 \odot \left(\prod_{j=1}^{n-1} x_j(2 - x_j) \right) \odot x_n$$
$$= \left(\prod_{j=1}^{n-1} x_j(2 - x_j) \right) \odot (x_0 \odot x_n).$$

The only possible values of the big product are 0 or 1, and only when it is equal to 1 there is a possibility that the entire expression becomes non-zero. Furthermore, $1 \odot x_0 \odot x_n = x_0 \odot x_n = x_0 x_n(x_0 + x_n - x_0 x_n)$, yielding

$$[F_{10}^n(x)]_i = x_i x_{i+n}(x_i + x_{i+n} - x_i x_{i+n}) \prod_{j=1}^{n-1} x_{i+j}(2 - x_{i+j}).$$

4.5 Rule 12

Rule 12 with the local function $f_{12}(u, v) = uv(2 - u)$ has the property $f(0, v) = f(v, 0) = 0$. This means that if 0 is present in $x_0, x_1, \ldots, x_n$ then

$$f_{12}^n(x_0, x_1, \ldots, x_n) = 0.$$

To get non-zero output of f_{12}, therefore, its arguments must include only 1's and 2's. However, $f(2, 1) = f(2, 2) = 0$, meaning that the presence of pairs 21 or 22 in $(x_0, x_1, \ldots, x_n)$ will also cause the output to be zero. This leaves $1, 1, \ldots, 1$ and $1, 1, \ldots, 1, 2$ as the only configurations producing non-zero output, and it is easy to check that

$$f_{12}^n(1, 1, \ldots, 1) = 1 \quad \text{and} \quad f_{12}^n(1, 1, \ldots, 1, 2) = 2.$$

Indicator function of $(x_0, x_1, \ldots, x_{n-1}) = (1, 1, \ldots, 1)$ is $\prod_{j=0}^{n-1} x_j(2 - x_j)$, and if we multiply it by x_n, we will get the desired result,

$$f_{12}^n(x_0, x_1, \ldots, x_n) = x_n \prod_{j=0}^{n-1} x_j(2 - x_j),$$

hence

$$[F_{12}^n(x)]_i = x_{i+n} \prod_{j=0}^{n-1} x_{i+j}(2 - x_{i+j}).$$

4.6 Idempotent Rules 13–16

Rule 13 has the local function $f_{13} = \max(u, v)$. It is both commutative and idempotent, thus we can write

$$f_{13}^n(x_0, x_1, \ldots, x_n) = x_0 \odot x_1 \odot \ldots \odot x_n.$$

Due to commutativity, we can sort x_i's on the right hand side of the above in an increasing order and then use idempotency. If all three symbols $0, 1, 2$ are present among them, we will get

$$f_{13}^n(x_0, x_1, \ldots, x_n) = 0 \odot 1 \odot 2 = 2.$$

If only two different symbols a and b are present among $(x_0, x_1, \ldots, x_n)$, we get

$$f_{13}^n(x_0, x_1, \ldots, x_n) = a \odot b = \max(a, b).$$

In all cases, therefore, f_{13}^n will return the largest value of its arguments,

$$f_{13}^n(x_0, x_1, \ldots, x_n) = \max(x_0, x_1, \ldots, x_n),$$

and

$$[F_{13}^n(x)]_i = \max\{x_{i+j}, j = 0, 1, \ldots, n\}.$$

Note that one could also use polynomial representation of f_{13}. Although is it rather unwieldy, namely $f_{13}(u, v) = u + v - \frac{5}{2}uv - \frac{1}{2}u^2v^2 + u^2v + uv^2$, polynomial expression for $[F_{13}^n(x)]_i$ could be obtained as well. We will not pursue this here because the expression obtained above is much simpler.

For rule 14, $f_{14}(u, v) = \frac{1}{2}uv(3uv - 5u - 5v + 9)$. Since it is idempotent,

$$f_{14}^n(x_0, x_1, \ldots, x_n) = x_0 \odot x_1 \odot \ldots \odot x_n.$$

This rule is also commutative. Because of this and because $0 \odot v = 0$ for any v, if 0 appears in $x_0, x_1, \ldots, x_n$, then $f_{14}^n(x_0, x_1, \ldots, x_n) = 0$. We also have $1 \odot 2 = 0$, which means that the only possibility to obtain non-zero value of $f_{14}^n(x_0, x_1, \ldots, x_n)$ is to have $x_0, x_1, \ldots, x_n$ consisting of all 1's or all 2's. The indicator functions for all 1's and all 2's are, respectively, $\prod_{j=0}^n x_j(2 - x_j)$ and $\prod_{j=0}^n \frac{1}{2}x_{i+j}(x_{i+j} - 1)$, which immediately yields the solution formula

$$[F_{14}^n(x)]_i = \prod_{j=0}^n x_{i+j}(2 - x_{i+j}) + 2\prod_{j=0}^n \frac{1}{2}x_{i+j}(x_{i+j} - 1).$$

Rule 15 is idempotent and non-commutative, with $f_{15}(u, v) = \frac{1}{2}u(uv^2 - uv - v^2 - 2u + v + 4)$. We have $f_{15}(0, v) = 0$ or $0 \odot v = 0$, hence

$$0 \odot x_1 \odot \ldots \odot x_n = 0 \odot x_2 \odot \ldots \odot x_n = \ldots = 0 \odot x_n = 0.$$

Moreover, since also $1 \odot v = 1$, then by the same token

$$1 \odot x_1 \odot \ldots \odot x_n = 1.$$

Let us now observe that $f_{15}(2,v) = v(v-1) \in \{0,2\}$. This means that if $x_0, x_1, \ldots, x_n$ starts with 2, the only possibility for $f_{15}^n(x_0, x_1, \ldots, x_n)$ to return non-zero value is that it consists of all 2's. We thus have

$$f_{15}^n(x_0, x_1, \ldots, x_n) = \begin{cases} 1 & \text{if } x_0 = 1, \\ 2 & \text{if } (x_0, x_1, \ldots, x_n) = (2, 2, \ldots, 2), \\ 0 & \text{otherwise.} \end{cases}$$

The indicator function for $x_0 = 1$ is $x_0(2-x_0)$, and for all 2's it is $\prod_{j=0}^n \frac{1}{2} x_j(x_j - 1)$. This yields

$$f_{15}^n(x_0, x_1, \ldots, x_n) = x_0(2-x_0) + 2\prod_{j=0}^n \frac{1}{2} x_j(x_j-1),$$

and hence

$$[F_{15}^n(x)]_i = x_i(2-x_i) + 2\prod_{j=0}^n \frac{1}{2} x_{i+j}(x_{i+j}-1).$$

Another idempotent and non-commutative semigroup is G_{16} with the local function $f_{16}(u,v) = 1 + (u-1)(v-1)^2$. Straightforward calculations verify that

$$\begin{aligned} x_0 \odot x_1 &= 1 + (x_0-1)(x_1-1)^2, \\ x_0 \odot x_1 \odot x_2 &= 1 + (x_0-1)(x_1-1)^2(x_2-2)^2, \\ x_0 \odot x_1 \odot x_2 \cdot x_3 &= 1 + (x_0-1)(x_1-1)^2(x_2-1)^2(x_3-1)^2, \end{aligned}$$

etc. One can thus show by induction that

$$x_0 \odot x_1 \odot \ldots \odot x_n = 1 + (x_0-1)\prod_{j=1}^n (x_j-1)^2,$$

hence

$$[F_{16}^n(x)]_i = 1 + (x_i-1)\prod_{j=1}^n (x_{i+j}-1)^2.$$

4.7 Rule 18

Rule 18 with $f_{18}(u,v) = \frac{1}{2}u(uv-2u-v+4)$ is non-commutative but idempotent, so Proposition 1 can be used. First note that $0 \odot v = 0$, $1 \odot v = 1$, and $2 \odot v = v$. Using this and associativity, we can easily see that

$$\begin{aligned} &0 \odot \ldots = 0, && 1 \odot \ldots = 1, \\ &2 \odot 0 \odot \ldots = 0, && 2 \odot 1 \odot \ldots = 1, \\ &2 \odot 2 \odot 0 \odot \ldots = 0, && 2 \odot 2 \odot 1 \odot \ldots = 1, \\ &2 \odot 2 \odot 2 \odot 0 \odot \ldots = 0, && 2 \odot 2 \odot 2 \odot 1 \odot \ldots = 1, \\ &\ldots && \ldots \\ &\underbrace{2 \odot 2 \odot \ldots \odot 2}_{n} \odot 0 = 0, && \underbrace{2 \odot 2 \odot \ldots \odot 2}_{n} \odot 1 = 1. \end{aligned}$$

It is clear that the above list contains all possible configurations of $(x_0, x_1, \ldots, x_n)$ except the configuration consisting of all 2's, for which we have

$$\underbrace{2 \odot 2 \odot \ldots \odot 2}_{n+1} = 2.$$

This means that the only possibility to produce 1 as output of f_{18}^n is to have its arguments starting with 1 or with a block of 1's terminated by 2. The only possibility to get output 2 is to have all 2's as input. Define indicator function

$$H(k) = \begin{cases} x_0(2 - x_0) & k = 0, \\ x_n(2 - x_n) \prod_{j=0}^{n-1} \frac{1}{2} x_j(x_j - 1) & k > 0. \end{cases}$$

We can see that $H(k) = 1$ if the configuration starts with 1 and $k = 0$. If, for $k > 1$, it starts with k 1's terminated by 2, we have $H(k) = 1$ as well. In all other cases $H(k) = 0$. In order to obtain 1 as output of $f_{18}^n(x_0, x_1, \ldots, x_n)$ we want

$$H(0) = 1 \quad \text{or} \quad H(1) = 1 \quad \text{or} \quad \ldots \quad \text{or} \quad H(n) = 1.$$

Since in Boolean logic $p \vee q = \sim (\sim p \wedge \sim q)$, the above is equivalent to

$$1 - \prod_{k=0}^{n} (1 - H(k)) = 1.$$

Indicator function of all 2's is

$$\prod_{j=0}^{n} \frac{1}{2} x_j(x_j - 1),$$

and we need to multiply it by 2 to get the correct value of the output. Combining all of this together we obtain

$$f_{18}^n(x_0, x_1, \ldots, x_n) = 1 - \prod_{k=0}^{n} (1 - H(k)) + 2 \prod_{j=0}^{n} \frac{1}{2} x_j(x_j - 1).$$

The final solution formula, therefore, can be written as

$$[F_{18}^n(x)]_i = 1 - \prod_{k=0}^{n} (1 - H(i,k)) + 2 \prod_{j=0}^{n} \frac{1}{2} x_{i+j}(x_{i+j} - 1),$$

where

$$H(i,n) = \begin{cases} x_i(2 - x_i) & n = 0, \\ x_{i+n}(2 - x_{i+n}) \prod_{j=0}^{n-1} \frac{1}{2} x_{i+j}(x_{i+j} - 1) & n > 0. \end{cases}$$

5 Concluding Remarks

We have demonstrated that all CA defined by semigroups with 3 elements are solvable. What are the possible uses of such solution formulae? Since they exhibit explicit dependence of the state of site i at iteration n on the initial configuration, they can be used to compute various quantities of interest along the orbit of the given initial configuration.

For example, let us assume that the initial configuration is drawn from a Bernoulli distribution such that $Pr(x_i = k) = p_k$ for $k = 0, 1, 2$, where $p_0, p_1, p_2 \in [0, 1]$ and $p_0 + p_1 + p_2 = 1$. By taking the expected value of both sides of the solution formula and by using basic properties of expected values, one can obtain [3,4] the expected value of the state of site i after n iterations of the CA as a function of probabilities p_0, p_1, p_2. Probabilities of occurrences of finite block of symbols can also be computed by a similar method [3]. The solution formulae are thus very useful to study statistical properties of the corresponding CA.

Another possible use of the results presented here would be the investigation of finite size effects. If one takes as the initial configuration a periodic configuration with period L, then it is equivalent to what is often called "finite lattice with periodic boundary conditions". As shown in [3], one can use the solution formulae to study how various properties of the orbit of such configuration depend on the size of the lattice L. The author plans to report relevant results elsewhere in the near future.

Acknowledgments. The author acknowledges comments made by anonymous referees. Their thorough and careful reading of the manuscript helped to eliminate numerous typos and to correct the derivation of the formula for rule 3.

Appendix: summary of solutions

$$[F_1^n(x)]_i = \sum_{j=0}^{n} \binom{n}{j} x_{i+j} \mod 3, \quad [F_2^n(x)]_i = 1 + \prod_{j=0}^{n} (x_{i+j}^2 - x_{i+j} - 1)^{\binom{n}{j}},$$

$$[F_3^n(x)]_i = \begin{cases} 2x_i(x_i - 2)x_{i+1}(x_{i+1} - 2) & n = 1, \\ 0 & n > 1, \end{cases} \quad [F_4^n(x)]_i = 1 + \prod_{j=0}^{n} (x_{i+j} - 1)^{\binom{n}{j}},$$

$$[F_5^n(x)]_i = 1 + \prod_{j=0}^{n} (x_{i+j}^2 - 3x_{i+j} + 1)^{\binom{n}{j}} - \prod_{j=0}^{n} x_{i+j}(2 - x_{i+j}),$$

$$[F_6^n(x)]_i = 1 + \prod_{j=0}^{n} (x_{i+j}^2 - 3x_{i+j} + 1)^{\binom{n}{j}}, \qquad [F_7^n(x)]_i = 2,$$

$$[F_8^n(x)]_i = \prod_{j=0}^{n} x_{i+j}(2 - x_{i+j}), \quad [F_9^n(x)]_i = \prod_{j=0}^{n} \frac{1}{2} x_{i+j}(3 - x_{i+j}),$$

$$[F_{10}^n(x)]_i = x_i x_{i+n}(x_i + x_{i+n} - x_i x_{i+n}) \prod_{j=1}^{n-1} x_{i+j}(2 - x_{i+j}),$$

$$[F_{11}^n(x)]_i = 1 + (x_i - 1)^2, \quad [F_{12}^n(x)]_i = x_{i+n} \prod_{j=0}^{n-1} x_{i+j}(2 - x_{i+j}),$$

$$[F_{13}^n(x)]_i = \max\{x_{i+j}, j = 0, 1, \ldots, n\},$$

$$[F_{14}^n(x)]_i = \prod_{j=0}^{n} x_{i+j}(2 - x_{i+j}) + 2 \prod_{j=0}^{n} \frac{1}{2} x_{i+j}(x_{i+j} - 1),$$

$$[F_{15}^n(x)]_i = x_i(2 - x_i) + 2 \prod_{j=0}^{n} \frac{1}{2} x_{i+j}(x_{i+j} - 1),$$

$$[F_{16}^n(x)]_i = 1 + (x_i - 1) \prod_{j=1}^{n} (x_{i+j} - 1)^2, \quad [F_{17}^n(x)]_i = x_i,$$

$$[F_{18}^n(x)]_i = 1 - \prod_{k=0}^{n} (1 - H(i,k)) + 2 \prod_{j=0}^{n} \frac{1}{2} x_{i+j}(x_{i+j} - 1),$$

where

$$H(i,n) = \begin{cases} x_i(2 - x_i) & n = 0, \\ x_{i+n}(2 - x_{i+n}) \prod_{j=0}^{n-1} \frac{1}{2} x_{i+j}(x_{i+j} - 1) & n > 0. \end{cases}$$

References

1. Distler, A.: Classification and enumeration of finite semigroups. Ph.D. thesis, University of St Andrews (2010)
2. Distler, A., Jefferson, C., Kelsey, T., Kotthoff, L.: The semigroups of order 10. In: Milano, M. (ed.) CP 2012. LNCS, vol. 7514, pp. 883–899. Springer, Heidelberg (2012). https://doi.org/10.1007/978-3-642-33558-7_63
3. Fukś, H.: Solvable cellular automata - methods and applications. Springer (2023). https://doi.org/10.1007/978-3-031-38700-5
4. Fukś, H., Midgley-Volpato, J.: An example of a deterministic cellular automaton exhibiting linear-exponential convergence to the steady state. Acta Phys. Pol. B **9**(1), 49–62 (2016). https://doi.org/10.5506/APhysPolBSupp.9
5. Fukś, H., Procyk, R.: Explorations of ternary cellular automata and ternary density classification problems. Acta Physica Polonica Supp. **12**(1), 75–89 (2019). https://doi.org/10.5506/APhysPolBSupp.12.75
6. Hadeler, K.-P., Müller, J.: Cellular Automata: Analysis and Applications. SMM, Springer, Cham (2017). https://doi.org/10.1007/978-3-319-53043-7

7. Vollmar, R.: Algorithmen in Zellularautomaten: eine Einführung. Teubner, Stuttgart (1979)
8. Wolfram, S.: Statistical mechanics of cellular automata. Rev. Mod. Phys. **55**, 601–644 (1983). https://doi.org/10.1103/RevModPhys.55.601
9. Wolnik, B., De Baets, B.: Ternary reversible number-conserving cellular automata are trivial. Inf. Sci. **513**, 180–189 (2020). https://doi.org/10.1016/j.ins.2019.10.068

A Sequential Solution to the Density Classification Task Using an Intermediate Alphabet

Pacôme Perrotin[1(✉)], Pedro Paulo Balbi[1,2], and Eurico Ruivo[1,2]

[1] Pós-Graduação em Engenharia Elétrica e Computação, Universidade Presbiteriana Mackenzie, Rua da Consolação 896, São Paulo 01302-907, SP, Brazil
pacome.perrotin@gmail.com, {pedrob,eurico.ruivo}@mackenzie.br

[2] Faculdade de Computação e Informática, Universidade Presbiteriana Mackenzie, Rua da Consolação 896, São Paulo 01302-907, SP, Brazil

Abstract. We present a sequential cellular automaton of radius $\frac{1}{2}$ as a solution to the density classification task that makes use of an intermediate alphabet, and converges to a clean fixed point with no remaining auxiliary or intermediate information. We extend this solution to arbitrary finite alphabets and to configurations in higher dimensions.

Keywords: Cellular automata · Density classification task · Sequential update

2020 Mathematics Subject Classification. 68Q80

1 Introduction

Cellular automata are computational models characterised by a local rule uniformly applied over a configuration. The straightforwardness of their definition makes them the subject of a wide array of applications to the modeling of complex physical phenomena [1,7,14,20].

Among some of the theoretical questions studied on cellular automata, classification tasks [15] can be compared to decision problems defined on Turing machines. Such a task is defined by a function that assigns any initial configuration $x \in \mathbb{B}^n$ to a binary value b. A cellular automaton is a solution to a classification task if while executed on the initial configuration x it converges to the uniform configuration b^n, and this configuration is a fixed point. The two most studied classification tasks are the parity classification task, where b is 1 if and only if the initial configuration contains an odd number of 1s, and the density classification task, where b is the symbol in strict majority in the initial configuration.

P. P. Balbi and E. Ruivo—Contributing authors.

Published by Springer Nature Switzerland AG 2026
S. Riva and A. Richard (Eds.): AUTOMATA 2025, LNCS 15831, pp. 107–122, 2026.
https://doi.org/10.1007/978-3-032-01570-9_8

Various solutions to the parity classification task exist [2,5,12,16,19], including a pure solution in the form of a cellular automaton of radius 4 [3]. However, the density classification task has been proven to not have such a pure solution [10]. The current state of the art contains various solutions approaching the problem from different angles, including changing the local rule during the computation [13] or using multiple tracks in parallel to provide a solution [8]. Solutions have also been constructed by using a continuous space of values [4,11], or by using a stochastic approach [6].

This paper is structured by first detailing the specifications of the variant of the density classification task presently under investigation. We then offer a detailed and illustrated description of our novel solution, and lastly we offer generalisations to the solution to larger alphabets and configurations in more dimensions.

In addition to formal proofs, we tested the one-dimensional binary solution on all initial configurations up to size 30, the source code for which can be freely accessed online [17], written in Rust.

2 Definitions

- *Configuration:*
  For Σ a finite alphabet and n a positive integer, we define a *configuration* of size n any $x \in \Sigma^{\{0,\dots,n-1\}}$. For any integer $0 \leq i < n$, we denote x_i the cell of index i in the configuration x. Indexes of configurations are always defined modulo n, i.e., $x_{-1} = x_{n-1}$, and $x_{n+1} = x_1$.
- *Cellular Automaton:*
  For r a positive integer, we refer to *local function* of radius r any function $f : \Sigma^{\{-r,\dots,0,\dots,r\}} \to \Sigma$. For f such a local function, and n a positive integer, the *Cellular Automaton* F defined by f is $F : \Sigma^{\{0,\dots,n-1\}} \to \Sigma^{\{0,\dots,n-1\}}$, where $F(x)_i = f(x_{i-r},\dots,x_i,\dots,x_{i+r})$. We define the particular case of a local function of radius $\frac{1}{2}$ as a local function $f : \Sigma^{\{-1,0\}} \to \Sigma$.
- *Sequential Update Schedule:*
  For x a configuration of size n, f a local function of radius r, and $i < n$ a non-negative integer, we say that the *update of i in x* is the configuration x', where $x'_k = f(x_{k-r},\dots,x_{k+r})$, if and only if $k = i$, and $x'_k = x_k$ otherwise. The *sequential* update of x under f is the configuration obtained by updating every cell in $\{0,\dots,n-1\}$ in order, and in sequence.
- *Fixed Point:*
  For any configurations x and y, x is said to converge to y if and only if $F^k(x) = y$ for some positive integer k. We call x a *fixed point* if $F(x) = x$. Note that if x is a fixed point, then the sequential update of x is also x.

3 The Problem and the General Description of the Solution

3.1 The Problem

In this paper, we focus on a non-standard solution of the density classification task, as it relies on a variant cellular automaton and the use of an intermediate alphabet, that is, the full alphabet Σ of the solution is a superset of the input alphabet, $\mathbb{B}$.

The formulation of the problem is as follows: for any finite initial configuration over $\mathbb{B}$ that has a defined density (a symbol that outnumbers every other one), then the lattice of the cellular automaton must converge to the uniform configuration containing only that symbol, which must be a fixed point. If the initial solution does not have a defined density, then no expectation is set on the convergence.

Since there is no imposition on what would happen in between the initial configuration and the fixed point, a solution to the problem is free to use any number of symbols from its extended alphabet. Solutions relying on this freedom have been found in the past, namely [8]. This particular solution uses two tracks, one that contains the initial configuration and the second that converges to the desired fixed point, the former guiding the convergence of the latter. We consider the solution presented herein as an improvement because it always converges to a fixed point with no remaining auxiliary or intermediate information, whereas that two-tracks solution only ensures this clean result in one of its tracks.

3.2 The Overall Idea of the Solution

Our solution is a cellular automaton of radius $\frac{1}{2}$ (the reference cell being the one on the right), updated sequentially, meaning that the local rule is applied using the value of the current cell, plus the value of the cell to its left, while the cellular automaton as a whole is updated from left to right. In essence, this cellular automaton simulates an operating head that moves along the configuration while updating an internal memory and transforming the configuration as it proceeds.

With its radius $\frac{1}{2}$, our solution can appear to belong in the family of one-way cellular automata [9]. However, it is updated sequentially and not in parallel, and operates on cyclic configurations.

In the following, a cycle is a complete loop of the operating head around the configuration. This cellular automaton tries to remove exactly one 0 and one 1 from the configuration per cycle, storing them in its internal memory. It then discards this pair when a cycle is complete. The detection of the end of a cycle is done thanks to an internal counter. At the end of a cycle, if only one symbol was found (say, a 0), it then means that there is no more of the other symbol in the configuration (so, no more 1s). Since symbols have been removed in equal amounts, the cellular automaton can now converge to the uniform configuration containing the symbol it still holds in memory (here, it would converge to 0^n). All these extra pieces of information – the internal memory, the internal counter, and the marker that allows to know which symbols have been removed from the configuration – are encoded using the aforementioned intermediate alphabet.

So, alongside the Boolean alphabet $\mathbb{B} = \{0, 1\}$, based upon which the initial configuration and the final fixed points are defined, a key aspect of the solution is that it relies on an intermediate alphabet composed of the following 16 triplets:

$$\begin{pmatrix} \circ \\ 0 \\ \{0\} \end{pmatrix}, \begin{pmatrix} \circ \\ 0 \\ \mathbb{B} \end{pmatrix}, \begin{pmatrix} \circ \\ 1 \\ \{1\} \end{pmatrix}, \begin{pmatrix} \circ \\ 1 \\ \mathbb{B} \end{pmatrix}, \begin{pmatrix} \circ \\ X \\ \varnothing \end{pmatrix}, \begin{pmatrix} \circ \\ X \\ \{0\} \end{pmatrix}, \begin{pmatrix} \circ \\ X \\ \{1\} \end{pmatrix}, \begin{pmatrix} \circ \\ X \\ \mathbb{B} \end{pmatrix}, \begin{pmatrix} \bullet \\ 0 \\ \{0\} \end{pmatrix}, \begin{pmatrix} \bullet \\ 0 \\ \mathbb{B} \end{pmatrix}, \begin{pmatrix} \bullet \\ 1 \\ \{1\} \end{pmatrix},$$
$$\begin{pmatrix} \bullet \\ 1 \\ \mathbb{B} \end{pmatrix}, \begin{pmatrix} \bullet \\ X \\ \varnothing \end{pmatrix}, \begin{pmatrix} \bullet \\ X \\ \{0\} \end{pmatrix}, \begin{pmatrix} \bullet \\ X \\ \{1\} \end{pmatrix} \text{ and } \begin{pmatrix} \bullet \\ X \\ \mathbb{B} \end{pmatrix}.$$

Therefore, the intermediate alphabet is actually composed of triplets of symbols, organised in three layers, one on top of the other.

At the top, the symbols $\{\circ, \bullet\}$ form an internal counter of the number of cycles. Each cycle has a uniform top layer, with either only $\circ$ symbols or only $\bullet$ symbols, and is always succeeded by a cycle with a uniform top layer using the opposite symbol. Alternating between these two symbols at each new cycle allows the solution to tell if any triplet and its left neighbour originate from the same cycle.

In the middle layer, the symbol in $\{0, 1, X\}$ represents the value contained at any particular location of the configuration. The symbol X indicates the positions in the configuration where a 0 or a 1 has been removed. There is no X in the initial configuration; they are used to replace binary symbols from this layer as the automaton removes them from the configuration over time.

As for the bottom layer, the symbols $\{\varnothing, \{0\}, \{1\}, \mathbb{B}\}$ are related to the memory of the moving head of the machine encoded in the cellular automaton. This memory is a set that can store one individual 0 and one individual 1, which are taken from the configuration. A memory of value $\varnothing$ means no symbol has yet been taken from the configuration in the current cycle, while a memory of $\{0\}$ (respectively, $\{1\}$) means that only a 0 symbol (respectively, a 1 symbol) has been taken in the current cycle, and a memory of $\mathbb{B}$ means both a 0 and a 1 have been taken in the current cycle. While a memory symbol appears at the bottom layer of every intermediate symbol of a configuration, not all of them are meaningful. The memory symbol considered to be the actual memory of the automaton (its *active memory*) is the one that has been added most recently in the configuration.

Based on the previous description of the layers, it is clear that there are indeed $2 \times 3 \times 4 = 24$ possible triplets; however, since the triplets $\begin{pmatrix} \circ \\ 0 \\ \varnothing \end{pmatrix}$, $\begin{pmatrix} \circ \\ 0 \\ \{1\} \end{pmatrix}$, $\begin{pmatrix} \circ \\ 1 \\ \varnothing \end{pmatrix}$, $\begin{pmatrix} \circ \\ 1 \\ \{0\} \end{pmatrix}$, $\begin{pmatrix} \bullet \\ 0 \\ \varnothing \end{pmatrix}$, $\begin{pmatrix} \bullet \\ 0 \\ \{1\} \end{pmatrix}$, $\begin{pmatrix} \bullet \\ 1 \\ \varnothing \end{pmatrix}$ and $\begin{pmatrix} \bullet \\ 1 \\ \{0\} \end{pmatrix}$ are never used, they are not considered part of the intermediate alphabet, bringing the total down from 24 to 16.

A warning should be made to the reader at this point: from now on we will refer to the triplets of the intermediate alphabet as its *symbols*, which should not be confused with the individual symbols they are made of, as already mentioned; so, in a sense we will be stretching the meaning of the word 'symbol' associated to the components of the intermediate alphabet, just to preserve the standard jargon associated to the notion of an alphabet, that is usually said to be composed of symbols.

3.3 Mechanics of the Process

Since the constructed cellular automaton must have 0^n and 1^n as fixed points, this implies that the state transitions $00 \mapsto 0$ and $11 \mapsto 1$ must be part of the local rule. This represents an action embedded in the rule that we can refer to as *fixed point preservation*; other actions are represented in phases of the process which we refer to as *kickstart*, *propagation*, *swap* and *convergence*, as explained below.

- The *kickstart* phase is applied when 01 or 10 is detected on the initial configuration. These patterns are proof that the configuration is not uniform, and thus the cellular automaton kickstarts its computation of the density of the configuration by inserting a symbol from the intermediate alphabet. In particular, the neighbourhood 01 maps to $\begin{pmatrix} \circ \\ X \\ \{1\} \end{pmatrix}$ and 10 maps to $\begin{pmatrix} \circ \\ X \\ \{0\} \end{pmatrix}$. In the 01 case, the resulting symbol $\begin{pmatrix} \circ \\ X \\ \{1\} \end{pmatrix}$ shows that the symbol 1 is no longer in the configuration at this location, has been replaced by X, and has been placed in the active memory $\{1\}$. Furthermore, we initialise the internal counter to the value $\circ$, which indicates an odd number of cycles. An equivalent logic applies to the case 10, where the 0 is removed and placed in memory instead.

- The *propagation* phase applies directly after the kickstart phase, but also in any case of the form ab where a is an intermediate symbol and b is either in $\mathbb{B}$ or is an intermediate symbol, but with a different internal counter from a. The propagation phase represents the majority of the updates once the process has started, and its function is to propagate the counter from the left to the right, and also to remove the current character of the configuration and to add it to the memory, if possible.

  For example, the pair $\begin{pmatrix} \circ \\ X \\ \{1\} \end{pmatrix}$ 0 maps to the symbol $\begin{pmatrix} \circ \\ X \\ \mathbb{B} \end{pmatrix}$. In essence, the current symbol 0 has been replaced by an intermediate symbol, in which the symbol 0 has been removed and placed in the memory, and the counter $\circ$ has been propagated from the left. The memory is now $\mathbb{B} = \{0, 1\}$, which means a complete pair has been collected. Another typical case of the propagation phase is associated to the neighbourhood $\begin{pmatrix} \bullet \\ 0 \\ \{0\} \end{pmatrix} \begin{pmatrix} \circ \\ 0 \\ \mathbb{B} \end{pmatrix}$, which maps to $\begin{pmatrix} \bullet \\ 0 \\ \{0\} \end{pmatrix}$; here, the new character is obtained by propagating the counter and the memory from the left. As the current character 0 is already present in the memory, it is not removed. Note that the previous memory $\mathbb{B}$ date from the previous cycle, as indicated by the outdated counter $\circ$, and can thus be deleted in the process of the propagation.

  To reiterate, the propagation phase serves two purposes: to propagate the current counter and the active memory from left to right, and to remove any character it can out of the configuration and place them in the active memory.

- The *swap* phase happens any time where the updated cell is at the right hand side of another cell with an identical counter, such as in $\begin{pmatrix}\circ\\ 0\\ \mathbb{B}\end{pmatrix}\begin{pmatrix}\circ\\ X\\ \{0\}\end{pmatrix}$. What happens now depends on the state of the active memory. As a reminder, the active memory is the memory contained in the cell to the left of the cell which is to be updated. Since in this example, the active memory is $\mathbb{B}$, it is erased and the internal counter increased, therefore leading to the symbol $\begin{pmatrix}\bullet\\ X\\ \varnothing\end{pmatrix}$. This serves two purposes: the $\{0, 1\}$ pair that was harvested from the configuration in the previous cycle is deleted, and the internal counter is updated, allowing for another propagation phase.

  Two remaining cases are possible: the active memory could be empty, or a singleton. If the memory is empty, this is the situation where the initial configuration had an equal amount of 0s and 1s. As discussed previously, the solution is not required to converge in this case and thus this is classified as an undefined behaviour. However, if the active memory is a singleton $\{b\}$, the automaton now has to converge to the uniform configuration b^n. This is done by simply updating to the symbol b. For example, the neighbourhood $\begin{pmatrix}\bullet\\ 1\\ \{1\}\end{pmatrix}\begin{pmatrix}\bullet\\ X\\ \varnothing\end{pmatrix}$ would be updated to the symbol 1. The rest of the convergence is achieved through the next and final phase.

- The *convergence* phase is straightforward, and happens at any time where the left hand symbol is in $\mathbb{B}$ and the one at the right is an intermediate symbol, in which case the left hand symbol is simply propagated, as happens, for example, with the neighbourhood $0\begin{pmatrix}\circ\\ X\\ \{0\}\end{pmatrix}$ which maps to 0. This simple propagation method leads to a uniform configuration, in our example 0^n, which is a fixed point and concludes the execution of the process.

A more formal specification of the local rule is presented in Table 1. Executions of the solution on configurations of size 7 and 13 are represented in Figs. 1 and 2, respectively.

4 Proofs

For what follows, we first introduce a few technical terms:

- F is the solution previously introduced in the paper.
- For any configuration x of length n, $F(x)$ denotes the update of x through the solution.
- For any integer $k \in \mathbb{N}$, $F^k(x)$ is the repetition of the application of F on x, k times.
- Since our solution works in the sequential update schedule, we will use a notation to denote parts of an update. For any integer $i \in \{1, \ldots, n\}$, $F^{k,i}(x)$ denotes the configuration obtained after k applications of function F, followed by the application of F's local rule on cells 1 to i, in order. In effect, $F^{k,n}(x)$ is equivalent to $F^{k+1}(x)$. We denote $|x|_0$ and $|x|_1$ the number of 0 and 1 symbols in the configuration x.

Table 1. Table detailing the different cases of the proposed solution to the density classification task using an intermediate alphabet. The propagation phase is described by 4 different sets of cases, and the swap phase by 2. The symbol '?' in patterns represents a wildcard.

Pattern	Case name	Example
$00 \mapsto 0,\ 11 \mapsto 1$	Fixed point behaviour	$00 \mapsto 0$
$0\ 1 \mapsto \begin{pmatrix} \circ \\ X \\ \{1\} \end{pmatrix},\ 1\ 0 \mapsto \begin{pmatrix} \circ \\ X \\ \{0\} \end{pmatrix}$	Kickstart	$0\ 1 \mapsto \begin{pmatrix} \circ \\ X \\ \{1\} \end{pmatrix}$
$\forall M \subseteq \mathbb{B},\ b \in \mathbb{B} \setminus M,\ c \in \{\bullet, \circ\},\ \begin{pmatrix} c? \\ M \end{pmatrix} b \mapsto \begin{pmatrix} c \\ X \\ M \cup \{b\} \end{pmatrix}$	First propagation phase and removing a character	$\begin{pmatrix} \circ \\ 0 \\ \{0\} \end{pmatrix} 1 \mapsto \begin{pmatrix} \circ \\ X \\ \mathbb{B} \end{pmatrix}$
$\forall M \subseteq \mathbb{B},\ b \in \overline{M},\ c \in \{\bullet, \circ\},\ \begin{pmatrix} c? \\ M \end{pmatrix} b \mapsto \begin{pmatrix} c \\ b \\ M \end{pmatrix}$	First propagation phase, without removing a character	$\begin{pmatrix} \bullet \\ 1 \\ \{1\} \end{pmatrix} 1 \mapsto \begin{pmatrix} \bullet \\ 1 \\ \{1\} \end{pmatrix}$
$\forall c, c' \in \{\bullet, \circ\},\ c \neq c',\ \begin{pmatrix} c? \\ \mathbb{B} \end{pmatrix} \begin{pmatrix} c? \\ ? \end{pmatrix} \mapsto \begin{pmatrix} c' \\ X \\ \varnothing \end{pmatrix}$	Swap phase and resetting the memory	$\begin{pmatrix} \bullet \\ X \\ \mathbb{B} \end{pmatrix} \begin{pmatrix} \bullet \\ X \\ \{0\} \end{pmatrix} \mapsto \begin{pmatrix} \circ \\ X \\ \varnothing \end{pmatrix}$
$\forall M \subseteq \mathbb{B},\ b \in \mathbb{B} \setminus M,\ c, c' \in \{\bullet, \circ\},\ c \neq c',\ \begin{pmatrix} c? \\ M \end{pmatrix} \begin{pmatrix} c' \\ b \\ ? \end{pmatrix} \mapsto \begin{pmatrix} c \\ X \\ M \cup \{b\} \end{pmatrix}$	Propagation phase and removing a character	$\begin{pmatrix} \bullet \\ X \\ \varnothing \end{pmatrix} \begin{pmatrix} \circ \\ 1 \\ \mathbb{B} \end{pmatrix} \mapsto \begin{pmatrix} \bullet \\ X \\ \{1\} \end{pmatrix}$
$\forall M \subseteq \mathbb{B},\ b \in \overline{M},\ c, c' \in \{\bullet, \circ\},\ c \neq c',\ \begin{pmatrix} c? \\ M \end{pmatrix} \begin{pmatrix} c' \\ b \\ ? \end{pmatrix} \mapsto \begin{pmatrix} c \\ b \\ M \end{pmatrix}$	Propagation phase, without removing a character	$\begin{pmatrix} \circ \\ X \\ \mathbb{B} \end{pmatrix} \begin{pmatrix} \bullet \\ X \\ \{0\} \end{pmatrix} \mapsto \begin{pmatrix} \circ \\ X \\ \mathbb{B} \end{pmatrix}$
$\forall b \in \mathbb{B},\ c \in \{\bullet, \circ\},\ \begin{pmatrix} c? \\ \{b\} \end{pmatrix} \begin{pmatrix} c? \\ ? \end{pmatrix} \mapsto b$	Swap phase and starting the convergence	$\begin{pmatrix} \circ \\ 0 \\ \{0\} \end{pmatrix} \begin{pmatrix} \circ \\ X \\ \varnothing \end{pmatrix} \mapsto 0$
$\forall b \in \mathbb{B},\ b \begin{pmatrix} ?? \\ ? \end{pmatrix} \mapsto b$	Convergence phase	$1 \begin{pmatrix} \circ \\ 1 \\ \mathbb{B} \end{pmatrix} \mapsto 1$

We call the *active cell* the cell to the left of the next cell to be updated. If we consider some configuration $F^{k,i}(x)$ taken at some point of an execution, the active cell is the cell number i. If the symbol contained in that cell is from the intermediate alphabet, its memory part is called the *active memory* of the automata.

For the lemma that follows, we specify that a propagation phase starts when the first symbol with an updated internal counter is inserted, and lasts until the configuration has a uniform internal counter. The convergence phase at the end of an execution is not considered as a propagation phase. We refer to as a rule case as an application of the local rule. For example, by propagation rule case we mean the application of the local rule in the propagation phase.

Lemma 1. *Throughout any propagation phase, the count of* 0 *and* 1 *symbols in the configuration plus the symbols contained in the active memory are preserved.*

Proof. At the start of the propagation phase, the active memory is $\varnothing$. Thus, the count of 0 and 1 symbols at this point is exactly what is contained in the configuration. Starting from there and at each step, the local rule attempts to remove the local symbol in the configuration and to place it in memory, if

0	0	0	1	0	1	0
0	0	0	$\circ$ X $\{1\}$	$\circ$ X $\mathbb{B}$	$\circ$ 1 $\mathbb{B}$	$\circ$ 0 $\mathbb{B}$
$\circ$ 0 $\mathbb{B}$	$\circ$ 0 $\mathbb{B}$	$\circ$ 0 $\mathbb{B}$	$\bullet$ X $\varnothing$	$\bullet$ X $\varnothing$	$\bullet$ X $\{1\}$	$\bullet$ X $\mathbb{B}$
$\bullet$ 0 $\mathbb{B}$	$\bullet$ 0 $\mathbb{B}$	$\bullet$ 0 $\mathbb{B}$	$\circ$ X $\varnothing$	$\circ$ X $\varnothing$	$\circ$ X $\varnothing$	$\circ$ X $\varnothing$
$\circ$ X $\{0\}$	$\circ$ 0 $\{0\}$	$\circ$ 0 $\{0\}$	0	0	0	0
0	0	0	0	0	0	0

Fig. 1. An execution of the proposed solution to a configuration of size 7, in the form of a table. The first row contains the initial configuration, and the execution operates from top to bottom. The first propagation phase starts at line 2, column 4. This propagation phase is followed by a second one with internal counter $\bullet$, and together they remove two symbols 0 and two symbols 1 from the configuration, leaving only 0 symbols. The third propagation phase ends with the active memory $\{0\}$, which leads to the convergence phase starting at line 5.

possible. If this is the case, the removed symbol would then be contained in the active memory, preserving the count. If no symbol is taken, the active memory is simply copied over and the configuration is not altered, thus conserving the count. □

Lemma 2. *Let x be a configuration and k and i be integers such that $F^{k,i}(x)$ is a configuration which has completed p propagation phases and has not started a convergence phase. The count of 0 and 1 symbols in the configuration and the active memory of $F^{k,i}(x)$ are $|x|_0 - p$ and $|x|_1 - p$.*

Proof. We observe that at the end of a propagation phase, if the active memory is $\mathbb{B}$, a swap is applied that starts a new propagation phase and resets the active memory to $\varnothing$. Thus, if at the end of a propagation phase the count of the 0 and 1 symbols shared between the configuration and the active memory was $(|F^{k,i}(x)|_0, |F^{k,i}(x)|_1)$, the count starting in the new propagation phase has to be $(|F^{k,i}(x)|_0 - 1, |F^{k,i}(x)|_1) - 1$. Lemma 1 then tells us that this count is preserved until the start of the next propagation phase.

0	0	0	1	0	1	1	0	1	1	0	1	0
0	0	0	$\circ$ X $\{1\}$	$\circ$ X $\mathbb{B}$	$\circ$ 1 $\mathbb{B}$	$\circ$ 1 $\mathbb{B}$	$\circ$ 0 $\mathbb{B}$	$\circ$ 1 $\mathbb{B}$	$\circ$ 1 $\mathbb{B}$	$\circ$ 0 $\mathbb{B}$	$\circ$ 1 $\mathbb{B}$	$\circ$ 0 $\mathbb{B}$
$\circ$ 0 $\mathbb{B}$	$\circ$ 0 $\mathbb{B}$	$\circ$ 0 $\mathbb{B}$	$\bullet$ X $\varnothing$	$\bullet$ X $\varnothing$	$\bullet$ X $\{1\}$	$\bullet$ 1 $\{1\}$	$\bullet$ X $\mathbb{B}$	$\bullet$ 1 $\mathbb{B}$	$\bullet$ 1 $\mathbb{B}$	$\bullet$ 0 $\mathbb{B}$	$\bullet$ 1 $\mathbb{B}$	$\bullet$ 0 $\mathbb{B}$
$\bullet$ 0 $\mathbb{B}$	$\bullet$ 0 $\mathbb{B}$	$\bullet$ 0 $\mathbb{B}$	$\circ$ X $\varnothing$	$\circ$ X $\varnothing$	$\circ$ X $\varnothing$	$\circ$ X $\{1\}$	$\circ$ X $\{1\}$	$\circ$ 1 $\{1\}$	$\circ$ 1 $\{1\}$	$\circ$ X $\mathbb{B}$	$\circ$ 1 $\mathbb{B}$	$\circ$ 0 $\mathbb{B}$
$\circ$ 0 $\mathbb{B}$	$\circ$ 0 $\mathbb{B}$	$\circ$ 0 $\mathbb{B}$	$\bullet$ X $\varnothing$	$\bullet$ X $\varnothing$	$\bullet$ X $\varnothing$	$\bullet$ X $\varnothing$	$\bullet$ X $\varnothing$	$\bullet$ X $\{1\}$	$\bullet$ 1 $\{1\}$	$\bullet$ X $\{1\}$	$\bullet$ 1 $\{1\}$	$\bullet$ X $\mathbb{B}$
$\bullet$ 0 $\mathbb{B}$	$\bullet$ 0 $\mathbb{B}$	$\bullet$ 0 $\mathbb{B}$	$\circ$ X $\varnothing$	$\circ$ X $\varnothing$	$\circ$ X $\varnothing$	$\circ$ X $\varnothing$	$\circ$ X $\varnothing$	$\circ$ X $\varnothing$	$\circ$ X $\{1\}$	$\circ$ X $\{1\}$	$\circ$ 1 $\{1\}$	$\circ$ X $\{1\}$
$\circ$ X $\mathbb{B}$	$\circ$ 0 $\mathbb{B}$	$\circ$ 0 $\mathbb{B}$	$\bullet$ X $\varnothing$	$\bullet$ X $\varnothing$	$\bullet$ X $\varnothing$	$\bullet$ X $\varnothing$	$\bullet$ X $\varnothing$	$\bullet$ X $\varnothing$	$\bullet$ X $\varnothing$	$\bullet$ X $\varnothing$	$\bullet$ X $\{1\}$	$\bullet$ X $\{1\}$
$\bullet$ X $\{1\}$	$\bullet$ X $\mathbb{B}$	$\bullet$ 0 $\mathbb{B}$	$\circ$ X $\varnothing$	$\circ$ X $\varnothing$	$\circ$ X $\varnothing$	$\circ$ X $\varnothing$	$\circ$ X $\varnothing$	$\circ$ X $\varnothing$	$\circ$ X $\varnothing$	$\circ$ X $\varnothing$	$\circ$ X $\varnothing$	$\circ$ X $\varnothing$
$\circ$ X $\varnothing$	$\circ$ X $\varnothing$	$\circ$ X $\{0\}$	0	0	0	0	0	0	0	0	0	0
0	0	0	0	0	0	0	0	0	0	0	0	0

Fig. 2. An execution of the proposed solution to a configuration of size 13, in the form of a table. The first row contains the initial configuration, and the execution operates from top to bottom. This execution contains a total of 7 propagation phases, which is also the count of 1 symbols in the starting configuration, plus one.

Assuming that $|x|_0$ and $|x|_1$ are both higher than p, a sequence of p propagation phases is observed, which implies a final count of $|x|_0 - p$ and $|x|_1 - p$. □

Theorem 1. *The sequential cellular automaton F is a solution to the density classification task using an intermediate alphabet.*

Proof. Let $x \in \mathbb{B}^n$ be an initial configuration. If $|x|_0 = |x|_1$, then no special behaviour is expected. We now assume that $|x_0| \neq |x_1|$. If x is uniform in value, then it is a fixed point of F, which is a required behaviour. We now assume that x is not uniform.

This implies that a pattern 01 or 10 appears somewhere in the configuration, which implies that the kickstart rule case applies at some point, which in turns implies a number of propagation phases. We now argue that exactly $min(|x|_0, |x|_1) + 1$ propagation phases happen in the execution, followed by a convergence phase.

As shown in Lemma 2, the succession of p propagation phases removes p symbols 0 and 1 from the configuration and the active memory. We argue that as long as the configuration and active memory contains a symbol 0 and 1 at the beginning of a propagation phase, then the active memory will be $\mathbb{B}$ at the end of a propagation phase. This can be seen because all propagation rule cases try to capture symbols from the configuration into the memory at any occasions, and all symbols of the configurations are considered this way during a propagation phase. Thus, as long as the configuration and active memory contains both a 0 and 1, another propagation phase will follow the current one. It follows that a sequence of $min(|x|_0, |x|_1)$ propagation phases happen in a sequence, after which there will be no more 0 or 1 left in the configuration and active memory, which leads to an extra propagation phase which ends with an active memory of the form $\{b\}$, which then leads to a convergence phase.

When this is the case, we argue that the remaining symbol (either 0 and 1) had a greater count in the initial configuration than the other one, which implies that it was the majority symbol in the initial configuration. Furthermore, at the end of the last configuration phase, the active memory $\{b\}$ contains the symbol in majority, and the following convergence phase turns the configuration into the fixed point b^n, which proves that F is a sequential solution to the density classification task, using an intermediate alphabet. □

5 Generalisations

This solution is versatile enough to be generalised to support any finite alphabet to compute a density over, and also to support configurations in higher dimensions. In this section we present the necessary changes to realise these generalisations, along with proofs of their correctness.

5.1 Larger Alphabets

Let us consider S some finite alphabet. The generalisation of the density classification task over that alphabet is the task of converging to the uniform configuration s^n if the symbol $s \in S$ is in strict majority over the input configuration $x \in S^n$ of size n. Such a uniform configuration must be a fixed point.

We denote F_S the generalised solution, working on the extended alphabet $\Sigma = S \cup (\{\circ, \bullet\} \times (S \cup \{X\}) \times 2^S)$, where 2^S stands for the power set of S, the set of all the subsets of S. This intermediate alphabet grows exponentially in the size of the input alphabet S. Similarly to the binary case, F_S is a sequential cellular automaton of radius $\frac{1}{2}$.

The rule cases are similar to the ones in the binary solution. For any symbol $s \in S$, the rule $s\ s \mapsto s$ ensures that the uniform configurations are fixed points.

Any mismatch $s, s' \in S$ leads to the kickstart rule case $s\ s' \mapsto \binom{\overset{\circ}{X}}{\{s'\}}$. The propagation phases operate as normal, moving symbols from the configuration into the active memory when possible. The swap cases lead to another propagation phase as long as the active memory contains more than one symbol, and to a convergence phase if the memory contains exactly one symbol. An empty active memory at the end of a propagation phase leads to undefined behaviour.

Theorem 2. *The sequential cellular automaton F_S is a solution to the density classification task over the set S using an intermediate alphabet.*

Proof. We follow the steps of the proof in the binary case, the main difference being that we count the number of propagation phases in a different way. In each propagation phase, the active memory accumulates one of each symbol of S still in the configuration, and the propagation phases stop when the active memory is a singleton at the end of propagation. Such an event happens when each symbol that is not in majority in the initial configuration has been taken out. This time is exactly the maximum of the counts of the non-majority symbols, or the count of the second most present symbol in the initial configuration. After this exact amount of propagation phases, the configuration only contains X and the majority symbols, and an extra propagation phase leads to a convergence phase. □

5.2 Higher Dimensions

For $d \geq 1$ an integer, we generalise the density classification task over an alphabet S to any number d of dimensions. Instead of considering cyclic configurations, we here consider cuboids of sides $(n_1, n_2, \dots, n_d)$ in d dimensions, which associate a symbol in S to any coordinate $(x_1, x_2, \dots, x_d)$. The density task in higher dimensions then asks to replace all symbols of this cuboids by the symbol which is in strict majority in the initial configuration.

The generalisation of our solution on d-dimensional configurations, denoted $F_{S,d}$, is still a sequential rule, which explores the space of coordinates in an iterative order. We denote it $F_{S,d}$. For example, for $d = 2$ and $n_1 = n_2 = 3$, the update sequence is $((0,0),(1,0),(2,0),(0,1),(1,1),(2,1),(0,2),(1,2),(2,2))$.

The neighbourhood of our solution is extended to contain one neighbour per dimension, plus the cell itself. For $(x_1, x_2, \dots, x_d)$ the position of a given cell, the neighbours of this cell are those with coordinates $(x_1-1, x_2, \dots, x_d)$, $(x_1-1, x_2-1, x_3, \dots, x_d)$, $(x_1-1, x_2-1, x_3-1, x_4, \dots, x_d)$, ..., $(x_1-1, x_2-1, \dots, x_d-1)$, plus $(x_1, x_2, \dots, x_d)$, the cell itself. This neighbourhood is a subset of the Moore neighbourhood in d dimensions, as it always contains corners.

The local rule of $F_{S,d}$ is defined as the following generalisation of the one-dimensional solution over S. Firstly, the fixed point behaviour is applied when the neighbourhood is of a uniform value in S. Secondly, the kickstart rule case is applied if the neighbourhood only contains symbols in S but is not uniform.

Thirdly, the propagation phase must be applied by discerning which neighbour was the cell to be last updated in the sequence; or more precisely, it must determine what the active memory is. This is done by considering all the neighbours which are in the intermediate alphabet, and taking the larger memory, by comparing them by set inclusion. We then apply the one-dimensional local rule as if this active memory was in the cell to the left, and the present cell the cell to the right.

If both the present cells and all its neighbours are intermediate symbols with a uniform internal counter, we apply the swap rule case. The active memory is computed as before, by taking the maximum between the memories of the neighbours.

Finally, if the present cell is in the intermediate alphabet and has at least one neighbour with a value in S, we propagate that value to converge to a fixed point.

An execution of our generalised solution over a two dimensional configuration of size 9 over the alphabet $\{0, 1, 2\}$ is shown in Fig. 3.

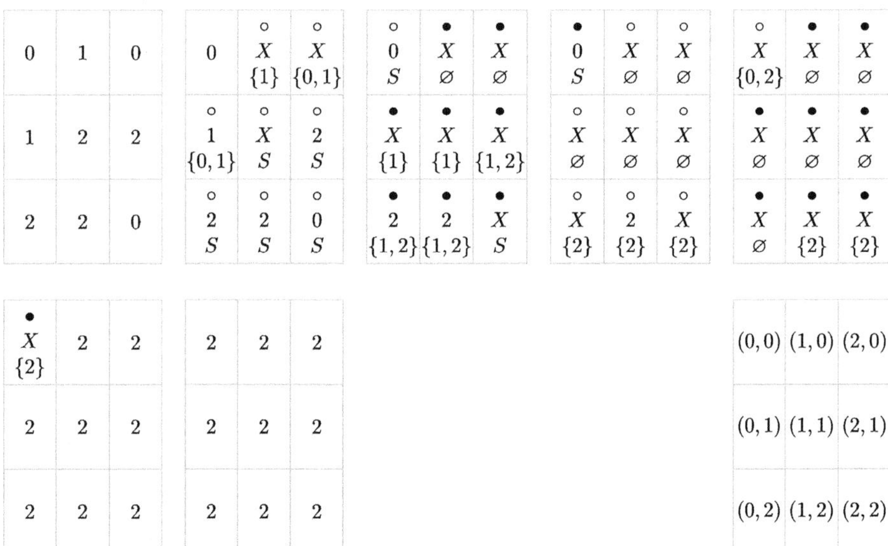

Fig. 3. An execution of $F_{\{0,1,2\},2}$ on a 3 by 3 configuration, with the set S of the input alphabet being $\{0, 1, 2\}$. This execution lasts for 7 configurations, which are illustrated from left to right, top to bottom. Within each configuration, the sequential order is from left to right, and from top to bottom. The element at the bottom right of the figure indicates the coordinates of the cells; for instance, the neighbours of $(0, 0)$ are the cells $(2, 0)$, $(2, 2)$ and $(0, 0)$ itself. As all these cells have the value 0 in the initial configuration, the cell $(0, 0)$ does not change value during the first update.

Theorem 3. *The sequential cellular automaton $F_{S,d}$ is a solution to the density classification task over the set S in d dimensions using an intermediate alphabet.*

Proof. This proof works by showing that $F_{S,d}$ boils down to the application of F_S to the d-dimensional configuration as if it were one-dimensional, by reconstructing the active memory from its neighborhood. We will show that this is the case on every phase of the solution.

First, observe that if the configuration is uniform over S, then it is a fixed point of $F_{S,d}$. However, if the configuration is non-uniform over S, then there exist two locations that differ. We claim that if two locations differ, then a kickstart rule case happens in the first update of the configuration. This is true because a path can be made from any two locations of the configuration only using jumps in the local neighbourhood of the cells. If the starting and ending points of such a path have different values, then this path is bound to have two consecutive values that differ, and those two values would be the value of a cell and one of its neighbours, which leads to a kickstart rule case when this cell is updated.

Let us assume that the intermediate symbol introduced in the kickstart rule case is in the cell of coordinates $(x_1, x_2, \dots x_d)$. Let us show that a propagation phase now starts and replaces the entire configuration with intermediate symbols.

If we assume that $x_1 < n_1 - 1$, then the next coordinate to be updated is $(x_1 + 1, x_2, \dots, x_d)$. This new cell has not been updated yet since the kickstart, and thus contains a symbol in S. The first cell in its neighbourhood is the active cell, and thus the propagation rule case is applied.

Let us now assume that $x_1 = n_1 - 1$, but that $x_2 < n_2 - 1$. This means that the next cell to be updated is of coordinates $(x_1 + 1, x_2 + 1, x_3, \dots, x_d)$. Similarly to before, this cell has not yet been updated and contains a symbol over S. Moreover, its neighbour at coordinate $(x_1, x_2+1, x_3, \dots, x_d)$ has not been updated either, and the neighbour at coordinate $(x_1, x_2, \dots, x_d)$ is the active cell, and contains an intermediate symbol. This means that we apply a propagation rule case; to do so, the local rule is defined to apply a propagation phase as in F_S by taking the active memory as the largest memory within its neighbourhood. As the memory only accumulates symbols throughout a propagation phase, taking the largest set (in the sense of set inclusion) is always a defined operation that computes the correct active memory. Note that the configuration symbol of the active cell (in $S \cup X$) is actually never relevant to apply the local rule, and it is not necessary to know its value. It follows that one step of propagation is applied as it would in the one-dimensional solution F_S.

This logic works for any number of dimensions; when the sequential order jumps in the direction of the k-th dimension, the $k - 1$ first neighbours of the new cell have not yet been updated in the current propagation phase, but the k-th neighbour is the active cell, the last cell to be updated. This means that the propagation phase operates as the one dimensional local rule would, up to the point where the entire configuration has been converted to the intermediate alphabet with a uniform internal counter. The new cell to be updated has the active cell within its neighbourhood, which means that it can accurately compute the active memory by taking the largest memory in its neighbourhood. If this active memory is a singleton, this means that the previous propagation phases removed all symbols except one, and the solution can converge. If the active memory is empty, then the density is not defined over the initial configuration and the behaviour is said to be undefined. If the active memory has size at least 2, then the solution starts a new propagation phase by emptying the memory and updating the internal counter.

Overall, this solution successfully explores a d-dimensional configuration to apply the local rule as if it were one-dimensional, therefore leading to the result. □

6 Simulating Arbitrary Cellular Automata

Our solution illustrates how an intermediate alphabet paired with a sequential update schedule allows one to solve the density classification task. We are confident that the same methods can be used to solve any consensus problem that can be solved by any parallel cellular automata. This section is speculative and reflects prospective ideas that could lead to future work in this area.

6.1 Simulating Larger Neighbourhoods

It is reasonable to think that a local function with neighbourhood $\{-1, 0\}$ and sequential update can use an intermediate alphabet to simulate a larger neighbourhood. To achieve this, we propagate the value of each cell to the right, allowing a cell to contain a larger collection of values of cells to its left. We then apply the simulated function over this array contained in a single symbol. This allows for the simulation of any cellular automaton with neighbourhood $\{-r, \ldots, 0\}$ for some integer r.

We can then use this simulated cellular automaton to simulate any cellular automaton in a sequential update schedule by having each cell to apply the local function of the cell at the center of its neighbourhood, instead of its own. Since the local function has neighbourhood $\{-r, \ldots, 0\}$, the cell at index 0 in the simulator automaton would compute the local function of the cell at index $\lceil \frac{r}{2} \rceil$ in the simulated automaton. This implies a shift of $\lceil \frac{r}{2} \rceil$ to the right at each step of the simulation, which is not an issue when converging to a uniform fixed point.

Using this reasoning, we conjecture that any sequential one-dimensional cellular automata can be simulated by a sequential cellular automata of neighbourhood $\{-1, 0\}$ using an intermediate alphabet.

6.2 Simulating a Parallel Update Schedule

Once an arbitrary sequential cellular automaton can be simulated, we use it to simulate a parallel cellular automaton by increasing the number of symbols, so that updates can be done in a double-buffer strategy.

The configuration of the simulating automaton contains two configurations of the simulated automaton. One contains the initial configuration, the other is initialised to an arbitrary value. An extra bit of information in each cell indicates which configuration is current and which will serve to store its update. If the current configuration is contained in the first buffer, the new value of each cell is placed in the second buffer, allowing for an order-independent update of the entire configuration. Both buffers are swapped once per completed update of the configuration using a similar strategy used in the 'swap phase' of the solution presented in this paper.

In conjunction with the previous conjecture, we conjecture that any one-dimensional parallel cellular automata can be simulated by a sequential cellular automata of neighbourhood $\{-1, 0\}$ using an intermediate alphabet.

7 Closing Words

The presented solution pushes the boundary of the classification tasks known to be possible using cellular automata. It proves that using an intermediate alphabet together with a sequential update schedule is enough to solve the density classification task.

Following what the extensive literature available suggests, especially [18], we are of the opinion that a solution of the problem using the synchronous update schedule does not exist. Proving this conjecture would be a fitting continuation of the present work, and would confirm that the present solution is in fact one example of some minimal requirements that are sufficient to solve the density classification task.

Acknowledgements. P.P.B. thanks the Brazilian agencies CNPq (Conselho Nacional de Desenvolvimento Científico e Tecnológico) for the research grant PQ 303356/2022-7, and CAPES (Coordenação de Aperfeiçoamento de Pessoal de Nível Superior) for Mackenzie-PrInt research grant no 88887.310281/2018-00. P.P.B. and E.R. jointly thank CAPES for the research grant STIC-AmSud no. 88881.694458/2022-01, and P.P. thanks CAPES for the postdoc grant no. 88887.833212/2023-00.

References

1. Aburas, M.M., Ho, Y.M., Ramli, M.F., Ash'aari, Z.H.: The simulation and prediction of spatio-temporal urban growth trends using cellular automata modes: a review. Int. J. Appl. Earth Obs. Geoinf. **52**, 380–389 (2016)
2. Balbi, P.P., Ruivo, E., Faria, F.: Synchronous solution of the parity problem on cyclic configurations, with elementary cellular automaton rule 150, over a family of directed, non-circulant, regular graphs. Inf. Sci. **615**, 578–603 (2022)
3. Betel, H., de Oliveira, P.P.B., Flocchini, P.: Solving the parity problem in one-dimensional cellular automata. Nat. Comput. **12**, 323–337 (2013)
4. Briceno, R., de Espanés, P.M., Osses, A., Rapaport, I.: Solving the density classification problem with a large diffusion and small amplification cellular automaton. Physica D **261**, 70–80 (2013)

5. Faria, F., Ruivo, E., Balbi, P.P.: Generalisation of a synchronous solution of the parity problem on cyclic configurations over a non-circulant graph. Inf. Sci. **666**, 120387 (2024)
6. Fatès, N.A.: Stochastic cellular automata solve the density classification problem with an arbitrary precision. In: Symposium on Theoretical Aspects of Computer Science-STACS 2011, vol. 9, pp. 284–295. Schloss Dagstuhl–Leibniz-Zentrum fuer Informatik (2011)
7. Hoekstra, A.G., Kroc, J., Sloot, P.M.A.: Introduction to modeling of complex systems using cellular automata. In: Kroc, J., Sloot, P.M.A., Hoekstra, A.G. (eds.) Simulating Complex Systems by Cellular Automata. UCS, pp. 1–16. Springer, Heidelberg (2010). https://doi.org/10.1007/978-3-642-12203-3_1
8. Kari, J., Le Gloannec, B.: Modified traffic cellular automaton for the density classification task. Fund. Inform. **116**(1–4), 141–156 (2012)
9. Kutrib, M.: Complexity of one-way cellular automata. In: Isokawa, T., Imai, K., Matsui, N., Peper, F., Umeo, H. (eds.) AUTOMATA 2014. LNCS, vol. 8996, pp. 3–18. Springer, Cham (2015). https://doi.org/10.1007/978-3-319-18812-6_1
10. Land, M., Belew, R.K.: No perfect two-state cellular automata for density classification exists. Phys. Rev. Lett. **74**(25), 5148 (1995)
11. Leal, L., Montealegre, P., Osses, A., Rapaport, I.: A large diffusion and small amplification dynamics for density classification on graphs. Int. J. Mod. Phys. C **34**(05), 2350056 (2023)
12. Lee, K.M., Xu, H., Chau, H.F.: Parity problem with a cellular automaton solution. Phys. Rev. E **64**(2), 026702 (2001)
13. Martins, C.L.M., de Oliveira, P.P.B.: Evolving sequential combinations of elementary cellular automata rules. In: Capcarrère, M.S., Freitas, A.A., Bentley, P.J., Johnson, C.G., Timmis, J. (eds.) ECAL 2005. LNCS (LNAI), vol. 3630, pp. 461–470. Springer, Heidelberg (2005). https://doi.org/10.1007/11553090_47
14. Mikler, A.R., Venkatachalam, S., Abbas, K.: Modeling infectious diseases using global stochastic cellular automata. J. Biol. Syst. **13**(04), 421–439 (2005)
15. Montalva-Medel, M., de Oliveira, P.P.B., Goles, E.: A portfolio of classification problems by one-dimensional cellular automata, over cyclic binary configurations and parallel update. Nat. Comput. **17**, 663–671 (2018)
16. Ninagawa, S.: Solving the parity problem with elementary cellular automaton rule 60. In: Proceedings of AUTOMATA and JAC, 2012 (2012)
17. Perrotin, P.: Density solution checker, August 2024. https://github.com/Demonagon/density_checker
18. Ruivo, E., Perrot, K., Balbi, P.P., Perrotin, P.: Negative results on density determination with one-dimensional cellular automata with block-sequential asynchronous updates. J. Comput. Sci. **82**, 102430 (2024)
19. Ruivo, E.L.P., de Oliveira, P.P.B.: A perfect solution to the parity problem with elementary cellular automaton 150 under asynchronous update. Inf. Sci. **493**, 138–151 (2019)
20. Wolf-Gladrow, D.A.: Lattice-Gas Cellular Automata and Lattice Boltzmann Models: An Introduction. Springer, Heidelberg (2004). https://doi.org/10.1007/b72010

Descriptive Complexity of Sensitivity of Cellular Automata

Tom Favereau[1(✉)] and Ville Salo[2]

[1] Mines Nancy, University of Lorraine, Nancy, France
tom.favereau@etu.mines-nancy.univ-lorraine.fr

[2] University of Turku, Turku, Finland
vosalo@utu.fi

Abstract. We study the computational complexity of determining whether a cellular automaton is sensitive to initial conditions. We show that this problem is Π_2^0-complete in dimension 1 and Σ_3^0-complete in dimension 2 and higher. This solves a question posed by Sablik and Theyssier.

Keywords: Cellular automata · Sensitivity · Arithmetical hierarchy

1 Introduction

Cellular automata are discrete dynamical systems that exhibit complex behavior despite their simple local rules. There have been numerous attempts to classify such systems, with the first notable classification proposed by Wolfram [9] for one-dimensional cellular automata. However, this classification lacked rigorous formality, which led Kůrka [2] to propose a more formal classification of one-dimensional cellular automata based on their sensitivity to initial conditions.

Other classification schemes have also been proposed, such as Culik's classification. The arithmetical complexity of Culik's classes has been established and demonstrated by Sutner in [8]. The decidability of Kůrka's classes, particularly the problem of sensitivity to initial conditions, was studied by Durand et al. [1], while the reversible case was addressed by Lukkarila [4].

Sablik and Theyssier [7] showed that Kůrka's classification no longer holds in higher dimensions and that additional classes must be introduced. In the same article, they investigated the arithmetical complexity of Kůrka's classes. They demonstrated that sensitivity to initial conditions is Π_2^0 in one dimension, but did not prove completeness, and showed Σ_3^0-hardness starting from dimension three, but the exact complexity of sensitivity within the arithmetical hierarchy was left open.

Understanding the dynamical properties of cellular automata, particularly their sensitivity to initial conditions, is crucial for characterizing their behavior. In this paper, we address these open questions and provide a precise characterization of the computational complexity of determining sensitivity across different

Published by Springer Nature Switzerland AG 2026
S. Riva and A. Richard (Eds.): AUTOMATA 2025, LNCS 15831, pp. 123–138, 2026.
https://doi.org/10.1007/978-3-032-01570-9_9

dimensions. Specifically, we demonstrate that sensitivity to initial conditions is Π_2^0-complete in one dimension and Σ_3^0-complete in two dimensions and higher. As a corollary, we provide a new proof that the finite nilpotency problem for cellular automata, originally proven by Sutner in [8], is Π_2^0-complete. Additionally, we explore an application of our results by constructing a cellular automaton whose sensitivity is equivalent to the truth of the twin prime conjecture. These findings not only fill gaps left by previous research but also expose the fundamental difference in complexity between one-dimensional and higher-dimensional cellular automata with respect to sensitivity.

Our main results establish a complete classification of the complexity of the sensitivity problem in cellular automata. We formally state them as follows.

For one-dimensional cellular automata, establish:

Theorem 1. *The problem of determining whether a one-dimensional cellular automaton is sensitive is Π_2^0-complete.*

For higher dimension, we establish:

Theorem 2. *For $d > 1$, the problem of determining whether a d-dimensional cellular automaton is sensitive is Σ_3^0-complete.*

The proofs of these theorems rely on embedding Turing machines into cellular automata and reducing the problems TOT and COF to the respective sensitivity problem. With these new results, the classification of cellular automata with respect to sensitivity can be summarized in Table 1. Formal definitions and preliminaries are provided in Sect. 2. We present the proof of Theorem 1 in Sect. 3, and the proof of Theorem 2 in Sect. 4. An application is given in Sect. 5.

Table 1. Descriptive complexity of Kůrka's classification of cellular automata. The set $\mathcal{E}$ denotes the equicontinuity points. The notation Π_2^0-c indicates Π_2^0-completeness, while Σ_1^0-? signifies that completeness is unknown. A question mark (?) indicates that both completeness and the position in the hierarchy are unknown. Our contributions are highlighted with an asterisk.

	$\mathcal{E} = A^{\mathbb{Z}^d}$	$\mathcal{E} \neq \emptyset$	$\mathcal{E} = \emptyset$	Sensitive	Expansive
$d = 1$	Σ_1^0-c	Σ_2^0-c*	Π_2^0-c*	Π_2^0-c*	Σ_1^0-?
$d > 1$	Σ_1^0-c	?	?	Σ_3^0-c*	Σ_1^0-?

2 Preliminaries

We will first recall some basic definitions that we will need throughout this document.

Definition 1 (Cellular Automaton). *A* ***cellular automaton*** *is a quadruple (d, S, N, f) where d is the dimension of the automaton, S is a finite set of states, N is a finite subset of $\mathbb{Z}^d$ called the neighborhood, and $f : S^N \to S$ is the local transition function. This induces a global function $F : S^{\mathbb{Z}^d} \to S^{\mathbb{Z}^d}$.*

The sensitivity to initial conditions is a property of dynamical systems that states that for any configuration, we can always find an arbitrarily close configuration that tends to diverge from our original configuration. To formalize this we endow $S^{\mathbb{Z}^d}$ with the following metric:

$$d(x, y) = 2^{-\min\{\|n\|_\infty | x(n) \neq y(n)\}} \tag{1}$$

where $\|n\|_\infty = \max_{1 \leq i \leq d} |n_i|$ denotes the supremum norm on $\mathbb{Z}^d$.

We formalize the concept of sensitivity in the following definition:

Definition 2 (Sensitivity). *A cellular automaton F is* ***sensitive*** *to initial conditions if there exists $\epsilon > 0$ such that for all configurations x and $\delta > 0$, there exists $y \in B_\delta(x)$ and $n \in \mathbb{N}$ such that $d(F^n(x), F^n(y)) > \epsilon$.*

In one dimension, a famous result states a connection between sensitivity and having words that block information, i.e., blocking words. Blocking words are characterized by a length that no information can cross. Indeed, to truly prevent information from propagating, such words must have a length larger than the automaton's radius.

Given a set $K \subset \mathbb{Z}^d$ and a word $w \in S^K$, we write $w \sqsubset_K u$ if $u \in S^{\mathbb{Z}^d}$ contains w at position K, and we define the *cylinder*:

$$\text{Cyl}(w, K) = \{u \in S^{\mathbb{Z}^d} \mid w \sqsubset_K u\} \tag{2}$$

We provide a definition of an m-blocking word:

Definition 3 (m-blocking word). *A word $w \in S^*$ together with an integer p is* ***m-blocking*** *if for any configurations $u, v \in Cyl(w, [0, |w| - 1])$, for all $n \in \mathbb{N}, F^n(u)_{|[p,p+m]} = F^n(v)_{|[p,p+m]}$.*

Hence, we can state the well-known characterization of sensitivity in one dimension:

Theorem 3 (Kůrka [3]). *A one-dimensional cellular automaton with radius r is not sensitive if and only if it has an r-blocking word.*

We will also need a notion of blocking word in higher dimensions. In dimension d, we want an m-blocking word to be any pattern that contains a subpattern of size m^d that no information can enter.

We define the *shift action* by:

$$\sigma^p(x)_u = x_{u+p}, \quad \forall x \in S^{\mathbb{Z}^d}, \ \forall u, p \in \mathbb{Z}^d \tag{3}$$

$$\sigma^p(K) = \{u + p \mid u \in K\}, \quad \forall K \subset \mathbb{Z}^d, \ \forall p \in \mathbb{Z}^d \tag{4}$$

Definition 4 (Higher dimensional m-blocking word). *For any finite subset $K \subset \mathbb{Z}^d$ together with a vector $p \in \mathbb{Z}^d$ such that $\sigma^p([0,m]^d) \subseteq K$, a word $w \in S^K$ is* **m-blocking** *if for any configurations u, v containing w at the position K, for all $n \in \mathbb{N}$, $F^n(u)_{|\sigma^p([0,m]^d)} = F^n(v)_{|\sigma^p([0,m]^d)}$.*

With that definition, we state the following lemma that shows how one can extend the blocking word characterization for higher-dimensional cellular automata.

Lemma 1. *A cellular automaton is not sensitive if and only if it has arbitrarily large blocking words.*

Proof. If F is a sensitive cellular automaton, there exists $\epsilon > 0$ such that for all x and $\delta > 0$, there exists $y \in B_\delta(x)$ and n such that $d(F^n(x), F^n(y)) > \epsilon$. This means that there exists $m > -\log_2(\epsilon)$ such that arbitrarily close configurations will eventually differ on $[0,m]^d$, hence there is no m-blocking word.

Conversely, if F is not sensitive, for every $\epsilon > 0$ and $m > -\log_2(\epsilon)$, we can find a pattern π such that every configuration that matches with π at position 0 will never differ on $[0,m]^d$. Hence, we have arbitrarily large blocking words. □

Turing machines are abstract computational models that provide a formal definition of a computable function. These machines can perform basic operations such as reading, writing, and moving the head. Their power lies in their ability to simulate any algorithm or computational process. We will use them to prove our complexity results.

A Turing machine is formally defined as a 5-tuple (Q, A, q_i, q_h, δ) where Q is a finite set of states, including an initial state q_i and a halting state q_h; A is a finite alphabet that contains at least the blank symbol $\sqcup$ and the symbol 1; and $\delta : Q \times A \to Q \times A \times \{-1, 0, 1\}$ is the transition function, such that for all $a \in A$, $\delta(q_h, a) = (q_h, a, 0)$. Inputs are natural numbers n represented in unary as bi-infinite tapes containing only blanks and a block of n consecutive 1s, i.e., the tape content is $\sqcup^\infty 1^n \sqcup^\infty$, with the head initially positioned on the first 1.

The transition function δ determines the machine's behavior: given a current state and a symbol under the head, it specifies the next state, the symbol to write, and the direction to move the head (-1 for left, 0 for stay, 1 for right).

Fix an enumeration of Turing machines; we denote by M_e the e-th Turing machine. Let $W_e := \{x \mid M_e \text{ halts on } x\}$ be the set of inputs on which M_e halts. We now introduce the two sets that we will use in our proof:

$$\mathrm{TOT} := \{e \mid W_e = \mathbb{N}\} \tag{5}$$

and

$$\mathrm{COF} := \{e \mid W_e \text{ is cofinite}\} \tag{6}$$

Lemma 2. *TOT is Π_2^0-complete and COF is Σ_3^0-complete.*

Proof. The reader can find a proof of these results in [6]. □

Let us note a basic result about Turing machines: semi-infinite tape Turing machines are equivalent to bi-infinite tape Turing machines.

Proposition 1. *Given a Turing machine M_2, there exists a semi-infinite Turing machine M_1 such that for all $x \in \mathbb{N}$, M_2 halts on x if and only if M_1 halts on x.*

Proof. The backward direction is trivial. For the converse, we can simulate any bi-infinite Turing machine on a semi-infinite tape by instructing the machine, when it wants to move left to 0, to copy all its non-blank symbols one step to the right. □

In particular, this proposition allows us to consider the sets TOT and COF as sets of indices of semi-infinite Turing machines.

Finally, we introduce our main tool for lifting results to higher dimensions: slicing.

Definition 5 (Slicing). *For any d-dimensional cellular automaton with global function F, we can construct a $(d+1)$-dimensional cellular automaton with the same function F, which corresponds to applying the d-dimensional cellular automaton independently on each hyperplane $x_{d+1} = k$ (called a **slice**).*

This construction often allows us to reduce a d-dimensional problem to a $(d+1)$-dimensional one.

3 One-Dimensional Cellular Automata

In this section, we prove our first result: the Π_2^0-completeness of the sensitivity problem for one-dimensional cellular automata. We begin with a simple lemma.

Lemma 3. *The problem of determining whether a given cellular automaton has an m-blocking word is in Σ_2^0.*

Proof. Observe that in the definition of a blocking word, we only need to quantify over finite objects. Hence, having an m-blocking word can be written as:

$$\begin{aligned} &\exists K \subset \mathbb{Z}^d, \exists p \in \mathbb{Z}^d, \exists w \in S^K, \forall u, v \in (S^d)^*, n \in \mathbb{N}, \\ &\quad (\sigma^p([0,m]^d) \subset K \wedge w \sqsubset_K u \wedge w \sqsubset_K v) \\ &\quad \implies F^n(u)_{|\sigma^p([0,m]^d)} = F^n(v)_{|\sigma^p([0,m]^d)} \end{aligned} \tag{7}$$

This formulation clearly places the problem in Σ_2^0. □

3.1 Upper Bound on Complexity of the Sensitivity Problem

The sensitivity problem for one-dimensional cellular automata is in Π_2^0. The proof follows directly from Lemma 3. We note that this result was already known from Sablik and Theyssier [7].

Lemma 4. *The problem of determining whether a one-dimensional cellular automaton is sensitive to initial conditions is in Π_2^0.*

Proof. A cellular automaton is sensitive to initial conditions if and only if it does not have a blocking word of any length. This is clearly a Π_2^0 formula, as it negates a Σ_2^0 formula (from Lemma 3). □

3.2 Construction of G_e

To prove Π_2^0-hardness, we reduce from TOT, which is known to be Π_2^0-hard. Given a number e, we denote the associated Turing machine by $M_e = (Q, A, q_i, q_h, \delta)$.

It is important to note that we consider configurations starting from any state and with any distribution of symbols—not just those that result from a valid evolution of the Turing machine from its initial state. This includes configurations that do not correspond to any correct computation. Such 'degenerate' configurations arise because, in a cellular automaton, any configuration can serve as an initial one. We will explain how to address this issue in the following sections of the construction.

We construct a cellular automaton G_e as follows:

The state set of G_e is $(1 \cup \{\sqcup\}) \times ((Q \cup \{\sqcup\}) \times A) \times (\{<, >, p, \sqcup\} \cup X)$, where: $<$ and $>$ are delimiter symbols that partition the space into computational blocks and $X = \{x_r, x_l, x_0\}$ is a set of elements that handle the extension of the computational zone and restart the Turing machine on the input tape to prevent degenerate configurations. G_e has radius one.

It is a three-tape cellular automaton with a witness input tape, a working tape, and a delimiter tape.

The cellular automaton G_e simulates multiple copies of M_e, where each copy operates within its own computational block, delimited by sequences of $<$ and $>$ symbols. A typical configuration is shown in Fig. 1.

…	$>$	$>$	$>$	$>$	x_l	$<$	$<$	$<$	$>$	$>$	x_r	$<$	$<$	…
…	a'	a'	b'	q, b'	c'	c'	d'	d'	a'	b'	q, c'	d'	a'	…
…	a	a	b	b	c	c	d	d	a	b	c	d	a	…

Fig. 1. Structure of computational blocks in G_e. The upper row shows the delimiters and machine heads, while the lower rows show the tape content.

The transition rules of G_e enforce the following behaviors:

1. The set X contains x_r, which moves to the right on computational blocks, x_l, which moves to the left, and x_0, which moves to the left while resetting the computation on the witness tape. Symbols move back and forth in the computational zone and always try to extend it to the right when possible. When this happens, the Turing machine restarts on the input tape (eventually eliminating degenerate configurations).

2. < and > delimit computational blocks. x_r can only move to the right if it is to the left of a <; otherwise, it becomes an x_l. Similarly x_0 and x_l can only move to the left if they are to the right of a >; otherwise, they become an x_r.
3. The blank symbol on the witness tape propagates to the right on the computational block, preventing the input from being divided by a blank.
4. When a machine halts, it writes a blank symbol that propagates throughout the computational block.
5. The x symbol can extend its computational block if and only if the machine to its right has been destroyed.
6. p is a particle that always travels to the right on blank symbols of the first tape and gets destroyed when it encounters non-blank cells. It allows us to establish sensitivity.

We provide the complete rule of the cellular automaton G_e in Fig. 2.

3.3 Lower Bound and Π_2^0-Hardness

Lemma 5. *For any $e \in \mathbb{N}$, the Turing machine M_e halts on all inputs if and only if the cellular automaton G_e is sensitive.*

Proof. We now prove that $e \in \mathrm{TOT}$ if and only if G_e is sensitive.

If $e \in$ TOT: We need to show that G_e is sensitive. Let w be any word. We can take $y \in \mathrm{Cyl}(w)$ such that y has only blank symbols on all tapes to the right of w, and to the left, there is only one p particle moving to the right and blank symbols.

Since $e \in \mathrm{TOT}$, all computational blocks in w will eventually be destroyed. Indeed, in the rightmost computational block in w, the x symbols will eventually be inserted and then be able to extend the computational block arbitrarily far, allowing the Turing machine to compute on its input without being restarted and with arbitrary large space. Hence, the rightmost Turing machine will halt and erase itself in finitely many steps, leaving space for the machine to its left. Therefore, in finitely many steps, w will become blank. Thus, the particle we placed to the left of w can pass through w if the particle is placed far enough. Therefore, since we can choose whether or not to place the particle, this establishes sensitivity.

If $e \notin TOT$: Then there exists an input n such that M_e runs forever on n without halting. Consider the word pattern uu where u is a computational block of size at least radius of G_e containing input n. The machine simulated in the second copy of u will never halt and will never be destroyed. Consequently, the machine in the first copy of u remains confined to its computational block and likewise never halts. This creates a barrier that no information can cross. Therefore uu is an r-blocking word, proving that G_e is not sensitive. □

Thus, we have shown that G_e is sensitive if and only if $e \in \mathrm{TOT}$.

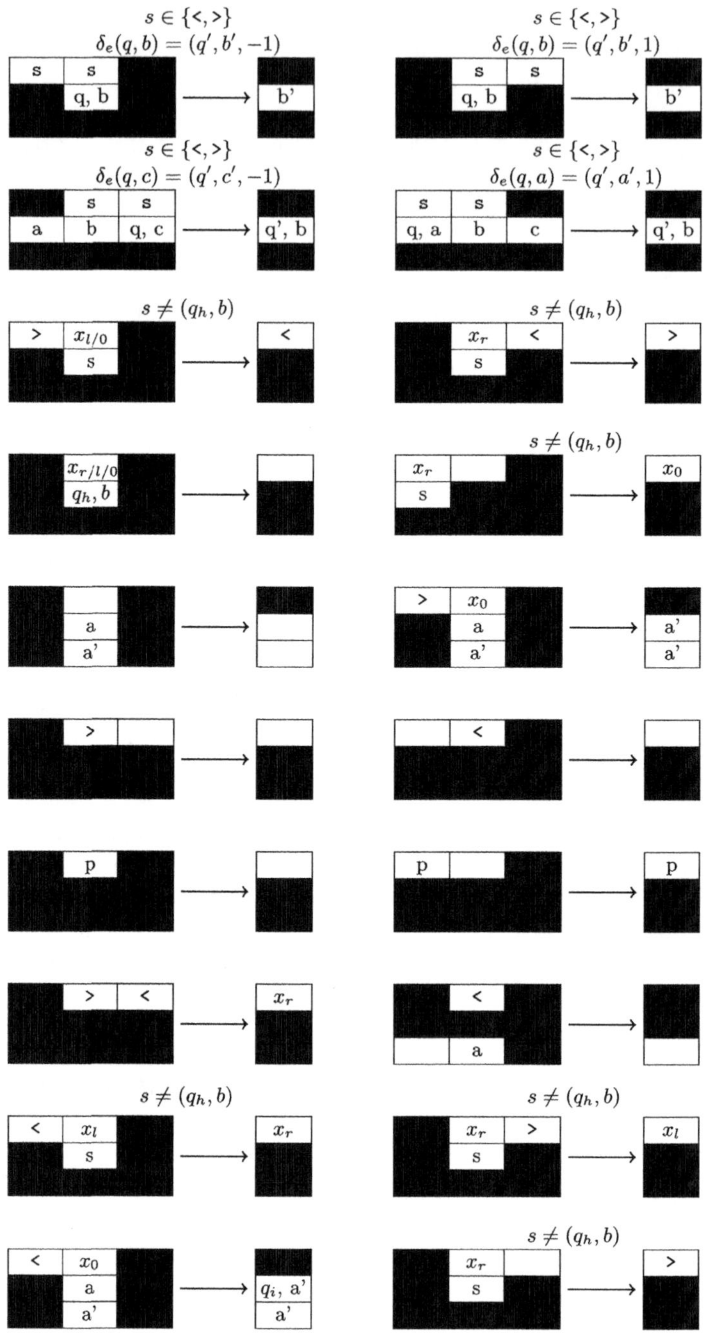

Fig. 2. Complete transition function of the cellular automaton G_e. Black cells act as wildcards and can match any state in the neighborhood. When no rule applies, the cell remains unchanged.

Proof (Theorem 1). By Lemma 4, we know that the sensitivity problem is in Π_2^0, and by Lemma 5, we have hardness. We conclude that determining sensitivity for one-dimensional cellular automata is Π_2^0-complete. This proves the theorem. □

As a corollary of these constructions, we obtain a new proof of Sutner's result on finite nilpotency [8].

Corollary 1. *The problem of determining whether a cellular automaton is nilpotent on finite configurations is* Π_2^0*-complete.*

Proof. Given a one-dimensional cellular automaton G of radius r, finite nilpotency is a Π_2^0 property. This is because finite configurations can be encoded by a finite set along with the position of the top-rightmost non-zero cell. Consequently, the function S that takes the code of a finite configuration c and returns the code of $G(c)$ is recursive. Therefore finite nilpotency can be written as:

$$\forall e \in \mathbb{N}, \quad \exists n \in \mathbb{N}, \quad S^n(e) = \text{Code}(0) \tag{8}$$

We obtain hardness by reducing TOT and removing particle p in our construction of G_e. Hence, from our previous proof, all finite patterns P will eventually become blank if and only if the given Turing machine halts on every input. We can then lift the result to higher dimensions using slices. For any d and a d-dimensional cellular automaton G which is finitely nilpotent. Consider the slice version of G. Any finite configuration on $A^{\mathbb{Z}^{d+1}}$ is finite on every slice and non-null on finitely many. Therefore, the slice version of G is finitely nilpotent if and only if G is. By induction, finite nilpotency is Π_2^0-complete. □

4 Higher Dimensional Cellular Automata

In this section, we extend our analysis to cellular automata in two or more dimensions and prove Theorem 2.

4.1 Upper Bound: Σ_3^0

We begin by showing that for any $d > 1$, the sensitivity problem for d-dimensional cellular automata belongs to the class Σ_3^0 of the arithmetical hierarchy. First, we recall a crucial lemma from our previous discussion, Lemma 1: A cellular automaton is not sensitive if and only if it has an arbitrarily large blocking word. We then state the following lemma.

Lemma 6. *For any* $d > 1$*, the problem of determining whether a* d*-dimensional cellular automaton is sensitive is* Σ_3^0.

Proof. Recall that the property "there exists an M-blocking word" is Σ_2^0 by Lemma 3. Therefore, by Lemma 1, being non-sensitive is Π_3^0, as it requires the existence of M-blocking words for all sufficiently large M. Consequently, being sensitive is Σ_3^0. This establishes that the sensitivity problem is at most Σ_3^0. □

4.2 Lower Bound: Σ_3^0-Hardness

In this section, we aim to prove the following result:

Theorem 4. *The problem of determining whether a two-dimensional cellular automaton is sensitive is Σ_3^0-complete.*

To prove Σ_3^0-hardness, we reduce from the Cofinite Set (COF) problem, which is known to be Σ_3^0-hard. For each e, let $M_e = (Q, A, q_i, q_h, \delta)$ be the associated Turing machine. We construct a 2D cellular automaton G_e as follows:

The states of G_e are $(A \cup \{\sqcup\}) \times (Q \cup \{\sqcup\}) \times (T \cup \{\sqcup\}) \times (P \cup \{\sqcup\}) \times \{\text{red1}, \text{red2}, \text{red3}, \text{red4}, \text{white}, \text{green}\}$.

Where $P = \{p, p_r, p_l, q_r, q_l, p_{ru}, p_{rd}, p_{lu}, p_{ld}, q_{ru}, q_{rd}, q_{lu}, q_{ld}\}$ is a set of particles, $T = Q \cup \{t_h\}$, with Q a set of states for tentacles and t_h a signal for halting. The colors red, white, and green delimit the computational zones.

G_e operates using the von Neumann neighborhood.

We describe the cellular automaton's behavior as follows:

Each red cell can have at most two red neighbors. A red cell marked with 1 can have either a 1 neighbor to the west and a 1 neighbor to the east, a 2 neighbor to the west and a 1 neighbor to the east, or a 4 neighbor to the north and a 1 neighbor to the west. Other marker rules are given Fig. 3. Consequently given a finite configuration, after finitely many steps, the only remaining red zones are the ones forming rectangular loops (Lemma 7), these rectangles will form the tape of Turing machines.

P is a set of particles, that move on white or green cells. There are two types of particles: p particles, which send a signal to a Turing machine to process one step of computation, and q particles, which place a Turing machine at the beginning of the tape in the initial state. The particles p and q are divided into right and left particles (p_r, p_l) that move to the right and left, respectively. When they meet at the beginning of a tape, they send a signal into that tape. If a particle meets an obstacle (i.e. a red zone) it divides into an up particle and a down particle (p_{ru}, p_{lu}, p_{rd}, p_{ld}) that follow the red loop and reform when meeting again.

When a p-signal enters a red zone, it follows the loop guided by the 1, 2, 3, and 4 markers. When it encounters a Turing machine head, it allows the head to process one step of computation and is erased after meeting the first head or if there is no head on the zone. The Turing machine head is guided along the loop by the markers. If it encounters another head on the tape, it erases that head (i.e. the most advanced particle on the zone is erased). When it halts, it erases itself and the red zone.

When a machine runs out of space, it requests the creation of a tentacle that operates with T symbols on green zones. Tentacles always grow to the east, or to the north if there is a red zone in the eastward position. These extension rules define local rules, and tentacles can be defined as green zones respecting these rules. The set T contains copies of states of M_e and includes a signal t_h that is sent when the machine halts to destroy the connected red zone. By the first rules, when two green zones meet, they erase each other. If a particle reaches the end of the red zone (meaning it has not found any Turing machine head), it continues into the green zone.

We give below the main rules of the cellular automaton G_e in Fig. 3.

Lemma 7. *Given a finite configuration, after finitely many steps all red zones will form rectangular loops, and all green zones will become tentalces. This process is illustrated in Fig. 4.*

Proof. Given a finite configuration, each green cell that does not follow the local rules will eventually become white. Therefore, after finitely many steps, all green zones that violate local rules will be erased. The only remaining connected green zones will be those that comply with the local rules, which take the form of tentacles.

Now consider the 5-state cellular automaton with states $\{0, 1, 2, 3, 4\}$ governed by the transition rules `red1`, `red2`, `red3`, `red4`, and `white`, as shown in Fig. 3. Given a 0-finite configuration, the local rules constrain any connected non-zero zone to form a spiral (the proof is omitted). There are two possibilities: either the spiral closes into a rectangular loop, or it spirals indefinitely. In the latter case, the inward-spiraling zone creates a conflict at its center. Because no non-zero cell can be created the whole non-zero zone will be erased. □

Lemma 8. *Given a finite configuration, we can send particles from outside the configuration to meet at any position outside the red zones within the configuration after the red zones have stabilized.*

Proof. Consider a finite configuration in which the only red zones are rectangular loops, and suppose there is a single right-moving particle (possibly split) to the left of a left-moving particle (possibly split), both located outside the red zones. This configuration has a preimage. This follows from the fact that red zones are rectangular, allowing us to trace the evolution backward using the local rules. Moreover, since the right-moving particle is to the left of the left-moving one, they could not have met in the past. We place the particles at the desired meeting point and trace the consecutive preimages of the configuration backward. This allows us to determine where to initially place the particles outside the configuration so that they meet as intended. We only need to place them sufficiently far from the configuration to ensure that the red zones have time to evolve into rectangular loops. □

Lemma 9. *For any $e \in \mathbb{N}$, the Turing machine M_e halts on all but finitely many inputs if and only if the associated cellular automaton G_e is sensitive.*

Proof. We prove that $e \in \mathrm{COF}$ if and only if G_e is sensitive. Let x be any finite configuration, by Lemma 7 in finite time all red zone will be rectangular red loops. These rectangular loops will be our Turing machines tapes and the input of a Turing machines will the length of its loop/tape divided by two.

If $e \in COF$: Let x be any finite configuration. In finite time it will be constituted of rectangular red loops, white zones, and tentacles. For any accessible red zone

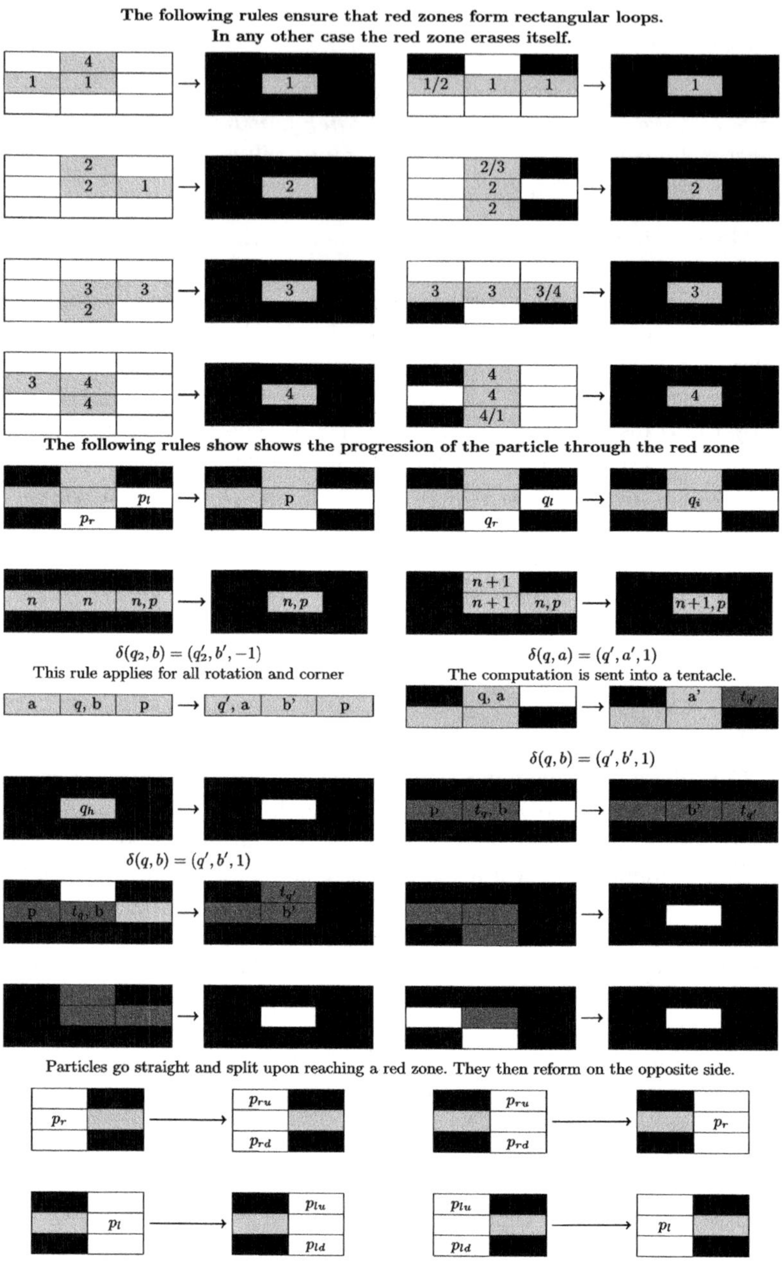

Fig. 3. Main rules for the transition function of the 2-dimensional cellular automaton G_e. Black cells act as wildcards and can match any state in the neighborhood. All rules specify the next state of the center cell, except for the last one, which applies to a full neighborhood configuration (but remains a local rule). When no rule applies, the cell remains unchanged. (Color figure online)

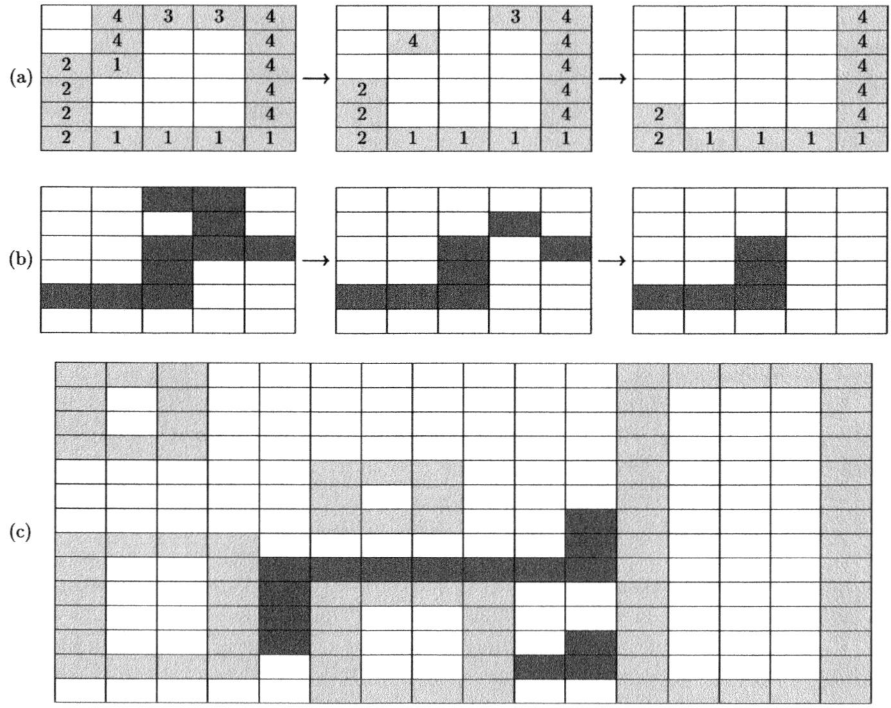

Fig. 4. Illustration of the stabilization process. (a) Defective red regions are progressively eliminated. (b) Green regions are removed in parallel. (c) A representative configuration after the system has stabilized. (Color figure online)

(not inside another), we can send a particles q to place a Turing machine on the zone. We can then send processing particles in those zones. Because inaccessible zones are surrounded by red zones, if these zones are sufficiently large, they must be surrounded by a large red area. Since $e \in \mathrm{COF}$, there exists an N such that for all $y > N$, M_e halts on y. These machines might not have enough space to complete their computation, but they can request a tentacle. Since we control which zone is allowed to compute by sending a particle, we can prevent conflicts in the green zone by ensuring that only one red zone is permitted to compute at a time. Therefore, any sufficiently large block will have its border destroyed because the Turing on that tape will eventually halt, allowing us to send particles through it. by Lemma 1, G_e is sensitive.

If $e \notin \mathrm{COF}$*:* Then there exist infinitely many y such that $M_e(y)$ does not halt. We can construct arbitrarily large blocking words as follows: For any $M > 0$, choose $y > M$ such that $M_e(y)$ does not halt. Construct a red rectangle with perimeter $2y$. This rectangle forms an M-blocking word, as:

1. The Turing machine simulating $M_e(y)$ will never halt, so the rectangle will never be destroyed. 2. No particles can penetrate the red border. 3. The interior of the rectangle is inaccessible to any external influence.

Since we can construct such blocking words for arbitrarily large M, by Lemma 1, G_e is not sensitive. □

Proof (Theorem 4). By Lemma 6, we know that the sensitivity problem for two-dimensional cellular automata is Σ_3^0, and by Lemma 9, we have established hardness. Hence, the theorem is proved. □

Proof (Theorem 2). By Lemma 6, we know that the sensitivity problem for d-dimensional cellular automata is in Σ_3^0. We prove Σ_3^0-hardness by reducing from the two-dimensional case using a slicing argument.

Let G_d be a d-dimensional cellular automaton, and let G_{d+1} be its slice extension to dimension $d+1$. Suppose w_d is an m-blocking word for G_d over some finite set $K \subset \mathbb{Z}^d$. Then the word

$$w_{d+1}(x, x_{d+1}) = w_d(x), \quad \forall x_{d+1} \in [0, m-1], \quad \forall x \in K \tag{9}$$

defines an m-blocking word for G_{d+1}. Therefore, if G_d is not sensitive, neither is G_{d+1}.

Conversely, if G_d is sensitive, then it does not admit arbitrarily large blocking words, so information can propagate in slices. Hence, G_{d+1} is also sensitive. By induction on d, this proves the theorem. □

This construction establishes a reduction from COF to the sensitivity problem, proving that the latter is Σ_3^0-hard. Combined with our earlier upper bound, this shows that the sensitivity problem for $d > 1$ dimensional cellular automata is Σ_3^0-complete.

5 Application

In this section, we explore an application of our results in number theory, specifically in relation to the twin prime conjecture. While we do not believe this to be a suitable approach for solving the twin prime conjecture, we argue that it demonstrates a concrete application of the arithmetical hierarchy that is not often explored. Furthermore, this construction illustrates how complexity classifications can provide unexpected connections between different areas of mathematics.

Proposition 2. *The twin prime conjecture is a Π_2^0 statement in the arithmetical hierarchy.*

Proof. The twin prime conjecture can be stated as:

$$\forall n, \exists p (p > n \wedge \mathrm{Prime}(p) \wedge \mathrm{Prime}(p+2)) \tag{10}$$

□

We construct a Turing machine M that, given an input n in unary (represented by a string of 0s), halts if and only if it finds a pair of twin primes larger than or equal to n.

Theorem 5. *There exists a cellular automaton G that is sensitive to initial conditions if and only if the twin prime conjecture is true.*

Proof. By our construction, the Turing machine M halts on all inputs if and only if the twin prime conjecture is true. Using our reduction from the TOT problem to the sensitivity problem for cellular automata, we can construct a cellular automaton G that is sensitive to initial conditions if and only if M halts on all inputs. Therefore, G is sensitive to initial conditions if and only if the twin prime conjecture is true. □

Remark 1. The construction used in Theorem 1 can be adapted to any Π_2^0 statement. For example, one could replace the twin prime conjecture with the Riemann Hypothesis or Goldbach's conjecture—although these are actually Π_1^0 statements and therefore technically simpler, the method still applies. More interestingly, it also applies to statements like $P = NP$, which is known to be Π_2^0 [5]. However, in this article we focus on a single illustrative example.

We have implemented this cellular automaton, which can be explored interactively at the following URL: https://tom-favereau.github.io/misc/ca.html. The source code for the automaton is also available on GitHub at: https://github.com/tom-favereau/twin_prime_automaton.

6 Conclusion and Future Work

In this paper, we have established the precise complexity of determining sensitivity to initial conditions for cellular automata within the arithmetical hierarchy. Specifically, we have shown that this problem is Π_2^0-complete for one-dimensional cellular automata and Σ_3^0-complete for cellular automata of dimension two and higher. These results provide a complete characterization of the complexity of the sensitivity problem across all dimensions.

Additionally, we have provided a new proof of Sutner's result stating that the problem of determining finite nilpotency for one-dimensional cellular automata is Π_2^0-complete. We have also constructed a cellular automaton that is sensitive to initial conditions if and only if the twin prime conjecture is true.

As a corollary to our main results, we can conclude that the problem of determining non-sensitivity is Σ_2^0-complete for one-dimensional cellular automata and Π_3^0-complete for higher dimensions. This complementary result completes our analysis of Kůrka's classes.

However, it is important to note that our reductions are not reversible. Consequently, the complexity of the sensitivity problem for reversible cellular automata remains an open question. This presents an interesting avenue for future research, as reversible cellular automata form an important subclass with unique properties and applications.

Furthermore, our work does not address the case of expansive cellular automata, which constitute the final class in Kůrka's classification. For expansive cellular automata, we know they are at the level Σ_1^0 of the arithmetical hierarchy, yet the question of the decidability or undecidability of the problem is a well-known open problem in the field. This gap in our understanding presents another significant direction for future investigations.

Additionally, the complexity of determining the existence of equicontinuity points in cellular automata remains unknown, and it is possible that it might be analytical. This presents another important direction for future research, as having equicontinuity points can be seen as a two-dimensional Kůrka class.

Question 1. What is the complexity of determining whether a d-dimensional reversible cellular automaton is sensitive to initial conditions?

Question 2. What is the complexity of determining the existence of equicontinuity points for a d-dimensional cellular automaton?

Question 3. What is the complexity of determining whether a one-dimensional cellular automaton is expansive?

In conclusion, while our results provide a comprehensive complexity analysis for the sensitivity problem for general cellular automata, they also highlight important open questions and future directions.

References

1. Durand, B., Formenti, E., Varouchas, G.: On undecidability of equicontinuity classification for cellular automata. Discrete Mathematics & Theoretical Computer Science. DMTCS Proceedings vol. AB, Discrete Models for Complex Systems (DMCS'03), 2, January 2003. https://doi.org/10.46298/dmtcs.2302, https://dmtcs.episciences.org/2302
2. Kůrka, P.: Languages, equicontinuity and attractors in cellular automata. Ergodic Theory Dynam. Systems **17**(2), 417–433 (1997). https://doi.org/10.1017/S014338579706985X
3. Kůrka, P.: Topological dynamics of cellular automata. In: Marcus, B., Rosenthal, J. (eds.) Codes, Systems, and Graphical Models, pp. 447–485. Springer, New York (2001)
4. Lukkarila, V.: On Undecidable Dynamical Properties of Reversible One-Dimensional Cellular Automata. Ph.D. thesis, University of Turku (2010)
5. Madore, D.: How to formulate the P vs NP problem as a formal statement inside the language of arithmetic? https://math.stackexchange.com/q/1765741 (2016), math StackExchange. Accessed 05 May 2025
6. Rogers, H.: Theory of recursive functions and effective computability. MIT Press, Cambridge (1987)
7. Sablik, M., Theyssier, G.: Topological dynamics of cellular automata: Dimension matters. Theory Comput. Syst. **48**(4), 693–714 (2011). https://doi.org/10.1007/s00224-010-9255-x, https://doi.org/10.1007/s00224-010-9255-x
8. Sutner, K.: A note on Culik-Yu classes. Complex Systems **3**(1), 107–115 (1989)
9. Wolfram, S.: Statistical mechanics of cellular automata. Rev. Mod. Phys. **55**, 601–644 (1983). https://doi.org/10.1103/RevModPhys.55.601, https://link.aps.org/doi/10.1103/RevModPhys.55.601

Conditions for Cyclic Attractors for a Class of Discrete n-Dimensional Repressilators

Honglu Sun[1], Maxime Folschette[2(✉)], Morgan Magnin[1], and Elisa Tonello[3]

[1] Nantes Université, École Centrale Nantes, CNRS, LS2N, UMR 6004, 44000 Nantes, France
[2] Univ. Lille, CNRS, Centrale Lille, UMR 9189 CRIStAL, 59000 Lille, France
Maxime.Folschette@centralelille.fr
[3] Department of Mathematics and Computer Science, Freie Universität Berlin, Berlin, Germany

Abstract. Repressilators are biological regulatory networks in which components interact only in terms of negative influences. They are of interest in biology, since their oscillatory behavior can inform the design of gene therapies. Although sustained oscillations are ensured in 3-dimensional repressilators, that is, in systems made of 3 genes, they do not always appear in higher dimensions, as their occurrence depends on the topology of the network and on the chosen parameters. Here we focus on discrete models, where the presence of at least one cyclic attractor is required for sustained oscillations. Even in a discrete framework, enumerating and simulating all possible models can quickly become computationally infeasible. In this paper, we provide a sufficient condition for the presence of sustained oscillations for a class of repressilators, based on the structure of their influence graphs. The condition applies in any dimension and independently of the parameters, that is, threshold labeling of the edges. We also study the coexistence of cyclic attractors and fixed points in dimension 4.

Keywords: Discrete regulatory networks · Interaction graph · Repressilators · Static analysis · Attractors

1 Introduction

Gene expression has generally two major steps: transcription, that generates mRNA from genes, and translation, that generates proteins from mRNA. A generated protein can be structural (giving it a particular structural property) or be an enzyme (catalyzing a certain reaction). Additionally, it can also serve to activate or inhibit other genes. These regulations (activation or inhibition) between genes give rise to *gene regulatory networks*, which play a key role in various cellular processes and pathways (Kauffman, 1969, Thomas, 1973, de Jong, 2002).

Published by Springer Nature Switzerland AG 2026
S. Riva and A. Richard (Eds.): AUTOMATA 2025, LNCS 15831, pp. 139–153, 2026.
https://doi.org/10.1007/978-3-032-01570-9_10

One major challenge associated to gene regulatory networks is the analysis of their dynamical properties. In the literature, various classes of these properties have been studied, such as the existence of oscillations or fixed points (Melkman et al., 2010, Akutsu et al., 2012, Comet et al., 2013), state reachability (Batt et al., 2008, Paulevé et al., 2012, Mendes et al., 2018), or more complex properties described by temporal logic (Bernot et al., 2004). Identifying the dynamical properties of gene regulatory networks enables the correction of inaccurate models, the prediction of a system's behavior, and even the discovery of new strategies for regulating specific parts of the network.

However, studying such properties often requires to exhaustively compute the dynamics of the model, either completely or partially. This computation can be very time-costly since it usually has an exponential complexity in the size of the model, which is typically determined by the number of genes. Several techniques exist to speed up the process (such as model reduction, see for instance (Naldi et al., 2011), but these do not reduce the inherent complexity of the problem. Thus, when possible, relying on static analysis is an interesting alternative. Static analysis consists in computing dynamical properties based only on the topology of the model, thus avoiding the exhaustive computation of the dynamics. This results in a drastic decrease in computational complexity although, so far, ad hoc techniques or properties must be found for each problem addressed (Paulevé and Richard, 2011, Gadouleau, 2020).

In the literature, different modeling frameworks have been applied to model gene regulatory networks, mainly including probabilistic, continuous, discrete or hybrid approaches (de Jong, 2002). This work uses Thomas' discrete modeling framework (Thomas, 1973, Thomas, 1991), where the continuous expressions of the genes are abstracted by an integer vector called a *state*, which describes the discrete expression levels of genes, so that the dynamics of the system can be represented by a state transition graph. One major advantage of using discrete modeling is its simplicity in implementation and analysis. Based on this discrete modeling framework, one can describe the dynamical properties in terms of the existence of different attractors (fixed points and cyclic attractors) in the state transition graph. The significance of attractors lies in their representation of the system's long-term behavior, which typically corresponds to the phenotype of a living organism.

This study considers the problem of determining to what extent the presence of a certain type of attractors (fixed points, cyclic attractors, or both) which generally depend on both the structure of the regulations and the specific modeling formalism, can be inferred solely from the topology of the *interaction graph*. The interaction graph of a gene regulatory network is a directed graph where the vertices represent the genes and the arcs represent the regulations between genes. We study a class of gene regulatory networks, called n-dimensional repressilators, which are n-dimensional networks with only inhibitions between genes. The 3-dimensional repressilator, consisting of a single negative feedback loop, was widely studied in synthetic biology because it can generate synthetic oscillations (Potvin-Trottier et al., 2016, Elowitz and Leibler, 2000). However, adding more genes to this network tends to improve the controllability of this model

(Page, 2019, Perez-Carrasco et al., 2018, Goh et al., 2008). In (Sun et al., 2023), a sufficient and necessary condition for the existence of a cyclic attractor in the particular case of 4-dimensional repressilators was discovered by machine learning models. Here we describe conditions for the existence of fixed points or cyclic attractors in n-dimensional repressilators without resorting to machine learning techniques. The first contribution is the formulation of a sufficient and necessary condition for the existence of fixed points in n-dimensional repressilators, which also leads to a sufficient condition for the existence of cyclic attractors. Note that this result has already been reported in (Richard and Ruet, 2013 Proposition 4) for a subclass of Boolean models. We then state a sufficient condition for the coexistence of fixed points and cyclic attractors in n-dimensional repressilators. Finally, we prove that this sufficient condition is also a necessary condition in the case of 4-dimensional repressilators, which is compatible with the results in (Sun et al., 2023).

2 Definitions

In this work, we consider a subset of multi-valued networks, also often called Thomas models (Thomas, 1973, Thomas, 1991). Indeed, we consider discrete networks on n species with interaction graphs admitting *inhibition interactions only*, and call these interaction graphs *repressilator* interaction graphs. We consider only repressilators without self-loops, and with the following dynamical rule: one in-neighbor is sufficient to decrease the target value. This means in particular that the asynchronous dynamics is uniquely defined by the interaction graph and the threshold assignment, that is, the labeling of the arcs indicating at which expression level the source gene starts expressing its influence on the target gene. The same assumption was also made in (Sun et al., 2023). However, contrary to the other assumptions of the same article, here we do not assume that every vertex is the regulator of at least one other vertex and that a different threshold exists for each target, and we do not limit the networks to 4 components.

To simplify the discussion, we assume, without loss of generality, that the directed graph underlying the interaction graph is connected. If this condition is not satisfied, the asynchronous dynamics associated to the interaction graph can be described as the Cartesian product of the asynchronous dynamics associated to each connected component. In particular, the dynamics admits a cyclic attractor if and only if any of the dynamics associated to a connected component admits a cyclic attractor.

Definition 1. *For a repressilator interaction graph* G, *let* $V = \{0, \dots, n-1\}$ *be the set of vertices, and* E *the set of directed edges. A* maximum level assignment $m\colon V \to \mathbb{N}\setminus\{0\}$ *associates a strictly positive maximum level to each vertex in* G. *For simplicity, for each vertex* $i \in V$, *we write* m_i *instead of* $m(i)$. *Thus,* $X = \{0, \dots, m_0\} \times \cdots \times \{0, \dots, m_{n-1}\}$ *is the state space of the dynamics associated to* G.

For convenience, in the rest of this paper, and since we model only negative regulations, if $i, j \in V$ are two vertices such that there is an edge $(i, j) \in E$, we say that i *inhibits* j, i is called an *inhibitor* of j, and the edge (i, j) is called an *inhibition*. Recall that the sign of a path in an interaction graph is the product of the sign of its arcs. Hence, in a repressilator graph, a cycle is negative if and only if it contains an odd number of arcs.

Definition 2. *Let* G *be an interaction graph and* m *a maximum level assignment. A* threshold assignment $t : E \to \mathbb{N}$ *associates a threshold to each edge in* G *so that, for each edge* $(i, j) \in E$, $0 < t(i, j) \leq m_i$.

Let $d(x, y)$ denote the Hamming distance between $x, y \in X$. Moreover, if $x \in X$ and $i \in V$, x_i denotes the ith component of state x.

Definition 3. *Given a repressilator interaction graph* G, *a maximum level assignment* m *and a threshold assignment* t, $\mathrm{AD}(\mathrm{G}, m, t)$ *is the associated* asynchronous state transition graph, *also called* asynchronous dynamics, *defined as follows: for* $i \in V$ *and* $x, y \in X$,

- *there is a transition from* x *to* y *with* $d(x, y) = 1$ *and* $y_i = x_i + 1$ *if and only if* $x_i < m_i$ *and* $x_j < t(j, i)$ *for all inhibitors* j *of* i;
- *there is a transition from* x *to* y *with* $d(x, y) = 1$ *and* $y_i = x_i - 1$ *if and only if* $x_i > 0$ *and there exists* j *an inhibitor of* i *such that* $x_j \geq t(j, i)$.

In a nutshell, any inhibition pushes the level of the target vertex towards zero, while, in absence of any inhibition, the level of the vertex is allowed to grow towards its maximum, in a stepwise fashion.

Definition 4. *An* attractor *of* $\mathrm{AD}(\mathrm{G}, m, t)$ *is a terminal strongly connected component of the state transition graph. Attractors are called* fixed points *if they consist of one state, and* cyclic attractors *otherwise.*

This definition is the classic definition of an attractor, modeling the long-term oscillating behavior of a system. The condition of strong connectedness ensures that all states within the attractor are mutually reachable, while terminality ensures that the system's dynamics cannot escape these sets (Comet et al., 2013).

Remark 1. The state x with $x_i = 0$ for all $i \in V$ has indegree zero in $\mathrm{AD}(\mathrm{G}, m, t)$ for all repressilator graphs G and threshold assignments t. In other words, the state where all vertices are at level 0 can only be a source state. This is a consequence of the fact that we only consider repressilators without self-loops: a state where only one vertex is at level 1 cannot see this vertex decrease, because no inhibitions are expressed.

More generally, consider the set $S = \{x \in X \mid x_i < t(i, k) \text{ for all } (i, k) \in E\}$. All states in this set contain only vertices values that are below the thresholds of the interaction graph, meaning that no inhibition is expressed. Thus, any dynamical transition from a state in S can only lead to a state with one increased value (first case in Definition 3). The consequence is that from any state in S, there exists a path of successive transitions that exits the set S. Moreover, there exists no transition from a state $y \in X \setminus S$ to a state $x \in S$, implying that the states in S cannot be part of an attractor.

For a graph G and a subset A of the vertices, we write $\mathrm{G}[A]$ for the subgraph of G induced by A.

We call a *subspace* a subset of the state space X obtained by fixing some vertices. In more detail, consider a set $C \subseteq V$ and a map $I\colon C \to \mathbb{N}$ that satisfies $I(i) \le m_i$ for all $i \in C$. Then the set $\kappa_{C,I} = \{x \in X \mid x_i = I(i) \text{ for all } i \in C\}$ is the subspace of X defined by C and I.

It is often useful to view a subspace $\kappa_{C,I}$ as a smaller state space contained in the state space X. Given a repressillator (G, m, t), one can consider the subgraph of the asynchronous dynamics $\mathrm{AD}(\mathrm{G}, m, t)$ induced by the vertices in $\kappa_{C,I}$, and ask whether the dynamics thus obtained can be viewed as the dynamics associated to some repressilator. This is not the case in general, but works when $I(i) = 0$ for all $i \in C$, as described in the following remark.

Remark 2. Given a subspace $\kappa_{C,I}$ with $I(i) = 0$ for all $i \in C$, consider the set of vertices $V' = V \setminus C$, and define a maximum level assignment m' as the restriction of m to V'. The subspace can be viewed as a state space via the isomorphism $\pi\colon \kappa_{C,I} \to X'$, with $X' = \prod_{i \in V \setminus C}\{0, \dots, m_i\}$, so that for all $x \in \kappa_{C,I}$, $\pi(x) = (x_i)_{i \in V \setminus C}$. In other words, this isomorphism projects the components of x onto the components in $V \setminus C$. We show that the subgraph of $\mathrm{AD}(\mathrm{G}, m, t)$ induced by the vertices in $\kappa_{C,I}$ (on the state space X', via the isomorphism π) is the dynamics $\mathrm{AD}(\mathrm{G}', m', t')$ associated to the repressilator interaction graph $\mathrm{G}' = \mathrm{G}[V']$ with threshold assignment t' given by the restriction of t to the edges in $\mathrm{G}[V']$ (edges that have both endpoints in V').

- Suppose that there is a transition in $\mathrm{AD}(\mathrm{G}', m', t')$ from x to y in $\kappa_{C,I}$, and that $y_i = x_i + 1$. Then i is in V', and the transition is also a transition in $\mathrm{AD}(\mathrm{G}, m, t)$. Hence $x_i < m_i = m'_i$ and $x_j < t(j,i) = t'(j,i)$ for all inhibitors j of i, and in particular, for all inhibitors in V'. Vice versa, take $x \in \kappa_{C,I}$ and suppose that $x_i < m'_i$ and $x_j < t'(j,i)$ for all inhibitors $j \in V'$ of i. Then $x_i < m_i$, and since $x_j = 0$ for all j outside of V', we have $x_j < t(j,i)$ for all inhibitors j of i in V. Hence a transition from x to y with $y_i = x_i + 1$ exists in $\mathrm{AD}(\mathrm{G}, m, t)$ and in its restriction to $\kappa_{C,I}$.
- Suppose that there is a transition in $\mathrm{AD}(\mathrm{G}', m', t')$ from x to y in $\kappa_{C,I}$, and that $y_i = x_i - 1$. Then i is in V', and the transition is also a transition in $\mathrm{AD}(\mathrm{G}, m, t)$. Hence $x_i > 0$ and there exists $j \in V$ inhibitor of i such that $x_j \ge t(j,i)$. Since $t(i,j) > 0$, j is not in C. Vice versa, take $x \in \kappa_{C,I}$ and suppose that $x_i > 0$ and $x_j \ge t'(j,i)$ for some inhibitor $j \in V'$ of i. Then there is a transition from x to y with $y_i = x_i - 1$ in $\mathrm{AD}(\mathrm{G}, m, t)$, and also in its restriction to $\kappa_{C,I}$.

2.1 Stable Dominating Sets

We now introduce a definition that will be useful for the of analysis of repressilator attractors.

Definition 5. *Let $A \subseteq V$ be a non-empty set of vertices. If there exists no edge $(i, j) \in E$ with $i \in A$ and $j \in A$, then A is called an* independent set*. If for all $j \in V \setminus A$, there exists $i \in A$ such that $(i, j) \in E$, then A is called a* dominating set*. If A is both an independent and dominating set, then it is called a* stable dominating set.

The set A of this definition is a set of vertices that do not inhibit each other, and that, taken together, inhibit all vertices outside of A. For $n = 1$, there is only one repressilator interaction graph, the graph with the empty set of edges E, and $A = V = \{0\}$ is its only stable dominating set. Note that the case $A = V$ cannot exist for $n > 1$ since we suppose in this work that the interaction graph is connected, thus preventing V to be a stable dominating set. For $n = 2$, a stable dominating set also always exists:

- If there is an edge from vertex 0 to vertex 1, then $A = \{0\}$ is a stable dominating set, whether an edge from 1 to 0 exists or not.
- If there is an edge from vertex 1 to vertex 0, then $A = \{1\}$ is a stable dominating set, which is not incompatible with the previous case as several stable dominating sets can coexist.
- The case where there is no edge is out of scope since we suppose that the interaction graph is connected. This case could be tackled by considering it as a composition of two models of size $n = 1$.

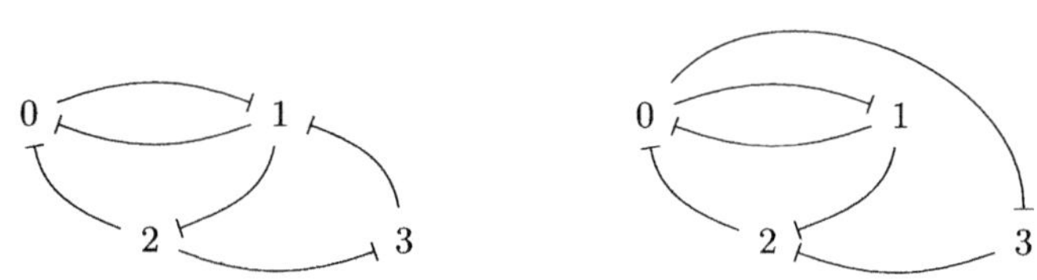

Fig. 1. Left: interaction graph always having a cyclic attractor. Right: interaction graph never having a cyclic attractor. Reproduced from (Sun et al., 2023, Fig. 5).

Example 1. Consider the graphs in Fig. 1. For the graph on the right, $A = \{1, 3\}$ is a stable dominating set (no edges between 1 and 3, while 0 and 2 are inhibited by 1). The graph on the left does not admit any stable dominating set: no single vertex inhibits all other vertices; considering pair of vertices, 0 and 3 are the only vertices that do not inhibit each other, but they do not inhibit vertex 2.

We will use the stable dominating sets of Definition 5 to characterize the fixed points of the dynamics. To this end, given a subset A of V, we define a state $\phi(A) \in X$ associated to A as follows:

$$\phi(A)_i = \begin{cases} m_i & \text{if } i \in A, \\ 0 & \text{otherwise,} \end{cases}$$

for all $i \in V$, where $\phi(A)_i$ is the i^{th}component of $\phi(A)$. Equivalently, for all $i \in V$, $\phi(A)_i = \mathbf{1}_A(i) \cdot m_i$, where $\mathbf{1}_A$ is the indicator function of A.

3 Results

3.1 Sufficient Condition for the Existence of Cyclic Attractors

The following theorem explains the rationale behind the name "stable dominating sets". The notion of stable dominating set is actually closely related to the notion of kernel as recalled in (Richard and Ruet, 2013), where it is used to prove the same result for a class of Boolean models. Here, the result is generalized to multi-valued networks.

Theorem 1. *A state $x \in X$ is a fixed point for the dynamics associated to a repressilator interaction graph* G *if and only if $x = \phi(A)$ for some stable dominating set $A \subseteq V$.*

Proof. (1) We first show that, if $A \subseteq V$ is a stable dominating set for G, then $\phi(A)$ is a fixed point.

For i in A, all the inhibitors of i are outside A. Hence, at $\phi(A)$, all inhibitors of i are below the threshold required for the inhibition, and $\phi(A)_i$ cannot decrease.

For i outside A, there is at least one inhibitor in A, at its maximum value, hence above the threshold. Therefore $\phi(A)_i$ cannot increase.

(2) Suppose now that x is a fixed point. Define $A = \{i \in V \mid x_i > 0\}$.

If i is in A, since x is a fixed point, all its repressors must be below the relative threshold. Moreover, since the value of x_i cannot increase and all its inihibitors are below threshold, the value of x_i must be maximum. Since all inhibitors B of vertices in A are below the threshold for the inhibition, and all components in A are at maximum levels, all components in B must be at zero, that is, all inhibitors of vertices in A must be outside A (A is an independent set).

If i is outside of A, since x_i is zero and cannot increase, it must have an inhibitor that is above threshold, that is, an inhibitor that is in A (A is a dominating set). □

It is noteworthy that the result of Theorem 1 is independent of the chosen threshold assignment.

Corollary 1. *The dynamics associated to a repressilator interaction graph* G *has a fixed point if and only if the graph* G *admits a stable dominating set.*

Corollary 2. *If a repressilator interaction graph* G *does not admit a stable dominating set, then it has a cyclic attractor.*

The previous corollary establishes a sufficient condition for the existence of cyclic attractors, based on the absence of fixed points. Before moving on to consider situations where fixed points and cyclic attractors coexist, we make some simple observations on the dynamics.

Proposition 1. *If A is a stable dominating set for* G *with maximum level assignment m, then, for any threshold assignment t and for any state x such that $x_i = 0$ for all $i \in V \setminus A$, there is a path from x to $\phi(A)$ in* $\mathrm{AD}(\mathrm{G}, m, t)$.

Proof. Since all the inhibitors of vertices in A are outside A, the components in A are free to increase to their maximum levels. □

Proposition 2. *If A is a stable dominating set for* G *with maximum level assignment m, then, for any threshold assignment t and for any state x such that $x_i = m_i$ for all $i \in A$, there is a path from x to $\phi(A)$ in* $\mathrm{AD}(\mathrm{G}, m, t)$.

Proof. All components outside A are inhibited by vertices in A in all states x that satisfy $x_i = m_i$ for all $i \in A$. □

We say that a vertex i *oscillates* in an attractor $\mathcal{A}$ if there exists x, y in $\mathcal{A}$ with $x_i \neq y_i$.

Proposition 3. *If a vertex i oscillates in an attractor $\mathcal{A}$, then*

(i) there exists a state $x \in \mathcal{A}$ such that $x_i = 0$;
(ii) there exists a state $x \in \mathcal{A}$ such that $x_i = m_i$.

Proof. If vertex i oscillates in an attractor $\mathcal{A}$, then there exist a transition between two states in $\mathcal{A}$ that decreases the value of component i. Say that this transition is from state x to state y. This means that at x component i is inhibited. Since the transition graph is asynchronous, x and y differ only in component i; therefore, since there are no self-inhibitions, component i is inhibited in state y as well, meaning that state y has a successor z with component i satisfying $z_i < y_i$, and component i can continue to decrease until 0 is reached.

The proof for point (ii) proceeds the same way. □

3.2 Coexistence of Fixed Points and Cyclic Attractors

We first give a sufficient condition for the coexistence of fixed points and cyclic attractors, valid in any dimension. In the next section, we show that the condition is also necessary for $n = 4$.

Theorem 2. *Consider a repressilator interaction graph* G *and suppose that there exists a stable dominating set A such that the subgraph* $\mathrm{G}[V \setminus A]$ *admits no stable dominating set. Take $B \neq \emptyset$ any minimal subset of $V \setminus A$ such that* $\mathrm{G}[B]$ *does not admit a stable dominating set. If all vertices in B inhibit all vertices in $V \setminus B$, then there exist a maximum level assignment m and a threshold assignment t such that the dynamics* $\mathrm{AD}(\mathrm{G}, m, t)$ *admits a cyclic attractor.*

Proof. Let $C = V \setminus B$ and consider a threshold assignment $t \colon E \to \mathbb{N}^+$ that satisfies the following property: for all $i, k \in B$ and $j \in C$ such that $(i, j) \in E$ and $(i, k) \in E$ are edges in G, $t(i, j) \leq t(i, k)$. That is, the thresholds for vertices in B to inhibit vertices in B cannot be below the thresholds of inhibitions of vertices in B to vertices in C.

Let $\kappa_{C,I}$ be the subspace of X such that $I(i) = 0$ for all $i \in C$, that is, where the vertices in C are fixed to zero. By Remark 2, the restriction AD$'$ of AD(G, m, t) to $\kappa_{C,I}$, defined on the state space X' via the isomorphism $\pi \colon \kappa_{C,I} \to X'$, admits G[$B$] as interaction graph. Hence, by Corollary 2, the dynamics AD$'$ admits a cyclic attractor.

Let $\mathcal{A}' \subseteq X'$ be a set of states that defines a cyclic attractor in AD$'$, and let $\mathcal{A} = \pi^{-1}(\mathcal{A}')$. We want to show that $\mathcal{A}$ is a cyclic attractor in AD(G, m, t).

Since $\mathcal{A}'$ is strongly connected, $\mathcal{A}$ is also strongly connected. To conclude the proof, we show that $\mathcal{A}$ is terminal, that is, it admits no outgoing transition.

For this, it is sufficient to show that, given a state x in $\mathcal{A}$, for all $j \in C$ there exists $i \in B$ such that $x_i \geq t(i, j)$, meaning that component j is inhibited by i and cannot change. Suppose by contradiction that, for some $j \in C$, $x_i < t(i, j)$ for all $i \in B$ (recall that j is inhibited by all vertices in B). Then, by definition of the threshold function t, if (i, k) is an edge in E with $k \in B$, we have $x_i < t(i, j) \leq t(i, k)$, that is, x_i is below the thresholds for the inhibition from i to any vertex in B. Now, recall that state $\pi(x)$ is part of the attractor $\mathcal{A}'$ of AD$'$. On the other hand, the state $\pi(x)$ satisfies the conditions of Remark 1 ($\pi_i(x) = x_i < t(i, k) = t'(i, k)$ for all $i, k \in B$ with (i, k) an edge in G[B]). Therefore $\pi(x)$ cannot be part of an attractor, a contradiction. □

Remark 3. The proof of the theorem provides a family of threshold assignments for which AD(G, m, t) admits both a fixed point and a cyclic attractor, under the stated hypotheses. In particular, we showed that we can always take the constant threshold assignment $t = 1$. The result applies therefore also to Boolean repressilators (systems that satisfy $m_i = 1$ for all $i \in V$).

Example 2. Consider the interaction graph G in Fig. 2, without taking into account the threshold assignment. This interaction graph contains the stable dominating set $A = \{4\}$, and the interaction graph G[$V \setminus A$] $=$ G[$\{0, 1, 2, 3\}$] contains no stable dominating set. Indeed, any singleton subset of $V \setminus A$ does not inhibit all other vertices in $V \setminus A$, and any subgraph with two or more vertices in $V \setminus A$ contains at least one edge. Consider $B = \{0, 1, 2\} \subset V \setminus A$; it is easy to see that B does not contain a stable dominating set for G[B] for the same reasons as above. Moreover, B is minimal for this property, since any interaction graph in dimension 1 or 2 always contains a stable dominating set, as explained after Definition 5. Finally, since each node in B inhibits all nodes in $V \setminus B = \{3, 4\}$, then Theorem 2 applies: there exists a threshold assignment such that the asynchronous dynamics of G admits a cyclic attractor. An example of such an assignment is the one given in Fig. 2, that produces an asynchronous dynamics containing both the fixed point 00004, and the following cyclic attractor:

$$\{00300, 01300, 02300, 03000, 03100, 03200, 03300, \\ 10300, 11300, 12300, 13000, 13100, 13200, 13300, \\ 20300, 21300, 22300, 23000, 23100, 23200, 23300, \\ 30000, 30100, 30200, 30300, 31000, 31100, 31200, 31300, \\ 32000, 32100, 32200, 32300, 33000, 33100, 33200\}$$

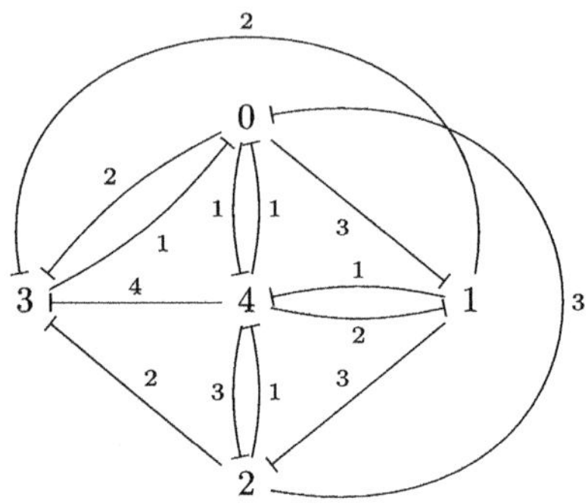

Fig. 2. Interaction graph of dimension 5 with a threshold assignment.

3.3 Case $n = 3$

We first characterize the only possible cyclic attractor in dimension $n = 3$, which will be used in later proofs.

Remark 4. Consider a repressilator G with set of vertices V of size 3, and suppose that, for some maximum level assignment m and threshold assignment t, $\mathrm{AD}(\mathrm{G}, m, t)$ admits a cyclic attractor $\mathcal{A}$ where all three vertices oscillate. Then G consists in an isolated cycle. To see this, first observe that all 3 vertices must have an incoming edge. Then, suppose for a contradiction that one vertex i is the source of two edges which target the other two vertices. Then $\{i\}$ is a stable dominating set. By Proposition 3, there exists a state $x \in \mathcal{A}$ with $x_i = m_i$. Then, by Proposition 2, there is a path in $\mathrm{AD}(\mathrm{G}, m, t)$ from x to $\phi(\{i\})$, which is a fixed point by Theorem 1, a contradiction.

The remark implies, in particular, that in a cyclic attractor in dimension 3, for each pair of vertices i and j that oscillate in the attractor, there exists $x \in \mathcal{A}$ such that $x_i = 0$ and $x_j = 0$.

Note that this property does not hold in general for attractors in higher dimensions. Consider for instance the repressilator interaction graph with 6 vertices defined in Fig. 3. The asynchronous dynamics associated to this graph has one cyclic attractor with states:

$$\{010200, 011200, 012000, 012100, 012200,\\ 100002, 100012, 100020, 100021, 100022,\\ 110000, 110001, 110002, 110010, 110011, 110012, 110020,\\ 110021, 110100, 110200, 111000, 111100, 111200, 112000, 112100\}$$

Taking $i = 0$ and $j = 1$, we observe that both vertices oscillate in the attractor, but the attractor does not contain a state x with $x_i = x_j = 0$.

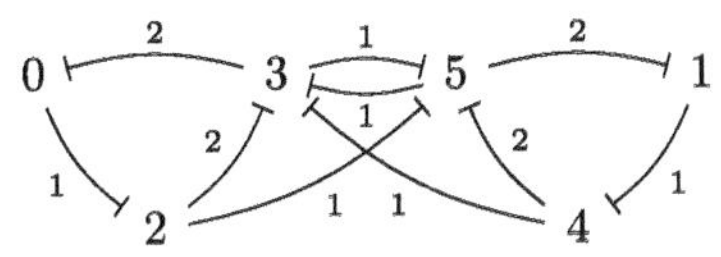

Fig. 3. Interaction graph of dimension 6 with a threshold assignment.

3.4 Case $n = 4$

In dimension $n = 4$, we can fully characterize the repressilator interaction graphs that admit a dynamics with a cyclic attractor. We start by showing that, in dimension 4, if the dynamics has a cyclic attractor, then the interaction graph cannot have a stable dominating set that contains more than one vertex. Intuitively, a stable dominating set cannot intersect the negative cycle associated to the cyclic attractor.

Lemma 1. *Consider $n = 4$. Suppose that* AD(G, m, t) *has a cyclic attractor. Then* G *cannot have a stable dominating set of cardinality two or larger.*

Proof. Observe first that, by (Richard, 2010, Theorem 1), G must admit a negative cycle, therefore a cycle C of length 3.

Since all pairs of vertices in C are connected by at least one edge, any stable dominating set A intersects C in at most one vertex. Suppose that A contains two vertices, and therefore a vertex i in C and a vertex j outside C. Write $A = \{i, j\}$ and $C = \{i, k, h\}$.

Suppose that the vertices in C are the only vertices that oscillate in the attractor. Then j is fixed in the attractor. If j is not the target of any vertex, then the value of component j is fixed to m_j in all attractors. Since we assumed that the directed graph underlying G is connected, j must be an inhibitor of at least one vertex in $\{k, h\}$, meaning that the value of its target is fixed to zero in any attractor, which precludes the existence of a cyclic attractor.

Therefore j is the target of either k or h. Assume without loss of generality that j is the target of k. By Proposition 3 (ii), the attractor contains a state x with $x_k = m_k$, that is, where component k is at maximum level and, therefore, above the threshold for inhibition of j. Since j is fixed in the attractor, its fixed value must be 0. That is, the attractor is contained in the 3-dimensional subspace $S = \{x \in X \mid x_j = 0\}$. By Remark 2, the restriction of the dynamics to S is exactly a repressilator dynamics associated to the interaction graph $\mathrm{G}[C]$. Since it admits a cyclic attractor, by Remark 4 $\mathrm{G}[C]$ consists of an isolated cycle. Moreover, there exists a state x in the attractor where $x_i = m_i$ and $x_k = x_h = 0$. This means that j is not inhibited in x, a contradiction. Therefore all four vertices must oscillate in the attractor.

By definition of a stable dominating set, k and h are inhibited by either i or j. On the other hand, neither i or j can be an inhibitor of both k and h. Indeed, suppose that i inhibits both k and h (the same proof works if we take j as the inhibitor). By Proposition 3 (ii), we can take a state x in the attractor where $x_i = m_i$ and both components k and h are inhibited. By the definition of the dynamics, the attractor contains therefore a state y where $y_k = y_h = 0$. On the other hand, since i does not inhibit j, the value of component j can increase to m_j. That is, the attractor contains a state z that satisfies $z_i = m_i$, $z_j = m_j$. By Proposition 2, there is a path from z to the fixed point $\phi(A)$, a contradiction.

We can therefore assume that i inhibits k and j inhibits h. Since i, k, h form a cycle and h is not inhibited by i, h inhibits i.

Suppose that there is no edge $(k, i) \in E$. Using Proposition 3, take a state x in the attractor where $x_j = m_j$. Since j inhibits h, there also exists a state y in the attractor where $y_j = m_j$ and $y_h = 0$. Since i is only inhibited by h, then there exists a state z in the attractor where $z_j = m_j$, $z_h = 0$ and $z_i = m_i$. By Proposition 2, there is a path from z to the fixed point $\phi(A)$, which is a contradiction.

Suppose now that there is an edge $(k, i) \in E$. If there also exists an edge $(k, j) \in E$, then $A' = \{k\}$ is also a stable dominating set; using Proposition 3, there exists a state $x \in X$ so that $x_k = m_k$ and by Proposition 2, there is a path from x to $\phi(A')$, a contradiction. Finally, if there is an edge $(k, i) \in E$ but $(k, j) \notin E$, then this means that $A'' = \{k, j\}$ is also a stable dominating set, and that vertex $k \in A''$ inhibits vertices $i, h \in V \setminus A''$; as shown above, this also leads to a contradiction. □

Theorem 3. *For $n = 4$, if $\mathrm{AD}(\mathrm{G}, m, t)$ admits both a fixed point and a cyclic attractor for some maximum level assignment m and threshold assignment t, then* G *satisfies the conditions of Theorem 2. More precisely:*

1. *$\mathrm{AD}(\mathrm{G}, m, t)$ admits exactly one fixed point, with a stable dominating set A of size one;*
2. *$\mathrm{G}[B]$ with $B = V \setminus A$ has no stable dominating set, and B is minimal for this property;*
3. *all vertices in B inhibit the vertex in A.*

In addition, $\mathrm{AD}(\mathrm{G}, m, t)$ has exactly one cyclic attractor.

Proof. Consider the minimum subspace $\kappa_{C,I}$ of X that contains the cyclic attractor, meaning that all variables in $V \setminus C$ oscillate in the attractor. The interaction graph of the restriction of the dynamics to $\kappa_{C,I}$ is a subgraph of $\mathrm{G}[V \setminus C]$. By

(Richard, 2010, Theorem 1), $G[V \setminus C]$ must admit a negative cycle. Since loops are excluded and all arcs are negative, $G[V \setminus C]$, and therefore G, must contain a cycle of length 3. In particular, C has cardinality at most one, and at least three vertices oscillate in the cyclic attractor.

(1) By Theorem 1, G has a stable dominating set A. By Lemma 1, A has size one. Say $A = \{i\}$. By Proposition 2 and Proposition 3, i does not oscillate in the cyclic attractor. Therefore this attractor oscillates in exactly three dimensions, and there is only one stable dominating set, and therefore only one fixed point (by Theorem 1).

(2) We know that i is fixed in the cyclic attractor, and, by Proposition 2, cannot be fixed at maximum level. Therefore, it must be inhibited in all states in the attractor. Since it is inhibited and fixed in the attractor, it must take value zero in all states in the attractor. That is, the attractor is contained in $S = \{x \in X \mid x_i = 0\}$.

Therefore the vertices in B form a cycle. By Remark 2, the restriction of the dynamics to S is a repressilator dynamics associated to the interaction graph $G[B]$, and by Remark 4, $G[B]$ is an isolated cycle, and has no stable dominating set while all proper subsets of B admit a stable dominating set.

(3) Suppose that a vertex $j \in B$ does not inhibit i. By Remark 4 there exists a state x in the attractor where the components corresponding to $B \setminus \{j\}$ are zero, and i is not inhibited and is free to increase, a contradiction.

Finally, again by Remark 4, the cyclic attractor is unique (all cyclic attractors contain the state where the vertex in A is zero, two vertices in B are zero and the remaining vertex is at maximum level). □

4 Conclusion

Repressilators are biological networks composed only of inhibitions between components, used in synthetic biology for their ability to exhibit oscillatory behavior. However, in dimensions higher than 3, not all repressilators oscillate: in some cases, the attractors are all fixed points. In this paper, we propose a method to determine if a given repressilator of dimension n might present a cyclic attractor. This method is solely based on the interaction graph without threshold assignment, meaning that we avoid both the combinatorial explosion due to the computation of the state transition graph, and the enumeration of the possible threshold assignments.

A possible extension of this work could explore the applicability of a result analogous to Theorem 2 with a weaker premise, making it less specific and more widely applicable. Networks that are not repressilators and that might contain positive interactions could also be considered. A complete characterization of the asymptotic dynamics of repressilators in dimension 5 or higher also remains to be investigated. Linking the theory and results developed in this work to and-nets (such as in (Richard and Ruet, 2013) could prove beneficial to this aim.

Acknowledgments. ET was funded by the Deutsche Forschungsgemeinschaft (DFG, German Research Foundation) under Germany's Excellence Strategy âĂŞ The Berlin Mathematics Research Center MATH+ (EXC-2046/1, project ID: 390685689). HS was funded by the China Scholarship Council.

References

Akutsu, T., Kosub, S., Melkman, A.A., Tamura, T.: Finding a periodic attractor of a boolean network. IEEE/ACM Trans. Comput. Biol. Bioinf. **9**(5), 1410–1421 (2012)

Batt, G., de Jong, H., Page, M., Geiselmann, J.: Symbolic reachability analysis of genetic regulatory networks using discrete abstractions. Automatica **44**(4), 982–989 (2008)

Bernot, G., Comet, J.-P., Richard, A., Guespin, J.: Application of formal methods to biological regulatory networks: extending Thomas' asynchronous logical approach with temporal logic. J. Theor. Biol. **229**(3), 339–347 (2004)

Comet, J.-P., et al.: On circuit functionality in boolean networks. Bull. Math. Biol. **75**(6), 906–919 (2013)

de Jong, H.: Modeling and simulation of genetic regulatory systems: a literature review. J. Comput. Biol. **9**(1), 67–103 (2002)

Elowitz, M.B., Leibler, S.: A synthetic oscillatory network of transcriptional regulators. Nature **403**(6767), 335–338 (2000)

Gadouleau, M.: On the influence of the interaction graph on a finite dynamical system. Nat. Comput. **19**(1), 15–28 (2020)

Goh, K.-I., Kahng, B., Cho, K.-H.: Sustained oscillations in extended genetic oscillatory systems. Biophys. J . **94**(11), 4270–4276 (2008)

Kauffman, S.A.: Metabolic stability and epigenesis in randomly constructed genetic nets. J. Theor. Biol. **22**(3), 437–467 (1969)

Melkman, A.A., Tamura, T., Akutsu, T.: Determining a singleton attractor of an AND/OR Boolean network in O(1.587̂n) time. Inf. Process. Lett. **110**(14-15), 565–569 (2010)

Melkman, A.A., Tamura, T., Akutsu, T.: Determining a singleton attractor of an AND/OR Boolean network in O(1.587âŇČn) time. Inf. Process. Lett. **110**(14-15), 565–569 (2010)

Naldi, A., Remy, E., Thieffry, D., and Chaouiya, C.: Dynamically consistent reduction of logical regulatory graphs. Theoretical Comput. Sci. **412**(21), 2207–2218 (2011). Selected Papers from the 7th International Conference on Computational Methods in Systems Biology

Page, K.M.: Oscillations in well-mixed, deterministic feedback systems: beyond ring oscillators. J. Theor. Biol. **481**, 44–53 (2019)

Paulevé, L., Magnin, M., and Roux, O.: Static analysis of Biological Regulatory Networks dynamics using abstract interpretation. Mathematical Structures in Computer Science, pp. 1–35 (2012)

Paulevé, L. and Richard, A. (2012). Static analysis of boolean networks based on interaction graphs: a survey. Electron. Notes Theoretical Comput. Sci. **284**, 93–104. Proceedings of the 2nd International Workshop on Static Analysis and Systems Biology (SASB 2011)

Perez-Carrasco, R., Barnes, C.P., Schaerli, Y., Isalan, M., Briscoe, J., Page, K.M.: Combining a toggle switch and a repressilator within the ac-dc circuit generates distinct dynamical behaviors. Cell Syst. **6**(4), 521–530 (2018)

Potvin-Trottier, L., Lord, N.D., Vinnicombe, G., Paulsson, J.: Synchronous long-term oscillations in a synthetic gene circuit. Nature **538**(7626), 514–517 (2016)

Richard, A.: Negative circuits and sustained oscillations in asynchronous automata networks. Adv. Appl. Math. **44**(4), 378–392 (2010)

Richard, A., Ruet, P.: From kernels in directed graphs to fixed points and negative cycles in boolean networks. Discret. Appl. Math. **161**(7), 1106–1117 (2013)

Sun, H., Folschette, M., Magnin, M.: Condition for periodic attractor in 4-dimensional repressilators. In: Pang, J., Niehren, J. (eds.) 21st International Conference on Computational Methods in Systems Biology (CMSB 2023), pp. 184–201. Cham. Springer Nature Switzerland (2023)

Thomas, R.: Boolean formalization of genetic control circuits. J. Theor. Biol. **42**(3), 563–585 (1973)

Thomas, R.: Regulatory networks seen as asynchronous automata: a logical description. J. Theor. Biol. **153**(1), 1–23 (1991)

Symbol Frequencies in Surjective Cellular Automata

Benjamin Hellouin de Menibus[1], Ville Salo[2], and Ilkka Törmä[2(✉)]

[1] Laboratoire Interdisciplinaire des Sciences du Numérique, Université Paris-Saclay, CNRS, Orsay, France
hellouin@lisn.fr

[2] Department of Mathematics and Statistics, University of Turku, Turku, Finland
vosalo@utu.fi, iatorm@utu.fi

Abstract. We study the behavior of probability measures under iteration of a surjective cellular automaton. We solve the following question in the negative: if the initial measure is ergodic and has full support, do all weak-* limit points of the sequence of measures have full support as well? The initial measure of our solution is not a product measure, and in this case the question remains open. To this end, we present a tool for studying the frequencies of symbols in preimages of surjective cellular automata, and prove some basic results about it. However, we show that by itself it is not enough to solve the stricter question in the positive.

Keywords: Cellular automata · Surjective cellular automata · Measures · Iteration · Frequency

1 Introduction

We study the asymptotic behavior of cellular automata (CA) iterated on random initial configurations. Formally, we take a CA F on a state set Σ and a shift invariant probability measure μ on $\Sigma^{\mathbb{Z}}$ – such as the uniform measure λ where each cell is chosen in an i.i.d. uniform manner – and study the asymptotic properties of the sequence $(F^t\mu)_{t\in\mathbb{N}}$. This asymptotic behavior may be computationally very complex [5] and related properties are generally undecidable [1].

Surjective CA are better-behaved in this regard. Despite the fact that they are capable of universal computation in some settings, their behavior on probability measures has a much more combinatorial and dynamical structure. For example, every surjective CA keeps the uniform measure invariant, so in particular properties of $(F^t\lambda)_{t\in\mathbb{N}}$ are completely understood. Another very important property is that the image of a measure under a surjective CA cannot have a lower measure-theoretical entropy. A survey of this structure can be found in [4].

Let us provide examples of asymptotic behavior. It may happen that F has a non-uniform invariant measure μ, in which case $F^t\mu = \mu$ stays "away" from the uniform measure; this happens e.g. when $F = \mathrm{Id}$, or more generally when the CA

Published by Springer Nature Switzerland AG 2026
S. Riva and A. Richard (Eds.): AUTOMATA 2025, LNCS 15831, pp. 154–170, 2026.
https://doi.org/10.1007/978-3-032-01570-9_11

has some conserved quantity [3]. Other types of CA may exhibit *randomization*, where for a large class of initial measures the sequence $(F^t\mu)_{t\in\mathbb{N}}$ tends, either directly or on average, toward the uniform measure. As the latter is the measure of maximum entropy on $\Sigma^{\mathbb{Z}}$, the intuition is that as time goes on, $F^t\mu$ tends to a measure of maximum disorder. Measure randomization has been studied extensively (see [6,8] among others).

Uniform measures and Gibbs measures [4] are among the few cases of initial measures for which nontrivial results about iteration of general surjective CA are known. These two families, as well as the fact that surjective CA cannot decrease entropy, are examples of phenomena where $(F^t\mu)_{t\in\mathbb{N}}$ cannot go "further away" from the uniform measure and that the identity CA is extremal in this sense. In this article, we provide new examples and counterexamples of this phenomenon.

Our main motivation is the following question, which is hinted at in [1, Section 7] and relayed to us explicitly by Guillaume Theyssier (personal communication). For a probability measure μ and a finite word u, we denote by $\mu([u])$ the probability that u appears at position 0.

Question 1. Let F be a surjective CA on $\Sigma^{\mathbb{Z}}$ and μ a product measure of full support, meaning $\mu([u]) > 0$ for all words u. Does $F^t\mu([u]) \not\to 0$ hold for all u?

This article represents an attempt at resolving Question 1 that ultimately failed, but produced interesting partial results and counterexamples. For example, the intuition of not going further away from the uniform measure may suggest a stronger statement, that is,

$$\forall u \in \Sigma^n, |F\mu([u]) - \lambda([u])| \leq \max_{w\in\Sigma^n} |\mu([w]) - \lambda([w])|, \tag{1}$$

where $\lambda([u]) = |\Sigma|^{-n}$. We show that this is false (Theorem 1). However, a failed attempt led us to introduce a value called *correlation* for which the phenomenon holds (Theorems 4 and 5) and which does not seem to be a consequence of existing results, although we did not find a clear application.

Orthogonally to these results, we also show that Question 1 is false if the measure μ is merely assumed to be ergodic instead of a product measure. We construct an explicit counterexample in which the two-neighbor XOR automaton F satisfies $F^t([1]) \longrightarrow 0$ (Theorem 2). We also provide an example of the XOR automaton giving a different limit behavior (Theorem 3).

2 Definitions

Cellular Automata. We consider one-dimensional cellular automata over a finite alphabet Σ. A *cellular automaton* (CA for short) is a function $F : \Sigma^{\mathbb{Z}} \to \Sigma^{\mathbb{Z}}$ defined by a *local rule* $f : \Sigma^N \to \Sigma$ of some finite *neighborhood* $N \subset \mathbb{Z}$ by $F(x)_i = f(x|_{N+i})$ for all $x \in \Sigma^{\mathbb{Z}}$ and $i \in \mathbb{Z}$. The identity CA is defined by $\mathrm{Id}(x_i) = x_i$. The shift CA σ is defined by $\sigma(x_i) = x_{i+1}$.

Unless explicitly stated, we only consider CA with neighborhoods $N = \{0, 1, \ldots, r\}$ for some *(one-sided) radius* $r \geq 0$. The notions we study are invariant under composition with shifts, and one-sided neighborhoods simplify the calculations. We may apply a one-sided CA F to a word $w \in \Sigma^n$ of length $n \geq r+1$ to obtain a word $F(w) \in \Sigma^{n-r}$ by the formula $F(w)_i = f(w_{[i,i+r]})$.

For a word $w \in \Sigma^*$ and $A \subset \Sigma$, we denote by $|w|$ its length and by $|w|_A$ the number of occurrences of A-symbols in w. For single symbols $a \in \Sigma$, we write $|w|_a = |w|_{\{a\}}$. The *cylinder* corresponding to w, denoted $[w]$, is the set of configurations $x \in \Sigma^{\mathbb{Z}}$ such that $x_{[0,|w|-1]} = w$.

Surjectivity and Probability Measures. See [7] for a general reference on CA and probability measures. Through the article, probability measures on $\Sigma^{\mathbb{Z}}$ are assumed to be σ-invariant. In this case a probability measure μ is entirely described by its value on cylinders $\mu([u])$, $u \in \Sigma^*$. We say μ is σ-*ergodic* if $\frac{1}{N}\sum_{k=0}^{N-1} \mu(A \cap T^{-k}(B)) \overset{N\to\infty}{\longrightarrow} \mu(A)\mu(B)$ holds for all Borel sets $A, B \subseteq \Sigma^{\mathbb{Z}}$.

The simplest example is the uniform measure λ where $\lambda([u]) = |\Sigma|^{-|u|}$. In general, any function $\pi : \Sigma \to [0,1]$ with $\sum_{a\in\Sigma} \pi(a) = 1$ defines a product measure μ with $\mu([u]) = \prod_{i=0}^{|u|-1} \pi(u_i)$. When $\Sigma = \{0,1\}$, the product measure with a density p of 1-symbols is denoted by μ_p. It is also called the Bernoulli measure with parameter p. For $a \in \Sigma$, the Dirac measure with support ${}^\infty a^\infty$, denoted δ_a, is defined by $\delta_a([a^n]) = 1$ and $\delta_a([u]) = 0$ for all $u \in \Sigma^* \setminus a^*$.

The image under a CA F of a probability measure μ is given by $F\mu([u]) = \mu(F^{-1}([u]))$ for any $u \in \Sigma^*$. We call ν the weak-* limit of the sequence $(F^t\mu)_{t\in\mathbb{N}}$ if $F^t\mu([u]) \longrightarrow \nu([u])$ for all words $u \in \Sigma^*$. The sequence $(F^t\mu)_{t\in\mathbb{N}}$ does not always admit a single weak-* limit, but it has weak-* limit points by compactness.

A surjective CA F satisfies a *balance property*: $|F^{-1}(w)| = |\Sigma|^r$ holds for all words $w \in \Sigma^*$. This implies that $F\lambda = \lambda$.

The measure-theoretical entropy of a shift-invariant probability measure μ is $h(\mu) = \lim_{n\to\infty} \sum_{w\in\Sigma^n} -\mu([w]) \log \mu([w])$. In particular, we have $h(\lambda) = \log(|\Sigma|)$, which is the highest possible entropy. For any function $\pi : \Sigma \to [0,1]$ with $\sum_{a\in\Sigma} \pi(a) = 1$, the product measure defined by π is the unique measure of maximum entropy among those measures μ with $\mu([a]) = \pi(a)$ for all $a \in \Sigma$. For any CA F, entropy may not increase: $h(F\mu) \leq h(\mu)$. If F is surjective, it preserves entropy: $h(F\mu) = h(\mu)$ [7, Theorem 6].

3 Limit Measures Not of Full Support

We show that if one considers an arbitrary sequence of surjective CA, instead of the iterations of a single CA, the answer to Question 1 is negative.

Theorem 1. *There exists $0 < p < 1$, a sequence $(F_n)_{n\in\mathbb{N}}$ of reversible binary cellular automata and a word $w \in \{0,1\}^*$ such that $F_n\mu_p([w]) \longrightarrow 0$. In particular, no weak-* limit point of $(F_n\mu_p)_{n\in\mathbb{N}}$ has full support.*

Proof. Take a small $p > 0$, and for $n \in \mathbb{N}$, let $w_n = (10)^n0$ and $\alpha(n) = n/\mu_p(w_n) + |w_n|$. For each $k \geq 2/p$, define two subsets of $\{0,1\}^k$:

$$A_k = \{w \in \{0,1\}^k \mid kp/2 \leq |w|_1 \leq 3kp/2, w_n \text{ does not occur in } w\}$$

$$B_k = \{(110a_1)(110a_2)\cdots(110a_{\lfloor k/4 \rfloor})0^{k-4\lfloor k/4 \rfloor} \mid a_i \in \{0,1\}\}$$

We also fix an injection $E_k : A_k \to B_k$. This is possible, since

$$|A_k| \leq \sum_{m=pk/2}^{3pk/2} \binom{k}{m} \leq pk \binom{k}{3pk/2} \leq pk \cdot 2^{kH(3p/2)} \leq 2^{\lfloor k/4 \rfloor} = |B_k|,$$

where $H(x) = -x \log_2 x - (1-x)\log_2(1-x)$ is the binary entropy function, as long as p is small enough. Finally, we have $A_k \cap B_k = \emptyset$, because every $w \in B_k$ satisfies $|w|_1 \geq 2\lfloor k/4 \rfloor \geq k/3 > 3kp/2$ as long as p is small enough.

We are now ready to define the CA F_n. The idea is that a μ_p-random configuration consists mostly of words in A_k, and we use the injection f_k to change them into words of B_k, which contain no occurrences of the word 1111.

The CA F_n behaves as follows on a configuration $x \in \{0,1\}^{\mathbb{Z}}$. Let $I = \{i \in \mathbb{Z} \mid x_{[i,i+|w_n|-1]} = w_n\}$ be the set of occurrences of w_n. For any two consecutive elements $i_1 < i_2 \in I$, the word $w_n v = x_{[i_1,i_2-1]}$ is called an *n-interval*. Denote $k = i_2 - i_1$. This n-interval is *short* if $k < 2n/p$, *medium* if $2n/p \leq k \leq \alpha(n) + |w_n|$, and *long* if $k > \alpha(n) + |w_n|$.

- If an interval is medium and $v \in A_k$, then F_n replaces v by $E_k(v) \in B_k$. Such intervals are called *p-common*.
- If an interval is medium and $v \in E_k(A_k)$, then F_n replaces v by $E_k^{-1}(v) \in A_k$.
- F_n acts as the identity in any other situation.

Then F_n is a well-defined CA with neighborhood $[-r, r]$ for $r = \alpha(n) + |w_n|$. It cannot create or destroy occurrences of w_n. It satisfies $F_n^{-1} = F_n$, and is in particular reversible.

We claim that $w = 1111$ does not occur in the support of any weak-* limit point of $F_n\mu_p$, or equivalently, $(F_n\mu_p)([1111]) \longrightarrow 0$ as $n \longrightarrow \infty$. Namely, consider a configuration $x \in \{0,1\}^{\mathbb{Z}}$ with $F_n(x) \in [1111]$. Almost surely with respect to μ_p, x partitions $\mathbb{Z}$ into n-intervals of finite length. In any occurrence of 1111, only the rightmost symbol can overlap an occurrence of w_n. Thus, the three leftmost symbols overlap the non-w_n part of a n-interval of some length k. This interval cannot be p-common, as no word of B_k contains more than two consecutive 1-symbols. Thus, $(F_n\mu_p)([1111])$ is at most the probability that the n-interval that contains the origin is not p-common.

An n-interval is not p-common if it is short, long, or medium but not in A_k.

- The probability of being short is at most the probability of seeing an occurrence of w_n in a μ_p-random word of length $2n/p$, which is upper-bounded by $2n/p \cdot \mu_p(w_n) = 2np^{n+1}(1-p)^{n+1}$.
- Since the mean length of an n-interval is $1/\mu_p(w_n)$, by Markov's inequality the probability of being long is at most $1/n$.
- By Hoeffding's bound [2], the probability of a medium n-interval to not be p-common is at most $2\exp(-pn)$.

Each of these tends to 0 as $n \longrightarrow \infty$, hence $(F_n\mu_p)([1111])$ does as well. □

Orthogonally to Theorem 1, we can also weaken Question 1 by removing the condition that μ be a product measure. We show that the answer becomes negative if we only assume ergodicity.

Theorem 2. *Let F be the two-neighbor XOR automaton. There exists an ergodic full-support measure μ on $\{0,1\}^{\mathbb{Z}}$ such that $(F^n\mu)_{n\in\mathbb{N}}$ weak-* converges to the Dirac measure δ_0.*

Without the ergodicity requirement, the result would be much easier. We could choose μ as the measure that picks n from a full-support distribution on $\mathbb{N}$, and then a uniformly random spatially 2^n-periodic configuration. Because $F^{2^n}(x) = {}^\infty 0^\infty$ when x is spatially 2^n-periodic, $F^n\mu$ weak-* converges to δ_0.

Proof. The idea is that we group the configuration into intervals of length 2, then group those into intervals of length 8, etc. The lengths form the sequence $2^{t(n)}$ where $t(n) = n(n+1)/2$. For each such interval we flip a biased coin, and with probability tending to 1 as n grows, constrain it to be locally $2^{t(n-1)}$-periodic. After $2^{t(n-1)}$ applications of XOR, such an interval is mostly 0s.

Definition of μ: We define a measure ν on an auxiliary dynamical system (X,T) and a measurable factor map $\phi : (X,T) \to (\{0,1\}^{\mathbb{Z}}, \sigma)$, and let $\mu = \phi\nu$. The space X is a subset of an infinite product of subshifts: $X \subset \{0,1\}^{\mathbb{Z}} \times \prod_{n\geq 1} X_n$, where each X_n is a subshift over the alphabet $\Sigma_n = \{0,1,\ldots,2^{t(n)}-1\}$ defined as the orbit of the periodic point ${}^\infty 012\cdots(2^{t(n)}-1)^\infty$. Points of X are denoted $x = (x^*, x^1, x^2, \ldots)$ where $x^* \in \{0,1\}^{\mathbb{Z}}$ and $x^n \in X_n$. We require for all $n \in \mathbb{N}$ and $i \in \mathbb{Z}$ that $x_i^n \equiv x_i^{n+1} \bmod 2^{t(n)}$. The dynamics T is just the left shift on each component, and the factor map ϕ is the projection $\phi(x) = x^*$.

Let $(p_n)_{n\geq 1}$ be an increasing sequence with $0 < p_n < 1$, $p_n \longrightarrow 1$ and $\prod_n p_n = 0$, such as $p_n = 1 - 1/(n+1)$. We define the measure ν on X by describing how to sample a ν-random configuration $x \in X$. We construct the components x^n sequentially. When $x^1, \ldots, x^{n-1}$ have been fixed, there are 2^n choices for the configuration x^n. We pick one of them with uniform probability.

For $n \geq 1$, each position $i \in \mathbb{Z}$ with $x_i^n = 0$ defines an *n-block*, which is the interval $\{i, i+1, \ldots, i+2^{t(n)}-1\}$. Each singleton $\{i\}$ is a 0-block. For $n \geq 1$, each level-n block consists of 2^n consecutive $(n-1)$-blocks, called its *children*.

To sample x^*, we choose some 0-block $i \in \mathbb{Z}$ as the *anchor* and pick x_i^* to be 0 or 1 each with probability 1/2. Suppose then that we have picked the value of $x^*|_I$ for some n-block $I \subset \mathbb{Z}$ containing i. Let J be the $(n+1)$-block containing I, and let $K_1, \ldots, K_{2^n-1}$ be its children other than I. Then, with probability p_n we choose $x^*|_{K_i} = x^*|_I$ for all i, and with probability $1-p_n$ we pick each $x^*|_{K_i}$ by choosing the leftmost 0-block of K_i as a temporary anchor and repeating the above process with independent random choices. With probability 1, the entire configuration x^* is eventually specified (the converse happens if for all large enough n, the n-block containing i is the left/rightmost one in its $(n+1)$-block; in this case we specify a half-line of x^*). This concludes the definition of ν.

We prove that the distribution of ν is independent of the choice of the anchor. Let $i_1 \leq i_2$ be two anchors. Almost surely the components $x^1, x^2, \ldots$ are such that i_1 and i_2 are contained in some n-block I. We proceed by induction on the minimal such n. For $n = 0$ we have $i_1 = i_2$ and the claim is trivial. For $n \geq 1$, let $I_1 \neq I_2$ be the children of I that contain i_1 and i_2, respectively. The process that starts at i_1 samples I_1, which by the induction hypothesis has the same distribution as I_2 in the i_2-originated process. With probability p_n, the i_1-process copies the contents of I_1 to every child of I, and with probability $1 - p_n$ it samples the other children independently, and by the induction hypothesis, identically to the i_2-process. The i_2-process behaves symmetrically, and we see that they produce identical distributions on $x^*|_I$. After $x^*|_I$ has been sampled, both processes are identical, so the distributions over x^* are identical. It also follows that ν is T-invariant, and its image μ is shift-invariant.

Properties of μ: The measure μ has full support: for any word $w \in \{0,1\}^{2^{t(n)}}$, there is a nonzero probability for $\{0, \dots, 2^{t(n)} - 1\}$ to be an n-block, none of its sub-blocks to be copied from their neighbors, and the randomly chosen bits to result in w.

We prove that $F^n \mu \longrightarrow \delta_0$. Recall that the two-neighbor XOR satisfies $F^{2^k}(x)_i \equiv x_i + x_{i+2^k} \bmod 2$ for all $k \geq 0$, $x \in \{0,1\}^{\mathbb{Z}}$ and $i \in \mathbb{Z}$. Consider a ν-random configuration $x = (x^*, x^1, x^2, \dots)$ and let $n \geq 1$. Let I be the $(n+2)$-block containing the position 0. With probability at least $1 - (2^{n+1} + 2^n)/(2^{n+2} \cdot 2^{n+1}) = 1 - 2^{-(n+2)} - 2^{-(n+3)}$, the n-block containing 0 is not among the $2^{n+1} + 2^n$ rightmost n-blocks in I. Independently, with probability at least $p_n p_{n+1}$, all n-blocks in I have equal contents in x^*. If both events happen, we have $x^*_i = x^*_{2^{t(n)}+i}$ for each $0 \leq i < 2^{t(n+1)}$, and hence $F^k(x^*)_0 = 0$ for all $2^{t(n)} \leq k < 2^{t(n+1)}$. Both probabilities tend to 1 as n grows, so $F^n \mu$ weak-* converges to δ_0.

We show that μ is ergodic by first showing that ν is ergodic, which means that $\frac{1}{N} \sum_{k=0}^{N-1} \nu(A \cap T^{-k}(B))$ converges to $\nu(A)\nu(B)$ as N grows, for all Borel sets $A, B \subseteq X$. By a standard argument (based on the fact that for every Borel set A and $\epsilon > 0$ there exists a finite union of cylinder sets C with $\nu(A \triangle C) < \epsilon$) it suffices to prove this when A and B are cylinder sets with domain $D = \{0, 1, \dots, 2^{t(n)} - 1\}$ on the components x^* and $x^1, \dots, x^n$ for some $n \geq 0$. For $0 \leq i < 2^{t(n)}$, let $P_i = \{x \in X \mid x^n_0 = i\}$. Since A and B are cylinder sets, we have $A \subseteq P_i$ and $B \subseteq P_j$ for some i, j. We assume $i = j = 0$, the general case being similar. Then we have $\nu(A \cap T^{-k}(B) \mid P_i) = 0$ whenever $i \neq 0$ or $k \not\equiv 0 \bmod 2^{t(n)}$, and $\nu(A \mid P_0) = 2^{t(n)} \nu(A)$ and analogously for B.

Let us condition on P_0. Fix a large $M \geq n$ and let $0 \leq \ell < 2^{t(M)-t(n)}$ vary. The domains of A and $T^{-\ell 2^{t(n)}}(B)$ coincide with some n-blocks, and lie in some M-blocks; possibly the same one. The sequence of directions (which child to choose) to reach the domain of A from its M-block is given by the representation of ℓ_A in the mixed base $b = (2^M, 2^{M-1}, \dots, 2^{n+1})$, where $\ell_A 2^{t(n)}$ is the distance from the left end of the M-block to the left end of A. We define ℓ_B similarly for the domain of $T^{-\ell 2^n}(B)$. Then $\ell_B - \ell_A \equiv \ell \mod 2^{t(M)-t(n)}$, so for a fraction of $0 \leq \ell < 2^{t(M)-t(n)}$ that tends to 1 as M grows, the base-b representations of ℓ_A and ℓ_B differ in at least $(M-n)/3$ digits; call this set $I \subset \{0, \dots, M-n\}$. With probability at least $1 - p_n p_{n+1} \cdots p_{n+(M-n)/3}$, which also tends to 1, for some $i \in I$ the children of the $(n+i)$-block containing A are sampled independently.

Thus, regardless of whether the M-blocks that contain A and $T^{-\ell 2^{t(n)}}(B)$ are the same, copies of each other, or independently sampled, for such an ℓ the n-blocks that make up the domains of A and $T^{-\ell 2^n}(B)$ are sampled independently. Then $\nu(A \cap T^{-\ell 2^{t(n)}}(B) \mid P_0) = \nu(A \mid P_0)\nu(T^{-\ell 2^{t(n)}}(B) \mid P_0) = 2^{2t(n)}\nu(A)\nu(B)$.

Altogether this implies that

$$\begin{aligned}
&\frac{1}{2^{t(M)}} \sum_{k=0}^{2^{t(M)}-1} \nu(A \cap T^{-k}(B)) \\
&= \frac{1}{2^{t(M)}} \sum_{k=0}^{2^{t(M)}-1} \sum_{i=0}^{2^{t(n)}-1} \nu(A \cap T^{-k}(B)|P_i)\nu(P_i) \\
&= \frac{1}{2^{t(M)+t(n)}} \sum_{\ell=0}^{2^{t(M)-t(n)}-1} \nu(A \cap T^{-\ell 2^{t(n)}}(B)|P_0)
\end{aligned}$$

is close to $\nu(A)\nu(B)$. Hence ν is T-ergodic, and μ is shift-ergodic. □

Again somewhat orthogonally to both of the above theorems, we can produce a different limit behavior by iterating XOR on a single initial ergodic measure, at the cost of having to pass to a fixed subsequence.

Theorem 3. *Let F be the two-neighbor XOR automaton and $0 \leq \alpha \leq 1$. There exists an ergodic full-support measure μ on $\{0,1\}^{\mathbb{Z}}$ such that the sequence $(F^{2^{n(n+1)/2}}\mu)_{n \in \mathbb{N}}$ weak-* converges to $\alpha\delta_0 + (1-\alpha)\delta_1$.*

Proof. We use the same construction of the measures ν and μ as in the proof of Theorem 2, but modified as follows. When sampling x^*, suppose we have sampled an n-block I containing the anchor and are considering the $(n+1)$-block J. With probability $1 - p_n$, we sample each child of J independently, as before. With probability αp_n, all children of J are filled with $x^*|_I$. With probability $(1-\alpha)p_n$, the children of J alternate between $x^*|_I$ and its symbolwise negation.

This distribution is also independent of the position of the anchor; the proof is the same as in Theorem 2, with the additional observation that the distribution of the contents of n-blocks in x^* is invariant under cellwise negation. This latter property can be easily proved by induction on n. The proofs of the shift-invariance, ergodicity and full support of μ are then exactly as before.

As for the limit points, take a ν-random configuration $x = (x^*, x^1, x^2, \ldots)$ and let $n \geq 1$. Let I be the $(n+1)$-block containing the origin. With probability $1 - 2^{-n+1}$, the n-block containing the origin is not one of the two rightmost children of I. Independently, with probability αp_n, the children of I have equal contents in x^*, and with probability $(1-\alpha)p_n$ they alternate between some word and its symbolwise negation. As n grows, the probability of $x^*_i = x^*_{2^{t(n)}+i}$, and hence $F^{2^{t(n)}}(x)_i = 0$, for all $0 \leq i < 2^{t(n)}$ tends to α, and the probability of $F^{2^{t(n)}}(x)_i = 1$ for all $0 \leq i < 2^{t(n)}$ tends to $1-\alpha$. This implies the claim. □

4 Correlation

In this section, we introduce a notion called correlation and prove that, among surjective CA of a given radius r, the identity CA has the highest (A, A)-correlation of order 1 and of any high enough order.

Let us first provide some motivation. Suppose that you are trying to prove Eq. (1) in the particular case where μ is a product measure. Without loss of generality, we consider $F\mu([b])$ where $b \in \Sigma$ is a single letter. Then

$$F\mu([b]) = \mu(F^{-1}([b])) = \sum_{f(w)=b} \mu[w] = \sum_{f(w)=b} \prod_{a\in\Sigma} (\mu[a])^{|w|_a} \tag{2}$$

Thus the values $F\mu([b])$ depend of the number and repartition of occurrences of each letter a in the pre-images of b under F, that is, the values of $|w|_a$ for $w \in f^{-1}(b)$ (notice that, by the balance property, the number of such words does not depend on b), and we would be looking to compare this repartition with the case $F = \mathrm{Id}$. As a first step, we try to count the total number of occurrences in all preimages without considering the repartition: this is the intuition behind correlation, which is essentially an additive version of Eq. (2).

4.1 Definition and Basic Properties

Definition 1. *Let F be a CA of radius at most r, and let $A, B \subseteq \Sigma$.*

For $0 \le k \le r+1$, we denote $N_B^A(F, r, k)$ the number of words that contain exactly k symbols in A and map to B under the radius-r local function. In other words, $N_B^A(F, r, k) = |\{w \in \Sigma^{r+1} \mid F(w)_0 \in B, |w|_A = k\}|$.

The (A, B, r)-histogram *of F is the list $H_B^A(F, r) = (N_B^A(F, r, k))_{0\le k\le r+1}$.*

The (A, B, r)-correlation of order m *of F is the m'th moment of the histogram, that is,*

$$C_B^A(F, r, m) = \sum_{k=0}^{r+1} k^m N_B^A(F, r, k).$$

The (A, B, r)-correlation of order 1 is simply called the (A, B, r)-correlation.

We drop r from these definitions if it is clear from the context; for example, we may discuss the (A, B)-correlation and denote it by $C_B^A(F, 1)$.

We also have the simpler formula

$$C_B^A(F, r, m) = \sum_{w\in f^{-1}(B)} |w|_A^m. \tag{3}$$

In particular, the (A, B, r)-correlation $C_B^A(F, r, 1)$ is the total number of A-symbols in all preimages of B-symbols, and (with the convention $0^0 = 1$) the correlation of order 0 is $C_B^A(F, r, 0) = |f^{-1}(B)|$. If F is surjective, the balance property gives $C_B^A(F, r, 0) = |B| \cdot |\Sigma|^r$.

Example 1. Consider the (non-surjective) radius-2 CA F with state set $\Sigma = \{0, 1, 2\}$ defined by the local rule

$$f(a,b,c) = \begin{cases} 2, & \text{if } b = c, \\ 1, & \text{if } b \neq c \text{ and } a = 0, \\ 0, & \text{otherwise.} \end{cases}$$

For $A = \{0\}$ and $B = \{0, 2\}$, the quantity $N_B^A(F, 1)$ is the number of words $w \in \Sigma^3$ that satisfy $f(w) \in \{0, 2\}$ and $|w|_0 = 1$. These words are exactly 011, 022, 101, 102, 110, 120, 201, 202, 210, and 220. Hence $N_B^A(F, 1) = 10$.

The full (A, B)-histogram of F is $(8, 10, 2, 1)$. Its sum, $8 + 10 + 2 + 1 = 21$, equals the number of words in $f^{-1}(B)$. The first moment of the histogram, $0 \cdot 8 + 1 \cdot 10 + 2 \cdot 2 + 3 \cdot 1 = 17$, equals $C_B^A(F, 1)$, the (A, B)-correlation of F.

Lemma 1. *Let F be a radius-r CA on $\Sigma^{\mathbb{Z}}$, let $A \subseteq \Sigma$ and $0 < p < 1$, and let $\mu_{A,p}$ be the product measure with $\mu_{A,p}([a]) = p/|A|$ for all $a \in A$ and $\mu_{a,p}([b]) = (1-p)/(|\Sigma| - |A|)$ for all $b \notin A$. Then we have*

$$\sum_{a \in A} F\mu_{A,p}([a]) = \sum_{\ell=0}^{r+1} p^\ell \left(\sum_{k=0}^{\ell} \frac{(-1)^{\ell-k} \binom{r+1-k}{r+1-\ell} N_A^A(F, r, k)}{|A|^k (|\Sigma| - |A|)^{r+1-k}} \right). \tag{4}$$

In particular, this implies that the (A, A)-histogram of a CA F completely determines the values $\sum_{a \in A} F\mu_{A,p}([a])$ for $0 < p < 1$.

Proof. We compute

$$\begin{aligned}
\sum_{a \in A} F\mu_{A,p}([a]) &= \sum_{a \in A} \sum_{w \in F^{-1}([a])} \prod_{i=0}^{r} \mu_{A,p}(w_i) \\
&= \sum_{k=0}^{r+1} \sum_{a \in A} \sum_{\substack{w \in F^{-1}([a]) \\ |w|_A = k}} \left(\frac{p}{|A|}\right)^k \left(\frac{1-p}{|\Sigma| - |A|}\right)^{r+1-k} \\
&= \sum_{k=0}^{r+1} \frac{N_A^A(F, k)}{|A|^k (|\Sigma| - |A|)^{r+1-k}} \cdot p^k (1-p)^{r+1-k} \\
&= \sum_{k=0}^{r+1} \frac{N_A^A(F, k)}{|A|^k (|\Sigma| - |A|)^{r+1-k}} \cdot p^k \sum_{\ell=0}^{r+1-k} \binom{r+1-k}{\ell} (-p)^{r+1-k-\ell} \\
&= \sum_{\ell=0}^{r+1} p^{r+1-\ell} \left(\sum_{k=0}^{r+1-\ell} \frac{(-1)^{r+1-k-\ell} \binom{r+1-k}{\ell} N_A^A(F, k)}{|A|^k (|\Sigma| - |A|)^{r+1-k}} \right).
\end{aligned}$$

The change of variables $\ell \to r + 1 - \ell$ gives the claim. □

The (A, B)-correlation of a CA is defined for a fixed radius. We also present a normalized definition that is independent of the radius.

Lemma 2. *Let F be a radius-r CA on $\Sigma^{\mathbb{Z}}$, $A, B \subseteq \Sigma$ and $m, k \geq 0$. Then*

$$C_B^A(F, r+k+1, m) = |\Sigma| \cdot C_B^A(F, r+k, m) + |A| \sum_{i=0}^{m-1} \binom{m}{i} C_B^A(F, r+k, i). \quad (5)$$

Proof. Let $f_k : \Sigma^{r+k+1} \to \Sigma$ be the radius-$(r+k)$ local rule. By Equation (3),

$$\begin{aligned} C_B^A(F, r+k+1, m) &= \sum_{w \in f_k^{-1}(B)} \sum_{s \in \Sigma} |ws|_A^m \\ &= \sum_{w \in f_k^{-1}(B)} |A| \cdot (1 + |w|_A)^m + |\Sigma \setminus A| \cdot |w|_A^m \\ &= |\Sigma| \cdot C_B^A(F, r+k, m) + |A| \sum_{w \in f_k^{-1}(B)} \sum_{i=0}^{m-1} \binom{m}{i} |w|_A^i \\ &= |\Sigma| \cdot C_B^A(F, r+k, m) + |A| \sum_{i=0}^{m-1} \binom{m}{i} C_B^A(F, r+k, i), \end{aligned}$$

which is exactly the claim. □

Definition 2. *Let F be a CA on $\Sigma^{\mathbb{Z}}$ and $A, B \subseteq \Sigma$. We extend the definition of $C_B^A(F, r, m)$, the (A, B, r)-correlation of order m of F, to all $m, r \geq 0$ as follows. For r at least the radius of F, we use Definition 1. For smaller r, we apply Eq. 5 recursively, with k negative. The* normalized (A, B)-correlation *of order m of F is $\bar{C}_B^A(F, m) = C_B^A(F, 0, m)$. We denote $\bar{C}_B^A(F, 1) = \bar{C}_B^A(F)$.*

By induction on $0 \leq k \leq r$ and using Eq. 5, we can prove that

$$C_B^A(F, r-k, m) = \frac{C_B^A(F, r, m)}{|\Sigma|^k} - |A| \sum_{i=0}^{m-1} \binom{m}{i} \sum_{t=1}^{k} \frac{C_B^A(F, r-t, i)}{|\Sigma|^{k+1-t}}.$$

With $m = 1$ and $k = r$, since $C_B^A(F, r-t, 0) = |f^{-1}(B)|/|\Sigma|^t$, this gives

$$\bar{C}_B^A(F) = \frac{C_B^A(F, r, 1)}{|\Sigma|^r} - r \frac{|A| \cdot |f^{-1}(B)|}{|\Sigma|^{r+1}}. \quad (6)$$

We could produce analogous formulas for $\bar{C}_B^A(F, m)$ with $m \geq 2$, expressed in terms of $C_B^A(F, r, m)$ and $\bar{C}_B^A(F, i)$ for $0 \leq i < m$, but they quickly become unwieldy. Note that $\bar{C}_B^A(F)$ may be negative.

Example 2. Let us continue Example 1, where we computed $C_B^A(F, 2, 1) = 17$ and $|f^{-1}(B)| = 21$. Plugging into Eq. 6 these values and $|\Sigma| = 3$, $|A| = 1$ and $r = 2$, we get $\bar{C}_B^A(F) = 3^{-2} \cdot 17 - 2 \cdot 3^{-3} \cdot 1 \cdot 21 = 1/3$.

If F is a radius-r surjective CA, the balance property implies $|f^{-1}(B)| = |B| \cdot |\Sigma|^r$. Then Eq. 6 becomes

$$\bar{C}_B^A(F) = \frac{C_B^A(F, r, 1)}{|\Sigma|^r} - r\frac{|A| \cdot |B|}{|\Sigma|}. \quad (7)$$

In particular, for a fixed r and surjective F the conversion from $C_B^A(F, r, 1)$ to $\bar{C}_B^A(F)$ is given by a monotone function.

Example 3. For non-surjective CA of radius $r \geq 1$, the conversion from (A, B, r)-correlation to normalized (A, B)-correlation may not be monotone. Take $\Sigma = \{0, 1\}$ and $r = 2$. Define F and G by the local functions $f, g : \Sigma^3 \to \Sigma$, where $f(w) = 1$ if and only if $|w|_1 \leq 2$, and $g(w) = 1$ if and only if $|w|_1 = 2$. Now we have $C_1^1(F, 2, 1) = 9 > 6 = C_1^1(G, 2, 1)$ and $\bar{C}_1^1(F) = 1/2 < 3/4 = \bar{C}_1^1(G)$.

The following result can be seen as evidence that our definition of the normalized (A, B)-correlation is the "correct" way to remove the dependence on r from the (A, B, r)-correlation.

Proposition 1. *Let $A, B \subseteq \Sigma$. For each $r \geq 0$, the average of the normalized (A, B)-correlation of order 1 among all radius-r CA on $\Sigma^{\mathbb{Z}}$ is $|A| \cdot |B|/|\Sigma|$.*

Proof. For a radius-r CA F with local rule f, let I_f be the indicator function of $f^{-1}(B)$, that is, $I_f(w) = 1$ if $w \in f^{-1}(B)$ and $I_f(w) = 0$ otherwise for all $w \in \Sigma^{r+1}$. Then $|f^{-1}(B)| = \sum_{w \in \Sigma^{r+1}} I_f(w)$. From Eq. 3 we have

$$C_B^A(F, r, 1) = \sum_{w \in f^{-1}(B)} |w|_A = \sum_{w \in \Sigma^{r+1}} I_f(w) \cdot |w|_A.$$

Combining these with Eq. 6, we have

$$\bar{C}_B^A(F) = \sum_{w \in \Sigma^{r+1}} I_f(w) \left(|\Sigma|^{-r}|w|_A - r|\Sigma|^{-r-1}|A|\right).$$

For each w, the average of $I_f(w)$ over all f is $|B|/|\Sigma|$. The average of $\bar{C}_B^A(F)$ over all f is thus

$$\sum_{w \in \Sigma^{r+1}} \frac{|B|}{|\Sigma|} \left(|\Sigma|^{-r}|w|_A - r|\Sigma|^{-r-1}|A|\right) = |B|(r+1)\frac{|A|}{|\Sigma|} - r\frac{|A| \cdot |B|}{|\Sigma|} = \frac{|A| \cdot |B|}{|\Sigma|},$$

as claimed. □

4.2 Upper Bound for Order 1

In this section we show that the identity CA has the highest normalized (A, A)-correlation among all surjective CA. A similar computation would yield that the minimum is reached by any permutation τ of Σ that minimizes $|\tau(A) \cap A|$. When

$A \cap B = \emptyset$ and $|A| = |B|$, the identity has the lowest (A, B)-correlation, while the highest is reached by any permutation τ with $\tau(A) = B$.

A direct computation gives $\bar{C}_A^A(\mathrm{Id}) = |A|$. As expected, it is higher than $|A|^2/|\Sigma|$, the average of the normalized (A, A)-correlation of a randomly chosen CA as per Proposition 1. Equation 7 now gives for all $r \geq 0$ that

$$C_A^A(\mathrm{Id}, r, 1) = (|\Sigma| + r|A|)|A| \cdot |\Sigma|^{r-1}. \tag{8}$$

Lemma 3. *For each integer $n \geq 0$ and real $a \geq 0$, we have*

$$\sum_{k=0}^{n} k^2 a^k \binom{n}{k} = na(na+1)(a+1)^{n-2}.$$

Proof. We apply double counting. The left hand side counts the ways of choosing a subset $S \subseteq \{1, \ldots, n\}$ and then a function $f : \{0, 1\} \to S$, where each choice is given the weight $a^{|S|}$.

We can also choose first the function $f : \{0, 1\} \to \{1, \ldots, n\}$ and then the remaining $m \geq 0$ elements of S. There are $n(n-1)$ choices for an injective f, and each contributes $\sum_{m=0}^{n-2} a^{m+2}\binom{n-2}{m} = a^2(a+1)^{n-2}$ to the total weight. For a non-injective f, there are n choices, and each contributes $\sum_{m=0}^{n-1} a^{m+1}\binom{n-1}{m} = a(a+1)^{n-1}$ to the total weight. Thus the total weight is

$$n(n-1) \cdot a^2(a+1)^{n-2} + n \cdot a(a+1)^{n-1} = na(na+1)(a+1)^{n-2},$$

which is exactly the right hand side. □

Theorem 4. *If F is a surjective CA of radius at most r, then $C_A^A(F, r, 1) \leq C_A^A(\mathrm{Id}, r, 1)$, and hence $\bar{C}_A^A(F) \leq \bar{C}_A^A(\mathrm{Id}) = |A|$.*

Proof. For $n \geq 1$, denote by $F_n : \Sigma^{n+r} \to \Sigma^n$ the CA F applied to words of length $n + r$. We define the (A, A, r)-correlation of F_n as $C_A^A(F_n, r, 1) = \sum_{w \in \Sigma^{n+r}} |w|_A \cdot |F_n(w)|_A$. We prove the desired bound by expressing $C_A^A(F_n, r, 1)$ in terms of the correlation $C_A^A(F, r, 1)$, proving an upper bound on $C_A^A(F_n, r, 1)$ that depends on n, and letting n go to infinity.

For the first step, we define the set of words $W_n^i = \{w \in \Sigma^{n+r} \mid F_n(w)_i \in A\}$. Since r is the radius of F, a given word $w \in \Sigma^{n+r}$ belongs to W_n^i if and only if $F(w_{[i,i+r]}) \in A$; the other coordinates of w are irrelevant. We rewrite the definition of $C_A^A(F_n, r, 1)$ as

$$\begin{aligned}
C_A^A(F_n, r, 1) &= \sum_{i=0}^{n-1} \sum_{w \in W_n^i} |w|_A \\
&= \sum_{i=0}^{n-1} \sum_{w \in W_n^i} (|w_{[0,i-1]}|_A + |w_{[i,i+r]}|_A + |w_{[i+r+1,n+r-1]}|_A) \\
&= \sum_{i=0}^{n-1} \left(|\Sigma|^{n-1} C_A^A(F, r, 1) + |A||\Sigma|^r |\Sigma|^{n-1}(n-1)\frac{|A|}{|\Sigma|} \right) \\
&= n|\Sigma|^{n-1}(C_A^A(F, r, 1) + (n-1)|A|^2|\Sigma|^{r-1}).
\end{aligned}$$

The second-to-last equality follows from two considerations. The first term of the inner sum comes from $|w_{[i,i+r]}|_A$ for $w \in W_n^i$. Each subword $w_{[i,i+r]}$ occurs exactly $|\Sigma|^{n-1}$ times in the sum, since we have $n-1$ "irrelevant" coordinates that do not affect the condition $w \in W_n^i$. The second term comes from $|w_{[0,i-1]}|_A + |w_{[i+r+1,n+r-1]}|_A$ for $w \in W_n^i$, or in other words, the irrelevant coordinates. Each of the $|\Sigma|^{n-1}$ words over these coordinates occurs exactly $|F^{-1}(A)| = |A||\Sigma|^r$ times, and their average A-weight is $(n-1)\frac{|A|}{|\Sigma|}$. With some rearranging, we obtain

$$C_A^A(F, r, 1) = \frac{C_A^A(F_n, r, 1)}{n|\Sigma|^{n-1}} - (n-1)|A|^2|\Sigma|^{r-1}. \tag{9}$$

Next, we prove the upper bound on $C_A^A(F_n, r, 1)$. Define two integer vectors $\boldsymbol{u}_n = (|w|_A)_{w \in \Sigma^{n+r}}$ and $\boldsymbol{v}_n = (|F_n(w)|_A)_{w \in \Sigma^{n+r}}$ in $\mathbb{R}^{|\Sigma|^{n+r}}$, with the words in Σ^{n+r} enumerated in some consistent order. It is immediate from the definition that $C_A^A(F_n, r, 1) = \boldsymbol{u}_n \cdot \boldsymbol{v}_n$. Since F_n is a balanced function, the weight of each word $w \in \Sigma^n$ is enumerated in $\boldsymbol{v}_n$ exactly $|\Sigma|^r$ times. Using these facts and the Cauchy-Schwarz inequality, we compute

$$C_A^A(F_n, r, 1) \leq \|u_n\| \cdot \|v_n\| = \sqrt{\left(\sum_{w \in \Sigma^{n+r}} |w|_A^2\right)\left(|\Sigma|^r \sum_{v \in \Sigma^n} |v|_A^2\right)}. \tag{10}$$

Consider the rightmost sum $s = \sum_{v \in \Sigma^n} |v|_A^2$. Grouping the words by their A-weight and denoting $B = \Sigma \setminus A$, we have

$$\begin{aligned} s &= \sum_{k=0}^{n} k^2 |A|^k |B|^{n-k} \binom{n}{k} = |B|^n \sum_{k=0}^{n} k^2 \left(\frac{|A|}{|B|}\right)^k \binom{n}{k} \\ &= n|B|^n \frac{|A|}{|B|}\left(n\frac{|A|}{|B|} + 1\right)\left(\frac{|A|}{|B|} + 1\right)^{n-2} = n|A|((n-1)|A| + |\Sigma|)|\Sigma|^{n-2} \end{aligned}$$

by Lemma 3. Applying this to both sums in (10), we obtain

$$C_A^A(F_n, r, 1) \leq |A||\Sigma|^{n+r-2}\sqrt{n(n+r)((n-1)|A| + |\Sigma|)((n+r-1)|A| + |\Sigma|)}. \tag{11}$$

We now combine (9) and (11) to get an upper bound for $C_A^A(F, r, 1)$, which holds for all $n \geq 1$. For the sake of notational convenience, we express the bound in terms of the quantity $C_A^A(F, r, 1)/(|A||\Sigma|^{r-1}) + |A|$:

$$\begin{aligned} \frac{C_A^A(F, r, 1)}{|A||\Sigma|^{r-1}} + |A| &\leq \sqrt{\frac{(n+r)((n-1)|A| + |\Sigma|)((n+r-1)|A| + |\Sigma|)}{n}} - n|A| \\ &= \frac{(n+r)((n-1)|A| + |\Sigma|)((n+r-1)|A| + |\Sigma|) - |A|^2 n^3}{\sqrt{n(n+r)((n-1)|A| + |\Sigma|)((n+r-1)|A| + |\Sigma|)} + |A|n^2} \\ &= \frac{2\,A|((r-1)|A| + |\Sigma|)n^2 + O(n)}{|A|n^2(\sqrt{o(n) + 1} + 1)} \xrightarrow{n \to \infty} (r-1)|A| + |\Sigma| \end{aligned}$$

The claim follows from this bound and Eq. 8. □

Example 4. Theorem 4 generally does not hold for non-surjective CA. Namely, let $A \subsetneq \Sigma$, and let F be a radius-r local rule whose image is contained in A. Its (A, A, r)-correlation is $C_A^A(F, r, 1) = \sum_{w \in \Sigma^{r+1}} |w|_A = (r+1)|A| \cdot |\Sigma|^r$, which is strictly larger than $C_A^A(\mathrm{Id}, r, 1) = (|\Sigma| + r|A|)|A| \cdot |\Sigma|^{r-1}$.

4.3 Upper Bound for High Enough Orders

Theorem 5. *If F is a surjective CA of radius at most r, then $C_A^A(F, r, m) \leq C_A^A(\mathrm{Id}, r, m)$ and $\bar{C}_A^A(F, m) \leq \bar{C}_A^A(\mathrm{Id}, m)$ for large enough m (depending on r).*

Proof. If F and Id have the same (A, A, r)-histogram, then they have the same (A, A, r)-correlation of every order m. If not, take the maximal $k_0 \in \{0, \ldots, r+1\}$ for which $N_A^A(F, r, k_0) \neq N_A^A(\mathrm{Id}, r, k_0)$. If $N_A^A(F, r, k_0) < N_A^A(\mathrm{Id}, r, k_0)$, then

$$\begin{aligned} C_A^A(\mathrm{Id}, r, m) - C_A^A(F, r, m) &= \sum_{i=0}^{r+1} (N_A^A(\mathrm{Id}, r, i) - N_A^A(F, r, i)) i^m \\ &= (N_A^A(\mathrm{Id}, r, k_0) - N_A^A(F, r, k_0)) k^m + O((k_0 - 1)^m), \end{aligned}$$

which is strictly positive for large enough m.

It remains to prove that $N_A^A(F, r, k_0) < N_A^A(\mathrm{Id}, r, k_0)$. Suppose for a contradiction that $N_A^A(F, r, k_0) > N_A^A(\mathrm{Id}, r, k_0)$. Choose a small $p > 0$ and consider the measure $\mu_{A,1-p}$ of Lemma 1. From the proof of the Lemma applied to F and Id,

$$\begin{aligned} &\mu_{A,1-p}(F^{-1}(A)) - \mu_{A,1-p}(A) \\ &= \sum_{k=0}^{r+1} \frac{N_A^A(F, r, k) - N_A^A(\mathrm{Id}, r, k)}{|A|^k (|\Sigma| - |A|)^{r+1-k}} \cdot (1-p)^k p^{r+1-k} \\ &= \frac{N_A^A(F, r, k_0) - N_A^A(\mathrm{Id}, r, k_0)}{|A|^{k_0} (|\Sigma| - |A|)^{r+1-k_0}} \cdot (1-p)^{k_0} p^{r+1-k_0} + O(p^{r+1-k_0+1}). \end{aligned}$$

When p is small enough (in particular $p < |A|/|\Sigma|$), this is strictly positive, so $q = (F\mu_{A,1-p})(A) > \mu_{A,1-p}(A) = 1 - p$. For the entropies, this implies

$$\begin{aligned} h(F\mu_{A,p}) &\leq -q \log \frac{q}{|A|} - (1-q) \log \frac{1-q}{|\Sigma| - |A|} \\ &< -(1-p) \log \frac{1-p}{|A|} - p \log \frac{p}{|\Sigma| - |A|} = h(\mu_{A,1-p}). \end{aligned}$$

But a surjective CA must preserve entropy, a contradiction. □

4.4 State Conservation

Histograms also provide a characterization for the existence of certain conserved quantities for surjective CA. Recall that a *conserved quantity* of radius r for a CA F is a function $\phi : \Sigma^{r+1} \to \mathbb{R}$ such that for all $p \geq 1$ and all spatially p-periodic configurations $x \in \Sigma^{\mathbb{Z}}$, we have $\sum_{i=0}^{p-1} \phi(x_{[i,i+r]}) = \sum_{i=0}^{p-1} \phi(F(x)_{[i,i+r]})$. Conserved quantities have a connection to invariant measures, which manifests as follows in the case of surjective CA and radius-0 conserved quantities.

Theorem 6 (Theorem 1 in [3]). *A surjective CA $F : \Sigma^{\mathbb{Z}} \to \Sigma^{\mathbb{Z}}$ preserves a full-support product measure μ if and only if it conserves the radius-0 quantity $\phi(a) = -\log \mu(a)$.*

Theorem 7. *Let F be a CA of radius at most r, and $A \subseteq \Sigma$. If F conserves the total number of A-symbols, then $H_A^A(F, r) = H_A^A(\mathrm{Id}, r)$. The converse holds if F is surjective.*

Proof. Suppose first that F conserves the number of A-symbols. Choose a transcendental $0 < p < 1$ and let $\mu_{A,p}$ be the measure of Lemma 1. Then we have $\mu_{A,p}(F^{-1}(A)) = p$. Equation (4) now becomes

$$p = \mu_{A,p}(F^{-1}(A)) = \sum_{\ell=0}^{r+1} p^{\ell} \left(\sum_{k=0}^{\ell} \frac{(-1)^{\ell-k} \binom{r+1-k}{r+1-\ell} N_A^A(F, r, k)}{|A|^k (|\Sigma| - |A|)^{r+1-k}} \right).$$

This is a polynomial equation in p, and since p is transcendental, the equation must be trivial: the coefficient of $p^{r+1-\ell}$ in the last sum must equal 1 when $\ell = 1$, and 0 otherwise. The case $\ell = 0$ fixes the value of $N_A^A(F, r, 0)$, then $\ell = 1$ fixes the value of $N_A^A(F, r, 1)$, and so on up to $N_A^A(F, r + 1)$. Hence all A-preserving CA of radius at most r, including Id, have the same (A, A, r)-histogram.

Suppose then that F is surjective and $H_A^A(F, r) = H_A^A(\mathrm{Id}, r)$. Let $0 < p < 1$. Lemma 1 gives $F\mu_{A,p}(A) = \mathrm{Id}\mu_{A,p}(A) = \mu_{A,p}(A) = p$. Since F is surjective, it preserves entropy, so $h(F\mu_{A,p}) = h(\mu_{A,p})$. But $\mu_{A,p}$ is the unique measure of maximum entropy among all measures μ with $\mu(A) = p$. Hence F preserves $\mu_{A,p}$. Theorem 6 implies that F conserves the number of A-symbols. □

Example 5. The second claim of Theorem 7 does not hold for non-surjective cellular automata. Namely, take $\Sigma = \{0, 1, 2\}$ and consider the radius-1 CA F with local rule $f : \Sigma^2 \to \Sigma$, where $f(a, b) = b$ if $\{a, b\} = \{0, 1\}$ and $f(a, b) = a$ otherwise. We have $H_0^0(F, 1) = (0, 2, 1) = H_0^0(\mathrm{Id}, 1)$, but F does not conserve the total number of 0-symbols, since $F({}^{\infty}(012)^{\infty}) = {}^{\infty}(112)^{\infty}$.

5 Open Questions

We state the following questions mainly for F the two-neighbor XOR automaton, although they are of interest for other surjective CA as well.

Question 2. Can we find a weakly mixing shift-invariant measure μ such that $F^n(\mu) \xrightarrow{n} \delta_0$?

Question 3. Starting from an ergodic shift-invariant measure μ, what can be said about the set of weak-* limit points of $F^n(\mu)$?

For the previous question, even the case where μ is a non-uniform Bernoulli measure is still largely open. Since measure-theoretical entropy is upper semicontinuous with respect to weak-* convergence, any weak-* limit point must have positive entropy, so in particular $F^n\mu \xrightarrow{n\to\infty} \delta_0$ is not possible, but we do not know whether it is possible to find a word w such that $(F^n\mu)([w]) \xrightarrow{n\to\infty} 0$.

For a computability point of view, we can see that any complexity in the limit measure in Theorem 3 was present in the initial measure and the CA itself is not doing any significant computation. Is this a restriction caused by surjectivity?

Question 4. Starting from a computable shift-invariant measure μ, is it possible to have an uncomputable weak*-limit point for $F^n(\mu)$? Alternatively, is it possible that the μ-limit set $\{w \in \Sigma^* \mid F^n([w]) \not\to 0\}$ is uncomputable?

Based on computer searches, it seems likely that the gap between Theorem 4 and Theorem 5 can be closed, at least in the binary case.

Conjecture 1 (Domination of prefix sums). For a surjective binary CA F with radius r and $0 \leq n \leq r+1$, we have

$$\sum_{k=0}^{n} N_1^1(F, r, k) \geq \sum_{k=0}^{n} N_1^1(\mathrm{Id}, r, k).$$

This would imply $C_1^1(F, r, m) \leq C_1^1(\mathrm{Id}, r, m)$ for all positive integers m.

Acknowledgments. This work started during a stay of the first author at Turku University, and Benjamin Hellouin is grateful to Jarkko Kari for the invitation (and the orienteering). Ilkka Törmä was supported by the Academy of Finland under grant 359921.

Disclosure of Interests. The authors have no competing interests to declare that are relevant to the content of this article.

References

1. Boyer, L., Delacourt, M., Poupet, V., Sablik, M., Theyssier, G.: μ-limit sets of cellular automata from a computational complexity perspective. J. Comput. Syst. Sci. **81**(8), 1623–1647 (2015)
2. Hoeffding, W.: Probability inequalities for sums of bounded random variables. J. Am. Stat. Assoc. **58**, 13–30 (1963)
3. Kari, J., Taati, S.: Conservation laws and invariant measures in surjective cellular automata. In: Automata 2011—17th International Workshop on Cellular Automata and Discrete Complex Systems, Discrete Math. Theor. Comput. Sci. Proc., vol. AP, pp. 113–122. Assoc. Discrete Math. Theor. Comput. Sci., Nancy (2012)
4. Kari, J., Taati, S.: Statistical mechanics of surjective cellular automata. J. Stat. Phys. **160**, 1198–1243 (2015)
5. Hellouin de Menibus, B., Sablik, M.: Characterisation of sets of limit measures after iteration of a cellular automaton on an initial measure. arXiv e-prints (2013)

6. Hellouin de Menibus, B., Salo, V., Theyssier, G.: Characterizing asymptotic randomization in abelian cellular automata. Ergodic Theory Dynamical Syst. **40**(4), 923–952 (2020)
7. Pivato, M.: Ergodic theory of cellular automata. In: Cellular automata, pp. 373–418. Encycl. Complex. Syst. Sci., Springer, New York (2018). https://doi.org/10.1007/978-1-4939-8700-9_178
8. Pivato, M., Yassawi, R.: Limit measures for affine cellular automata. Ergodic Theory Dynam. Systems **22**(4), 1269–1287 (2002)

Solving "Pseudo-injective" Polynomial Equations over Finite Dynamical Systems

Antonio E. Porreca(✉) and Marius Rolland(✉)

Aix-Marseille Université CNRS, LIS, Marseille, France
marius.rolland@lis-lab.fr

Abstract. We consider the semiring of abstract finite dynamical systems up to isomorphism, with the operations of alternative and synchronous execution. We continue searching for efficient algorithms for solving polynomial equations of the form $P(X) = B$, with a constant side B, with the goal of decomposing complex behaviors into simpler systems. Taking inspiration from the characterization of injective polynomials P over dynamical systems, which is based on a condition on the lengths of limit cycles of their coefficients, we introduce a more general notion of pseudo-injectivity by relaxing this constraint. We prove that the associated equations can be solved efficiently, even in certain cases where the input is encoded in an exponentially more compact way.

Keywords: Finite dynamical systems · Functional digraphs · Graph direct product

1 Introduction

Abstract finite discrete-time dynamical systems (FDDS) are pairs (X, f) where X is a finite set of states and $f: X \to X$ is a transition function (when f is implied, we denote (X, f) simply as X). These objects focus on the dynamics of concrete deterministic models, such as finite cellular automata [1], automata networks [7], or reaction systems [6], by hiding their specific aspects.

We often identify these systems with their transition digraphs, which have uniform out-degree one (Fig. 1). These graphs are also known as functional digraphs [9]. Their general shape is a collection of cycles, where each node of a cycle is the root of a finite in-tree (a directed tree with the edges pointing toward the root). The nodes of the cycles are periodic states, while the others are transient states.

The set $(\mathbb{D}, +, \times)$ of FDDS up to isomorphism, with the alternative execution of two systems as *addition* and the synchronous parallel execution of two FDDS as *multiplication*, is a commutative semiring [3]. As all semirings, we can define a semiring of polynomials over $\mathbb{D}$ and the associated polynomial equations.

Although it has already been proven that general polynomial equations over $\mathbb{D}$ (with variables on both sides of the equation) are undecidable, it is easily proved that, if one side of the equation is constant, then the problem becomes

Published by Springer Nature Switzerland AG 2026
S. Riva and A. Richard (Eds.): AUTOMATA 2025, LNCS 15831, pp. 171–187, 2026.
https://doi.org/10.1007/978-3-032-01570-9_12

decidable (there is just a finite number of possible solutions) [3]. This variant of the problem is actually in NP: since sums and products can be computed in polynomial time, we can just guess the values of the variables (their size is bounded by the constant side of the equation), evaluate the polynomial, and compare it with the constant side (isomorphism of functional digraphs can be checked in linear time [10]).

However, more restricted equations are not yet classified in terms of complexity. For example, we do not know if monomial equations of the form $AX = B$ are NP-hard, in P, or possible candidates for an intermediate difficulty. However, it has been proved that we can find in polynomial time with respect to the size of the inputs (A, B and $\log k$) the (unique) connected solution of $AX^k = B$ for all positive integer k [5]. Furthermore, the equation $AX = B$ has also been investigated for the case where A and B are sums of cycles (without transient states) with a sub-exponential algorithm for counting the number of solutions [2]. It has also been shown that, when the polynomial $P = \sum_{i=0}^{m} A_i X^i$ is *injective*, the equation $P(X) = B$ can be solved in polynomial time. The injective polynomials are exactly those where the coefficient A_i of a non-constant monomial (*i.e.*, with $i > 1$) is *cancelable* (Fig. 1), that is, it has a fixed point [12]. We are interested in finding a generalization of this result to a larger class of polynomials.

We can reformulate the condition of injectivity by saying that there exists an $i \geq 1$ such that A_i is cancelable (*i.e.*, $A_i B = A_i C$ if and only $B = C$ for all B, C) [12]. If an FDDS A is cancelable, then it satisfies the following property: denoting by $L(A)$ the set of all cycle lengths in A, it is always the case that $\ell(A) = \min(L(A))$ divides all elements of $L(A)$. We call *pseudo-cancelable* an element which verifies this property, without being necessarily cancelable (Fig. 1).

In this paper we first prove that equations of the form $AX = B$ can be solved in polynomial time if A is pseudo-cancelable, then generalize this result to a polynomial-time algorithm for equations of the form $P(X) = B$ where $P = \sum_{i=0}^{m} A_i X^i$ is a polynomial such that $\sum_{i=1}^{m} A_i$ (*i.e.*, the sum of coefficient of non constant terms) is pseudo-cancelable. We refer to this kind of polynomial as *pseudo-injective*.

2 Definitions

The set of FDDS *up to isomorphism*, with mutually exclusive alternative execution as *sum* and synchronous parallel execution as *product*, forms a semiring [3], denoted by $\mathbb{D}$. The two operations above define a notion of algebraic decomposition of FDDS.

The semiring of function digraphs, with disjoint union for sum and direct product for multiplication, is isomorphic to $\mathbb{D}$. We recall [8] that the direct product of two graphs A, B is the graph C such that $V(C) = V(A) \times V(B)$ and

$$E(C) = \{((u, u'), (v, v')) \mid (u, v) \in E(A), (u', v') \in E(B)\}.$$

An example of the product of two FDDS is depicted in Fig. 1. As for natural numbers, we sometimes employ the partial operation of subtraction, by writing $A - B = C$ if and only if $A = B + C$.

Then, an FDDS can be seen as the sum of connected components, where each component consists of a cycle, representing the periodic behavior, and in-trees (trees directed from leaf to root) rooted in the cycle, representing the transient behavior. Given two FDDS A, B, if there exists another FDDS C such that $A + C = B$ then we say that A is a submultiset of B (more precisely, the connected components of A are a submultiset of the connected components of B).

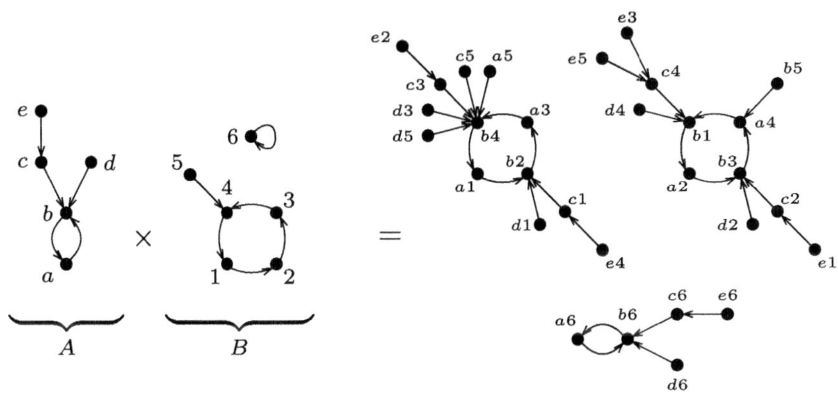

Fig. 1. Product of two FDDS A and B, where the states are given a temporary label in order to show how the result is computed (for brevity, the vertices (u, v) of the product are denoted here by uv). Remark that B is cancelable (state 6 is a fixed point) and AB is pseudo-cancelable ($L(AB) = \{2, 4\}$ and $\ell(AB) = \min(L(AB)) = 2$). A is also trivially pseudo-cancelable, since it is connected ($L(A) = \{2\}$ and $\ell(A) = 2$).

The structure of the product is algebraically rich. For example, this semiring does not admit unique factorizations into irreducibles, *i.e.*, there exist four irreducible FDDS A, B, C, D such that $A \neq C$ and $A \neq D$ but $AB = CD$; furthermore, polynomial equations of the form $P(X) = B$ may have multiple solutions (in other words, not all polynomials are injective). Moreover, while the periodic behavior of a product is easy to analyze, its transient behavior demands much more work. Indeed, the product of two connected FDDS A, B, having cycles of length p and q respectively, generates $\gcd(p, q)$ connected components, each with a cycle of size $\mathrm{lcm}(p, q)$ [8]. In order to analyze the (generally more complex) transient behaviors, we use the notion of unroll introduced in [11].

Definition 1 (Unroll). *Let $A = (X, f)$ be an FDDS. For each state $u \in X$ and $k \in \mathbb{N}$, we denote by $f^{-k}(u) = \{v \in X \mid f^k(v) = u\}$ the set of k-th preimages of u. For each u in a cycle of A, we call the* unroll tree of A in u *the infinite tree $\mathbf{t}_u = (V, E)$ having vertices $V = \{(s, k) \mid s \in f^{-k}(u), k \in \mathbb{N}\}$ and* *edges* $E = \{((v,k),(f(v),k-1))\} \subseteq V^2$. *We call* unroll of A, *denoted* $\mathcal{U}(A)$, *the set of its unroll trees.*

An unroll tree contains exactly one infinite branch, onto which are periodically rooted the trees representing the transient behaviors of the corresponding connected component. Remark that the set of unrolls *up to isomorphism* (which will be used in the rest of this paper, unless otherwise specified) with the disjoint union as sum and the levelwise product defined in [11] (and already exploited in [5,12]) is also a semiring, denoted by $\mathbb{U}$. In addition, the operation of unrolling an FDDS is a semiring homomorphism $\mathbb{D} \to \mathbb{U}$.

An interesting aspect of $\mathbb{U}$ is the existence of a total order compatible with the product [11], that is, for three unroll trees $\mathbf{t}_1, \mathbf{t}_2, \mathbf{t}$ we have $\mathbf{t}_1 \leq \mathbf{t}_2$ if and only if $\mathbf{t}_1\mathbf{t} \leq \mathbf{t}_2\mathbf{t}$. This feature has been exploited in order to describe polynomial algorithms for solving certain classes of equations of the form $AX = B$ or $P(X) = B$ with specific conditions on A, X, P or B [5,11,12]. Thanks to this order, it is also possible to prove that all univariate polynomials of $\mathbb{U}$ are injective [11,12] and, in particular, that the quotient of two unrolls (or unroll trees) is unique when it exists.

Remark that an order compatible with the product does not exist on FDDS. Indeed, if such an order existed, then all FDDS would be cancelable; however, the cancelable elements in $\mathbb{D}$, are exactly the FDDS that admit a fixed point [11, Theorem 30].

In this article, we focus our attention on the lengths of the cycles of an FDDS. Denote by $L(A)$ the set of cycle lengths of all connected components of A, and denote $\ell(A) = \min(L(A))$. Since least common multiples are important when dealing with the product of connected components, it is useful to introduce the following notion of "anti-lcm".

Definition 2 (anti-lcm). *Let a, b be positive integers with factorizations into primes $\prod_{i=1}^n p_i^{a_i}$ and $\prod_{i=1}^n p_i^{b_i}$ respectively and such that a divides b. Then, the* anti-lcm of b with respect to a *is*

$$\operatorname{alcm}_a b = \prod_{\substack{i=1 \\ b_i > a_i}}^{n} p_i^{b_i}.$$

That is, when computing $\operatorname{alcm}_a b$ we consider the factorization of b into primes and discard the primes having the same exponent in a (we always have $b_i \geq a_i$ for all i, since a divides b by hypothesis). For instance, if $a = 12 = 2^2 \times 3^1$ and $b = 252 = 2^2 \times 3^2 \times 7^1$, then we discard the factor 2^2 from b and obtain $\operatorname{alcm}_a b = 3^2 \times 7^1 = 63$. An important aspect of this notion (which justifies the name "anti-lcm") is that the anti-lcm of $\operatorname{lcm}(a,b)$ with respect to a is the smallest integer c such that $\operatorname{lcm}(a,c) = \operatorname{lcm}(a,b)$.

Since in the rest of the paper most uses of alcm will be with parameters such as $\ell(A)$ and $\ell(B)$, in order to improve the readability we introduce the shorter notation $\operatorname{alcm}_A B$ for $\operatorname{alcm}_{\ell(A)} \ell(B)$ whenever A and B are FDDS.

From the characterization of cancelable elements of $\mathbb{D}$, we remark that if A is cancelable, then every $a \in L(A)$ is a multiple of $\ell(a)$. By dropping the cancelability requirement, we say that an FDDS A is *pseudo-cancelable* if every $a \in L(A)$ is multiple of $\ell(a)$ (Fig. 1). Moreover, we call a polynomial $P = \sum_{i=0}^{m} A_i X_i$ over $\mathbb{D}$ *pseudo-injective* if the sum of the coefficients of its non-constant terms $\sum_{i=1}^{m} A_i$ is pseudo-cancelable; notice that this is indeed a generalization of the actual injectivity condition [12].

3 The Complexity of Solving Polynomial Equations

The main goal of this section is to prove the following theorem:

Theorem 1. *Let B be an FDDS and $P = \sum_{i=0}^{m} A_i X_i$ be a pseudo-injective polynomial. Then, we can solve $P(X) = B$ in polynomial time with respect to the size (number of states) of B plus the sizes of the coefficients of P.*

We begin by proving that this is true for equations $AX = B$ where A, X and B are sums of cycles (*i.e.*, their underlying transition functions are permutations). To this end, we prove that every cycle in X must satisfy a certain condition on its size. For brevity, in the following we denote by C_i the cycle with length i; remark that all sums of cycles A can be written as $A = \sum_{i \in L(A)} a_i C_i$, where a_i is the number of occurrences of C_i in A. We also denote by $\operatorname{Div}(p)$ the set of divisors of p.

Lemma 2. *Let A, B and X be sums of cycles with A pseudo-cancelable. If $AX = B$ then there exists a divisor k of $\ell(A)$ satisfying $k \times \operatorname{alcm}_A B \in L(X)$ and $\gcd(k, \operatorname{alcm}_A B) = 1$.*

Proof. Since $AX = B$, by definition of product there exist $a \in L(A)$ and $x \in L(X)$ such that $\ell(B) = \operatorname{lcm}(a, x)$. Furthermore, since B contains all products of cycles from A with cycles from X, in particular we have $\operatorname{lcm}(\ell(A), x) \in L(B)$. It follows that $\operatorname{lcm}(\ell(A), x) \geq \ell(B)$. Since A is pseudo-cancelable, necessarily $\ell(A)$ divides a and thus $\operatorname{lcm}(\ell(A), x)$ divides $\operatorname{lcm}(a, x)$. Then $\operatorname{lcm}(\ell(A), x) \leq \operatorname{lcm}(a, x) = \ell(B)$ and therefore $\operatorname{lcm}(\ell(A), x) = \ell(B)$. This implies that the primes in the factorization of $\ell(B)$ whose exponent is larger than in $\ell(A)$ must belong to the factorization of x. Hence, $\operatorname{alcm}_A B$ divides x and therefore $x = k \times \operatorname{alcm}_A B$ for some integer k. Since x divides $\ell(B)$, no prime in k appears in $\operatorname{alcm}_A B$ (otherwise their exponent in x would be larger than in b) and thus $\gcd(k, \operatorname{alcm}_A B) = 1$ and k divides $\ell(B)/\operatorname{alcm}_A B$. Finally,

$$\ell(B)/\operatorname{alcm}_A B = \prod_{\substack{i=1 \\ a_i = b_i}}^{n} p_i^{a_i}$$

and thus this number divides $\ell(A)$, implying that k is also a divisor of $\ell(A)$. □

Corollary 3. *If $AX = B$, where A and B are two sum of cycles and A is pseudo-cancelable, then for each cycle $C_x \in X$ which verifies $C_{\ell(B)} \in AC_x$ there exists a divisor k of $\ell(A)$ satisfying $k \times \operatorname{alcm}_A B = x$ and $\gcd(k, \operatorname{alcm}_A B) = 1$.*

Although Lemma 2 and Corollary 3 partially describe a cycle of X, there still remains an unknown, namely the value of k. Nevertheless, as we show in the following lemma, we can fix $k = 1$.

Lemma 4. *Let $A = \sum_{i \in L(A)} a_i C_i$ and B, X be sums of cycles with A pseudo-cancelable and let $k \in \operatorname{Div}(\ell(A))$ such that $\gcd(k, \operatorname{alcm}_A B) = 1$. Then, we have $A(X + C_{k \times \operatorname{alcm}_A B}) = B$ if and only if $A(X + dC_{(k/d) \times \operatorname{alcm}_A B}) = B$ for all $d \in \operatorname{Div}(k)$.*

Proof. Let $x = k \times \operatorname{alcm}_A B$, $d \in \operatorname{Div}(k)$ and $a \in L(A)$. Since A is pseudo-cancelable, we have $\ell(A) \in \operatorname{Div}(a)$. Furthermore, from the definition of k, we deduce that $k \in \operatorname{Div}(a)$ and also $d \in \operatorname{Div}(a)$. Consequently,

$$\gcd(x, a) = \gcd(\operatorname{alcm}_A B, a) \gcd(k, a) = k \times \gcd(\operatorname{alcm}_A B, a).$$

In addition, we have $k = \gcd(k, a) = \gcd(d \times (k/d), a) = d \times \gcd(k/d, a)$ and $\operatorname{lcm}(x, a) = \operatorname{lcm}(\operatorname{alcm}_A B, a)$. By consequence,

$$\begin{aligned}
C_a C_x &= \gcd(x, a) C_{\operatorname{lcm}(x,a)} \\
&= k \times \gcd(\operatorname{alcm}_A B, a) \times C_{\operatorname{lcm}(\operatorname{alcm}_A B, a)} \\
&= d \times \gcd(k/d, a) \times \gcd(\operatorname{alcm}_A B, a) \times C_{\operatorname{lcm}(\operatorname{alcm}_A B, a)} \\
&= d \times \gcd((k/d) \times \operatorname{alcm}_A B, a) \times C_{\operatorname{lcm}((k/d) \times \operatorname{alcm}_A B, a)} \\
&= C_a \times dC_{\operatorname{lcm}((k/d) \times \operatorname{alcm}_A B, a)}
\end{aligned}$$

This implies

$$\begin{aligned}
AC_x &= \sum_{i \in L(A)} a_i C_i C_x \\
&= \sum_{i \in L(A)} a_i d C_i C_{\operatorname{lcm}((k/d) \times \operatorname{alcm}_A B, a)} \\
&= AdC_{\operatorname{lcm}((k/d) \times \operatorname{alcm}_A B, a)}
\end{aligned}$$

and the lemma follows. □

We can now formulate an algorithm for the resolution of $AX = B$ working under the hypothesis that A and B are sums of cycles and A is pseudo-cancelable.

Algorithm 5. *Given two sums of cycles A and B with A pseudo-cancelable, we can compute X such that $AX = B$, if any exists, in the following way:*

1. *Check if $|A| \leq |B|$.*
2. *Let C be a cycle of length $\operatorname{alcm}_A B$.*
3. *Check if AC is a submultiset of B.*

4. Add C to X.
5. Set $B \leftarrow B - AC$.
6. If $B \neq \emptyset$ then go to 1; otherwise return X.

This algorithm runs in polynomial time with respect to the number of states of A and B. In fact, the number of iterations is bounded by $n = |B|$. Moreover, all the instructions in the loop only require polynomial time. Indeed, line 1 is $\mathcal{O}(n)$ time. Then, we can compute $\operatorname{alcm}_A B$ simply by counting up to $\ell(B)$ and construct C in $\mathcal{O}(n)$ time, since $n \geq \operatorname{alcm}_A B$. Thus, line 2 is executed in $\mathcal{O}(n)$ time. Then, we can compute AC in $\mathcal{O}(n^2)$ time, and its size is bounded by n^2. It follows that checking if AC is a submultiset of B and removing AC from B requires $\mathcal{O}(n^3)$ time. We deduce that lines 3 and 5 are executed in $\mathcal{O}(n^3)$ time. All the other instructions only require constant time.

Furthermore, the solution X computed by Algorithm 5 is correct. Indeed, if m is the number of iterations of the algorithm, C_i the cycle computed in the i-th iteration and B_i the value of B at the beginning of the i-th iteration, we have $AC_m = B_m$. Inductively, we have $B_i = AC_i + B_{i+1}$. Since $B_{i+1} = A\sum_{j=i+1}^{m} C_j$, it follows that $B_i = A\sum_{j=i}^{m} C_j$.

All that remains to prove in order to show the correctness of the algorithm is that, if a solution exists, then the algorithm finds it.

Lemma 6. *Let A and B be sums of cycles with A pseudo-cancelable. If the equation $AX = B$ has solutions, then Algorithm 5 finds one maximizing the number of connected components (equivalently, minimizing the cycle lengths).*

Proof. Suppose that $AX = B$. Thus, by Lemma 2, there exist k_1 and X_1 such that $X = X_1 + C$ with $C = C_{k_1 \times \operatorname{alcm}_A B}$. Accordingly, we have $AX_1 = B_1$ with $B_1 = B - AC$. Consequently, by Lemma 4, the sum of cycles $Y = X_1 + k_1 C_{\operatorname{alcm}_A B}$ satisfies $AY = B$. This implies $B_1 = B - Ak_1 C_{\operatorname{alcm}_A B}$.

The number of cycles with length $\ell(B)$ generated by AC is

$$\sum_{\substack{a \in L(A) \\ a \mid \ell(B)}} \gcd(\operatorname{alcm}_A B, a) k_1$$

whereas the number generated by $AC_{\operatorname{alcm}_A B}$ is

$$\sum_{\substack{a \in L(A) \\ a \mid \ell(B)}} \gcd(\operatorname{alcm}_A B, a).$$

We deduce that the value of $\ell(B)$ in line 2. of the algorithm is the same between the first iteration and the k_1th iteration of the loop. This implies that the result contains $k_1 C_{\operatorname{alcm}_A B}$ at the end the k_1th iteration of the loop.

The lemma follows by induction. Remark that the solution Y constructed at each step replaces one cycle by the maximum number of cycles of minimum compatible length while still satisfying the equation; this implies that the solution found by the algorithm maximizes the number of connected components □

This proves the correctness of Algorithm 5:

Proposition 7. *Given two sums of cycles A and B with A pseudo-cancelable, we can solve in polynomial time the equation $AX = B$.*

We can now extend our result to the case of equations $P(X) = B$ where B and all coefficients of P are sums of cycles. First, we generalize Lemma 2 as follows:

Lemma 8. *Let B and Y be two sums of cycles and $P = \sum_{i=0}^{m} A_i X^i$ be a pseudo-injective polynomial where each coefficient is a sum of cycles. Let A_c be a coefficient of P such that $\ell(A_c) = \ell(\sum_{i=1}^{m} A_i)$. Then $P(Y) = B$ implies the existence of $k \in \mathrm{Div}(\ell(A_c))$ such that $k \times \mathrm{alcm}_{A_c} B - A_0 \in L(Y)$ and $\gcd(k, \mathrm{alcm}_{A_c} B - A_0) = 1$.*

Proof. Suppose $P(Y) = B$. Thus, $P(Y) - A_0 = B'$ with $B' = B - A_0$. Therefore, there exist $i \in \{1, \ldots, m\}$, $a \in L(A_i)$ and $y \in L(Y)$ such that $\ell(B') = \mathrm{lcm}(a, y)$. Furthermore, for all $j \in \{1, \ldots, m\}$ we have $\mathrm{lcm}(\ell(A_j), y) \in L(B')$. It follow that $\mathrm{lcm}(\ell(A_j), y) \geq \ell(B')$ for all j. By hypothesis on P, $\ell(A_c)$ divides a. Thus, $\mathrm{lcm}(\ell(A_c), y) \leq \mathrm{lcm}(a, y) = \ell(B')$. We deduce that $\mathrm{lcm}(\ell(A_c), y) = \ell(B')$ and therefore $y = k\, \mathrm{alcm}_{A_c} B'$ with $k \in \mathrm{Div}(\ell(A_c))$ and $\gcd(k, \mathrm{alcm}_{A_c} B') = 1$. □

Thus, we can generalize Lemma 4 as follows.

Lemma 9. *Let B, Y be two sums of cycles and $P = \sum_{i=0}^{m} A_i X^i$ be a pseudo-injective polynomial where each coefficient is a sum of cycles. Let A_c be a coefficient of P such that $\ell(A_c) = \ell(\sum_{i=1}^{m} A_i)$. Let $k \in \mathrm{Div}(\ell(A_c))$ such that $k \times \mathrm{alcm}_{A_c} B - A_0 \in L(Y)$ and $\gcd(k, \mathrm{alcm}_{A_c} B - A_0) = 1$. Then, we have $P(Y + C_{k \times \mathrm{alcm}_{A_c} B}) = B$ if and only if $P(Y + dC_{(k/d) \times \mathrm{alcm}_{A_c} B}) = B$ for all $d \in \mathrm{Div}(k)$.*

Proof. Let $y = k \times \mathrm{alcm}_{A_c} B$, $d \in \mathrm{Div}(k)$ and $a \in L(\sum_{i=1}^{m} A_i)$. Then, we have $\ell(A_c) \in \mathrm{Div}(a)$. Furthermore, from the definition of k, we deduce that k and d divide a. Consequently, from the proof of Lemma 4, it follows that

$$C_a C_y^j = C_a C_y^{j-1} (dC_{(k/d) \times \mathrm{alcm}_{A_c} B}) = C_a (dC_{(k/d) \times \mathrm{alcm}_{A_c} B})^j$$

for all natural numbers j. Thus by summing, $A_j C_y^j = A_j (dC_{(k/d) \times \mathrm{alcm}_{A_c} B})^j$ for all j. We conclude that $P(Y + C_y) = P(Y + dC_{(k/d) \times \mathrm{alcm}_{A_c} B})$. □

We deduce that an adaptation of Algorithm 5 can solve in polynomial time the equation $P(Y) = B$ if P is a pseudo-injective polynomial (Fig. 2 shows an example run).

Algorithm 10. *Given a sum of cycles B and a pseudo-injective polynomial $P = \sum_{i=0}^{m} A_i X^i$ where each coefficient is a sum of cycles, we can compute Y such that $P(Y) = B$, if any exists, in the following way:*

1. *Check if A_0 is a submultiset of B.*

2. *Set* $B \leftarrow B - A_0$*,* $P \leftarrow P - A_0$ *and* $Y \leftarrow \mathbf{0}$*.*
3. *Let* C *be a cycle of length* $\mathrm{alcm}_{(\sum_{i=1}^{m} A_i)} B$*.*
4. *Check if* $|P(Y+C)| = \sum_{i=1}^{m} |A_i||Y+C|^i$ *is bounded by* $|B|$*.*[1]
5. *Compute* $P(Y+C)$ *and check if* $P(Y+C) - P(Y)$ *is a submultiset of* B*.*
6. *Set* $B \leftarrow B - (P(Y+C) - P(Y))$ *and* $Y \leftarrow Y + C$*.*
7. *If* $B \neq \emptyset$ *then go back to 3, otherwise return* Y*.*

B	Y	C	$P(Y+C)$	$P(Y)$	$P(Y+C) - P(Y)$
$16C_2 + 4C_4 + 18C_6 + C_{12}$	$\mathbf{0}$	C_1	$C_2 + C_4 + C_6$	$\mathbf{0}$	$C_2 + C_4 + C_6$
$15C_2 + 3C_4 + 17C_6 + C_{12}$	C_1	C_1	$4C_2 + 2C_4 + 2C_6$	$C_2 + C_4 + C_6$	$3C_2 + C_4 + C_6$
$12C_2 + 2C_4 + 16C_6 + C_{12}$	$2C_1$	C_1	$9C_2 + 3C_4 + 3C_6$	$4C_2 + 2C_4 + 2C_6$	$5C_2 + C_4 + C_6$
$7C_2 + C_4 + 15C_6 + C_{12}$	$3C_1$	C_1	$16C_2 + 4C_4 + 4C_6$	$9C_2 + 3C_4 + 3C_6$	$7C_2 + C_4 + C_6$
$14C_6 + C_{12}$	$4C_1$	C_3	$16C_2 + 4C_4 + 18C_6 + C_{12}$	$16C_2 + 4C_4 + 4C_6$	$14C_6 + C_{12}$
$\mathbf{0}$	$4C_1 + C_3$				

Fig. 2. A run of Algorithm 10 on equation $C_2X^2 + (C_4 + C_6)X = 16C_2 + 4C_4 + 18C_6 + C_{12}$, where each line of the table corresponds to an iteration of lines 3–7. This run gives the solution $Y = 4C_1 + C_3$. Remark that this equation also has the solutions $2C_2 + C_3$ and $2C_1 + C_2 + C_3$, but Algorithm 10 finds the solution which maximizes the number of connected components.

Notice that the test in step 4 is needed, since m can in principle be larger than $|B|$ and then $|Y + C| > 1$ would imply $|P(Y + C)| \geq 2^m \geq 2^{|B|}$, which would demand exponential computation time. The test itself must be performed by using fast exponentiation and stopping as soon as an intermediate result exceeds $|B|$ in order to guarantee polynomial time. It follows that steps 4, 5 and 6 require polynomial time with respect to the size of the input. We conclude that this algorithm is polynomial-time. In addition, as for Algorithm 5, if the algorithm returns Y then $P(Y) = B$. Finally, we can extend Lemma 6 by exploiting Lemmas 8 and 9 (instead of Lemmas 2 and 4) and by replacing the products by A with evaluations of P for the other direction.

Proposition 11. *Given a sum of cycles* B *and a pseudo-injective polynomial* $P = \sum_{i=0}^{m} A_i X^i$ *where each coefficient is a sum of cycles, we can find* Y *such that* $P(Y) = B$*, if one exists, in polynomial time with respect to the number of states of the input.*

[1] Remark that $|A + B| = |A| + |B|$ and $|A \times B| = |A| \times |B|$ for all FDDS A, B by the definitions of sum and product (in other words, the size function $|\cdot| : \mathbb{D} \to \mathbb{N}$ is a semiring homomorphism).

We can now consider the case where $A_0, \dots, A_m$ and B are not just sums of cycles. As in the previous case, our main idea is to iteratively construct the solution. At this end, we recall the notation introduced in [12], namely, the function $(X)(p)$, which denotes the multiset of connected components of FDDS X with cycles of length p, and the function $(X)\{p\}$, denoting the multiset of connected components of X with cycles of length *dividing* p. In the rest of this section, we denote unroll trees with bold lowercase letters.

Lemma 12. *Let $P = \sum_{i=0}^{m} A_i X^i$ be a pseudo-injective polynomial and B an FDDS. Let c such that $\ell(A_c) = \ell(\sum_{i=1}^{m} A_i)$ and let $A = \sum_{i=1}^{m} A_i$. Let*

$$\mathbf{a} = \min(\mathcal{U}((A)\{\ell(B - A_0)\})) \qquad \mathbf{b} = \min(\mathcal{U}((B - A_0)\{\ell(B - A_0)\}))$$

be minimal with respect to the order on trees [11, Section 3.1]. If there exists Y such that $P(Y) = B$ then Y contains a connected component C with minimal unroll tree $\mathbf{t} = \mathbf{b}/\mathbf{a}$ and cycle length $k \times \operatorname{lcm}(\operatorname{alcm}_{A_c} B, p))$, where p is the minimal period of $\mathbf{t}$ and $k > 0$ is an integer in $\operatorname{Div}(\ell(A_c))$ such that $\gcd(k, \operatorname{lcm}(\operatorname{alcm}_A B, p)) = 1$.

Proof. We assume that there exists an FDDS Y such that $P(Y) = B$. Then, there exists a connected component C of Y such that $P(C)$ contains a connected component D of $(B)\{\ell(B)\}$ having $\min(\mathcal{U}(D)) = \min(\mathcal{U}((B)\{\ell(B)\}))$. Hence $P(Y) - A_0 = B'$ with $B' = B - A_0$. Then, since $(\cdot)\{\ell(B')\}$ is an endomorphism [12], it follows that $\sum_{i=1}^{m} (A_i)\{\ell(B')\}((Y)\{\ell(B')\})^i = (B')\{\ell(B')\}$. Thus, since unroll is a homomorphism $\mathbb{D} \to \mathbb{U}$ [11], we have

$$\sum_{i=1}^{m} \mathcal{U}((A_i)\{\ell(B')\}) \times (\mathcal{U}((Y)\{\ell(B')\}))^i = \mathcal{U}((B')\{\ell(B')\}).$$

Consequently, by minimality of $\mathbf{a}$ and $\mathbf{b}$, we deduce that there exists $\mathbf{t}$ such that $\mathbf{at} = \mathbf{b}$. Moreover, since $\mathbf{a}$ and $\mathbf{b}$ are periodic, $\mathbf{t}$ is also periodic and thus an unroll tree with minimal period p, and all possible periods of $\mathbf{t}$ are multiples of p [5]. Therefore $\min(\mathcal{U}(C)) = \mathbf{t}$ and the cycle length c of C is a multiple of p. By a reasoning similar to the proof of Lemma 8, c is a multiple of $\operatorname{alcm}_A B$ and thus a multiple of $\operatorname{lcm}(\operatorname{alcm}_A B, p)$. Then, there exists a divisor k of $\ell(A)$ such that $c = k \times \operatorname{lcm}(\operatorname{alcm}_A B, p)$ with $\gcd(k, \operatorname{lcm}(\operatorname{alcm}_A B, p) = 1$. □

Hence, we can easily generalize Lemma 9 like this:

Lemma 13. *Let $P = \sum_{i=0}^{m} A_i X^i$ be a pseudo-injective polynomial and B an FDDS. Let c such that $\ell(A_c) = \ell(\sum_{i=1}^{m} A_i)$ and let $A = \sum_{i=1}^{m} A_i$. Let*

$$\mathbf{a} = \min(\mathcal{U}((A)\{\ell(B - A_0)\})) \qquad \mathbf{b} = \min(\mathcal{U}((B - A_0)\{\ell(B - A_0)\})).$$

Then we have $P(Y + C) = B$ if and only if $P(Y + dC') = B$ for all $d \in \operatorname{Div}(k)$, where C and C' are two connected components such that:

– *the quotient*

$$\frac{\min(\mathcal{U}((B - A_0)\{\ell(B - A_0)\}))}{\min(\mathcal{U}((\sum_{i=1}^{m} A_i)\{\ell(B - A_0)\}))}$$

is well-defined and C *and* C' *have this quotient as their minimal unroll tree and its period is* p*;*
– C *has a cycle length of* $k \times \operatorname{lcm}(\operatorname{alcm}_{A_c} B - A_0, p)$*;*
– C' *has a cycle length of* $(k/d) \times \operatorname{lcm}(\operatorname{alcm}_{A_c} B - A_0, p)$.

Thus, if we replace line 3 of Algorithm 10 by:

3.1 Compute $\mathbf{x} = \dfrac{\min(\mathcal{U}((B)\{\ell(B)\}))}{\min(\mathcal{U}((\sum_{i=1}^{n} A_i)\{\ell(B)\}))}$ by [5, Algorithm 3] if it exists; otherwise, abort the computation.
3.2 Let p be the minimal period of $\mathbf{x}$.
3.3 Create C the connected component whose cycle length is $\operatorname{lcm}(p, \operatorname{alcm}_{A_c} B)$ such that $\mathbf{x} \in \mathcal{U}(C)$.

we obtain a polynomial algorithm, since the new lines can also be executed efficiently. As before, the algorithm only returns correct solutions. Proving that the algorithm does always find a solution when one exists requires a straightforward generalization of Lemma 6 (obtained by multiplying the value of $\operatorname{alcm}_A B$ by p in the proof). This concludes the proof of Theorem 1.

Remark that a direct consequence of Lemmas 12 and 13 is that the equations considered in this section have a unique solution with the maximum number of connected components (which is returned by the three algorithms described above); this solution minimizes the lengths of the cycles. Symmetrically, there is a unique solution *minimizing* the number of connected components.

4 Equations with Cycles Encoded Compactly

We will reexamine the cases of equations over sums of cycles, but with a different encoding. Indeed, although until now we have represented sums of cycles as explicit graphs (equivalent to a unary coding of the number of states in terms of size) in order to conserve the dynamical point of view, we can also represent them more compactly. Here we choose an encoding as arrays of pairs (n, l) where l is the cycle length and n is the number of copies of this cycle; if A is an FDDS encoded this way, we denote by $A[i].l$ the i-th cycle length, and by $A[i].n$ its number of occurrences. We will prove that equations over sums of cycles can be solved efficiently even under this coding, while the input size is sometimes reduced exponentially.

We introduce the following adaptation of Algorithm 5.

Algorithm 14. *Given two sums of cycles* A *and* B *with* A *pseudo-cancelable, we can compute* X *such that* $AX = B$*, if any exists, in the following way:*

1. *Let* $min = 0$.
2. *Sort* A *and* B *by length of the cycles.*
3. *Check if the number of states of* A *is less than that of* B.
4. *Let* $p = \operatorname{alcm}_{A[0].l}(B[min].l)$.
5. *Let* d *be the number of cycles of length* $B[min].l$ *in the product* AC_p.
6. *Let* S *be sum of cycles such that* $S.n = B[min].n/d$ *and* $S.l = p$.
7. *Check if* AS *is a submultiset of* B.
8. *Add* S *to* X.
9. *Remove* AS *from* B *and set* $min \leftarrow \min\{i \mid B[i].n > 0\}$, *if the set is nonempty, and go back to 3; otherwise, return* X.

Lemma 15. *Algorithm 14 is correct.*

Proof. For reasons similar to Algorithm 5, if the algorithm returns a solution, then it is correct. For the other direction, if there exists a solution X such that $AX = B$, then by Lemma 6 there exists a solution $Y = \sum_{i=1}^{m} k_i C_{\operatorname{alcm}_A B_i}$ where B_i is the value of B at the beginning of the i-th iteration. From Corollary 3, it follows that, in AY, the term $Ak_1 C_{\operatorname{alcm}_A B_1}$ contains all cycles of B with length $\ell(B)$. Therefore k_1 is divisible by the number of cycles of $AC_{\operatorname{alcm}_A B_1}$ having length $\ell(B)$. By induction, the lemma follows. □

Before the analysis of the complexity of Algorithm 14, we define an efficient procedure for computing $\operatorname{alcm}_a b$ for $a, b > 0$ with a dividing b (line 4), which does not require factoring either b or a. This procedure is similar to Algorithm 8 in [13].

Algorithm 16. `computing` $\operatorname{alcm}_a b$

1: $quot_1 \leftarrow b/a$
2: $l_1 \leftarrow \operatorname{lcm}(quot_1, a)$
3: $quot_2 \leftarrow b/l_1$
4: $prod \leftarrow a \times quot_2$
5: $l_2 \leftarrow \operatorname{lcm}(prod, b)$
6: $res_1 \leftarrow l_2/b$
7: $g \leftarrow \gcd(b, prod)$
8: $quot_3 \leftarrow b/g$
9: $quot_4 \leftarrow quot_1/quot_3$
10: $pow \leftarrow quot_4^{\lceil \log_2 b \rceil}$
11: $res_2 \leftarrow \gcd(b, pow)$
12: **return** $res_1 \times res_2$

Lemma 17. *Algorithm 16 is correct and executes in* $\mathcal{O}((\log b)^2)$ *time.*

Proof. Let $a = \prod_{i=1}^{n} p_i^{a_i}$ and $b = \prod_{i=1}^{n} p_i^{b_i}$ with p_i the i-th prime and large enough n. Figure 3 shows the decomposition into primes of the variables of the algorithm; the terms of the factorization are grouped in order to make the calculations performed in each step more explicit. Line 11 of the algorithm is the only step that needs an argument more sophisticated than just an arithmetic computation in order to show that

$$\gcd(b, pow) = \prod_{\substack{i=1 \\ 0<2a_i<b_i}}^{n} p_i^{b_i} \prod_{\substack{i=1 \\ 0<a_i<b_i\leq 2a_i}}^{n} p_i^{b_i}$$

$$quot_1 = \prod_{\substack{i=1 \\ a_i=0}}^{n} p_i^{b_i} \prod_{\substack{i=1 \\ 0<a_i<b_i}}^{n} p_i^{b_i-a_i}$$

$$l_1 = \prod_{\substack{i=1 \\ a_i=0}}^{n} p_i^{b_i} \prod_{\substack{i=1 \\ 0<2a_i\leq b_i}}^{n} p_i^{b_i-a_i} \prod_{\substack{i=1 \\ a_i<b_i<2a_i}}^{n} p_i^{a_i}$$

$$quot_2 = \prod_{\substack{i=1 \\ 0<2a_i<b_i}}^{n} p_i^{a_i} \prod_{\substack{i=1 \\ a_i<b_i<2a_i}}^{n} p_i^{b_i-a_i}$$

$$prod = \prod_{\substack{i=1 \\ a_i=b_i}}^{n} p_i^{a_i} \prod_{\substack{i=1 \\ 0<2a_i<b_i}}^{n} p_i^{2a_i} \prod_{\substack{i=1 \\ a_i<b_i\leq 2a_i}}^{n} p_i^{b_i}$$

$$l_2 = \prod_{\substack{i=1 \\ a_i=b_i}}^{n} p_i^{a_i} \prod_{\substack{i=1 \\ 0<2a_i<b_i}}^{n} p_i^{b_i} \prod_{\substack{i=1 \\ a_i<b_i\leq 2a_i}}^{n} p_i^{b_i}$$

$$res_1 = \prod_{\substack{i=1 \\ a_i=0}}^{n} p_i^{b_i}$$

$$g = \prod_{\substack{i=1 \\ a_i=b_i}}^{n} p_i^{b_i} \prod_{\substack{i=1 \\ a_i<b_i\leq 2a_i}}^{n} p_i^{b_i} \prod_{\substack{i=1 \\ b_i>2a_i}}^{n} p_i^{2a_i}$$

$$quot_3 = \prod_{\substack{i=1 \\ a_i=0}}^{n} p_i^{b_i} \prod_{\substack{i=1 \\ b_i>2a_i}}^{n} p_i^{b_i-2a_i}$$

$$quot_4 = \prod_{\substack{i=1 \\ b_i>2a_i>0}}^{n} p_i^{a_i} \prod_{\substack{i=1 \\ 0<a_i<b_i\leq 2a_i}}^{n} p_i^{b_i-a_i}$$

$$pow = \prod_{\substack{i=1 \\ 0<2a_i<b_i}}^{n} p_i^{a_i\lceil\log_2 b\rceil} \prod_{\substack{i=1 \\ 0<a_i<b_i\leq 2a_i}}^{n} p_i^{(b_i-a_i)\lceil\log_2 b\rceil}$$

$$res_2 = \prod_{\substack{i=1 \\ 0<2a_i<b_i}}^{n} p_i^{b_i} \prod_{\substack{i=1 \\ 0<a_i<b_i\leq 2a_i}}^{n} p_i^{b_i} = \prod_{\substack{i=1 \\ 0<a_i<b_i}}^{n} p_i^{b_i}$$

$$res_1 \times res_2 = \prod_{\substack{i=1 \\ a_i<b_i}}^{n} p_i^{b_i} = \mathrm{alcm}_a b$$

Fig. 3. The decomposition into primes of each variable occurring in Algorithm 16, which proves the correctness of its output.

which implies that res_2 gets the correct value for the computation of the result in the last line. Remark that $\lceil\log_2 b\rceil \geq b_i$ for all i. Indeed, $p_i^{b_i} \leq b$ and since $p_i \geq 2$, we have $b_i \leq b_i \log_2 p_i \leq \log_2 b \leq \lceil\log_2 b\rceil$. This implies $a_i\lceil\log_2 b\rceil \geq b_i$ if $a_i > 0$, which gives the first term of the product. For the second term, since $b_i > a_i$, we have $a_i \leq b_i - 1$ and thus $(b_i - a_i)\lceil\log_2 b\rceil \geq \lceil\log_2 b\rceil \geq b_i$.

In order to analyze the complexity of the algorithm, remark that the input integers are bounded by b and that each variable in lines 1–9 is obtained by constant number of products, divisions, gcd and lcm; as a consequence, they are all bounded by a constant power c of b. Assuming a constant-time model for basic arithmetic operations, the gcd and lcm operations require time $\mathcal{O}(\log b)$. In particular, this is the case for $quot_4$: hence, pow is computed in time $\mathcal{O}(\log\log b)$ using fast exponentiation and is bounded by $b^{c\lceil\log_2\rceil}$, therefore its size is $\mathcal{O}((\log b)^2)$. Line 11 then requires $\mathcal{O}((\log b)^2)$ time, which gives the promised complexity bound. □

Lemma 18. *The complexity of Algorithm 14 is $\mathcal{O}(c^2 \times (\log c + (\log d)^2))$ where c is the maximum number of distinct cycle lengths of A and B, and d is the length of the longest cycle.*

Proof. First of all, the number of iterations is bounded by the number of elements (distinct cycle lengths) of array B, hence by c. Secondly, the product of two sums of cycles, where all cycle lengths of the second term are identical, can be performed in $\mathcal{O}(c(\log d + \log c))$ time. Indeed, for each pair of elements C_1, C_2, we just have to compute the gcd and the lcm of $C_1.l$ and $C_2.l$ and multiply the gcd by $C_1.n$ and $C_2.n$. Then, we sort the array containing the result of all the multiplications according to the cycle lengths and group together all cycles with the same length by summing their multiplicities. This implies that line 5 and the computation of AS require $\mathcal{O}(c(\log d + \log c))$ time. Furthermore, since the number of elements of AS is bounded by the number of elements of A (since S is only one element) and since B can be sorted, line 9 and verifying if AS is a submultiset of B are accomplished in $\mathcal{O}(c)$ time. Additionally, line 3 requires $\mathcal{O}(c)$ time, since it is just an array traversal. Beside, by Lemma 17, we execute line 4 in $\mathcal{O}((\log_2 d)^2)$ time. Finally, all the other operations in the loop only require constant time, therefore the complexity of the loop is $\mathcal{O}(c^2 \times (\log c + \log d) + c \times (\log_2 d)^2)$. Since the operations outside the loop require $\mathcal{O}(c \log c)$ time, the lemma follows. □

As an aside, Lemma 18 has the consequence that, when the FDDS of the equation $AX = B$ are sums of cycles represented explicitly as graphs, we can improve the runtime of Algorithm 5 by first converting the input to the compact encoding described above.

Corollary 19. *Let A and B be sums of cycles with A pseudo-cancelable. If A and B are given in input as graphs, then computing X such that $AX = B$ can be performed in $\mathcal{O}(n(\log n)^2)$ time.*

Proof. Translating a sum of cycles encoded as a graph into a sum of cycles encoded by a sorted array can be accomplished by a simple traversal, therefore in $\mathcal{O}(n \log n)$ in our context. Remark that the number of elements c of the array is $\mathcal{O}(\sqrt{n})$. Indeed, the smallest sum of cycles with c different cycles has $\sum_{i=1}^{c} i = c(c+1)/2$ states. At this point, by the Lemma 18, we conclude that the complexity of finding the solution X is $\mathcal{O}((\sqrt{n})^2(\log \sqrt{n} + (\log n)^2)) = \mathcal{O}(n(\log n)^2)$ time. □

We can now generalize Lemma 18 to equations of the form $P(X) = B$ with P a pseudo-injective polynomial and B a sum of cycles. For this, we represent the polynomial $P = A_1 X^{p_1} + \cdots + A_m X^{p_m}$ (where the number of states of each A_i is at least 1) as an array of pairs (p_i, A_i).

Algorithm 20. *Given a sum of cycles B and a pseudo-injective polynomial $P = \sum_{i=0}^{m} A_i X^i$ over sums of cycles encoded compactly, we can compute Y such that $P(Y) = B$, if any exists, as follows:*

1. *Set* $min \leftarrow 0, B \leftarrow B - A_0, P \leftarrow P - A_0, A \leftarrow \sum_{i=1}^{m} A_i$ *and* $X \leftarrow \mathbf{0}$.
2. *Sort A and B by length of the cycles.*
3. *Check if* $|A| \leq |B|$.
4. *Set* $l \leftarrow \mathrm{alcm}_{A[0].l}(B[min].l)$, $d \leftarrow 1$ *and* $d' \leftarrow B[min].n$.

5. *Set* $a_{init} \leftarrow P(Y)$ *and* $a_{end} \leftarrow P(Y+dC_l)$ *by computing progressively*[2] $P(Y+dC_l)$ *without exceeding the size of the original* B.
6. *Check if* $d \neq d'$.
7. *Sort the cycles of* a_{init} *and* a_{end} *by length and set* $rem \leftarrow a_{init} - a_{end}$.
8. *If* rem *is not a submultiset of* B *then set* $d \leftarrow \lfloor (d+d')/2 \rfloor$ *and go to 5. Otherwise if* $B[min].n - rem[0].n \neq 0$ *then set* $d' \leftarrow \lceil (d+d')/2 \rceil$ *and go to 5.*
9. *Otherwise add* (d, l) *to* Y.
10. *Remove* rem *from* B *and set* $min \leftarrow \min\{i \mid B[i].n > 0\}$, *if the set is nonempty, and go back to 3; otherwise, return* Y.

Theorem 21. *Let* P *be a pseudo-injective polynomial where each coefficient is a sum of cycles and* B *a sum of cycles. Then we can solve* $P(X) = B$ *in polynomial time.*

Proof. Thanks to Proposition 11 and by applying the same reasoning as Lemma 17, we can deduce that Algorithm 20 only outputs valid solutions.

Assume $B \neq \mathbf{0}$, $P = \sum_{i=0}^{m} A_i X^i$ and $P(Y) = B$ with $Y \neq \mathbf{0}$ and $Y \neq \mathbf{1}$. Then, without loss of generality, we can choose $m \leq \log_2 b$, where b is the number of states in B. Indeed, since $|Y^m| = |Y|^m$, we have $2^m \leq |Y^m| \leq b$ and thus $m \leq \log_2 b$. Observe that we can enumerate all natural numbers between 0 and m in polynomial time; indeed, the size of the representation of B is $\sum_{i=0}^{n-1} (\log_2 B[i].n + \log_2 B[i].l) = \log_2 \prod_{i=0}^{n-1} (B[i].n \times B[i].l)$ with $n = |L(B)|$, and $\log_2 b = \log_2 \sum_{i=0}^{n-1} (B[i].n \times B[i].l)$.

Let $X = \sum_{i=1}^{k} C_{x_i}$ be a sum of cycles and $j \geq 1$ be an integer. Then C_x^j is an element of X^j for each $x \in L(X)$. Since $C_p^q = p^{q-1} C_p$ for all positive integers p, q, we deduce that X^i is a submultiset of X^{i+1} for all integer $i \geq 0$ and thus, for all A, we AX^i is a submultiset of AX^{i+1}. Thanks to the two previous observations, line 5 can be executed in polynomial time. Since the number of iterations of Lines 5–8 perform a binary search ranging from 1 to $B[min].n$ and thus require at most $\log_2(B[min].n)$ iterations, this loop can be carried out in polynomial time.

Finally, since the number of iterations of lines 3–10 is bounded by $|L(B)|$, the statement of the theorem follows. □

5 Conclusions

In this paper, we enlarged the class of efficiently solvable polynomial equations over FDDS by generalizing the notion of injectivity of polynomials. Furthermore, we developed a procedure that allows us to carry over these results to a more compact representation when the FDDS involved are sums of cycles, not only without incurring an exponential slowdown, but even improving the efficiency of one of the aforementioned algorithms.

This work also highlighted the structure of solutions to equations over pseudo-injective polynomials (Lemmas 12 and 13), which we expect will be useful for efficiently counting and enumerating the set of solutions. We also believe

[2] See line 4 of Algorithm 10.

that a similar structure might be found among the solutions of other equations of the form $P(X) = B$, if the conditions on P are relaxed but other conditions on the divisibility of the lengths of the cycles of B are introduced. This could be useful for improving the efficiency of enumeration algorithms for other classes of equations [4].

A more in-depth investigation of compact representations of FDDS in the context of polynomial equations is also interesting, since in most applications the dynamics of the systems are not described explicitly, and the detection of simple dynamical properties usually becomes intractable, notably with a succinct encoding by Boolean circuits.

Another open problem is finding complexity lower bounds for different classes of equations. The exact complexity of solving equations of the form $AX = B$ or, more generally, $P(X) = B$ of a single variable, but without other restrictions, is still open. Is it an NP-hard problem or does it admit an efficient algorithm? Does this generalize to any constant number of variables? Furthermore, how much can we relax the constraints on the number of variables and the fact that the right-hand side of equations must be constant without them becoming intractable or even undecidable [3]?

Acknowledgments. This work has been partially supported by the HORIZON-MSCA-2022-SE-01 project 101131549 "Application-driven Challenges for Automata Networks and Complex Systems (ACANCOS)" and by the project ANR-24-CE48-7504 "ALARICE".

References

1. Betel, H., de Oliveira, P.P., Flocchini, P.: Solving the parity problem in one-dimensional cellular automata. Nat. Comput. **12**, 323–337 (2013). https://doi.org/10.1007/s11047-013-9374-9
2. Bridoux, F., Crespelle, C., Phan, T.H.D., Richard, A.: Dividing permutations in the semiring of functional digraphs. In: Gadouleau, M., Castillo-Ramirez, A. (eds.) AUTOMATA 2024. LNCS, vol. 14782, pp. 95–107. Springer, Cham (2024). https://doi.org/10.1007/978-3-031-65887-7_6
3. Dennunzio, A., Dorigatti, V., Formenti, E., Manzoni, L., Porreca, A.E.: Polynomial equations over finite, discrete-time dynamical systems. In: Mauri, G., El Yacoubi, S., Dennunzio, A., Nishinari, K., Manzoni, L. (eds.) ACRI 2018. LNCS, vol. 11115, pp. 298–306. Springer, Cham (2018). https://doi.org/10.1007/978-3-319-99813-8_27
4. Dennunzio, A., Formenti, E., Margara, L., Riva, S.: An algorithmic pipeline for solving equations over discrete dynamical systems modelling hypothesis on real phenomena. J. Comput. Sci. **66**, 101932 (2023)
5. Doré, F., Perrot, K., Porreca, A.E., Riva, S., Rolland, M.: Roots in the semiring of finite deterministic dynamical systems. arXiv e-prints (2025). https://arxiv.org/abs/2405.09236
6. Ehrenfeucht, A., Rozenberg, G.: Reaction systems. Fundamenta Informaticae **75**, 263–280 (2007). https://doi.org/10.3233/FUN-2007-751-415

7. Goles, E., Martìnez, S.: Neural and Automata Networks: Dynamical Behavior and Applications. Kluwer Academic Publishers (1990)
8. Hammack, R., Imrich, W., Klavžar, S.: Handbook of Product Graphs. Discrete Mathematics and Its Applications, 2nd edn. CRC Press (2011)
9. Harary, F.: The number of functional digraphs. Mathematische Annalen **138**, 203–210 (1959). https://doi.org/10.1007/BF01342903
10. Hopcroft, J.E., Wong, J.K.: Linear time algorithm for isomorphism of planar graphs (preliminary report). In: Proceedings of the Sixth Annual ACM Symposium on Theory of Computing, pp. 172–184 (1974)
11. Naquin, E., Gadouleau, M.: Factorisation in the semiring of finite dynamical systems. Theoret. Comput. Sci. **998**, 114509 (2024)
12. Porreca, A.E., Rolland, M.: Injectivity of polynomials over finite discrete dynamical systems. arXiv e-prints (2025). https://arxiv.org/abs/2502.02360
13. Riva, S.: Factorisation de Systèmes Dynamiques Discrets. Ph.D. thesis, Université Côte d'Azur and Università degli Studi di Milano-Bicocca (2022)

Self-orthogonal Cellular Automata

Luca Mariot(✉) and Federico Mazzone

Semantics, Cybersecurity and Services Group, University of Twente, Drienerlolaan 5, 7511GG Enschede, The Netherlands
{l.mariot,f.mazzone}@utwente.nl

Abstract. It is known that no-boundary Cellular Automata (CA) defined by bipermutive local rules give rise to Latin squares. In this paper, we study under which conditions the Latin square generated by a bipermutive CA is self-orthogonal, i.e. orthogonal to its transpose. We first enumerate all bipermutive CA over the binary alphabet up to diameter $d = 6$, remarking that only some linear rules give rise to self-orthogonal Latin squares. We then give a full theoretical characterization of self-orthogonal linear CA, by considering the square matrix obtained by stacking the transition matrices of the CA and of its transpose, and determining when it is invertible. Interestingly, the stacked matrix turns out to have a circulant structure, for which there exists an extensive body of results to characterize its invertibility. Further, for the case of the binary alphabet we prove that irreducibility is a sufficient condition for self-orthogonality, and we derive a simpler characterization which boils down to computing the parity of the central coefficients of the local rule.

Keywords: cellular automata · Latin squares · polynomials · resultant · circulant matrices

1 Introduction

Cellular Automata (CA) provide an interesting framework for the construction of cryptographic primitives, including pseudorandom number generators [6,14,28], S-boxes [8,22,24], and secret sharing schemes [10,19,25]. The case of secret sharing schemes is particularly interesting for the type of combinatorial structures that arise from the one-shot behavior of CA, which contrasts with the usual long-term and asymptotic approach employed in the literature to study the dynamical properties of CA. Among the set of works that studied the combinatorial structures generated by CA in the context of secret sharing, the research thread focused on Latin squares proved to be quite fruitful in the last few years. In particular, it is known that the Cayley table of a *bipermutive* CA (i.e. CA that are permutive in both the leftmost and rightmost coordinates of the local rule) is a Latin square, and that two bipermutive CA defined by linear local rules are orthogonal if and only if their associated polynomials are coprime [18]. This result gives a straightfoward way to implement threshold secret sharing schemes

Published by Springer Nature Switzerland AG 2026
S. Riva and A. Richard (Eds.): AUTOMATA 2025, LNCS 15831, pp. 188–204, 2026.
https://doi.org/10.1007/978-3-032-01570-9_13

where only two players are required in order to reconstruct the secret. Subsequent works explored different perspectives of this characterization of orthogonal CA, such as its specialization over more particular classes of Latin squares [9], the construction of Boolean functions with significant cryptographic properties [7], and the design subspace codes with optimal minimum distance [21].

In this paper, we take a different direction and consider the following problem: *when is the Latin square generated by a bipermutive CA self-orthogonal, i.e. orthogonal to its transpose?* Beside their own theoretical interest, self-orthogonal Latin squares are connected to several other types of combinatorial designs, including *resolvable Balanced Incomplete Block Designs* (BIBDs) [1]. In turn, resolvable BIBDs can be used to design anonymous secret sharing schemes [3] and Mutually Unbiased Bases (MUBs) for quantum error-correcting codes [13].

We start our investigation of self-orthogonal CA by first exhaustively enumerating all bipermutive CA over the binary alphabet up to diameter $d = 6$, and notice that among them only a few linear ones generate self-orthogonal Latin squares. We then provide a full theoretical characterization of self-orthogonal linear CA. In particular, we consider the square matrix obtained by stacking the transition matrix of the CA with that of its transpose, and studying under which conditions this matrix is invertible. Interestingly, we show that this stacked matrix is circulant, a remark that allows us to reduce the problem of its invertibility to the computation of the greatest common divisor of the polynomial associated with the local rule of the CA and the polynomial $X^{2(d-1)} - 1$. Additionally, we focus on the binary case where we prove that irreducibility of the polynomial associated to the local rule is a sufficient condition for self-orthogonality, and we derive a simpler characterization when the size of the stacked matrix is a power of 2. In particular, this characterization reduces the problem to determining the parity of the central coefficients of the linear local rule.

The rest of this paper is structured as follows. Section 2 covers the basic definitions and results about cellular automata and Latin squares used throughout the paper. Section 3 formally states the problem of finding self-orthogonal CA, and discusses the preliminary results obtained from the exhaustive search experiments of bipermutive CA up to diameter $d = 6$. Then, Sect. 4 formally analyzes the case where the underlying local rule is linear, deriving a general characterization result for linear self-orthogonal CA over a finite field, and providing more refined results for the binary case. Finally, Sect. 5 recaps the main contributions of the paper, and describes a few interesting directions for future research on the topic.

2 Background

This section recalls the background terminology and results that the rest of the paper is based upon. In particular, the section covers first the basic concepts and representations concerning cellular automata, and then it reviews the essential results related to combinatorial designs and orthogonal Latin squares.

2.1 Cellular Automata

A Cellular Automaton (CA) can be broadly conceived as a computational model defined by a regular lattice of cells. Commonly, this lattice is one-dimensional, although generalizations to more dimensions are possible. Each cell updates its state by evaluating a local rule on its neighborhood, which comprises the cell itself and some of its neighbors. A single step of computation amounts to applying in parallel the local rule at all cells.

Different settings can arise depending on how one addresses the update of the cells at the boundaries of the lattice. In this paper, we consider the *no boundary* and *periodic boundary* conditions, which lead us to the following definition:

Definition 1. *Let Σ be a finite set of size $q \in \mathbb{N}$, and let $d, n \in \mathbb{N}$ such that $d \leq n$. Further, let $f : \Sigma^d \to \Sigma$ be a d-variable mapping over Σ. Then, we define the following two models of* one-dimensional *CA over the alphabet Σ and with n input cells, equipped with the* local rule *f of* diameter *d:*

- No Boundary CA *(NBCA): $F : \Sigma^n \to \Sigma^{n-d+1}$ is defined for all $x \in \Sigma^n$ as:*

$$F(x_1, \dots, x_n) = (f(x_1, \dots, x_d), f(x_2, \dots, x_{d+1}), \dots, f(x_{n-d+1}, \dots, x_n)) . \tag{1}$$

- Periodic Boundary CA *(PBCA): $F : \Sigma^n \to \Sigma^n$ is defined for all $x \in \Sigma^n$ as:*

$$F(x_1, \dots, x_n) = (f(x_1, \dots, x_d), \dots, f(x_{n-d}, \dots, x_1), \dots, f(x_n, \dots, x_{d-1}) . \tag{2}$$

In general, the i-th output coordinate of a one-dimensional CA is determined by applying the local rule f to the neighborhood formed by the i-th input cells and the $d-1$ cells to its right. The difference between the NBCA and PBCA model is that in the former the local rule is applied only to those cells that have enough neighbours on the right, while in the latter it is applied to all cells by considering the lattice as the ring of integers modulo n.

The local map $f : \Sigma^d \to \Sigma$ is usually represented as a lookup table of q^d entries which specifies the output value $f(x)$ for each input vector $x \in \Sigma^d$. In this context, the most basic setting corresponds to *binary* CA, where the alphabet is the finite field of two elements $\Sigma = \mathbb{F}_2 = \{0, 1\}$. In particular, sum and multiplication in $\mathbb{F}_2$ corresponds respectively to the XOR (denoted as $\oplus$) and the logical AND (denoted by concatenation of the operands). A binary local rule can then be interpreted as a *Boolean function* $f : \mathbb{F}_2^d \to \mathbb{F}_2$ of d variables, where the input space is the d-dimensional vector space $\mathbb{F}_2^d$.

From a representation standpoint, the lookup table of f is the *truth table* representation of the Boolean function, and it can be uniquely identified by the 2^d-bit string $\Omega_f \in \mathbb{F}_2^{2^d}$ of its outputs, once the input vectors of $\mathbb{F}_2^d$ have been sorted in lexicographic order. In the CA literature, it is customary to refer to the *Wolfram code* of the local rule, which is simply the decimal encoding of Ω_f [27].

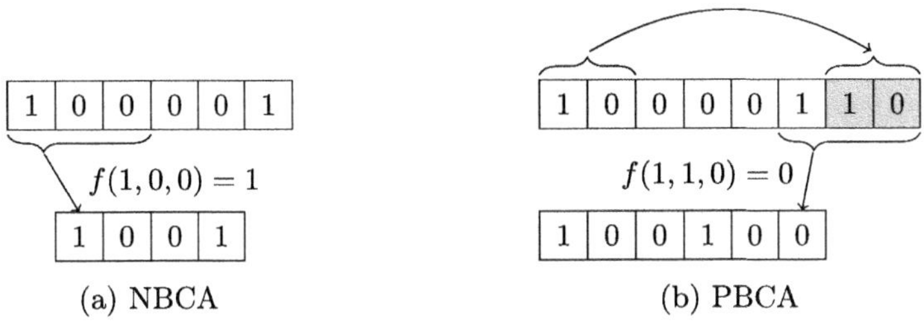

Fig. 1. Examples of NBCA and PBCA evaluations under local rule 150.

As an example, Fig. 1 displays an example of binary NBCA and PBCA of length $n = 6$ equipped with the linear local rule 150, which is defined for all $x = (x_1, x_2, x_3) \in \mathbb{F}_2^3$ as $f(x_1, x_2, x_3) = x_1 \oplus x_2 \oplus x_3$.

Another method to uniquely represent Boolean functions that we will use throughout the paper for the local rules of binary CA is the *Algebraic Normal Form* (ANF) [4]. Formally, the ANF of $f : \mathbb{F}_2^d \to \mathbb{F}_2$ is the multivariate polynomial P_f over the quotient ring $\mathbb{F}_2[x]/(x_1^2 \oplus x_1, \cdots, x_n^2 \oplus x_n)$ defined as follows:

$$P_f(x) = \bigoplus_{u \in \mathbb{F}_2^n} a_u x^u = \bigoplus_{u \in \mathbb{F}_2^n} a_u (x_1^{u_1} \cdots x_n^{u_n}) \text{ , with } a_u = \bigoplus_{x \in \mathbb{F}_2^n : x \preceq u} f(x) \text{ ,} \tag{3}$$

where $x \preceq u$ if and only if $x_i \leq u_i$ for all $i \in \{1, \ldots, n\}$. The *algebraic degree* of f is the size of the largest nonzero monomial in P_f. Functions of degree 1 are also called *affine*, and an affine function is *linear* if $a_{\underline{0}} = 0$.

Beside the binary case, in this paper we consider CA defined over the finite field $\mathbb{F}_q$ as an alphabet, mainly due the interest for applications in cryptography and coding theory [15]. In this case, the size q of the alphabet is a power of a prime number. Linear CA can be generalized also over the alphabet $\mathbb{F}_q$. Specifically, the function $f : \mathbb{F}_q^d \to \mathbb{F}_q$ is called linear if it is possible to write it as a linear combination of the input variables, that is:

$$f(x_1, \ldots, x_d) = a_1 x_1 + \ldots + a_d x_d \tag{4}$$

for all $x = (x_1, \ldots, x_d) \in \mathbb{F}_q^d$, where $a_1, \ldots a_d \in \mathbb{F}_q$. The global map of a CA $F : \mathbb{F}_q^n \to \mathbb{F}_q^{n-d+1}$ defined by the linear local rule f in Eq. (4) can be expressed as the linear transformation $F(x) = M_F \cdot x^\top$, where M_F is the $(n - d + 1) \times n$ *transition matrix* defined as:

$$M_F = \begin{pmatrix} a_1 \ldots a_{d-1} & a_d & 0 & \ldots\ldots\ldots & \ldots & 0 \\ 0 \;\; a_1 \;\; \ldots & a_{d-1} & a_d & 0 \;\ldots\ldots & \ldots & 0 \\ \vdots \;\; \vdots \;\; \vdots & \ddots & \vdots & \vdots \;\; \vdots \;\; \ddots & \vdots & \vdots \\ 0 \;\ldots\; \ldots & \ldots & \ldots & 0 \;\; a_1 \;\ldots & a_{d-1} & a_d \end{pmatrix} . \tag{5}$$

Further, one can naturally associate to the linear local rule f of Eq. (4) the polynomial $p_f \in \mathbb{F}_q[X]$ with the following form:

$$p_f(X) = a_1 + a_2 X + \ldots + a_d X^{d-1} . \tag{6}$$

In other words, we assign the coefficients $a_1, \dots, a_d \in \mathbb{F}_q$ to the increasing powers of the unknown X, thus obtaining a polynomial of degree at most $d-1$. From a coding-theoretic standpoint, M_F and p_f are respectively the generator matrix and the generator polynomial of a cyclic code [20].

Due to their connections with combinatorial designs and Latin squares, in this paper we also consider the specific class of *permutive* CA. Formally, a local rule $f : \Sigma^d \to \Sigma$ is permutive in the i-th coordinate (with $i \in \{1 \dots, d\}$) if, by fixing all other input coordinates $j \neq i$ to any constant value, the resulting restriction of f is a permutation over Σ. In the binary case $\Sigma = \mathbb{F}_2$, a permutive local rule $f : \mathbb{F}_2^d \to \mathbb{F}_2$ can be written as:

$$f(x_1, \dots, x_d) = x_i \oplus g(x_1, \dots, x_{i-1}, x_{i+1}, \dots, x_i) \ , \tag{7}$$

where $g : \mathbb{F}_2^{d-1} \to \mathbb{F}_2$ is a function of $d-1$ variables, also called the *generating function* of f [14].

A function f that is permutive in the first (respectively, the last) coordinate is also called *leftmost* (respectively, *rightmost*) *permutive.* If f is both leftmost and rightmost permutive, then it is called *bipermutive.* The aforementioned rule 150 is an example of bipermutive rule. Clearly, any linear rule over $\mathbb{F}_q^d$ of the form defined in Eq. (4) is bipermutive if and only if both a_1 and a_d are not null.

2.2 Latin Squares

In this section we cover only the basic facts related to Latin squares, referring the reader to [12,26] for a more thorough treatment of the subject. In what follows, we denote by $[n] = \{1, \dots, n\}$ the set of the first $n \in \mathbb{N}$ integer positive numbers. We start by giving the definition of Latin square:

Definition 2. *A Latin square of order $N \in \mathbb{N}$ is an $N \times N$ matrix L with entries from $[N]$ such that for all $i, j, k \in [N]$ with $j \neq k$, one has that $L(i,j) \neq L(i,k)$ and $L(j,i) \neq L(k,i)$.*

Intuitively, Definition 2 states that every number from 1 to N occurs exactly once in each row and in each column of a Latin square. Alternatively, each row and each column of L forms a permutation of $[N]$.

The next definition introduces orthogonal Latin squares:

Definition 3. *Two Latin squares L_1, L_2 of order $N \in \mathbb{N}$ are orthogonal if for all distinct pairs of coordinates $(i,j), (i',j') \in [N] \times [N]$ it holds that*

$$(L_1(i,j), L_2(i,j)) \neq (L_1(i',j'), L_2(i',j')) \ . \tag{8}$$

Thus, two Latin squares of the same order are orthogonal if their *superposition* yields all ordered pairs of the Cartesian product $[N] \times [N]$ exactly once.

We now briefly review the construction of orthogonal Latin squares based on CA proposed in [18]. To this end, we first introduce the *Cayley table* associated to a generic NBCA, which requires a bit more of notation on how we can encode

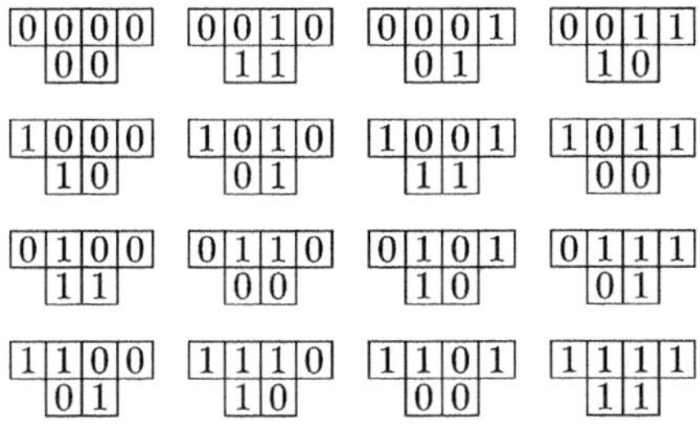

1	4	3	2
2	3	4	1
4	1	2	3
3	2	1	4

Fig. 2. Latin square of order 4 generated by rule 150.

$(d-1)$-cell blocks as integer numbers. Specifically, we assume that Σ^{d-1} is totally ordered, and that $\phi : \Sigma^{d-1} \to [N]$ is a monotone bijective mapping between Σ^{d-1} and $[N]$, where the latter inherits the usual order of natural numbers. The inverse mapping of ϕ is denoted by $\psi = \phi^{-1}$. This notation leads to the following definition:

Definition 4. *Let $F : \Sigma^{2(d-1)} \to \Sigma^{d-1}$ be a NBCA defined by the local rule $f : \Sigma^d \to \Sigma$ of diameter d over an alphabet Σ of q symbols. Setting $N = q^{d-1}$, the* Cayley table *associated to F is the $N \times N$ matrix C_F with entries from $[N]$ such that*

$$C_F(i,j) = \phi(F(\psi(i)||\psi(j))) \ , \tag{9}$$

for all $1 \leq i,j \leq N$, where $||$ denotes concatenation.

Intuitively, this means that the output of the CA corresponds to the entry of the Cayley table at the row and column coordinates respectively encoded by the left and the right half of the CA input configuration.

The next Lemma about CA and Latin squares has been independently rediscovered in multiple works under different guises [5,18]:

Lemma 1. *Let Σ be a finite alphabet of size q. The Cayley table C_F of a CA $F : \Sigma^{2(d-1)} \to \Sigma^{d-1}$ defined by a bipermutive local rule $f : \Sigma^d \to \Sigma$ is a Latin square of order $N = q^{d-1}$.*

To fix the ideas discussed so far with an example, Fig. 2 shows the Cayley table associated to the NBCA $F : \mathbb{F}_2^4 \to \mathbb{F}_2^2$ defined by rule 150. The bijective monotone mapping ϕ used here to encode pairs of bits $\phi(00) \mapsto 1$, $\phi(10) \mapsto 2$, $\phi(01) \mapsto 3$ and $\phi(11) \mapsto 4$.

When $\Sigma = \mathbb{F}_q$ is the finite field of order q, the result below proved in [18] gives a characterization of linear Orthogonal CA (or linear OCA), i.e. pairs of linear bipermutive CA whose associated Latin squares are also orthogonal:

Theorem 1. *Let $F, G : \mathbb{F}_q^{2(d-1)} \to \mathbb{F}_q^{d-1}$ be two linear bipermutive CA, and let $p_f, p_g \in \mathbb{F}_q[X]$ be the respective associated polynomials. Then, the corresponding Latin squares C_F and C_G of order $N = q^{d-1}$ are orthogonal if and only if $\gcd(p_f, p_g) = 1$, i.e. if and only if p_f and p_g are relatively prime.*

The proof of Theorem 1 stands on the observation that, in order for the Latin squares to be orthogonal, the square matrix obtained by stacking the transition matrices of F and G one on top of the other must be invertible. Crucially, the stacked matrix is the *Sylvester matrix* of the two polynomials p_f and p_g, and its determinant (also called the *resultant*) vanishes if and only if p_f and p_g have at least one common factor.

Theorem 1 gives a rather efficient method to check whether two linear CA are orthogonal: instead of generating exhaustively their associated Latin squares and checking if they are orthogonal, one can simply compute the greatest common divisor (e.g., by means of Euclid's algorithm) of the underlying polynomials.

We refer the reader to [18] for further results leveraging on Theorem 1, including how to count the number of all linear OCA of a given diameter d, and how to construct a maximal family of Mutually Orthogonal Latin Squares based on linear CA (also called MOCA).

3 Empirical Search of Self-orthogonal CA

A Latin square L is called *self-orthogonal* if it is orthogonal to its transpose $L^\top$ [1]. This definition can be naturally adapted to the case of Latin squares generated by CA, yielding the concept of *self-orthogonal CA*:

Definition 5. *Let $F : \Sigma^{2(d-1)} \to \Sigma^{d-1}$ be a NBCA over an alphabet Σ of size q defined by a bipermutive local rule $f : \Sigma^d \to \Sigma_q$ of diameter $d \in \mathbb{N}$. Then, F is a* self-orthogonal CA *if the Latin square S_F that it generates is self-orthogonal.*

Since we are mostly interested in applications to cryptography and coding theory, in what follows we focus on the case where the alphabet Σ is the finite field $\mathbb{F}_q$, thus with its cardinality q being the power of a prime number.

Clearly, one can check if a bipermutive NBCA is self-orthogonal by constructing the associated Latin square and superimposing it to its transpose, verifying that all ordered pairs in the Cartesian product of $(d-1)$-tuples occur exactly once. However, this procedure is exponential in the diameter of the automaton, since the NBCA F has to be evaluated over all $q^{2(d-1)}$ input configurations. Therefore, *we are interested in a more efficient characterization, which focuses on the properties of the underlying local rule.* This motivates the following problem, which we address in the remainder of the paper.

Problem 1. Let $F : \mathbb{F}_q^{2(d-1)} \to \mathbb{F}_q^{d-1}$ be a NBCA of diameter $d \in \mathbb{N}$, defined by a bipermutive local rule $f : \mathbb{F}_q^d \to \mathbb{F}_q$. What conditions must the local rule f satisfy for F to be self-orthogonal?

To get a general impression of this problem, let us start our investigation in an empirical manner. Consider the simplest case possible where the alphabet is binary (i.e., $\Sigma = \mathbb{F}_2 = \{0, 1\}$) and the diameter is $d = 3$, that is, the case of elementary CA. Here, up to complement and reversal of the inputs, there are only two bipermutive CA that give rise to Latin squares of order $2^{(3-1)} = 4$,

1,1	2,2	3,3	4,4
2,2	1,1	4,4	3,3
3,3	4,4	1,1	2,2
4,4	3,3	2,2	1,1

(a) Rule 90.

1,1	4,3	2,4	3,2
3,4	2,2	4,1	1,3
4,2	1,4	3,3	2,1
2,3	3,1	1,2	4,4

(b) Rule 150.

Fig. 3. Self-superposition of rule 90 and 150. Only rule 150 is self-orthogonal, since all 16 pairs in the Cartesian product of $[4] \times [4]$ occur exactly once.

namely those respectively defined by the linear local rules 90 and 150 [17]. By Theorem 1, these two Latin squares are orthogonal between each other, since the associated polynomials $1 + X^2$ and $1 + X + X^2$ do not have any factors in common. However, as depicted in Fig. 3, only rule 150 generates a self-orthogonal Latin square.

Indeed, a closer look shows that the square generated by rule 90 is symmetric (i.e. it equals its transpose), hence it cannot be self-orthogonal.

The finding above prompted us to perform a more systematic exploration of self-orthogonal CA. Hence, we set out to enumerate in an exhaustive manner all binary bipermutive CA up to diameter $d = 6$. For each local rule, we checked whether the corresponding bipermutive CA was self-orthogonal with the naive method mentioned earlier, i.e. by completely constructing the associated Latin square and its transpose, and checking whether all pairs in the Cartesian product occurred exactly once. As recalled in the previous section, there are $2^{2^{d-2}}$ bipermutive local rules of diameter d over $\mathbb{F}_2$, since the generating function is determined by the central $d-2$ variables. Therefore, for the largest problem instance of $d = 6$ we exhaustively checked $2^{16} = 65\,536$ rules for self-orthogonality. For each self-orthogonal Latin square found, we further checked whether it was generated by a nonlinear or linear rule, and in the latter case we computed the associated polynomial. Table 1 summarizes the results of the exhaustive search experiments, reporting for each diameter the corresponding number of bipermutive rule (#BCA), the number of self-orthogonal CA found (#SOCA), how many of them were linear or affine (#LIN/AFF) and the associated polynomials.

Two main facts stand out from the table: the first one is that, among those found, there are no self-orthogonal CA defined by nonlinear local rules. Indeed, the numbers in the columns #SOCA and #LIN coincide. The second fact is that the number of linear SOCA grows exponentially as the sequence of powers of 2. Actually, one can notice a straightforward symmetry from these exhaustive search experiments: if a rule $f : \mathbb{F}_2^d \to \mathbb{F}_2$ generates a self-orthogonal CA, then so does its complement $f_C : \mathbb{F}_2^d \to \mathbb{F}_2$ defined as $f(x)_C = f(x) \oplus 1$ for all $x \in \mathbb{F}_2^d$. This

Table 1. Exhaustive enumeration of self-orthogonal CA up to diameter $d = 6$.

d	#BCA	#SOCA	#LIN/AFF	Polynomials
3	4	2	2	$1 + X + X^2$
4	16	4	4	$1 + X + X^3$, $1 + X^2 + X^3$
5	256	8	8	$1 + X + X^4$, $1 + X^2 + X^4$ $1 + X^3 + X^4$, $1 + X + X^2 + X^3 + X^4$
6	65 336	16	16	$1 + X + X^5$, $1 + X^2 + X^5$ $1 + X^3 + X^5$, $1 + X^4 + X^5$ $1 + X + X^2 + X^3 + X^5$ $1 + X + X^2 + X^4 + X^5$ $1 + X + X^3 + X^4 + X^5$ $1 + X^2 + X^3 + X^4 + X^5$

is the reason why the polynomials reported in the last column amount to half of the number of linear self-orthogonal CA that have been found. The constant term in the ANF of the complemented local rule is simply neglected when considering the associated polynomial. A third fact is that for each considered diameter d *all irreducible polynomials of degree* $n = d - 1$ appear in the last column, suggesting that irreducibility is a sufficient condition for constructing a self-orthogonal CA.

4 Characterization of the Linear Case

Given the findings highlighted in the previous section concerning our exhaustive search experiments, we now narrow our attention to linear self-orthogonal CA, seeking a full algebraic characterization in the following subsections.

4.1 General Results for the Alphabet $\Sigma = \mathbb{F}_q$

Given a linear NBCA $F : \mathbb{F}_q^{2(d-1)} \to \mathbb{F}_q^{d-1}$, let us start by analyzing more in depth the meaning of computing the transpose of F. Transposing the Cayley table of the CA is equivalent to swap the left half and the right half of its input configuration, and then applying the global map F of the CA. Thus, the transpose CA $F^\top : \mathbb{F}_q^{2(d-1)} \to \mathbb{F}_q^{d-1}$ is defined for all $x, y \in \mathbb{F}_q^{d-1}$ as:

$$F^\top(x||y) = F(y||x) \ . \tag{10}$$

For all $x \in \mathbb{F}_q^n$ with $n \in \mathbb{N}$ even, the swap operation can be formalized as the linear transformation $P_s(x) = M_s \cdot x^\top$, where M_s is the $n \times n$ *permutation matrix*

$$M_s = \begin{pmatrix} 0\,0 \ldots 0\,1\,0 \ldots 0\,0 \\ 0\,0 \ldots 0\,0\,1 \ldots 0\,0 \\ \vdots\,\vdots\,\ddots\,\vdots\,\vdots\,\vdots\,\ddots\,\vdots\,\vdots \\ 0\,0 \ldots 0\,0\,0 \ldots 0\,1 \\ 1\,0 \ldots 0\,0\,0 \ldots 0\,0 \\ 0\,1 \ldots 0\,0\,0 \ldots 0\,0 \\ \vdots\,\vdots\,\ddots\,\vdots\,\vdots\,\vdots\,\ddots\,\vdots\,\vdots \\ 0\,0 \ldots 0\,1\,0 \ldots 0\,0 \end{pmatrix} . \tag{11}$$

Therefore, in the case of a linear CA $F : \mathbb{F}_q^{2(d-1)}$, the global map of its transpose $F^\top$ can also be expressed as a linear transformation $F^\top(x) = M_{F^\top} \cdot x^\top$, where $M_{F^\top}$ is the $(d-1) \times 2(d-1)$ matrix obtained by multiplying the transition matrix M_F of F with the permutation matrix M_s defined in Eq. (11):

$$M_{F^\top} = M_F \cdot M_s = \begin{pmatrix} a_1 & \ldots\ldots & a_d & 0 & \ldots\ldots\ldots\ldots & 0 \\ 0 & a_1 & \ldots\ldots & a_d & 0 & \ldots\ldots\ldots & 0 \\ \vdots & \vdots & \vdots & \ddots & \vdots & \vdots & \vdots & \ddots & \vdots & \vdots \\ 0 & \ldots\ldots\ldots\ldots & 0 & a_1 & \ldots\ldots & a_d \end{pmatrix} \cdot \begin{pmatrix} 0\,0 \ldots 0\,1\,0 \ldots 0\,0 \\ 0\,0 \ldots 0\,0\,1 \ldots 0\,0 \\ \vdots\,\vdots\,\ddots\,\vdots\,\vdots\,\vdots\,\ddots\,\vdots\,\vdots \\ 0\,0 \ldots 0\,0\,0 \ldots 0\,1 \\ 1\,0 \ldots 0\,0\,0 \ldots 0\,0 \\ 0\,1 \ldots 0\,0\,0 \ldots 0\,0 \\ \vdots\,\vdots\,\ddots\,\vdots\,\vdots\,\vdots\,\ddots\,\vdots\,\vdots \\ 0\,0 \ldots 0\,1\,0 \ldots 0\,0 \end{pmatrix} \tag{12}$$

In particular, Eq (12) can be rewritten as:

$$M_{F^\top} = M_F \cdot M_s = \begin{pmatrix} a_d & 0 & \ldots\ldots & 0 & a_1 & \ldots\ldots & a_{d-1} \\ a_{d-1} & a_d & \ldots\ldots & 0 & 0 & a_1 \ldots & a_{d-2} \\ \vdots & \vdots & \ddots\,\ddots & \vdots & \ddots & \ddots\,\ddots & \vdots \\ a_2 & a_3 & \ldots\ldots & a_d & 0 & 0 \ldots & a_1 \end{pmatrix} . \tag{13}$$

Equivalently, the transition matrix of the transpose CA of $F^\top$ is obtained by swapping the left and the right half of the transition matrix of F.

Consider now the $2(d-1) \times 2(d-1)$ square matrix $M_{F,F^\top}$ obtained by stacking M_F on top of $M_F^\top$:

$$M_{F,F^\top} = \begin{pmatrix} M_F \\ M_{F^\top} \end{pmatrix} = \begin{pmatrix} a_1 & \cdots\cdots & a_d & 0 & 0 & \cdots\cdots & 0 \\ 0 & a_1 & \cdots\cdots & a_d & 0 & \cdots\cdots & 0 \\ \vdots & \vdots & \ddots & \ddots & \vdots & \ddots\ddots\ddots & \vdots \\ 0 & 0 & \cdots\cdots & a_1 & \cdots\cdots\cdots & & a_d \\ a_d & 0 & \cdots\cdots & 0 & a_1 & \cdots\cdots & a_{d-1} \\ a_{d-1} & a_d & \cdots\cdots & 0 & 0 & a_1 \cdots & a_{d-2} \\ \vdots & \vdots & \ddots & \ddots & \vdots & \ddots\ddots\ddots & \vdots \\ a_2 & a_3 & \cdots\cdots & a_d & 0 & 0 \cdots & a_1 \end{pmatrix} . \tag{14}$$

Then, we can prove the following necessary and sufficient condition for the self-orthogonality of F:

Lemma 2. *The linear bipermutive CA $F : \mathbb{F}_q^{2(d-1)} \to \mathbb{F}_q^{d-1}$ is self-orthogonal if and only if the $2(d-1) \times 2(d-1)$ square matrix defined in Eq. (14) is invertible.*

Proof. The proof is analogous to the one of Theorem (1) reported in [18]. In particular, let M_F be the transition matrix of F, and let $F^\top : \mathbb{F}_q^{2(d-1)} \to \mathbb{F}_q^{d-1}$ be the transpose CA with $M_{F^\top}$ being its associated matrix. Then, F is self-orthogonal if and only if the superposed mapping $\mathcal{H} : \mathbb{F}_q^{d-1} \times \mathbb{F}_q^{d-1} \to \mathbb{F}_q^{d-1} \times \mathbb{F}_q^{d-1}$ defined for all $(x, y) \in \mathbb{F}_q^{2(d-1)} \times \mathbb{F}_q^{2(d-1)}$ as:

$$\mathcal{H}(x, y) = (F(x||y), F^\top(x||y)) = (w, z) \tag{15}$$

is bijective. The bijectivity of $\mathcal{H}$ amounts to the fact that the following system of $2(d-1)$ linear equations has exactly one solution for each possible assignment of the $2(d-1)$ variables:

$$\begin{cases} F(x||y) = M_F(x||y)^\top = w \\ F^\top(x||y) = M_{F^\top}(x||y)^\top = z \end{cases} . \tag{16}$$

In other words, the first half of the output w of $\mathcal{H}$ corresponds to the application of the CA F on the input obtained by concatenating x with y. Symmetrically, the second half z is obtained by computing the transpose CA $F^\top$ over the same concatenation. Finally, remark that the matrix associated to the system above is exactly the stacked matrix of Eq. (14). Hence, $\mathcal{H}$ is bijective if and only if the matrix (14) is invertible.

Differently from the case where we consider the orthogonality of the Latin squares generated by two distinct linear bipermutive CA, in our setting the square matrix defined in Eq. (14) is not of the Sylvester type. However, one can notice that this matrix is *circulant*. In particular, each row is the *cyclic right shift* of the row above. Formally, denoting $M_{F,F^\top} = (c_{ij})$ for all $i, j \in \{0, \cdots, n-1\}$, we have that $c_{i+1,j+1} = c_{i,j}$, where all indices are computed modulo $n = 2(d-1)$.

Fortunately, a great deal is known about circulant matrices, especially concerning their invertibility properties (see e.g. Section 13.2.4 of [23] for a summary of the main results). In particular, the set R_c of all $n \times n$ circulant matrices over a field is a ring, and thus it is closed under matrix addition and multiplication. Interestingly, the ring of circulant matrices is isomorphic to a quotient polynomial ring, as the next result shows:

Theorem 2 ([15]). *Let R_C be the ring of $n \times n$ circulant matrices over the finite field F_q, and let $R_P = \mathbb{F}_q[X]/(X^n - 1)$ be the quotient polynomial ring over $\mathbb{F}_q$ modulo $(X^n - 1)$. Given a matrix $M \in R_C$ whose first row is the vector $(c_1, \dots, c_n)$, the following mapping:*

$$\Phi : (c_1, \dots, c_n) \mapsto c(X) = c_1 + c_2 X + \dots + c_n X^{n-1} \mod X^n - 1 \tag{17}$$

is an isomorphism of rings between R_C and R_P.

Notice that the map Φ of Eq. (17) is exactly the same that we used to associate the polynomial $p_f(X)$ to a linear local rule f in Sect. 2.1. From the perspective of the circulant matrix, performing a right cyclic shift of the coefficients corresponds to multiplying the polynomial $c(X)$ by the monomial X, and then reducing the result modulo $X^n - 1$. Thus, in general, the i-th row of a circulant matrix is obtained by taking the coefficients of the following polynomial:

$$c_i(X) = X^i c(X) \mod X^n - 1 \ . \tag{18}$$

From a practical point of view, Theorem 2 states that one can check if a circulant matrix $M \in R_C$ is invertible by checking if the corresponding polynomial $c(X) = \Phi(M)$ is a *unit* in the quotient ring $\mathbb{F}_q[X]/(X^n - 1)$, that is if it has a multiplicative inverse $c^{-1}(X)$ such that $c(X) \cdot c^{-1}(X) = 1$. However, this is equivalent to computing the greatest common divisor of $c(X)$ and $X^n - 1$. In particular, $c(X)$ is invertible if and only if $\gcd(c(X), X^n - 1) = 1$. We have thus proved the following characterization result:

Theorem 3. *Let $F : \mathbb{F}_q^{2(d-1)} \to \mathbb{F}_q^{d-1}$ be a NBCA of size $n = 2(d-1)$ with a linear bipermutive rule $f : \mathbb{F}_q^d \to \mathbb{F}_q$ of diameter d and associated polynomial $p_f(X) \in \mathbb{F}_q[X]$. Then, F is self-orthogonal if and only if* $\gcd(p_f(X), X^n - 1) = 1$.

4.2 The Special Case $\Sigma = \mathbb{F}_2$

Theorem 3 gives an elegant way to check if a linear bipermutive CA over any finite field is self-orthogonal: instead of generating the full Latin square and the related transpose, one can simply apply Euclid's algorithm to check if the greatest common divisor of the associated polynomial with $X^n - 1$ is 1. This gives us a result analogous to the generic case addressed in [18], since the orthogonality of two CA is again related to the coprimality of two polynomials.

In this section, we consider the specific variant of Problem 1 when the underlying alphabet is the binary field $\mathbb{F}_2$, due to its particular interest for practical applications in cryptography and coding theory. Since we are working in characteristic 2, we have that $X^n - 1 = X^{2(d-1)} + 1 = (X^{d-1} + 1)^2$. If $p_f(X)$ has a non-trivial factor in common with $X^n - 1$, then it must also have a non-trivial factor in common with $X^{d-1} + 1$. Hence, in the particular case of $\mathbb{F}_2$, the condition provided in Theorem 3 is equivalent to $\gcd(p_f(X), X^{d-1} + 1) = 1$, and Theorem 3 can be restated as:

Corollary 1. *Let $F : \mathbb{F}_2^{2(d-1)} \to \mathbb{F}_2^{d-1}$ be a NBCA of size $n = 2(d-1)$ with a linear bipermutive rule $f : \mathbb{F}_2^d \to \mathbb{F}_2$ of diameter d and polynomial $p_f(X) \in \mathbb{F}_2[X]$. Then, F is self-orthogonal if and only if $\gcd(p_f(X), X^{d-1} + 1) = 1$.*

We now prove that irreducibility is sufficient for self-orthogonality in $\mathbb{F}_2$:

Lemma 3. *Let $F : \mathbb{F}_2^{2(d-1)} \to \mathbb{F}_2^{d-1}$ be a NBCA of size $n = 2(d-1)$ defined by a linear bipermutive rule $f : \mathbb{F}_2^d \to \mathbb{F}_2$ of diameter $d > 2$, with polynomial $p_f(X) \in \mathbb{F}_2[X]$. If $p_f(X)$ is irreducible, the NBCA F is self-orthogonal.*

Proof. By Corollary 1, we have to show that $\gcd(p_f(X), X^{d-1} + 1) = 1$. Since $X = 1$ is a root of $X^{d-1} + 1$, we can rewrite it as

$$X^{d-1} + 1 = (X+1)\, q(X) \ , \tag{19}$$

for some $q \in \mathbb{F}_2[X]$ with degree $d-2$. However, p_f is has degree $d-1$, thus it cannot be neither a factor of $X+1$ (as $d > 2$) nor of $q(X)$ in the right-hand side of Eq. (19). Because p_f is irreducible, we have $\gcd(p_f(X), X^{d-1} + 1) = 1$, and thus F is self-orthogonal.

Being a sufficient condition, Lemma 3 explains why all irreducible polynomials reported in Sect. 3 induce self-orthogonal linear CA.

We now consider another particular case, i.e. when the size of the stacked matrix in Eq. (14) is a power of 2.

Lemma 4. *Let $d = 2^t + 1$ for some t. Then, a linear bipermutive CA $F : \mathbb{F}_2^{2(d-1)} \to \mathbb{F}_2^{d-1}$ defined by the local rule $f : \mathbb{F}_2^d \to \mathbb{F}_2$ with associated polynomial $p_f(X)$ is self-orthogonal if and only if $p_f(1) \neq 0$.*

Proof. *Since $\mathbb{F}_2$ is a field of characteristic 2 and $d-1$ is a power of 2, we have that $X^{d-1} + 1 = X^{2^t} + 1 = (X+1)^{d-1}$. This easily follows by induction and by the fact that $X^2 + 1 = (X+1)^2$ in characteristic 2. Hence, by Corollary 1 F is self-orthogonal if and only if $\gcd(p_f(X), (X+1)^{d-1}) = 1$. Any nontrivial common divisor of $p_f(X)$ and $(X+1)^{d-1}$ must be of the form $(X+1)^k$ for some $k < d$. Therefore, $p_f(X)$ and $(X+1)^{d-1}$ do not share common factors if and only if $p_f(1) \neq 0$.*

The condition $p_f(1) \neq 0$ of Lemma 4 can be further refined in a very simple procedure: given a polynomial $f(X) \in \mathbb{F}_2[X]$, one needs to check the *parity* of its coefficients. Indeed, setting $X = 1$ means that we compute the XOR of all the coefficients of $f(X)$. Therefore, one has that $f(1) = 0$ if the number of coefficients of f set to 1 is even, and $f(1) = 1$ if it is odd.

Lemma 4 partly explains the numbers of linear self-orthogonal CA observed in the exhaustive search experiments of Sect. 3: in particular, the cases $d = 3$

and $d = 5$ yield square matrices whose size is a power of 2 (respectively, 2 and 4). Then, since we are considering linear bipermutive CA, we know that the leftmost and rightmost coefficients of the associated polynomials are always not null. Hence, the condition $f(1) \neq 0$ is determined only by the parity of the central $d-2$ coefficients. The number of combinations with an odd parity is exactly half of all 2^{d-2} combinations of the central coefficients, i.e. 2^{d-3}. We have thus obtained the following counting result:

Lemma 5. *Let $d = 2^t + 1$ for some t. Then, the number of self-orthogonal CA defined by linear bipermutive rules of the form $f : \mathbb{F}_2^d \to \mathbb{F}_2$ is 2^{d-3}.*

However, Lemma 5 does not account for the fact that the number of linear self-orthogonal CA seems also to follow the sequence 2^{d-3} when $d-1$ is not a power of 2. For this reason, we used Theorem 3 to extend our exhaustive search experiments, by generating all linear self-orthogonal CA up to diameter $d = 16$. As it can be seen from Table 2, the pattern of the sequence 2^{d-3} already breaks from diameter $d = 7$, which is the smallest case that we have not checked exhaustively in Sect. 3.

Table 2. Number of linear self-orthogonal CA up to diameter $d = 9$.

d	3	4	5	6	7	8	9
#LIN	1	2	4	8	12	24	64
d	10	11	12	13	14	15	16
#LIN	94	240	512	768	2048	3136	5062

The sequence does not seem to be already known in the Online Encyclopedia of Integer Sequences (OEIS). We leave the point of deriving a general recurrence equation for the number of linear self-orthogonal CA as an open problem for future research.

As a final remark, notice that Lemmas 3 and 4 hold over any finite field of characteristic 2. Therefore, they are directly applicable to self-orthogonal CA defined over any finite field $\mathbb{F}_{2^k}$ as an alphabet.

5 Conclusions and Open Problems

In this paper, we addressed the problem of determining when a bipermutive CA is self-orthogonal, i.e. when it generates a Latin square that is orthogonal to its transpose. We started with an empirical approach by enumerating all self-orthogonal binary CA up to diameter $d = 6$, noticing that only some linear CA are self-orthogonal. We thus tackled the linear case more systematically, proving a characterization that involves computing the greatest common divisor of the polynomial associated to the local rule and the polynomial $X^{2(d-1)} - 1$. Moreover, we looked at the binary case more in detail, proving that irreducibility is indeed a sufficient condition for self-orthogonality, as observed in our exhaustive search experiments. On the other hand, we showed a simpler characterization of linear self-orthogonal CA over the binary alphabet when the size of the matrix is a power of 2. In this case, the question whether the CA is self-orthogonal reduces to checking the parity of the central coefficients of the local rule.

To conclude, we take a step back on our results and focus on the main condition for self-orthogonality, i.e. the invertibility of the corresponding circulant matrix. Circulant matrices are already well known in the CA literature: indeed, the transition matrix of a linear PBCA is a circulant matrix, as noted for example by Bini et al. [2]. However, this connection remained relatively incospicuous in the literature, since most of the related works investigate the invertibility of *infinite* linear CA over a ring, and thus resort to the machinery of formal power series [11,16]. Thus, our work shows that *studying the self-orthogonality of linear bipermutive NBCA is equivalent to determining whether they are invertible as PBCA*. This remark gives an interesting link between the combinatorial perspective on bipermutive CA and their dynamical properties. One of the reviewers of this manuscript suggested that the same equivalence can be generalized to the nonlinear case, observing that the first and the second half of the output configuration of a bipermutive PBCA correspond respectively to the Latin square of the CA and its transpose.

For future work, there are several interesting directions to explore on the subject. In particular, the most evident open problem is to determine a counting formula for the number of linear self-orthogonal CA in the general case, which from our experiments seems to follow the sequence of the powers of 2. Further, it would be interesting to assess, even experimentally, if *nonlinear* self-orthogonal CA exist. Possibly, the spaces of rules of diameter up to $d = 6$ considered in this paper is too limited to grant the existence of nonlinear self-orthogonal CA. Finally, one general research direction to explore is whether CA can be used to construct families of *mutually self-orthogonal Latin squares* [1]. In particular, these objects can be used to obtain resolvable BIBDs, from which anonymous secret sharing schemes [3] and Mutually Unbiased Bases for quantum error-correcting codes [13] can be further constructed.

Acknowledgements. The authors thank the anonymous reviewers for providing useful comments and insights to improve the manuscript, and for suggesting that the equivalence between self-orthogonality and PBCA invertibility can be generalized to the nonlinear case. Luca Mariot was partially supported by the PRIN 2022 PNRR project entitled "Cellular Automata Synthesis for Cryptography Applications (CASCA)" (P2022MPFRT) funded by the European Union Next Generation EU.

References

1. Baker, R.D.: Resolvable bibd and sols. Discret. Math. **44**(1), 13–29 (1983)
2. Bini, D., Del Corso, G.M., Manzini, G., Margara, L.: Inversion of circulant matrices over Z_m. In: Larsen, K.G., Skyum, S., Winskel, G. (eds.) ICALP 1998. LNCS, vol. 1443, pp. 719–730. Springer, Heidelberg (1998). https://doi.org/10.1007/BFb0055096
3. Blundo, C., Stinson, D.R.: Anonymous secret sharing schemes. Discret. Appl. Math. **77**(1), 13–28 (1997)
4. Carlet, C.: Boolean Functions for Cryptography and Coding Theory. Cambridge University Press (2021)
5. Eloranta, K.: Partially permutive cellular automata. Nonlinearity **6**(6), 1009–1023 (1993)
6. Formenti, E., Imai, K., Martin, B., Yunès, J.-B.: Advances on random sequence generation by uniform cellular automata. In: Calude, C.S., Freivalds, R., Kazuo, I. (eds.) Computing with New Resources. LNCS, vol. 8808, pp. 56–70. Springer, Cham (2014). https://doi.org/10.1007/978-3-319-13350-8_5
7. Gadouleau, M., Mariot, L., Picek, S.: Bent functions in the partial spread class generated by linear recurring sequences. Des. Codes Cryptogr. **91**(1), 63–82 (2023)
8. Ghoshal, A., Sadhukhan, R., Patranabis, S., Datta, N., Picek, S., Mukhopadhyay, D.: Lightweight and side-channel secure 4×4 s-boxes from cellular automata rules. IACR Trans. Symmetric Cryptol. **2018**(3), 311–334 (2018)
9. Hammer, J.M., Lorch, J.: Diagonal cellular factor pair latin squares. Des. Codes Cryptogr. **91**(6), 2309–2322 (2023)
10. Herranz, J., Sáez, G.: Secret sharing schemes for (k, n)-consecutive access structures. In: Camenisch, J., Papadimitratos, P. (eds.) CANS 2018. LNCS, vol. 11124, pp. 463–480. Springer, Cham (2018). https://doi.org/10.1007/978-3-030-00434-7_23
11. Ito, M., Osato, N., Nasu, M.: Linear cellular automata over $\mathbb{Z}_m$. J. Comput. Syst. Sci. **27**(1), 125–140 (1983)
12. Keedwell, A.D., Dénes, J.: Latin squares and their applications. Elsevier (2015)
13. Kumar, A., Maitra, S.: Resolvable block designs in construction of approximate real MUBs that are sparse. Cryptogr. Commun. **14**(3), 527–549 (2022)
14. Leporati, A., Mariot, L.: Cryptographic properties of bipermutive cellular automata rules. J. Cell. Autom. **9**(5–6), 437–475 (2014)
15. Lidl, R., Niederreiter, H.: Introduction to Finite Fields and Their Applications. Cambridge University Press (1994)
16. Manzini, G., Margara, L.: Invertible linear cellular automata over z_m: algorithmic and dynamical aspects. J. Comput. Syst. Sci. **56**(1), 60–67 (1998)
17. Mariot, L., Formenti, E., Leporati, A.: Enumerating orthogonal Latin squares generated by bipermutive cellular automata. In: Dennunzio, A., Formenti, E., Manzoni, L., Porreca, A.E. (eds.) AUTOMATA 2017. LNCS, vol. 10248, pp. 151–164. Springer, Cham (2017). https://doi.org/10.1007/978-3-319-58631-1_12
18. Mariot, L., Gadouleau, M., Formenti, E., Leporati, A.: Mutually orthogonal Latin squares based on cellular automata. Des. Codes Cryptogr. **88**(2), 391–411 (2020)
19. Mariot, L., Leporati, A.: Sharing secrets by computing preimages of bipermutive cellular automata. In: Wąs, J., Sirakoulis, G.C., Bandini, S. (eds.) ACRI 2014. LNCS, vol. 8751, pp. 417–426. Springer, Cham (2014). https://doi.org/10.1007/978-3-319-11520-7_43

20. Mariot, L., Leporati, A.: A cryptographic and coding-theoretic perspective on the global rules of cellular automata. Nat. Comput. **17**, 487–498 (2018)
21. Mariot, L., Mazzone, F.: On the minimum distance of subspace codes generated by linear cellular automata. In: Manzoni, L., Mariot, L., Roy Chowdhury, D. (eds.) AUTOMATA 2023. LNCS, vol. 14152, pp. 105–119. Springer, Cham (2023). https://doi.org/10.1007/978-3-031-42250-8_8
22. Mariot, L., Picek, S., Leporati, A., Jakobovic, D.: Cellular automata based s-boxes. Cryptogr. Commun. **11**(1), 41–62 (2019)
23. Mullen, G.L., Panario, D.: Handbook of Finite Fields, vol. 17. CRC Press, Boca Raton (2013)
24. Picek, S., Mariot, L., Yang, B., Jakobovic, D., Mentens, N.: Design of S-boxes defined with cellular automata rules. In: Proceedings of the Computing Frontiers Conference, CF 2017, Siena, Italy, 15–17 May 2017, pp. 409–414. ACM (2017)
25. del Rey, Á.M., Mateus, J.P., Sánchez, G.R.: A secret sharing scheme based on cellular automata. Appl. Math. Comput. **170**(2), 1356–1364 (2005)
26. Stinson, D.R.: Combinatorial Designs - Constructions and Analysis. Springer, New York (2004). https://doi.org/10.1007/b97564
27. Wolfram, S.: Statistical mechanics of cellular automata. Rev. Mod. Phys. **55**(3), 601 (1983)
28. Wolfram, S.: Cryptography with cellular automata. In: Williams, H.C. (ed.) CRYPTO 1985. LNCS, vol. 218, pp. 429–432. Springer, Heidelberg (1986). https://doi.org/10.1007/3-540-39799-X_32

Timed Prediction Problem for Sandpile Models

Pablo Concha-Vega[1(✉)] and Kévin Perrot[1,2]

[1] Aix Marseille Univ, CNRS, LIS, Marseille, France
{pablo.concha-vega,kevin.perrot}@lis-lab.fr
[2] Université publique, Marseille, France

Abstract. We investigate the computational complexity of the *timed prediction problem* in two-dimensional sandpile models. This question refines the classical *prediction problem*, which asks whether a cell q will eventually become unstable after adding a grain at cell p from a given configuration. The prediction problem has been shown to be P-complete in several settings, including for subsets of the Moore neighborhood, but its complexity for the von Neumann neighborhood remains open. In a previous work, we provided a complete characterization of crossover gates (a key to the implementation of non-planar monotone circuits) for these small neighborhoods, leading to P-completeness proofs with only 4 and 5 neighbors among the eight adjacent cells. In this paper, we introduce the *timed* setting, where the goal is to determine whether cell q becomes unstable *exactly* at time t. We distinguish several cases: some neighborhoods support complete timed toolkits (including timed crossover gates) and exhibit P-completeness; others admit timed crossovers but suffer from synchronization issues; planar neighborhoods provably do not admit any timed crossover; and finally, for some remaining neighborhoods, we conjecture that no timed crossover is possible.

Keywords: Sandpile models · Discrete dynamical system · P-completeness

1 Introduction

Sandpiles are the canonical example of self-organized criticality [1], a phenomenon where complex, scale-invariant behavior emerges from simple local rules without any need for fine-tuning. Originally proposed in the context of statistical physics, sandpile models have also attracted interest from the perspective of computational complexity. A central question in this context is the *prediction problem*, which asks the following: starting from a stable configuration, and choosing two specific cells p and q, is it possible that adding a single grain at cell p will eventually cause cell q to become unstable (*i.e.*, ready to topple) at some point in time? This question captures the difficulty of anticipating the long-term effects of a simple perturbation.

Published by Springer Nature Switzerland AG 2026
S. Riva and A. Richard (Eds.): AUTOMATA 2025, LNCS 15831, pp. 205–220, 2026.
https://doi.org/10.1007/978-3-032-01570-9_14

Early foundational work by Moore and Nilsson [12] revealed that the computational power of sandpile dynamics depends strongly on the dimension of the grid. In dimension one, they showed that the prediction problem admits a fast parallel algorithm (in NC^3), while in dimension three or more it is P-complete, implying an inherent sequentiality in the dynamics. The two-dimensional case, however, remains open to this day. A significant obstacle to proving P-completeness in dimension two was identified by Gajardo and Goles [6], who showed that neither of the standard von Neumann nor Moore neighborhoods admit a crossover gate, which is a crucial component of all P-completeness proofs so far.

In a previous work [3], we systematically studied all subsets of the Moore neighborhood on the two-dimensional grid. By grouping them into equivalence classes under rotation and reflection, we identified which classes admit a *crossover*, and which do not. It follows that the former have a P-complete prediction problem, whereas the latter may be computationally easier to predict. In the present work, we extend this line of research by introducing a refined decision problem, which we call the *timed prediction problem*. This problem is similar in spirit to the original prediction problem, but with an important difference: a timestep t is now part of the input. More precisely, given a stable configuration, two cells p and q, and a time t, the question is whether adding a grain at cell p will cause cell q to become unstable after *exactly* t time steps.

We conduct a systematic study of the timed prediction problem across all subsets of the Moore neighborhood, following the equivalence classes approach of [3]. For each class, we seek to determine whether it admits a complete set of *timed* computational gadgets. Our results reveal a rich landscape: a large number of neighborhoods (planar ones) do not admit a timed crossover at all, which makes it unlikely for them to support a P-hardness reduction. On the other hand, we identify several new classes that do admit a complete timed toolkit, for which we establish the P-completeness of the timed prediction problem. A further group of neighborhoods admits a timed crossover gate, but encounters a difficulty when connecting gates consistently in time, a phenomenon we refer to as the *delay issue*. For the remaining classes, we conjecture that no timed crossover is possible.

2 Definitions and State of the Art

Notations. We write $\mathbb{N}_+ = \mathbb{N} \setminus \{0\}$ for the set of positive integers, and use $\subset_{\mathtt{fin}}$ to refer to finite subsets. Given any $d \in \mathbb{N}_+$, we denote by 0^d the d-dimensional tuple consisting entirely of zeros. The Heaviside step function $\mathtt{H}(\cdot)$ is defined by $\mathtt{H}(\alpha) = 1$ if $\alpha \geq 0$, and $\mathtt{H}(\alpha) = 0$ otherwise. For any $n \in \mathbb{N}_+$, we write $[n] = \{1, \dots, n\}$ and $[\![n]\!] = \{0, \dots, n-1\}$.

Sandpile Models. In this work, we consider sandpile dynamics restricted to two-dimensional square lattices $\mathbb{Z}^2$. A *sandpile model* is specified by a finite

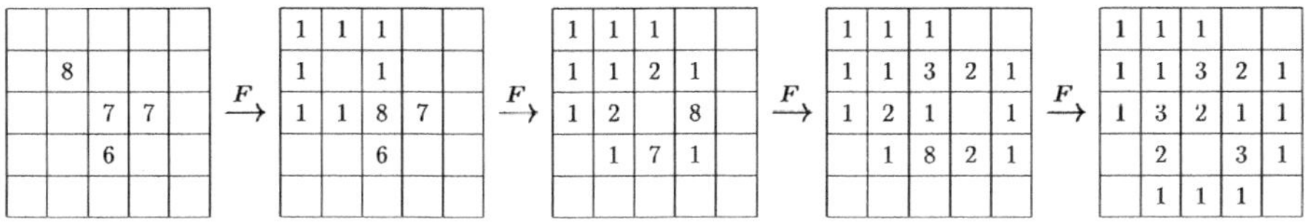

Fig. 1. Example of sandpile dynamics for Moore neighborhood $\mathcal{N}_{\mathtt{m}}$. The numbers indicate the amount of grains in every cell (blank is empty).

neighborhood $\mathcal{N} \subset_{\mathtt{fin}} \mathbb{Z}^2$, whose cardinality we denote by $\theta_{\mathcal{N}} = |\mathcal{N}|$. A *configuration* is a function $c : \mathbb{Z}^2 \to \mathbb{N}$ assigning to each cell $p \in \mathbb{Z}^2$ a number $c(p)$ of grains. The associated dynamics $F_{\mathcal{N}} : \mathbb{N}^{\mathbb{Z}^2} \to \mathbb{N}^{\mathbb{Z}^2}$ is defined cellwise by:

$$\forall p \in \mathbb{Z}^d : F_{\mathcal{N}}(c)(p) = \mathrm{c(p)} - \theta_{\mathcal{N}} \cdot \mathtt{H}\left(c(p) - \theta_{\mathcal{N}}\right) + \sum_{p' \in \mathcal{N}} \mathtt{H}\left(c(p - p') - \theta_{\mathcal{N}}\right).$$

In words, each cell reaching the threshold $\theta_{\mathcal{N}}$ *topples* or *fires*, sending one grain to each of its out-neighbors, whose relative positions are given by $\mathcal{N}$. This local rule is applied in parallel at every cell of the lattice. The most well-known neighborhoods, due to their simplicity and symmetries, are *von Neumann* and *Moore*, respectively defined as:

$$\mathcal{N}_{\mathtt{vn}} = \{(x, y) \in \mathbb{Z}^2 \mid |x| + |y| = 1\} \quad \text{and} \quad \mathcal{N}_{\mathtt{m}} = \{(x, y) \in \mathbb{Z}^2 \mid 1 \leq x^2 + y^2 \leq 2\}.$$

See an example in Fig. 1.

We restrict our study to neighborhoods $\mathcal{N} \subset_{\mathtt{fin}} \mathbb{Z}^2$ that span $\mathbb{Z}^2$ *i.e.*, such that $\mathcal{N} = \{p_1, p_2, \ldots, p_k\}$ and $\{a_1 \cdot p_1 + a_2 \cdot p_2 \cdots + a_k \cdot p_k \mid a_1, a_2, \ldots, a_k \in \mathbb{Z}\} = \mathbb{Z}^2$. Otherwise, the dynamics splits into independent subsystems, meaning that $\mathbb{Z}^2$ can be decomposed into sublattices for which the sand contents never interact. In this case, the global behavior becomes a product of independent sandpile dynamics over lower-dimensional components. Such separability would complicate our considerations, as crossovers could trivially arise between signals evolving in disconnected sublattices.

When it is clear from the context, we drop the subscript notations and simply denote θ and F the threshold and the evolution rule. The total number of sand grains in a configuration is denoted $\mathcal{G}(c) = \sum_{p \in \mathbb{Z}^2} c(p)$, it is invariant under F for any sandpile model: $\mathcal{G}(c) = \mathcal{G}(F(c))$. A configuration c is *finite* when it contains a finite number of sand grains ($\mathcal{G}(c) \in \mathbb{N}$), and *stable* when no toppling occurs ($\forall p \in \mathbb{Z}^2 : c(p) < \theta$). When $\mathcal{N}$ spans $\mathbb{Z}^2$, from any finite configuration c, the dynamics converges to a stable configuration denoted $c^\circ = \lim_{t \to \infty} F^t(c)$ (see *e.g.*, [5]). Note that it is customary to exclude the cell itself (at relative position 0^d) from its neighborhood, in order to avoid "trapping" one sand grain at each cell.

Prediction Problems and Crossovers. The problems are formulated for each sandpile model $\mathcal{N} \subset_{\texttt{fin}} \mathbb{Z}^2$. The asymptotic prediction of sandpile dynamics is the problem of computing the stable configuration c° reached from a given configuration c. It is classically restricted to an input configuration c which is finite and stable, and a position $p \in \mathbb{Z}^2$ on which *one* grain is added, and formalized as the following decision problems [5]. For any $p \in \mathbb{Z}^2$, let $1p$ be the configuration containing a unique grain at position p, and let $+$ denote the cell-wise addition of two configurations ($\forall p \in \mathbb{Z}^2, (c + c')(p) = c(p) + c'(p)$). It asks whether cell $q \in \mathbb{Z}^2$ topples during the evolution from $c + 1p$ to $(c + 1p)^\circ$.

$\mathcal{N}$-sandpile prediction problem ($\mathcal{N}$-**PRED**)
Input: a finite stable configuration $c \in \mathbb{N}^{\mathbb{Z}^2}$, and two positions $p, q \in \mathbb{Z}^d$.
Question: does $\exists t \in \mathbb{N}, F^t(c + 1p)(q) \geq \theta$?

We highlight the following problem, for which it is not clear yet whether it can be more difficult or less difficult than $\mathcal{N}$-**PRED** for some sandpile models $\mathcal{N}$. It asks whether cell q topples at time step t during the evolution from $c + 1p$.

$\mathcal{N}$-sandpile timed prediction problem ($\mathcal{N}$-**TIMED-PRED**)
Input: a finite stable config. $c \in \mathbb{N}^{\mathbb{Z}^2}$, two positions $p, q \in \mathbb{Z}^d$, and a time $t \in \mathbb{N}$.
Question: does $F^t(c + 1p)(q) \geq \theta$?

The general goal is to dichotomize the complexity of prediction problems based on the neighborhood $\mathcal{N}$: either in NC or P-complete for logspace reductions (see [10,11] for the definitions of NC, P, and their meaning within the theory of computational complexity). It is proven in [5] that all such problems lie in P (more precisely, the quantification over t can be upper bounded to a value polynomial in the size of c). On one hand, proofs that the problem belongs to NC typically involve either providing an efficient parallel algorithm, or reducing the problem to another one for which such an algorithm is known [5,7,9,12]. On the other hand, proofs of P-completeness rely on the so-called *Banks approach* [2], which consists in reducing from *monotone circuit value problem* (**MCVP**) by implementing the circuit computation via chains of reactions in the sandpile dynamics. In this context, it is required to build *wires*, *turns*, *and* gates, *or* gates, *diodes* and *crossover* gates [8]. In turns out that all gates are usually straightforward to design, except crossover gates. The inexistence of crossover gates is therefore a strong indication that such a reduction may not be possible, but it is relative to a precise definition of crossover gate (to prove that none exist), which enforces a precise (hence restrictive) consideration of what a *wire*, or more generally a *signal*, is. This topic is of much broader interest [4].

Definition 1 (Crossover gate). A *crossover gate* is a rectangular subset of the lattice on which a stable configuration is set, such that it transports signals from two pairs of opposite sides, independently from each other: two wires cross each other. Given a sandpile model $\mathcal{N}$, a crossover gate of size $M \times N$ is formally defined as a configuration $g : [\![M]\!] \times [\![N]\!] \to \{0, \ldots, \theta - 1\}$ together with four cells

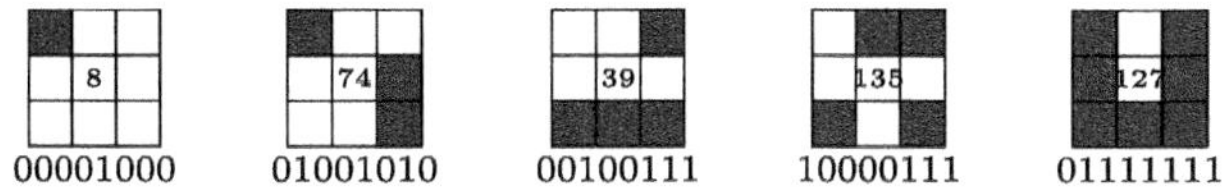

Fig. 2. Subsets of Moore neighborhood corresponding to $00001000 = 8$, $01001010 = 74$, $00100111 = 39$, $10000111 = 135$, $01111111 = 127$.

$n, e, s, w \in ([\![M]\!] \times [\![N]\!]) \setminus \{(0,0), (M-1,0), (0,N-1), (M-1,N-1)\}$ not in the corners, verifying the following constraints 1–5. For convenience, we denote the four sides of the gate as $S_0 = \{(0,y) \mid y \in [\![N]\!]\}$, $S_1 = \{(x,0) \mid x \in [\![M]\!]\}$, $S_2 = \{(M-1,y) \mid y \in [\![N]\!]\}$, $S_3 = \{(x,N-1) \mid x \in [\![M]\!]\}$.

1. n, s are on opposite sides, *i.e.* $\exists i_n, n \in S_{i_n}$, $\exists i_s, s \in S_{i_s}$ and $|i_n - i_s| = 2$;
2. w, e are on opposite sides, *i.e.* $\exists i_w, w \in S_{i_w}$, $\exists i_e, e \in S_{i_e}$ and $|i_w - i_e| = 2$;
3. n, e, s, w are on different sides, *i.e.* $\{i_n, i_e, i_s, i_w\} = \{0, 1, 2, 3\}$;
4. adding a grain at n eventually topples s, but no cell on the other sides, *i.e.* $\exists t \in \mathbb{N}, F^t(g + 1_n)(s) \geq \theta$, but $\forall p \in S_{i_w} \cup S_{i_e}, \forall t \in \mathbb{N}, F^t(g + 1_n)(p) < \theta$;
5. adding a grain at w eventually topples e, but no cell on the other sides, *i.e.* $\exists t \in \mathbb{N}, F^t(g + 1_w)(e) \geq \theta$, but $\forall p \in S_{i_n} \cup S_{i_s}, \forall t \in \mathbb{N}, F^t(g + 1_w)(p) < \theta$.

It is necessary to provide this formal definition, as we will state some impossibility results; however it is difficult to use in practice. In the following, no precise reference will be made to its constituents. The main tool we will employ is the *pair of firing graphs*, which is introduced at the beginning of Sect. 3.

For the timed prediction problem, a *timed crossover gate* is required. It is the same as a crossover gate, except that all quantifications over time t are bounded to a given value $T \in \mathbb{N}^+$ called the *delay* of the gate (which is part of the definition of the gate). That is, when adding a grain to one side (at n or w), the cell on the opposite side (s or e) must topple at time step T, and no cell on the other sides must topple before time step $T + 1$.

3 Timed Crossover Among Subsets of Moore

In this section we present an exhaustive study of the computational complexity of sandpile dynamics, by considering timed prediction problems ($\mathcal{N}$-**TIMED-PRED**) and timed crossover gates for every subset of the Moore neighborhood $\mathcal{N}_{\mathtt{m}}$. Observe that some of the 2^8 subsets of $\mathcal{N}_{\mathtt{m}}$ (which has 8 elements) do not span $\mathbb{Z}^2$, and the existence of a crossover gate is invariant by rotation and axial symmetries of the neighborhood. It reduces the number of neighborhoods to study to 43 equivalence classes, presented in [3, Table 1].

An example of timed crossover gate is presented on Fig. 3. We will show that while some neighborhoods do not support a crossover gate, they do admit a timed crossover gate and exhibit a P-complete timed prediction problem. It hints at the fact that predicting the dynamics at a precise time step may be harder than asymptotic prediction of the dynamics (the final stable configuration).

Definition 2 (Subset of Moore neighborhood). *Let* n, ne, e, se, s, sw, w, nw *denote the eight cardinal coordinates, starting with* north *and proceeding clockwise. We denote a subset of Moore neighborhood as an 8-bit string, where the i-th bit indicates whether the i-th coordinate in the list* n, e, s, w, nw, ne, se, sw, *is part of the neighborhood (bit 1), or not (bit 0). We also interpret 8-bit strings as numbers (converting them to decimal) with the least significant bit on the right, see Fig. 2.*

In this numbering scheme, the von Neumann neighborhood ($\mathcal{N}_{\text{vn}}$) corresponds to 11110000 (decimal 240), while the Moore neighborhood ($\mathcal{N}_{\text{m}}$) corresponds to 11111111 (decimal 255). Note that neighborhoods with numbers ≤ 15 consist exclusively of diagonal neighbors, and as a result, they do not span $\mathbb{Z}^2$.

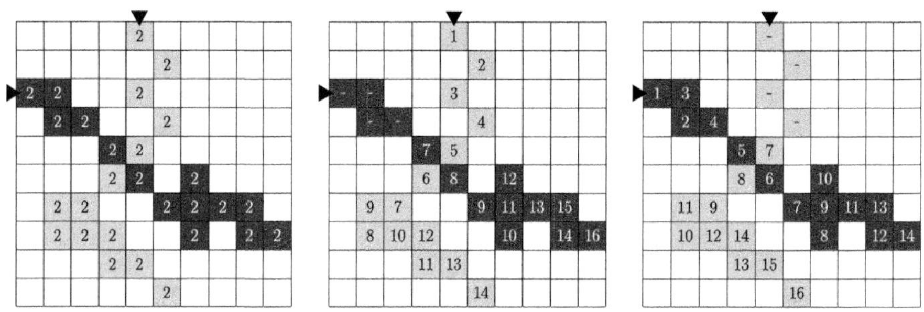

Fig. 3. Example of timed crossover gate of size 10×10 for neighborhood 131 (left). The delay of the gate is 14. We picture the timestamps of each cell, following a grain addition at n (center), and a grain addition at w (right).

Section Outline. We start this section by defining timed firing graphs (Subsect. 3.1), a tool that captures the timing and causal dependencies of topplings in a timed crossover. First we prove that timed crossover gates are impossible when the neighborhood is planar (Subsect. 3.2). Then we exhibit timed crossover gates for many neighborhoods. For some of them we prove that $\mathcal{N}$-**TIMED-PRED** is P-complete (Subsect. 3.3), and for others we are faced with a delay issue when trying to connect the different gates (Subsect. 3.4). The results of this section are summarized in Table 1.

3.1 Timed Firing Graphs

The causal structure of topplings is captured by the concept of firing graph, introduced in [6]. It is at the basis of our reasonings in this work. Given a neighborhood $\mathcal{N}$, we say that cell v_1 is an *in-neighbor* (resp. *out-neighbor*) of cell v_2 when $(v_2 - v_1) \in \mathcal{N}$ (resp. $(v_1 - v_2) \in \mathcal{N}$). Observe that v_1 may be both an in-neighbor and an out-neighbor of v_2. In particular, this is always the case for symmetric neighborhoods, such as von Neumann $\mathcal{N}_{\text{vn}}$ and Moore $\mathcal{N}_{\text{m}}$.

Table 1. Summary of results exposed in Sect. 3.

Section	3.3	3.4	3.5
Type	P-complete	Delay issue	Timed crossover impossibility (conjecture)
Neigborhoods	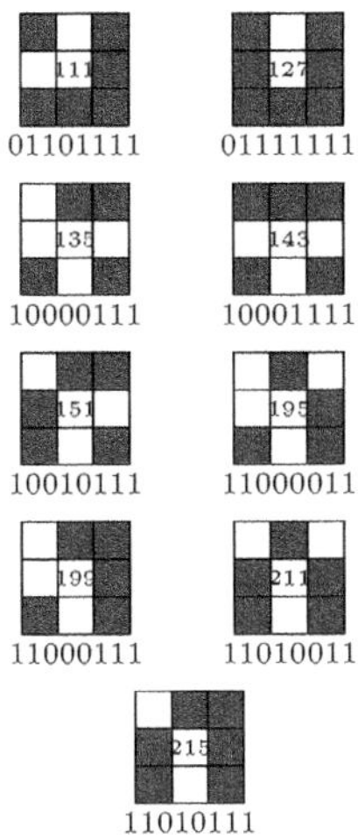 01101111, 01111111, 10000111, 10001111, 10010111, 11000011, 11000111, 11010011, 11010111	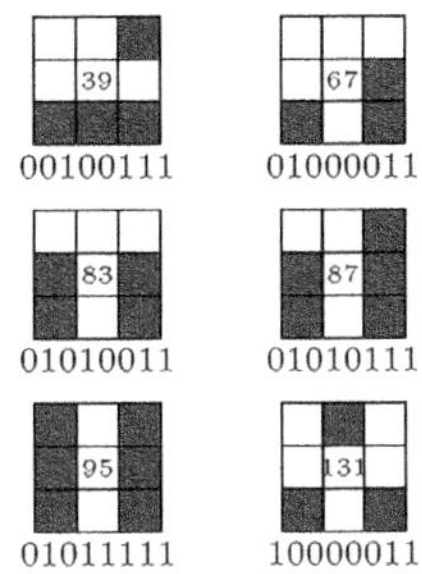 00100111, 01000011, 01010011, 01010111, 01011111, 10000011	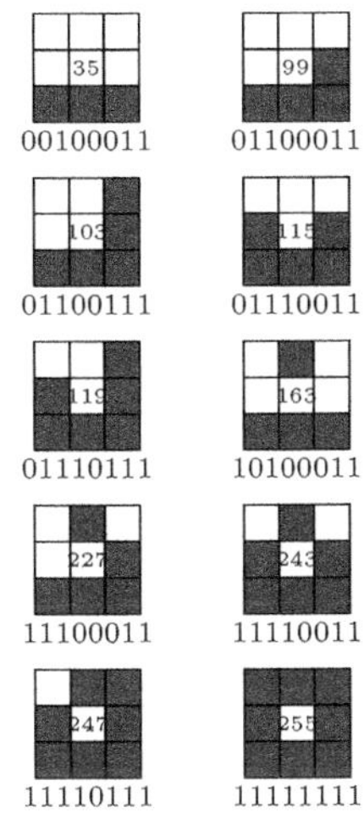 00100011, 01100011, 01100111, 01110011, 01110111, 10100011, 11100011, 11110011, 11110111, 11111111

Definition 3 (Firing graphs). Given a crossover gate g on cells n, s, w, e we define its two *firing graphs* $G^g_{ns} = (V_{ns}, A_{ns})$ and $G^g_{we} = (V_{we}, A_{we})$ as:

- V_{ns} (resp. V_{we}) is the set cells toppled after adding a grain at cell n (resp. w);
- we have $(v_1, v_2) \in A_{ns}$ (resp. A_{we}) when $v_1, v_2 \in V_{ns}$ (resp. V_{we}) verify:
  - v_1 is an in-neighbor of v_2 for $\mathcal{N}$, and
  - v_1 is fired strictly before v_2 after adding a grain at cell n (resp. w).

The endpoints of a firing graph are called *starting cells* (n and w) and *ending cells* (s and e) respectively. For every arc (v_1, v_2) in a firing graph, we call v_1 a *predecessor* of v_2, and v_2 a *successor* of v_1. The transitive and reflexive closure of the predecessor (resp. successor) relationship is the *ancestor* (resp. *descendant*) relationship. By definition, a predecessor is necessarily an in-neighbor, and a successor is necessarily an out-neighbor. The firing graph captures the *effective* causal relationships among cells within a given crossover gate, whereas the in-neighbor and out-neighbor relationships represent *potential* relationships.

The pair of firing graphs of a timed crossover gate may intersect (have vertices in common), because the wire in the perpendicular direction can be toppled (provided that it does so some steps behind compared to the 1 signal traversing the gate). We introduce the notion of *timed firing graphs*, which are subsets of the firing graphs. Given that the arcs of the firing graphs represent the causal relationship among toppled cells, it would be enough to discard the part not necessary to topple an ending cell, by restricting the corresponding firing graph to its ancestors. However, this inductive definition from the ending cell backwards, is not convenient for proofs by induction on the number of steps. We prefer the following definition, based on timestamps, which we denote $t_{ns} : V_{ns} \to \mathbb{N}$ and $t_{we} : V_{we} \to \mathbb{N}$ to distinguish the two firing graphs. In each firing graph, we take into account only cells toppling sufficiently early to belong to 1 signals. Recall that the timestamps of the two ending cells are equal to the delay T of the gate. Let $t_{ns}(v) = +\infty$ when t_{ns} is not defined for v. The same applies to t_{we}.

Definition 4 (Timed firing graphs). *Given a timed crossover gate g of delay $T \in \mathbb{N}_+$ on cells n, s, w, e, its two* timed firing graphs *are the induced subgraphs of its firing graphs, restricted to vertex sets:*

$$V_{ns}^T = \{v \in V_{ns} \mid t_{ns}(v) \leq t_{we}(v)\} \text{ and } V_{we}^T = \{v \in V_{we} \mid t_{we}(v) \leq t_{ns}(v)\}.$$

It is necessary that in a timed crossover gate, each of the two ending cells belongs only to its corresponding timed firing graph. The $\leq$ comparison among timestamps aims at discarding cells that have some lag (extra delay). The following Lemma generalizes Proposition 1 from [13], to the context of timed firing graphs.

Lemma 1. *If a sandpile model $\mathcal{N}$ admits a timed crossover gate, then it also admits a timed crossover gate g with timed firing graphs $G_{ns}^T = (V_{ns}^T, A_{ns}^T)$ and $G_{we}^T = (V_{we}^T, A_{we}^T)$, such that $V_{ns}^T \cap V_{we}^T = \emptyset$.*

Proof. The proof is constructive: given a timed crossover gate g' with timed firing graphs $G'^T_{ns} = (V'^T_{ns}, A'^T_{ns})$ and $G'^T_{we} = (V'^T_{we}, A'^T_{we})$, we:

1. remove all grains from vertices in the intersection $V'^T_{ns} \cap V'^T_{we}$ (which are intuitively useless), so that they do not topple anymore;
2. compensate for the missing predecessors in each timed firing graph: for each vertex in exactly one of V'^T_{ns} or V'^T_{we}, add as many grains to it as it had predecessors in $V'^T_{ns} \cap V'^T_{we}$.

We now argue that it gives another timed crossover gate with distinct timed firing graphs. By induction on successive time steps, we have the following three simple facts. First, the vertices in $V'^T_{ns} \cap V'^T_{we}$ do not topple anymore (this uses the fact that sandpile graphs are Eulerian, *i.e.* each vertex has equal in and out degree). Second, the vertices not in the intersection are still in their timed firing graph (thanks to the sand grains added at step 2, there is no lag in the topplings). Third, no new vertex appears in each timed firing graph, *i.e.* $V_{ns}^T \subseteq V'^T_{ns}$ and $V_{we}^T \subseteq V'^T_{we}$ (because the sand grains added at step 2 do not create successor relationships in the timed firing graph). Given that $n, s \in V'^T_{ns} \setminus V'^T_{we}$ and $w, e \in V'^T_{we} \cap V'^T_{ns}$, this still holds and the constructed configuration is indeed a timed crossover gate (it still performs a timed crossover of two signals), with sets of vertices $V_{ns}^T = V'^T_{ns} \setminus V'^T_{we}$ and $V_{we}^T = V'^T_{we} \setminus V'^T_{ns}$. □

3.2 Timed Crossover Impossibility: Planar Neighborhoods

As a corollary of Lemma 1, it is impossible to have a timed crossover gate when the neighborhood is planar.

Corollary 1. *If neighborhood $\mathcal{N}$ has a planar sandpile graph, then it does not admit a timed crossover gate.*

This proves that neighborhoods 66, 74, 82, 98, 90, 106, 130, 146, 192, 200, 202, 208, 210, 226, 234, 240, 242 and 250 do not admit a timed crossover gate.

3.3 Timed Crossover Possibility: P-Complete Neighborhoods

Neighborhoods studied in this subsection:

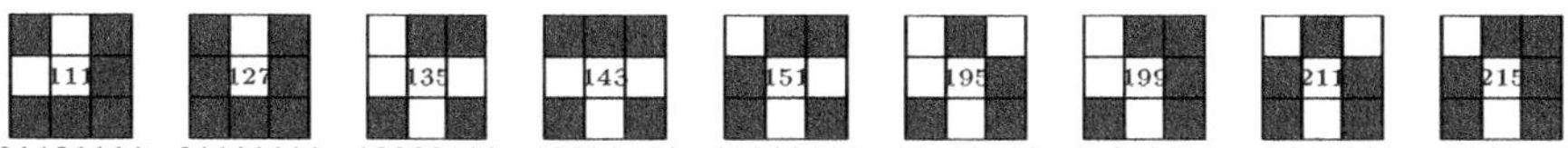

01101111 01111111 10000111 10001111 10010111 11000011 11000111 11010011 11010111

We now prove that some subsets of Moore neighborhood have a P-complete **$\mathcal{N}$-TIMED-PRED** problem. The proof is analogous to Theorem 2 from [3], but taking into account the delay of the gates.

Theorem 1. ***$\mathcal{N}$-TIMED-PRED*** *is* P*-complete for neighborhoods* 111, 127, 135, 143, 151, 195, 199, 211, 215.

Proof. For neighborhoods 135 and 143, this is a direct consequence of [3, Theorem 2], as they both have a P-complete prediction problem.

For the other neighborhoods, we prove P-completeness by reduction from monotone circuit value problem (**MCVP**) with gates of fan-in and fan-out two (problem **AM2CVP** in [10]), We consider an embedding of the monotone circuit on the two-dimensional grid (see Fig. 4), and replace all the elements by the corresponding sandpile gadgets of fixed size. For each neighborhood, we present a set of gates having a uniform delay (it takes the same number of steps for a signal to traverse each gate). Let us denote $d \in \mathbb{N}_+$ this *delay*, and z the peculiar delay of the starting constant 1 gate (time necessary for the single grain addition at p to reach the borders of the constant 1 gate). Following the Banks approach, a signal 1 is an avalanche (chain of topplings) reaching the edges of gates at time steps $(z + d \cdot T)_{T \in \mathbb{N}}$, and a signal 0 is a steady state or an avalanche reaching the edges of gates on time steps $z + d \cdot T + i$ with $i > 0$ (lags may accumulate). One can check on the layout of the **MCVP** instance on the grid (Fig. 4), that following a single grain addition, all the variable signals start synchronized (with avalanches for 1 signals, and steady wires for 0 signals). The uniform delay on all gates ensures that signals keep synchronized, because gates are placed on the diagonal: the two input signals are at the same distance from the origin. Every wire follows a shortest path in the grid toward the cell in question. The latter

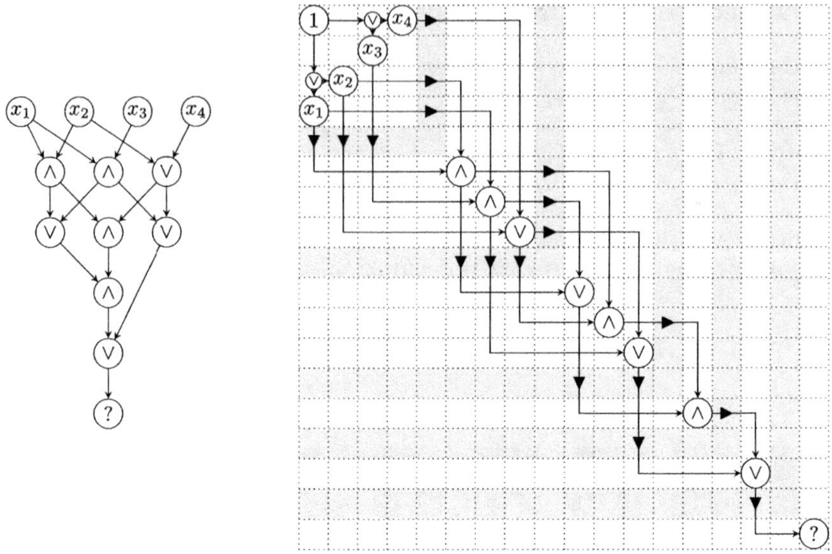

Fig. 4. Embedding of a **MCVP** instance of fan-in and fan-out two (left) on the grid (right). Diodes (represented as ▶ and ▼) are used systematically between layers in order to enforce the flow of information (and prevent it from going backward).

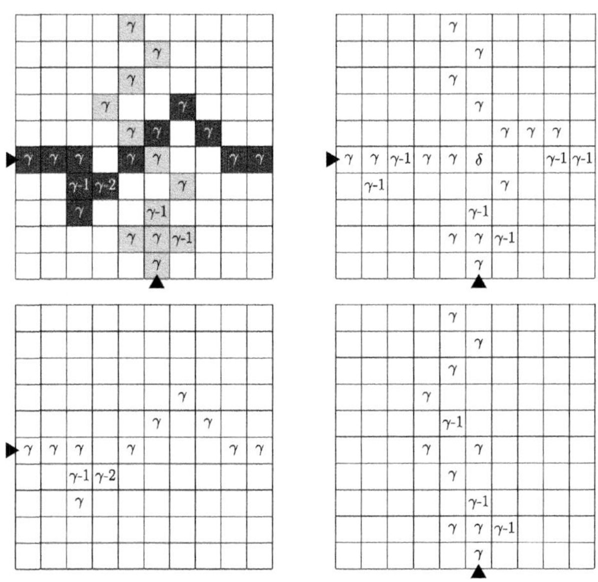

Fig. 5. Timed crossover gates (top left), *and* gates (top right, with $\delta = \theta_{\mathcal{N}} - 2$), *or* gates (top right, with $\delta = \theta_{\mathcal{N}} - 1$), horizontal diode (bottom left) and vertical diode (bottom right) for neighborhoods 111 and 127 with $\gamma = \theta_{\mathcal{N}} - 1$. The gates have size 10×10 and delay 12.

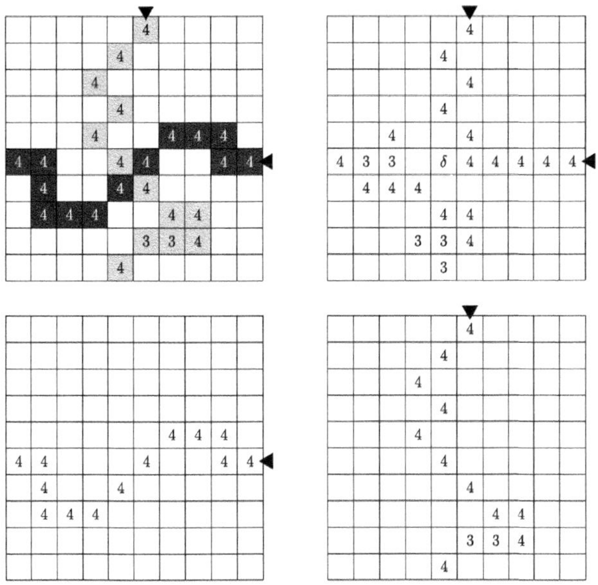

Fig. 6. Timed crossover gate (top left), *and* gate (top right, with $\delta = 3$), *or* gate (top right, with $\delta = 4$), horizontal diode (bottom left) and horizontal diode (bottom right) for neighborhood 151. The gates have size 10×10 and delay 13.

therefore topples at time step $z + d \cdot U + y$, with U the distance in the grid from the origin (top left cell) to the cell in question and y for its inner mechanism (precise distance to q), if and only if the **MCVP** outputs a signal 1.

The set of gates are presented as follows:

- on Fig. 5 for neighborhoods 111 and 127,
- on Fig. 6 for neighborhood 151,
- on Fig. 7 for neighborhoods 195, 211, 215 and 199.

For each neighborhood we present a crossover gate, an *and* gates, an *or* gate, and diodes. The constant 1 gate, turns and signal-duplication are derived from the *or* gate. The constant 0 gate is empty. □

3.4 Timed Crossover Possibility: Delay Issue

Neighborhoods studied in this subsection:

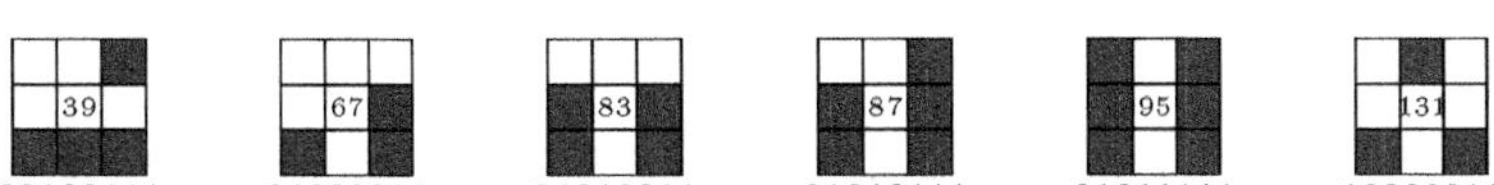

00100111 01000011 01010011 01010111 01011111 10000011

For multiple neighborhoods, we are able to construct a timed crossover gate, and even *and* and *or* gates, but we are faced with an issue when trying to plug

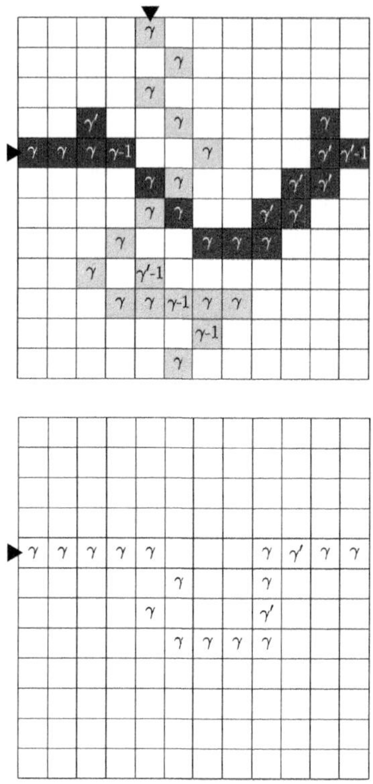

Fig. 7. Timed crossover gates (top left), *and* gates (top right, with $\delta = \theta_{\mathcal{N}} - 2$), *or* gates (top right, with $\delta = \theta_{\mathcal{N}} - 1$), horizontal diode (bottom left) and vertical diode (bottom right) for neighborhoods 195 (with $\gamma' = \theta_{\mathcal{N}} - 1$), 199 (with $\gamma' = \theta_{\mathcal{N}} - 2$), 211 (with $\gamma' = \theta_{\mathcal{N}} - 1$) and 215 (with $\gamma' = \theta_{\mathcal{N}} - 2$), with $\gamma = \theta_{\mathcal{N}} - 1$. The gates have size 12×12 and delay 17.

these gates together. Timed crossover gates for neighborhoods 39, 67, 83, 87 and 95 are presented on Fig. 8, and a timed crossover gate for neighborhood 131 is presented on Fig. 3.

Let us focus on neighborhood 39 as an example. On Fig. 9 we present an almost complete set of gates, of size 11×11 with delay 11. Inputs are located on the *west* and *north* borders, and outputs on the *east* and *south* borders. The north input and south output are identically located in every gate, and there are two possible locations of the west input and east output (size 11 is odd): either exactly in the middle of their respective borders (label A on Fig. 9), or one cell above (label B). They are meant to be plugged alternatively to each other horizontally (adapting the construction from Fig. 4), following a pattern of mono-labeled columns of gates (*i.e.*, in each column all the gates have label A or all the gates have label B). There are:

- *wires* (also *diodes*) labeled A and B,
- a *crossover* gate labeled A,

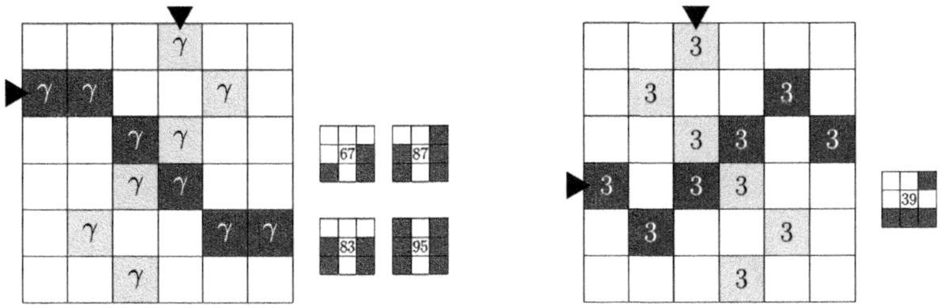

(a) Neighborhoods 67, 83, 87, and 95 (b) Neighborhoods 39

Fig. 8. Neighborhoods next to their timed crossover gate. Each non-empty cell contains $\gamma = \theta_{\mathcal{N}} - 1$ grains. The triangles indicate the direction in which the cells are toppled.

- an *or* gate labeled B,
- an *and* gate labeled B,
- a *constant* 1 gate labeled B is derived from the *or* gate,
- a *signal-duplication* gate labeled B is derived from the *or* gate,
- *turn* gates labeled B are derived from the *or* gate,
- a *constant* 0 gate is empty (labeled A and B).

Only a pair of gates is missing: *turn* gates labeled A. If turn gates labeled A exist, then we can connect all these gates together following this mono-labeled column approach (using zigzags to switch label) and prove the P-completeness of $\mathcal{N}$-**TIMED-PRED**. However, we show below that turn gates labeled A do not exist: the distance from the west input corresponding to label A to the south output is incompatible with the movements possible under a delay of 11. We do not know how to proceed with this reduction without turn gates labeled A.

The synchronization issue is explained by the fact that neighborhoods 39, 67, 83, 87, 95 and 131 are all in one of the two following cases:

- not having cell *north* nor *south* in the neighborhood,
- not having cell *west* nor *east* in the neighborhood.

Consequently, at each step of the avalanche process (chain of reaction of topplings), a signal must move along the perpendicular direction. For simplicity let us assume that neither cell *west* nor *east* are in the neighborhood, so that a signal must move along the y axis at each step. This induces a parity for the timestamps of signals: they have even timestamps on the cells $Y_2 = \{(x, y) \in \mathbb{Z}^2 \mid y \text{ is even}\}$ and odd timestamps on the other cells $\mathbb{Z}^2 \setminus Y_2$, or odd timestamps on Y_2 and even timestamps on $\mathbb{Z}^2 \setminus Y_2$.

It turns out that the *or/and* and *crossover* gates presented on Fig. 9 use a different combination of parities for the two input signals, because:

- *or/and* gates require the two signals to *meet* at synchronized timestamps,
- *crossover* gates require the two signals to *be adjacent along the y axis* at synchronized timestamps.

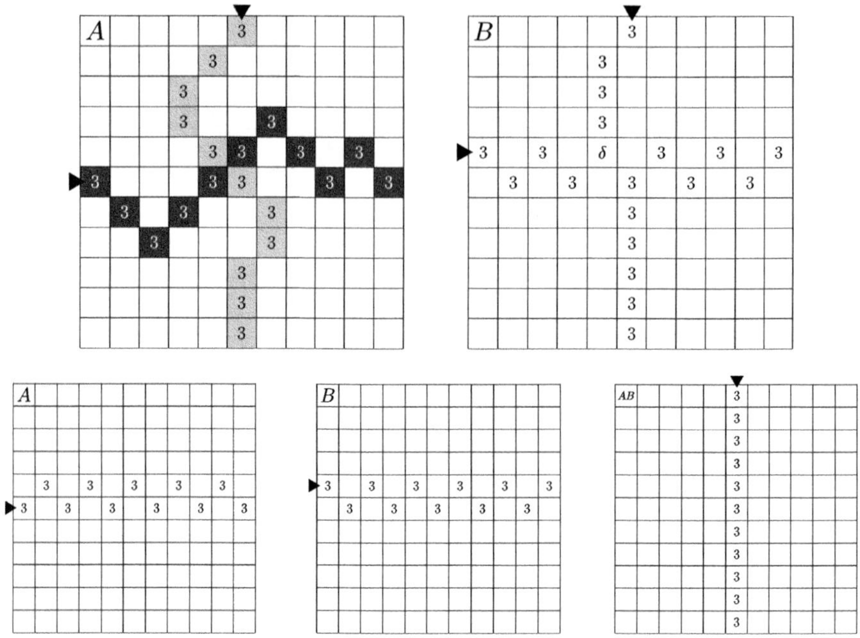

Fig. 9. An almost complete set of timed gates of size 11 × 11 and delay 11 for neighborhood 39. Timed crossover gate (top left, labeled A), *or* gate (top right, with $\delta = 3$, labeled B), *and* gate (top right, with $\delta = 2$, labeled B), horizontal diodes (bottom left and center, resp. labeled A and B) and vertical diode (bottom right, labeled both A and B).

This leads to an incompatibility in the synchronization between those gates for neighborhood 39. Neighborhoods 67, 83, 87 and 95 face a symmetric issue.

The case of 131 is different. It does not have the cell *west* nor *east* in the neighborhood, therefore it has a parity along the y axis, but the *crossover* gate requires the two signals to be adjacent along the x axis. So there is no apparent incompatibility. Nonetheless, we were not able to solve the synchronization issue for neighborhood 131.

3.5 Timed Crossover Impossibility: Conjectured

Neighborhoods studied in this subsection:

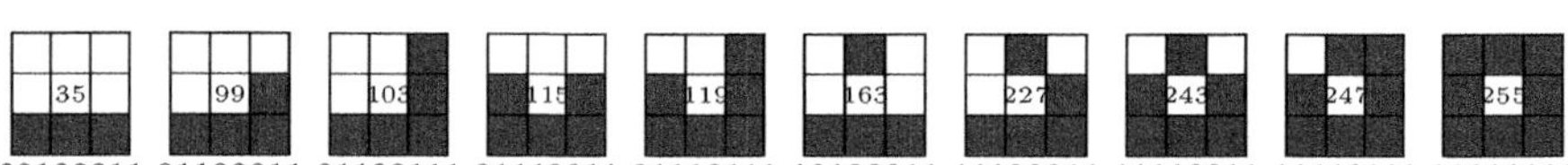

00100011 01100011 01100111 01110011 01110111 10100011 11100011 11110011 11110111 11111111

The difficulty to design a timed crossover gate for these neighborhoods lies in the fact that it is not possible to take advantage of the diagonal neighbors (in terms of delay) because the cell in-between the two diagonals is also an out-neighbor. We conjecture that this prevents to construct timed crossover gates for these neighborhoods, *i.e.* that they do not admit a timed crossover gate.

4 Conclusions

In this work we have considered the timed version of the sandpile prediction problem, asking whether, following a single grain addition on a stable configuration, a cell in question will topple or not at a precise time step $t \in \mathbb{N}$ which is part of the input. To study this problem, we have introduced the notion of timed firing graph, and timed crossover gate. The timed crossover gate allows for each of the two input cells to trigger an avalanche eventually toppling both output cells, provided there is a strictly positive lag on the output signal in the incorrect direction (not correspond to a crossing of two signal, *e.g.* from *north* to *south* the avalanche is allowed to topple the *east* cell if the delay of the signal from *north* to *south* is strictly smaller than the delay of the signal from *north* to *east*). This difference of delay aims at being embedded in a reduction from **MCVP** to $\mathcal{N}$-**TIMED-PRED** problem, according to the construction depicted on Fig. 4 (which has been designed with this purpose). It requires to have *wire*, *turns*, *and* and *or* gates with adequate delays, and with input and output cells that plug well to each other in order to keep the signals synchronized. Our results are partial; among the 255 non-empty subsets of the Moore neighborhood (the results are summarized on Table 1):

- 21 do not span $\mathbb{Z}^2$ and are therefore not relevant to our study,
- 52 admit a complete timed gates toolkit (including a timed crossover gate) and therefore have a P-complete timed prediction problem $\mathcal{N}$-**TIMED-PRED**,
- 99 have a planar sandpile structure and therefore do not admit a timed crossover gate,
- 34 admit a timed crossover gate, but one is faced with an issue in the delays when connecting the gates together,
- the 49 remaining neighborhoods (including Moore) are conjectured to do not admit a timed crossover gate.

Observe that a crossover gate is also a timed crossover gate, hence the 12 neighborhoods having a P-complete $\mathcal{N}$-**PRED** problem are part of the 52 neighborhoods having a P-complete $\mathcal{N}$-**TIMED-PRED** problem. It is notable that 40 neighborhoods (from 7 equivalence classes) do not admit a crossover gate, but do admit a complete timed gates toolkit allowing to prove the P-completeness of timed prediction problem. Intuitively, following the Banks approach, for these neighborhoods the embedding of the circuit evaluation in the sandpile dynamics is possible when one follows precisely the time steps, but asymptotically the sandpile will not stay in a configuration where the result of the circuit can be read out.

The precise characterization of the neighborhoods for which it is impossible to follow Banks approach in proving the P-completeness of $\mathcal{N}$-**TIMED-PRED** is still open, and does not seem to be captured by the existence of timed crossover gate as defined in Sect. 2. Proving that timed crossover gate do not exist for von Neumann and Moore neighborhoods would reveal more obstacles to the embedding of efficient computation within them.

Acknowledgments. The authors thank projects ANR-24-CE48-7504 ALARICE, HORIZON-MSCA-2022-SE-01 101131549 ACANCOS, STIC AmSud CAMA 22-STIC-02.

Disclosure of Interests. The authors have no competing interests to declare that are relevant to the content of this article.

References

1. Bak, P., Tang, C., Wiesenfeld, K.: Self-organized criticality: an explanation of the 1/f noise. Phys. Rev. Lett. **59**(4), 381 (1987)
2. Banks, E.R.: Information processing and transmission in cellular automata. Ph.D. thesis, Massachusetts Institute of Technology (1971)
3. Concha-Vega, P., Goles, E., Montealegre, P., Perrot, K.: Sandpiles prediction and crossover on $\mathbb{Z}^2$ within Moore neighborhood. Nat. Comput. **24**(1), 29–66 (2025). https://pageperso.lis-lab.fr/kevin.perrot/documents/crossing-moore-HAL.pdf
4. Delorme, M., Mazoyer, J.: Signals on cellular automata. In: Adamatzky, A. (ed.) Collision-Based Computing, pp. 231–275. Springer, London (2002). https://doi.org/10.1007/978-1-4471-0129-1_9
5. Formenti, E., Perrot, K.: How hard is it to predict sandpiles on lattices? A survey. Fund. Inform. **171**, 189–219 (2019)
6. Gajardo, A., Goles, E.: Crossing information in two-dimensional sandpiles. Theoret. Comput. Sci. **369**(1–3), 463–469 (2006)
7. Goles, E., Maldonado, D., Montealegre, P., Ollinger, N.: On the computational complexity of the freezing non-strict majority automata. In: Proceedings of AUTOMATA'2017. LNCS, vol. 10248, pp. 109–119 (2017). https://doi.org/10.1007/978-3-319-58631-1_9
8. Goles, E., Montealegre, P., Perrot, K., Theyssier, G.: On the complexity of two-dimensional signed majority cellular automata. J. Comput. Syst. Sci. **91**, 1–32 (2017)
9. Goles, E., Montealegre-Barba, P., Todinca, I.: The complexity of the bootstraping percolation and other problems. Theoret. Comput. Sci. **504**, 73–82 (2013)
10. Greenlaw, R., Hoover, H.J., Ruzzo, W.L.: Limits to Parallel Computation: P-Completeness Theory. Oxford University Press, Inc, Oxford (1995)
11. Jájá, J.: An Introduction to Parallel Algorithms. Addison-Wesley, Boston (1992)
12. Moore, C., Nilsson, M.: The computational complexity of sandpiles. J. Stat. Phys. **96**, 205–224 (1999)
13. Nguyen, V.-H., Perrot, K.: Any shape can ultimately cross information on two-dimensional abelian sandpile models. In: Baetens, J.M., Kutrib, M. (eds.) AUTOMATA 2018. LNCS, vol. 10875, pp. 127–142. Springer, Cham (2018). https://doi.org/10.1007/978-3-319-92675-9_10

Ergodicity of the Hard-Core PCA with a Random Walk Method

Jérôme Casse[1], Irène Marcovici[2], and Maxence Poutrel[2](✉)

[1] Université Paris-Saclay, CNRS, Laboratoire de mathématiques d'Orsay, 91405 Orsay, France
jerome.casse@universite-paris-saclay.fr

[2] Univ Rouen Normandie, CNRS, Normandie Univ, LMRS UMR 6085, 76000 Rouen, France
{irene.marcovici,maxence.poutrel1}@univ-rouen.fr

Abstract. The hard-core probabilistic cellular automaton has attracted a renewed interest in the last few years, thanks to its connection with the study of a combinatorial game on percolation configurations. We provide an alternative proof for the ergodicity of this PCA for a neighbourhood of size 2 and 3, using the notion of decorrelated islands introduced by Casse in 2023, together with some new ideas. This shortens the previous proofs and provides a more intuitive and unified approach.

Keywords: probabilistic cellular automata · ergodicity · percolation · hard-core model

1 Percolation Games and PCA

Percolation Games. Let us present the following percolation game on $\mathbb{Z}^2$, as in Ref. [5]. Consider two non-negative reals $\epsilon_0, \epsilon_1 \in [0,1]$ such that $0 \leq \epsilon_0 + \epsilon_1 \leq 1$. For each site of $\mathbb{Z}^2$ we assign independently one of the 3 following states:

- trap with probability ϵ_1;
- target with probability ϵ_0;
- open with probability $r = 1 - \epsilon_0 - \epsilon_1$.

This defines the random board on which two players compete. Fix an integer $n \geq 2$. The rule of the game is the following. At time 0, a token is placed at the starting position $(0,0)$, and then, the two players move it alternatively, from its current position (i,j) on the board to a site in the set $\mathrm{Out}(i,j) = \{(i+k, j+1) : k \in \{0,1,\ldots,n-1\}\}$, see Fig. 1. If the current player moves the token to a trap, that player loses the game immediately; if it moves it to a target, that player wins the game immediately; otherwise (i.e. if the destination site is open), the game continues with the other player's turn.

We can then ask the following question: with the best strategy for each player, what is the probability that the game never ends, so that there is a draw? The answer is 0 for the cases $n = 2$ [5] and $n = 3$ [1] when $0 < \epsilon_0 + \epsilon_1 \leq 1$. In this article, we give alternative proofs of these two results, using ideas developed by Casse [3]. For $n \geq 4$, the question remains open.

Published by Springer Nature Switzerland AG 2026
S. Riva and A. Richard (Eds.): AUTOMATA 2025, LNCS 15831, pp. 221–241, 2026.
https://doi.org/10.1007/978-3-032-01570-9_15

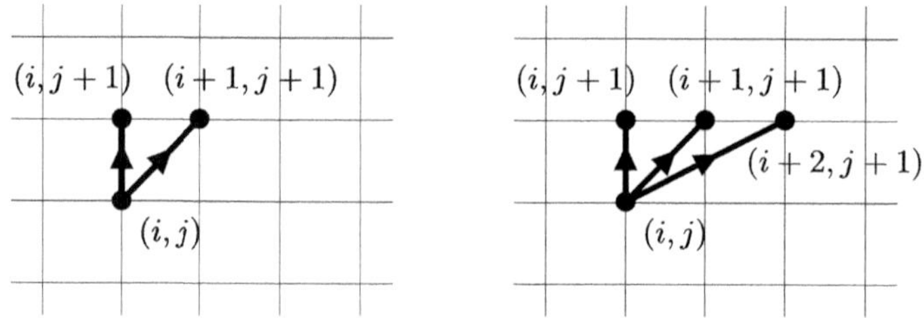

Fig. 1. The possible moves in the percolation game, for $n = 2$ on the left, and $n = 3$ on the right.

Associated PCA. To study the percolation game, we can associate to each site the outcome (win, lose or draw) of the current player (the one who moves out the token from this site) when both players play perfectly. If we know the outcomes of the sites of the set $\mathrm{Out}(i, j)$, it allows to find out the outcome of site (i, j). This leads to the introduction of a probabilistic cellular automaton (PCA) having a neighborhood of size n, with three states: 0 for the win, 1 for the lose and ? for the draw. Note that a trap can be interpreted as a win site, since if a player moves the token to a trap, the next player (the one who should have moved the token out from the trap site) wins; while a target can be interpreted as a lose site.

This PCA, denoted $\tilde{H}_n$ later in this article, defines a Markov chain $(X_i(t) : i \in \mathbb{Z})_{t \geq 0}$ on $\{0, 1, ?\}^{\mathbb{Z}}$, whose transition probabilities satisfy:

$$\mathbb{P}\left(X_i(t+1) = a \mid \forall k \in \{0, \ldots, n-1\},\, X_{i+k}(t) = 0\right) = \begin{cases} \epsilon_0 & \text{if } a = 0; \\ 1 - \epsilon_0 & \text{if } a = 1; \\ 0 & \text{if } a = ?. \end{cases}$$

$$\mathbb{P}\left(X_i(t+1) = a \mid \exists k \in \{0, \ldots, n-1\},\, X_{i+k}(t) = 1\right) = \begin{cases} 1 - \epsilon_1 & \text{if } a = 0; \\ \epsilon_1 & \text{if } a = 1; \\ 0 & \text{if } a = ?. \end{cases}$$

$$\mathbb{P}\left(X_i(t+1) = a \mid (X_i(t), \ldots, X_{i+n-1}(t)) \in \{0, ?\}^n \setminus \{(0, \ldots, 0)\}\right) = \begin{cases} \epsilon_0 & \text{if } a = 0; \\ \epsilon_1 & \text{if } a = 1; \\ r & \text{if } a = ?. \end{cases}$$

These transitions are illustrated on Fig. 2 for $n = 2$.

A PCA is *ergodic* if there is a unique probability measure μ_∞ such that the Markov chain $Z(t)$ of the PCA verifies: for any $\mu_0 \in \{0, 1\}^{\mathbb{Z}}$ such that the initial configuration $Z(0)$ is μ_0, the law of $Z(t)$ weakly converges to μ_∞. Here, the ergodicity of $\tilde{H}_n$ means that the status of site $(0, 0)$ does not depend on the assignment of traps and targets that are sufficiently far away on the board.

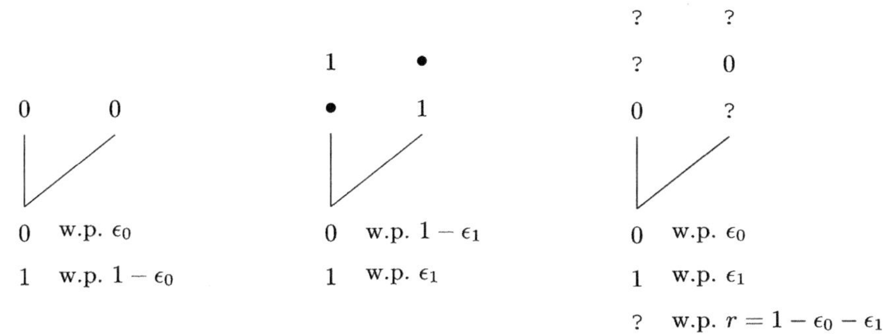

Fig. 2. Transition probability of the PCA $\tilde{H}_2$.

Observe that if for all $i \in \mathbb{Z}$, $X_i(0) \in \{0,1\}$, then for all $i \in \mathbb{Z}$, $t \geq 0$, $X_i(t) \neq ?$. In particular, if the PCA $\tilde{H}_n$ is ergodic, then its unique invariant measure does not contain the state ?, meaning that the probability of draw is null.

Theorem 1. *For $n \in \{2,3\}$ and $(\epsilon_0, \epsilon_1) \in [0, \frac{1}{2}]^2 \setminus \{(0,0)\}$, the PCA $\tilde{H}_n$ is ergodic, and so there is almost surely no draw in the percolation game.*

The result above was first proved for $n = 2$ using weight functions [5]. The method was then adapted for $n = 3$, with highly intricate computations [1]. The aim of the present article is to provide another shorter proof, based on the method of decorrelated islands [3].

Note that the PCA $\tilde{H}_n$ can be seen as the *envelope PCA* of the *hard-core PCA* H_n. By definition, it is the binary PCA whose associated Markov chain $X(t) = (X_i(t) : i \in \mathbb{Z}) \in \{0,1\}^{\mathbb{Z}}$ satisfies:

$$\mathbb{P}\left(X_i(t+1) = a \mid \forall k \in \{0,\ldots,n-1\}\, X_{i+k}(t) = 0\right) = \begin{cases} \epsilon_0 & \text{if } a = 0; \\ 1-\epsilon_0 & \text{if } a = 1. \end{cases}$$

$$\mathbb{P}\left(X_i(t+1) = a \mid \exists k \in \{0,\ldots,n-1\}\, X_{i+k}(t) = 1\right) = \begin{cases} 1-\epsilon_1 & \text{if } a = 0; \\ \epsilon_1 & \text{if } a = 1. \end{cases}$$

The transitions are illustrated on Fig. 3 for $n = 3$. The PCA H_n corresponds to the restriction of $\tilde{H}_n$ to configurations that do not contain the state ?. Envelope PCA are a practical tool to prove the ergodicity of PCA in the high noise regime, using the fact that the ergodicity of the envelope PCA implies the ergodicity of the associated PCA [2].

Finally, let us also mention that H_n can be seen as a CA with *double errors*: it is a PCA obtained from a deterministic CA, on which we add an error depending on the expected state (ϵ_0 if we expect a 1 and ϵ_1 if we expect a 0).

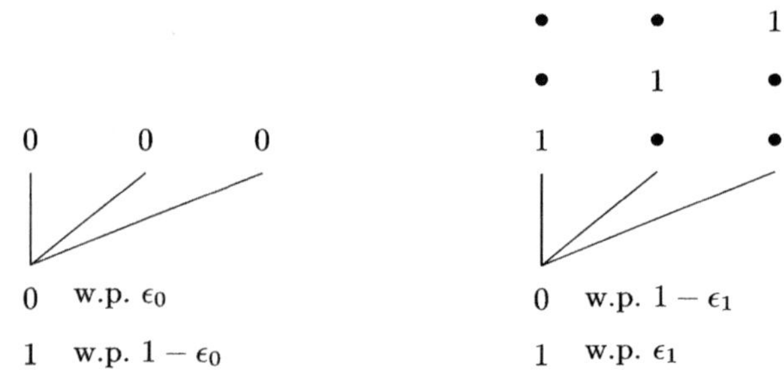

Fig. 3. Transition probability of the hard-core PCA H_3, where dots mean that there can be either a 0 or a 1.

Ergodicity of PCA. The ergodicity of PCA has been studied using various methods (coupling, entropy, Fourier analysis, weight functions ...) and still raises many questions, see [4,6–8] and the references therein. The hard-core PCA has attracted particular interest, since in addition to its connection to percolation games, it has long been known for its connection with statistical physics and with the enumeration of directed animals. For $\epsilon_1 = 0$, H_n has a Markovian invariant measure and its ergodicity is easier to prove [5], but for other values of the parameters, no general method is known.

Outline of the Article. In Sect. 2, we present the sketch of our proof of Theorem 1. In Sect. 2.1, we recall the notion of decorrelated islands introduced by Casse [3], then in Sect. 2.2, we explain the new idea that allows to handle the case of the hard-core PCA. In Sect. 3, we prove Theorem 1 for $n = 2$. This requires some computations that we present in details. In Sect. 4, we prove Theorem 1 when $n = 3$, using the same method.

2 Sketch of the Proof

2.1 Decorrelated Islands Method

Let us consider the evolution of the PCA $\tilde{H}_n$, from the initial configuration $?^{\mathbb{Z}}$.

- With probability $(\epsilon_0+\epsilon_1)^k$, the k consecutive cells of indices in $0,\ldots,k-1$ go from state ? to state 0 or 1, i.e. for all $i \in \{0,\ldots,k-1\}$, $X_i(1) \in \{0,1\}$. We call such a sequence of consecutive cells a *decorrelated island*, as the states of these cells do not depend on the initial configuration.
- Our goal is to study the evolution of the size of a decorrelated island, that is a (maximal) set of consecutive cells where the symbol ? does not appear. With probability 1, there exists a time $t_0 \geq 0$ when such a decorrelated island is created. For $t \geq t_0$, we denote by i_t and j_t the positions of the left and right boundary of the decorrelated island, respectively. So, cells between i_t and j_t are in state 0 or 1, while $i_t - 1$ and $j_t + 1$ are in state ?.

- If $j_t - i_t \to_{t\to\infty} \infty$ with positive probability, this means that the island grows, so that the symbols ? progressively disappear, implying that the PCA is ergodic.

To study the behaviour of the left boundary i_t, we only remember the states of the first m cells of the island, given by $f_t = (X_{i_t}, X_{1+i_t}, \dots, X_{m-1+i_t})$, with a well-chosen value of m, selected according to the size of the neighborhood n. We proceed in a similar way for the right boundary j_t. In the following, we will set $m = 2$ when $n = 2$, and $m = 4$ when $n = 3$.

This method, applied with $m = 1$, gives a sufficient ergodicity criterion for PCA with binary alphabet and two-size neighborhood [3]. This allows to handle the case of 12 out of 16 deterministic cellular automata with error $\epsilon > 0$. By taking $m = 2$, it also gives a new proof of the ergodicity of the PCA $\tilde{H}_2$ (and so of H_2) when $\epsilon_0 = \epsilon_1 > 0$.

2.2 The Main Improvement of the Method

In this article, we improve the method developed by Casse [3] to give a new and shorter proof of Theorem 1. The improvement consists in considering one or two time steps at once, according to the value of the states of the boundary, and not just one time step in every situation.

First, observe that in order to prove that $\mathbb{P}(j_t - i_t \to \infty)$ is positive, since the size of negative steps is bounded (by 1), it is enough to show that the mean asymptotic drift

$$D = \lim_{t\to\infty} \mathbb{E}[J_t] - \lim_{t\to\infty} \mathbb{E}[I_t]$$

of $(j_t - i_t)_{t\geq t_0}$ is positive, where J_t is the increment of (j_t), i.e. $J_t = j_{t+1} - j_t$ and I_t the one of (i_t). The following remark in fact allows one to restrict ourselves to the study of the right boundary.

Remark 1. Let us denote by $R = \lim_{t\to\infty} \mathbb{E}[J_t]$ the mean asymptotic drift of the right boundary. Using the symmetry of the transition rule of $\tilde{H}_n$ with respect to the left-right symmetry, while taking into account the fact that the neighborhood is not centered, it follows that $D = 2R + (n-1)$. Consequently, in the rest of the article, we focus only on the behaviour of the right boundary.

The innovation of the present work is to study the law of J_t and the one of $J_t + J_{t+1}$ according to the values of the states of the boundary f_t. This is summed up in the following lemma.

Lemma 1. *Consider a homogeneous Markov chain (j_t, f_t) on $\mathbb{Z} \times F$, where F is a finite set, and assume that the increment $J_t = j_{t+1} - j_t$ depends only on f_t. Precisely, assume that for any $f \in F$, for any $k \in \mathbb{Z}$, and for any $t \geq 0$,*

$$\mathbb{E}[J_t | f_t = f, j_t = k] = \mathbb{E}[j_1 | f_0 = f, j_0 = 0].$$

Then, if the limit $R = \lim_{t\to\infty} \mathbb{E}[J_t]$ exists and is finite, it satisfies:

$$R \geq \min_{f\in F} \max\left(\mathbb{E}[J_t | f_t = f], \frac{1}{2}\mathbb{E}[J_t + J_{t+1} | f_t = f]\right). \tag{1}$$

Proof. First, we split the set F into two disjoint parts:

$$F_1 = \left\{ f \in F : \mathbb{E}\left[J_0 | f_0 = f\right] \geq \frac{1}{2}\mathbb{E}\left[J_0 + J_1 | f_0 = f\right] \right\} \text{ and } F_2 = F \backslash F_1.$$

The set F_1 represents the states for which the mean increment is larger when we consider a single time step compared to two time steps, and F_2 those for which it is the reverse.

We now define another Markov chain $(\hat{j}_t, \hat{f}_t, w_t)_{t \geq 0}$ as follows:

- $(\hat{j}_0, \hat{f}_0, w_0) = (j_0, f_0, \mathbb{1}_{f_0 \in F_2})$,
- if $w_t = 0$, then $\hat{j}_{t+1} = j_{t+1}$, $\hat{f}_{t+1} = f_{t+1}$ and $w_{t+1} = \mathbb{1}_{f_{t+1} \in F_2}$,
- if $w_t = 1$, then $\hat{j}_{t+1} = j_t$, $\hat{f}_{t+1} = f_t$ and $w_{t+1} = 0$.

As a consequence:

$$\begin{aligned} \hat{J}_t = \hat{j}_{t+1} - \hat{j}_t = J_t \text{ when } w_t = 0 \text{ and } f_t \in F_1; \\ \hat{J}_t = 0 \text{ when } w_t = 1 \text{ and } f_t \in F_2; \\ \hat{J}_t = J_{t-1} + J_t \text{ when } w_t = 0 \text{ and } f_t \in F_2. \end{aligned}$$

So, compared to $(j_t, f_t)_{t \geq 0}$, the new Markov chain moves one step forward when $\hat{f}_t$ is in F_1, while when it is in F_2, the state does not change at the first time step (when $w_t = 1$) and then moves of the equivalent of two steps at a time (when $w_t = 0$). The variable w_t can thus be thought as a waiting time.

Let us now consider the value $\hat{R} = \lim_{t \to \infty} \mathbb{E}\left[\hat{J}_t\right]$. We show that $\hat{R} \geq M$, where M is the term on the right-hand side of (1). We have

$$\hat{R} = \sum_{f \in F_1} \tau(f, 0) \mathbb{E}\left[\hat{J}_t | \hat{f}_t = f, w_t = 0\right] + \sum_{f \in F_2} \left(\tau(f, 1) \times 0 + \tau(f, 0) \mathbb{E}\left[\hat{J}_t | \hat{f}_t = f, w_t = 0\right]\right)$$

where τ is the invariant measure of the Markov chain $(\hat{f}_t, w_t)_{t \geq 0}$, which exists since F is finite.

By definition of $(\hat{j}_t, \hat{f}_t, w_t)_{t \geq 0}$, we have for any $f \in F_1$,

$$\mathbb{E}\left[\hat{J}_t | \hat{f}_t = f, w_t = 0\right] = \max\left(\mathbb{E}\left[J_t | f_t = f\right], \frac{1}{2}\mathbb{E}\left[J_t + J_{t+1} | f_t = f\right]\right) \geq M$$

and for any $f \in F_2$,

$$\mathbb{E}\left[\hat{J}_t | \hat{f}_t = f, w_t = 0\right] = 2\max\left(\mathbb{E}\left[J_t | f_t = f\right], \frac{1}{2}\mathbb{E}\left[J_t + J_{t+1} | f_t = f\right]\right) \geq 2M.$$

By construction of the new Markov chain, for any $f \in F_2$, $\tau(f, 0) = \tau(f, 1)$. So we obtain $\hat{R} \geq M \sum_{(f,w) \in (F_1 \times \{0\}) \cup (F_2 \times \{0,1\})} \tau(f, w) = M$.

To conclude, we only need to prove that $R = \hat{R}$. We recall that the equality $(j_t, f_t) = (\hat{j}_t, \hat{f}_t)$ holds at least once in two, and by the ergodic theorem,

$$\hat{R} = \lim_{t\to\infty} \mathbb{E}\left[\hat{J}_t\right] = \lim_{t\to\infty} \frac{\mathbb{E}\left[\hat{j}_t - j_0\right]}{t} \quad \text{and } R = \lim_{t\to\infty} \mathbb{E}\left[J_t\right] = \lim_{t\to\infty} \frac{\mathbb{E}\left[j_t - j_0\right]}{t}.$$

So, we have $\hat{R} = R$. □

Using Remark 1 together with Lemma 1, we can then prove Theorem 1 by just showing that, for any $n \in \{2, 3\}$ and for every $t \geq t_0$,

$$R \geq \min_{f\in\{0,1\}^m} \left(\max\left(\mathbb{E}\left[J_t | f_t = f\right], \frac{1}{2}\mathbb{E}\left[J_t + J_{t+1} | f_t = f\right]\right)\right) > -\frac{n-1}{2}. \qquad (2)$$

Remark 2. We will actually prove the previous inequality not for (j_t) but for some modification $(\tilde{j}_t)$, introduced in Sects. 3.1 for $n = 2$ and in 4.1 for $n = 3$.

3 Proof of Theorem 1 When $n = 2$

3.1 Modified Boundary and Star State

To give a formal proof of Theorem 1, we now introduce two additional notions.

First, as mentioned in Remark 2, we define a slight modification of the position j_t, that depends on the states of the boundaries. To do so, let us consider a decorrelated island $(X_{i_t}, \ldots, X_{j_t})$ not reduced to a singleton at time t. To study the behaviour of its right boundary, we introduce the modified position $\tilde{j}_t$ defined by

$$\tilde{j}_t = \begin{cases} j_t & \text{if } (X_{-1+j_t}, X_{j_t}) \in \{(0,1),(1,1)\}; \\ j_t - \frac{1}{2} & \text{if } (X_{-1+j_t}, X_{j_t}) = (0,0); \\ j_t - 1 & \text{if } (X_{-1+j_t}, X_{j_t}) = (1,0). \end{cases}$$

As a result of this technical change, if $\epsilon_0 = \epsilon_1 = 0$ (error-free regime), then the deterministic drift satisfies $\tilde{J}_t = -1/2$ for any t, whereas J_t oscillates between 0 and -1. The purpose of this modification is therefore only to simplify the analysis. Note that the cells we will consider at time t in the right boundary will still be given by $f_t = (X_{-1+j_t}, X_{j_t})$. The modification $\tilde{i}_t$ of i_t is defined analogously, using the left-right symmetry of the transition rule.

Second, we introduce a star state, that we denote by $*$. This state will be used to encode the state of a cell of the decorrelated island whose exact value (0 or 1) is not remembered. Indeed, if we retain all the information about the island, the computation is too complex. The state $*$ will thus enable us to establish some bounds for the behaviour of the boundaries. This is different from the state ?, which represents a cell whose value is completely unknown.

3.2 Transition Probabilities

In this section, we study the behaviour of the Markov chain $(\tilde{\jmath}_t, f_t)$ where we recall that $f_t = (X_{-1+j_t}, X_{j_t})$. Our goal is to prove that

$$\mathbb{E}\left[\tilde{J}_t | f_t \in \{(0,1),(1,0),(1,1)\}\right] > -\frac{1}{2} \text{ and } \mathbb{E}\left[\tilde{J}_t + \tilde{J}_{t+1} | f_t = (0,0)\right] > -1, \quad (3)$$

which implies Eq. (2) when $n = 2$, and so Theorem 1 for $n = 2$.

In the following, we assume that $j_t - i_t \geq 5$. It is not a loss of generality to achieve the result, and it allows to avoid any problem of dependency between $(\tilde{\imath}_{t+1}, (X_{i_{t+1}}, X_{1+i_{t+1}}))$ and $(\tilde{\jmath}_{t+1}, (X_{-1+j_{t+1}}, X_{j_{t+1}}))$.

Case $f_t \in \{(0,1),(1,0),(1,1)\}$: For these three types of right boundaries, the transition probabilities are the same, as illustrated on Fig. 4.

More precisely, if $\tilde{\jmath}_t = \tilde{\jmath}$ and if $f_t = f$ belongs to $\{(0,1),(1,0),(1,1)\}$, then

$$(\tilde{\jmath}_{t+1}, f_{t+1}) = \begin{cases} (\tilde{\jmath} - 1, (1,0)) & \text{w.p. } \epsilon_1(1-\epsilon_1)r \\ (\tilde{\jmath} - \frac{1}{2}, (0,0)) & \text{w.p. } (1-\epsilon_1)^2 r \\ (\tilde{\jmath}, (0,1)) & \text{w.p. } (1-\epsilon_1)\epsilon_1 r \\ (\tilde{\jmath}, (1,1)) & \text{w.p. } \epsilon_1^2 r \\ (\tilde{\jmath}, (1,0)) & \text{w.p. } \epsilon_1\epsilon_0 r \\ (\tilde{\jmath} + \frac{1}{2}, (0,0)) & \text{w.p. } (1-\epsilon_1)\epsilon_0 r \\ (\tilde{\jmath} + 1, (0,1)) & \text{w.p. } (1-\epsilon_1)\epsilon_1 r \\ (\tilde{\jmath} + 1, (1,1)) & \text{w.p. } \epsilon_1^2 r \\ (\tilde{\jmath} + k + 1, (1,0)) & \text{w.p. } (\epsilon_0+\epsilon_1)^k \epsilon_1\epsilon_0 r \text{ for } k \geq 0 \\ (\tilde{\jmath} + k + \frac{3}{2}, (0,0)) & \text{w.p. } (\epsilon_0+\epsilon_1)^k \epsilon_0^2 r \text{ for } k \geq 0 \\ (\tilde{\jmath} + k + 2, (0,1)) & \text{w.p.} (\epsilon_0+\epsilon_1)^k \epsilon_0\epsilon_1 r \text{ for } k \geq 0 \\ (\tilde{\jmath} + k + 2, (1,1)) & \text{w.p. } (\epsilon_0+\epsilon_1)^k \epsilon_1^2 r \text{ for } k \geq 0 \end{cases} \quad (4)$$

Using Eq. (4), we can compute the mean increment in one time step for this type of boundary:

$$\begin{aligned} &\mathbb{E}\left[\tilde{J}_t | f_t = \{(0,1),(1,0),(1,1)\}\right] \\ &= -\epsilon_1(1-\epsilon_1)r - \frac{1}{2}(1-\epsilon_1)^2 r + \frac{1}{2}\epsilon_0(1-\epsilon_1)r + \cdots + \sum_{k=0}^{\infty}(k+2)\epsilon_1^2(1-r)^k r \\ &= -\frac{1}{2}r + \epsilon_1 r + \frac{1}{2}\epsilon_0(1-\epsilon_1)r + \frac{1}{2}\epsilon_1^2 r + \frac{1}{2}\epsilon_0^2 + \epsilon_0\epsilon_1 + \epsilon_1^2 + \frac{(1-r)^2}{r} \\ &= -\frac{1}{2} + \underbrace{\frac{1}{2}\epsilon_0 + \frac{1}{2}\epsilon_1 + \epsilon_1 r + \frac{1}{2}\epsilon_0(1-\epsilon_1)r + \frac{1}{2}\epsilon_1^2 r + \frac{1}{2}(1-r)^2 + \frac{1}{2}\epsilon_1^2 + \frac{(1-r)^2}{r}}_{>0}. \end{aligned} \quad (5)$$

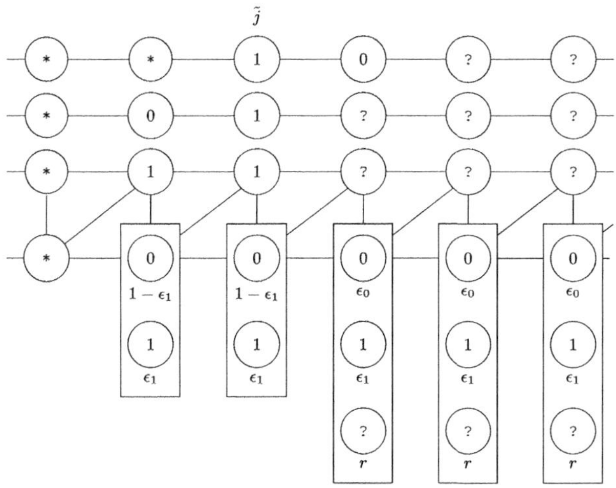

Fig. 4. Transition probabilities of the different cells when the state f of the boundary belongs to $\{(0,1),(1,0),(1,1)\}$. The first three lines correspond to the three cases $f=(1,0)$, $f=(0,1)$ and $f=(1,1)$. The boundary position j depends on the case, but the modified boundary $\tilde{j}$ is always the same. The boxes provide the different possible states of the cells with their respective probability.

This can be checked by hand or with the help of a computer algebra system.

Case $\boldsymbol{f_{t=(0,0)}}$: For this type of boundary, we look at the increment in two time steps. The first step is given on Fig. 5.

First Step: As illustrated on Fig. 5, if $\tilde{j}_t = \tilde{j}$ and if the state of the boundary satisfies $f_t = (0,0)$, then

$$(\tilde{j}_{t+1}, f_{t+1}) = \begin{cases} (\geq \tilde{j} - \frac{3}{2}, (*,0)) & \text{w.p. } \epsilon_0 r^2 \\ (\tilde{j} - \frac{3}{2}, (1,0)) & \text{w.p. } \epsilon_1\epsilon_0 r \\ (\tilde{j} - 1, (0,0)) & \text{w.p. } \epsilon_0^2 r \\ (\tilde{j} - \frac{1}{2}, (0,1)) & \text{w.p. } \epsilon_0(1-\epsilon_0) r \\ (\tilde{j} - \frac{1}{2}, (1,1)) & \text{w.p. } \epsilon_1(1-\epsilon_0) r \\ (\tilde{j} - \frac{1}{2}, (*,1)) & \text{w.p. } r(1-\epsilon_0) r \\ (\tilde{j} - \frac{1}{2}, (1,0)) & \text{w.p. } (1-\epsilon_0)\epsilon_0 r \\ (\tilde{j}, (0,0)) & \text{w.p. } \epsilon_0^2 r \\ (\tilde{j} + \frac{1}{2}, (0,1)) & \text{w.p. } \epsilon_0\epsilon_1 r \\ (\tilde{j} + \frac{1}{2}, (1,1)) & \text{w.p. } (1-\epsilon_0)\epsilon_1 r \\ (\tilde{j} + k + \frac{1}{2}, (1,0)) & \text{w.p. } (\epsilon_0+\epsilon_1)^k \epsilon_1\epsilon_0 r \\ (\tilde{j} + k + 1, (0,0)) & \text{w.p. } (\epsilon_0+\epsilon_1)^k \epsilon_0^2 r \\ (\tilde{j} + k + \frac{3}{2}, (0,1)) & \text{w.p. } (\epsilon_0+\epsilon_1)^k \epsilon_0\epsilon_1 r \\ (\tilde{j} + k + \frac{3}{2}, (1,1)) & \text{w.p. } (\epsilon_0+\epsilon_1)^k \epsilon_1^2 r \end{cases} \quad (6)$$

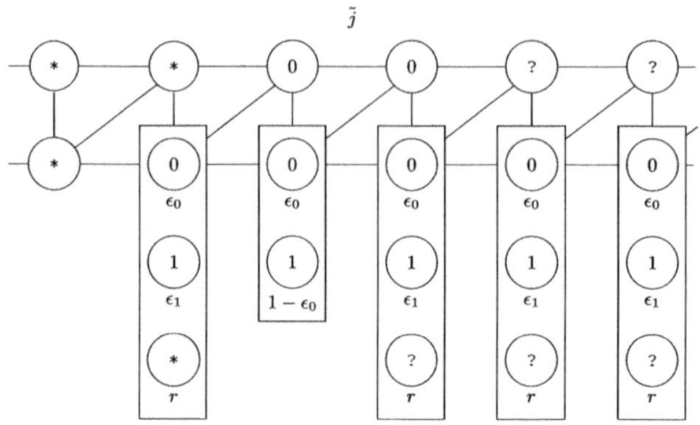

Fig. 5. Transition probabilities when the boundary is in state $(0, 0)$ and $\tilde{j}$ indicates the position of the boundary with the modification considered.

Remark 3. In the first case, which corresponds to a transition to $f_{t+1} = (*, 0)$, the value of $\tilde{j}_{t+1}$ can be equal to $\tilde{j} - 3/2$ if the boundary is in state $(1, 0)$ or to $\tilde{j} - 1$ if it is in state $(0, 0)$. As we want to bound by below the increment, we keep the lower bound $\tilde{j} - 3/2$ in that case.

Second Step: As the second step depends only on the first step through the value of f_{t+1}, the transitions given in Eq. (6) allow to deduce the mean increment for two time steps,

$$\begin{aligned}
&\mathbb{E}\left[\tilde{J}_t + \tilde{J}_{t+1} | f_t = (0,0)\right] \\
=&\mathbb{E}\left[\tilde{J}_t | f_t = (0,0)\right] + \mathbb{P}\left(f_{t+1} = (*,0) | f_t = (0,0)\right) \mathbb{E}\left[\tilde{J}_{t+1} | f_{t+1} = (*,0)\right] \\
&+ \mathbb{P}\left(f_{t+1} = (0,0) | f_t = (0,0)\right) \mathbb{E}\left[\tilde{J}_{t+1} | f_{t+1} = (0,0)\right] \\
&+ \mathbb{P}\left(f_{t+1} \in \{(0,1),(1,0),(1,1),(*,1)\} | f_t = (0,0)\right) \mathbb{E}\left[\tilde{J}_{t+1} | f_{t+1} = (0,1)\right].
\end{aligned} \tag{7}$$

The probability transitions of f_{t+1} are given by Eq. (6):

$$\begin{aligned}
&\mathbb{P}\left(f_{t+1} = (*,0) | f_t = (0,0)\right) = \epsilon_0 r^2, \\
&\mathbb{P}\left(f_{t+1} = (0,0) | f_t = (0,0)\right) = 2\epsilon_0^2 r + \sum_{k=0}^{\infty} \epsilon_0^2 (1-r)^k r = 2\epsilon_0^2 r + \epsilon_0^2, \text{ and, so,} \\
&\mathbb{P}\left(f_{t+1} \in \{(0,1),(1,0),(1,1),(*,1)\} | f_t = (0,0)\right) = 1 - \epsilon_0 r^2 - 2\epsilon_0^2 r - \epsilon_0^2.
\end{aligned}$$

Moreover, by Eq. (6), the mean increment in one time step when the boundary is in state $(0, 0)$ verify

$$\mathbb{E}\left[\tilde{J}_t | f_t = (0,0)\right] \geq -\frac{1}{2} r^2 - 2\epsilon_0 r + \epsilon_0^2 r + \frac{1}{2}\epsilon_1^2 + \frac{(1-r)^2}{r} \tag{8}$$

and, when it is in state $(*, 0)$ we have the following lower bound:

$$\mathbb{E}\left[\tilde{J}_t | f_t = (*,0)\right] \geq \min\left(\mathbb{E}\left[\tilde{J}_t | f_t = (0,0)\right], \mathbb{E}\left[\tilde{J}_t | f_t = (1,0)\right]\right) \geq -\frac{1}{2}r^2 - 2\epsilon_0 r + \epsilon_0^2 r + \frac{1}{2}\epsilon_1^2 + \frac{(1-r)^2}{r}. \tag{9}$$

Indeed,

$$\mathbb{E}\left[\tilde{J}_t | f_t = (1,0)\right] - \left(-\frac{1}{2}r^2 - 2\epsilon_0 r + \epsilon_0^2 r + \frac{1}{2}\epsilon_1^2 + \frac{(1-r)^2}{r}\right) = \frac{1}{2}(1-r)^2 + \frac{1}{2}\epsilon_1 r + \frac{1}{2}\epsilon_1^2 r + \frac{1}{2}\epsilon_0(1-\epsilon_1)r + \epsilon_0\left(\frac{3}{2} - \epsilon_0\right) r \geq 0. \tag{10}$$

Hence, as detailed in Appendix 6.1, we finally obtain that

$$\mathbb{E}\left[\tilde{J}_t + \tilde{J}_{t+1} | f_t = (0,0)\right] > -1. \tag{11}$$

Equations (5) and (11) imply Eq. (2) when $n = 2$, and so Theorem 1 for $n = 2$.

4 Proof of Theorem 1 When $n = 3$

In this Section, we consider the PCA $\tilde{H}_3$. The proof follows the same way as for $\tilde{H}_2$. The main difference is that we now consider a boundary f_t of size 4. Also, the definition of the modified boundary $\tilde{j}_t$ is slightly different.

4.1 Modified Boundary

Let us consider a decorrelated island $(X_{i_t}, \ldots, X_{j_t})$. We now define the modified boundary position $\tilde{j}_t$ by

$$\tilde{j}_t = \begin{cases} j_t & \text{if } X_{j_t} = 1, \\ j_t - 1 & \text{if } (X_{j_t-2}, X_{j_t-1}, X_{j_t}) = (0,0,0) \text{ or } (X_{j_t-1}, X_{j_t}) = (1,0), \\ j_t - 2 & \text{else, i.e. if } (X_{j_t-2}, X_{j_t-1}, X_{j_t}) = (1,0,0). \end{cases}$$

4.2 Transition Probabilities

For $n = 3$, we consider a right boundary made of the states of the 4 rightmost cells of the island, $f_t = (X_{-3+j_t}, X_{-2+j_t}, X_{-1+j_t}, X_{j_t})$, and in the following, we assume that $j_t - i_t \geq 9$. It is not a loss of generality to achieve the result, and it allows to avoid any problem of dependency between $(\tilde{j}_{t+1}, f_t)$ and its left counterpart.

We group the possibles states of the boundary into three subsets of configurations (two being reduced to a singleton): $\{(0,0,0,0)\}$, $\{(1,0,0,0)\}$ and

$$S_1 = \{(a_0, a_1, a_2, a_3) : a_0 \in \{0,1\} \text{ and } \exists k \in \{1,2,3\},\ a_k = 1\}.$$

The 14 configurations of this last set can be considered together, as their transition probabilities are the same. This is similar to the case $n = 2$, when $(0, 1)$, $(1, 0)$ and $(1, 1)$ were grouped.

Case $f_t \in S_1$: For this case, we can reduce the boundary to a length equal to 3, as the mean increment in one time step is enough. Hence, in the transition, we do not care about the value of $X_{j_{t+1}-3}$, as illustrated on Fig. 6. If $vj_t = \tilde{j}$ and $f_t = f \in S_1$, then, we have

$$\left(\tilde{j}_{t+1}, (X_{j_{t+1}-2}, X_{j_{t+1}-1}, X_{j_{t+1}})\right) =$$
$$\begin{cases} (\tilde{j} - 1 + k, (0,0,0)) & \text{w.p. } (1-\epsilon_1)^{3-k}\epsilon_0^k r \text{ for } k \in \{0,1,2\}; \\ (\tilde{j} + 2 + k, (0,0,0)) & \text{w.p. } (\epsilon_0+\epsilon_1)^k \epsilon_0^3 r \text{ for } k \in \mathbb{N}; \\ (\tilde{j} - l + k, \{0,1\}^{2-l} \times \{1\} \times \{0\}^l) & \text{w.p. } \epsilon_1(1-\epsilon_1)^{l-k}\epsilon_0^k r \text{ for } l \in \{0,1,2\} \text{ and } 0 \le k \le l; \\ (\tilde{j} - l + k, \{0,1\}^{2-l} \times \{1\} \times \{0\}^l) & \text{w.p. } (\epsilon_0+\epsilon_1)^{k-l-1}\epsilon_1\epsilon_0^l r \text{ for } l \in \{0,1\} \text{ and } l+1 \le k \le 2; \\ (\tilde{j} + 3 - l + k, \{0,1\}^{2-l} \times \{1\} \times \{0\}^l) & \text{w.p. } (\epsilon_0+\epsilon_1)^{k+2-l}\epsilon_1\epsilon_0^l r \text{ for } l \in \{0,1,2\} \text{ and } k \in \mathbb{N}; \end{cases}$$

We then obtain the following mean increment:

$$\mathbb{E}\left[\tilde{J}_t | f_t \in S_1\right] = \sum_{k=0}^{2} (-1+k)(1-\epsilon_1)^{3-k}\epsilon_0^k r + \dots$$
$$= -1 + \epsilon_0 + 2\epsilon_1 + \epsilon_0^2 + 3\epsilon_1^2(1-\epsilon_1) + \epsilon_0\epsilon_1(1-\epsilon_0) + \epsilon_1^4 + \epsilon_0^3\epsilon_1 + \frac{(1-r)^3}{r} > -1. \tag{12}$$

This can be checked by hand or with the help of a computer algebra system. Hence, we proved Eq. (2) for any $f \in S_1$. For the two others cases ($f = (0, 0, 0, 0)$ or $f = (1, 0, 0, 0)$), we have to consider two time steps. The case $f_t = (1, 0, 0, 0)$ is considered first.

Case $f_{t=(1,0,0,0)}$:
As illustrated on Fig. 7, if $\tilde{j}_t = \tilde{j}$ and $f_t = (1, 0, 0, 0)$, then

$$(\tilde{j}_{t+1}, f_{t+1}) =$$
$$\begin{cases} (\tilde{j} - 2 + k, (0,0,0,0)) & \text{w.p. } (1-\epsilon_1)^{3-k}\epsilon_0^{1+k} r \text{ for } k \in \{0,1,2,3\}; \\ (\tilde{j} - 2 + k, (1,0,0,0)) & \text{w.p. } \epsilon_1(1-\epsilon_1)^{2-k}\epsilon_0^{1+k} r \text{ for } k \in \{0,1,2\}; \\ (\tilde{j} + 1, (1,0,0,0)) & \text{w.p. } (1-\epsilon_0)\epsilon_0^3 r; \\ (\tilde{j} - 1 + k - l, \{0,1\}^{3-l} \times \{1\} \times \{0\}^l) & \text{w.p. } \epsilon_0^{k+1}\epsilon_1(1-\epsilon_1)^{l-(k+1)} r \text{ for } l \in \{1,2\} \text{ and } 0 \le k \le l-1; \\ (\tilde{j} - 1, \{0,1\}^{3-l} \times \{1\} \times \{0\}^l) & \text{w.p. } (1-\epsilon_0)\epsilon_0^l r \text{ for } l \in \{0,1,2\}; \\ (\tilde{j} - 1 + k - l, \{0,1\}^{3-l} \times \{1\} \times \{0\}^l) & \text{w.p. } (\epsilon_0+\epsilon_1)^{k-(l+1)}\epsilon_1\epsilon_0^l r \text{ for } l \in \{0,1,2\} \text{ and } l+1 \le k \le 3; \\ (\tilde{j} + 2 + k, (0,0,0,0)) & \text{w.p. } (\epsilon_0+\epsilon_1)^k \epsilon_0^4 r \text{ for } k \in \mathbb{N}; \\ (\tilde{j} + 2 + k, (1,0,0,0)) & \text{w.p. } (\epsilon_0+\epsilon_1)^k \epsilon_1\epsilon_0^3 r \text{ for } k \in \mathbb{N}; \\ (\tilde{j} + 3 + k - l, \{0,1\}^{3-l} \times \{1\} \times \{0\}^l) & \text{w.p. } (\epsilon_0+\epsilon_1)^{3+k-l}\epsilon_1\epsilon_0^l r \text{ for } l \in \{0,1,2\} \text{ and } k \in \mathbb{N}; \end{cases} \tag{13}$$

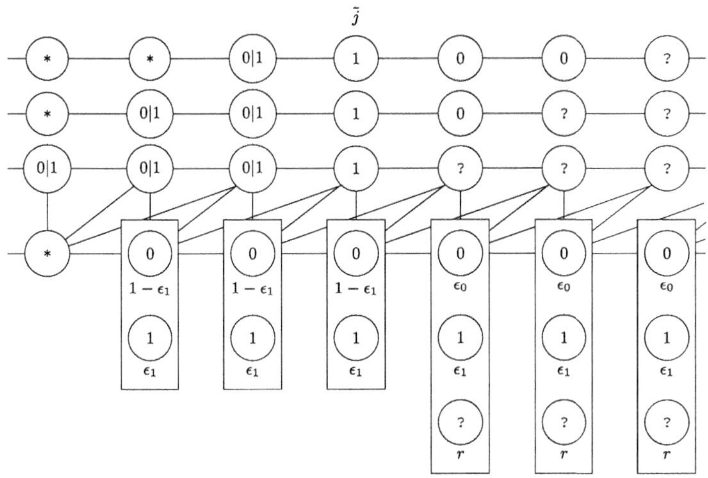

Fig. 6. Transition probabilities of the different cells when the state f of the boundary belongs to S_1. Precisely, the first line corresponds to $f \in \{(0,1,0,0),(1,1,0,0)\}$, the second line to $f \in \{0,1\}^2 \times \{1\} \times \{0\}$, and the third line to $f \in \{0,1\}^3 \times \{1\}$. The boundary position j depends on the case, but the modified boundary $\tilde{j}$ is always the same.

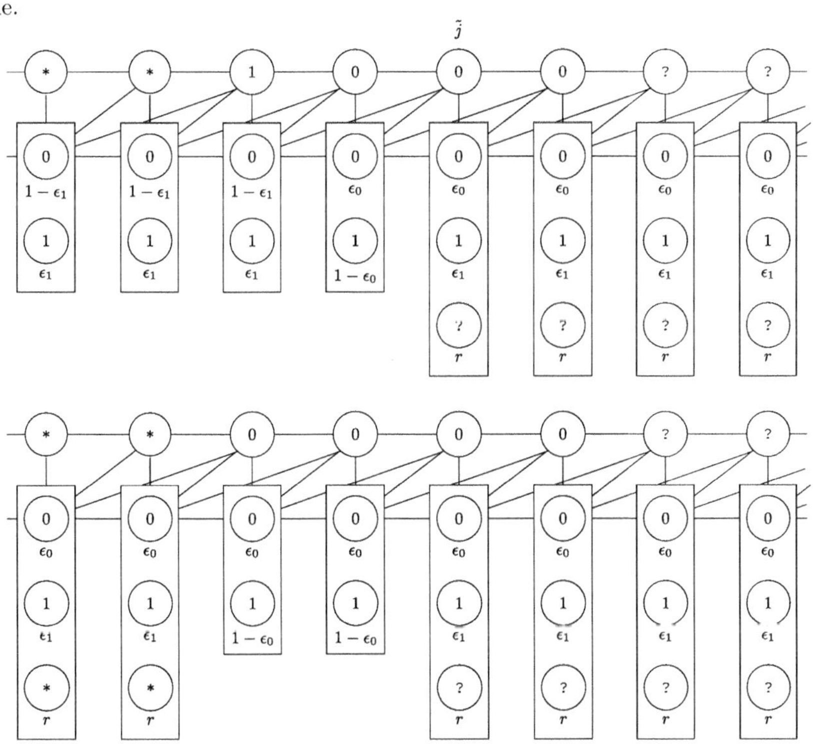

Fig. 7. Transition probabilities when the boundary is in state $(1,0,0,0)$, resp. $(0,0,0,0)$ and $\tilde{j}$ the position of the modified boundary.

We obtain then the following formula for the mean increment in two time steps when $f_t = (1, 0, 0, 0)$:

$$\begin{aligned}
&\mathbb{E}\left[\tilde{J}_t + \tilde{J}_{t+1} | f_t = (1,0,0,0)\right] \\
=&\mathbb{E}\left[\tilde{J}_t | f_t = (1,0,0,0)\right] + \mathbb{P}\left(f_{t+1} \in S_1 | f_t = (1,0,0,0)\right) \mathbb{E}\left[\tilde{J}_{t+1} | f_{t+1} \in S_1\right] \\
&+ \mathbb{P}\left(f_{t+1} = (1,0,0,0) | f_t = (1,0,0,0)\right) \mathbb{E}\left[\tilde{J}_{t+1} | f_{t+1} = (1,0,0,0)\right] \\
&+ \mathbb{P}\left(f_{t+1} = (0,0,0,0) | f_t = (1,0,0,0)\right) \mathbb{E}\left[\tilde{J}_{t+1} | f_{t+1} = (0,0,0,0)\right] \qquad (14)
\end{aligned}$$

From Eqs. (12) and (13), we have computed or we can compute all the previous terms except $\mathbb{E}\left[\tilde{J}_{t+1} | f_{t+1} = (0,0,0,0)\right]$. In particular, with the help of a computer algebra system, one finds

$$\mathbb{E}\left[\tilde{J}_t | f_t = (1,0,0,0)\right] = -1 - \epsilon_0 + \epsilon_1 + \epsilon_0^2 + \epsilon_1^2 + 2\epsilon_0\epsilon_1 + 2\epsilon_0^3 + 2\epsilon_0\epsilon_1^2 - \epsilon_0^4 - \epsilon_0\epsilon_1^3 + \frac{(1-r)^3}{r}. \quad (15)$$

For the missing term, we have to look at the transitions when $f_t = (0, 0, 0, 0)$.

Case f_t= (0, 0, 0, 0): If $\tilde{j}_t = j$ and $f_t = (0, 0, 0, 0)$, then

$$(\tilde{j}_{t+1}, f_{t+1}) = \begin{cases}
(\geq \tilde{j} - 3, (1, *, 0, 0)) & \text{w.p. } \epsilon_1 r \epsilon_0^2 r; \\
(\geq \tilde{j} - 3, \{0, *\} \times \{*\} \times \{0\}^2) & \text{w.p. } (1-\epsilon_1) r \epsilon_0^2 r; \\
(\tilde{j} - 2 + k, (*, 0, 0, 0)) & \text{w.p. } r\epsilon_0^3 r \text{ for } k \in \{0,1\}; \\
(\tilde{j} - 3, \{0, 1, *\} \times \{1\} \times \{0\}^2) & \text{w.p. } \epsilon_1 \epsilon_0^2 r; \\
(\tilde{j} - 2, \{0, 1, *\} \times \{1\} \times \{0\}^2) & \text{w.p. } (1-\epsilon_0)\epsilon_0^2 r; \\
(\tilde{j} - 2 + k, (0, 0, 0, 0)) & \text{w.p. } \epsilon_0^4 r \text{ for } k \in \{0,1,2,3\}; \\
(\tilde{j} - 2 + k, (1, 0, 0, 0)) & \text{w.p. } \epsilon_1 \epsilon_0^3 r \text{ for } k \in \{0,1\}; \\
(\tilde{j} - 2 + k, (1, 0, 0, 0)) & \text{w.p. } (1-\epsilon_0)\epsilon_0^3 r \text{ for } k \in \{2,3\}; \\
(\tilde{j} - 1, \{0, 1, *\}^2 \times \{0,1\} \times \{1\}) & \text{w.p. } (1-\epsilon_0) r; \\
(\tilde{j}, \{0, 1, *\} \times \{0,1\}^2 \times \{1\}) & \text{w.p. } \epsilon_1 r; \\
(\tilde{j} - 2, \{0, 1, *\}^2 \times \{1\} \times \{0\}) & \text{w.p. } (1-\epsilon_0)\epsilon_0 r; \\
(\tilde{j} - 1, \{0, 1, *\} \times \{0,1\} \times \{1\} \times \{0\}) & \text{w.p. } (1-\epsilon_0)\epsilon_0 r; \\
(\tilde{j} + 1 + k, \{0, 1\}^3 \times \{1\}) & \text{w.p. } (\epsilon_0 + \epsilon_1)^{k+1} \epsilon_1 r \text{ for } k \in \{0,1\}; \\
(\tilde{j} + k, \{0, 1\}^2 \times \{1\} \times \{0\}) & \text{w.p. } (\epsilon_0 + \epsilon_1)^{k} \epsilon_1 \epsilon_0 r \text{ for } k \in \{0,1\}; \\
(\tilde{j} - 1, \{0, 1\} \times \{1\} \times \{0\}^2) & \text{w.p. } (1-\epsilon_0)\epsilon_0^2 r \\
(\tilde{j}, \{0, 1\} \times \{1\} \times \{0\}^2) & \text{w.p. } \epsilon_1 \epsilon_0^2 r; \\
(\tilde{j} + 2 + k, (0, 0, 0, 0)) & \text{w.p. } (\epsilon_0 + \epsilon_1)^{k} \epsilon_0^4 r \text{ for } k \in \mathbb{N}; \\
(\tilde{j} + 2 + k, (1, 0, 0, 0)) & \text{w.p. } (\epsilon_0 + \epsilon_1)^{k} \epsilon_1 \epsilon_0^3 r \text{ for } k \in \mathbb{N}; \\
(\tilde{j} + 3 - l + k, \{0, 1\}^{4-l} \times \{1\} \times \{0\}^l) & \text{w.p. } (\epsilon_0 + \epsilon_1)^{k+3-l} \epsilon_1 \epsilon_0^l r \text{ for } l \in \{0,1,2\} \text{ and } k \in \mathbb{N}.
\end{cases} \quad (16)$$

This allows to find, with the help of a computer algebra system, the following lower bound, denoted by I_0, for $\mathbb{E}\left[\tilde{J}_t|f_t=(0,0,0,0)\right]$:

$$\begin{aligned}&\mathbb{E}\left[\tilde{J}_t|f_t=(0,0,0,0)\right]\\&\geq -1-\epsilon_0+\epsilon_1-\epsilon_0^2+\epsilon_1^2+3\epsilon_0\epsilon_1+6\epsilon_0^3+2\epsilon_0^2\epsilon_1-3\epsilon_0^4-3\epsilon_0^3\epsilon_1+\frac{(1-r)^3}{r}=I_0.\end{aligned} \tag{17}$$

Unfortunately, the lower bound I_0 is not greater than -1 for any ϵ_0 and ϵ_1.

Back to the Lower Bound of $\mathbb{E}\left[\tilde{J}\right]_t+\tilde{J}_{t+1}|f_{t=(1,0,0,0)}$. By putting the lower bound I_0 in the Eq. (14), see Appendix 6.2 for details, we find that

$$\mathbb{E}\left[\tilde{J}_t+\tilde{J}_{t+1}|f_t=(1,0,0,0)\right]>-2. \tag{18}$$

To conclude the proof, we now prove that the same inequality holds for $f_t=(0,0,0,0)$.

Lower Bound of $\mathbb{E}\left[\tilde{J}\right]_t+\tilde{J}_{t+1}|f_{t=(0,0,0,0)}$. Using Eq. (16), we obtain

$$\begin{aligned}&\mathbb{E}\left[\tilde{J}_t+\tilde{J}_{t+1}|f_t=(0,0,0,0)\right]\\=&\mathbb{E}\left[\tilde{J}_t|f_t=(0,0,0,0)\right]+\epsilon_1\epsilon_0^2r^2\mathbb{E}\left[\tilde{J}_{t+1}|f_{t+1}=(1,*,0,0)\right]\\&+\dots+\left(\sum_{l=0}^{2}\sum_{k=0}^{\infty}(1-r)^{k+3-l}\epsilon_0^l\epsilon_1\epsilon_0^l r\right)\mathbb{E}\left[\tilde{J}_{t+1}|f_{t+1}\in S_1\right].\end{aligned}$$

Finally, there are three terms that are not known and that we have to bound by below. For shortness, we denote by E^* the set $\{0,*\}\times\{*\}\times\{0\}^2$. By considering all the possible types of boundary in each subset, similarly as in Eq. (9), we obtain

$$\begin{aligned}&\mathbb{E}\left[\tilde{J}_t|f_t=(*,0,0,0)\right]\geq\min\left(\mathbb{E}\left[\tilde{J}_t|f_t=(0,0,0,0)\right],\mathbb{E}\left[\tilde{J}_t|f_t=(1,0,0,0)\right]\right);\\&\mathbb{E}\left[\tilde{J}_t|f_t=(1,*,0,0)\right]\geq\min\left(\mathbb{E}\left[\tilde{J}_t|f_t=(1,0,0,0)\right],\mathbb{E}\left[\tilde{J}_t|f_t\in S_1\right]\right);\\&\mathbb{E}\left[\tilde{J}_t|f_t\in E^*\right]\geq\min\left(\mathbb{E}\left[\tilde{J}_t|f_t=(0,0,0,0)\right],\mathbb{E}\left[\tilde{J}_t|f_t=(1,0,0,0)\right],\mathbb{E}\left[\tilde{J}_t|f_t\in S_1\right]\right).\end{aligned}$$

For any $(\epsilon_0,\epsilon_1)\in[0,\frac{1}{2}]^2$, we have, see Appendices 6.3 and 6.4, the two following inequalities:

$$\mathbb{E}\left[\tilde{J}_t|f_t\in S_1\right]\geq I_0 \text{ and } \mathbb{E}\left[\tilde{J}_t|f_t\in S_1\right]\geq\mathbb{E}\left[\tilde{J}_t|f_t=(1,0,0,0)\right].$$

Hence,

$$\begin{aligned}&\mathbb{E}\left[\tilde{J}_t|f_t=(*,0,0,0)\right]\geq\min\left(I_0,\mathbb{E}\left[\tilde{J}_t|f_t=(1,0,0,0)\right]\right);\\&\mathbb{E}\left[\tilde{J}_t|f_t=(1,*,0,0)\right]\geq\mathbb{E}\left[\tilde{J}_t|f_t=(1,0,0,0)\right];\\&\mathbb{E}\left[\tilde{J}_t|f_t\in E^*\right]\geq\min\left(I_0,\mathbb{E}\left[\tilde{J}_t|f_t=(1,0,0,0)\right]\right).\end{aligned}$$

Finally, we get

$$\begin{aligned}
&\mathbb{E}\left[\tilde{J}_t + \tilde{J}_{t+1} | f_t = (0,0,0,0)\right] \\
&\geq I_0 + \mathbb{P}\left(f_{t+1} = (0,0,0,0) | f_t = (0,0,0,0)\right) I_0 \\
&+ \mathbb{P}\left(f_{t+1} \in S_1 | f_t = (0,0,0,0)\right) \mathbb{E}\left[\tilde{J}_{t+1} | f_{t+1} \in S_1\right] \\
&+ \mathbb{P}\left(f_{t+1} \in \{(1,0,0,0),(1,*,0,0)\} | f_t = (0,0,0,0)\right) \mathbb{E}\left[\tilde{J}_{t+1} | f_{t+1} = (1,0,0,0)\right] \\
&+ \mathbb{P}\left(f_{t+1} = (*,0,0,0) \cup E^* | f_t = (0,0,0,0)\right) \min\left(I_0, \mathbb{E}\left[\tilde{J}_{t+1} | f_{t+1} = (1,0,0,0)\right]\right)
\end{aligned} \tag{19}$$

The value of $\min\left(I_0, \mathbb{E}\left[\tilde{J}_{t+1} | f_{t+1} = (1,0,0,0)\right]\right)$ can be the left or the right term, depending on the values of ϵ_0 and ϵ_1. Nevertheless, in Appendix 6.5, we prove that in both cases it is greater than -2, and so

$$\mathbb{E}\left[\tilde{J}_t + \tilde{J}_{t+1} | f_t = (0,0,0,0)\right] > -2. \tag{20}$$

Combined with Eqs. (12) and (18), it implies Eq. (2) when $n = 3$, and so Theorem 1 for $n = 3$.

5 Perspectives

We have proved the desired result for $n = 2$ and $n = 3$, by examining the behaviour of the boundaries of decorrelated islands. The ergodicity of the hard-core PCA for $n \geq 4$ is still an open question. Our method could be used to handle the case of larger values of n, but the computations are becoming increasingly complex with the size of the neighbourhood, so that the $n = 4$ case is already difficult to tackle. However, one can ask whether there could be an automated way of handling larger neighbourhoods, and perhaps also other classes of PCA.

Concerning specifically the hard-core PCA, it seems that for fixed ϵ_0, the mean increment in 1 (and 2) time step(s) is an increasing function in ϵ_1. If this is indeed the case, it could simplify the analysis.

6 Appendices

6.1 Lower Bound of $\mathbb{E}\left[\tilde{J}_t + \tilde{J}_{t+1} | f_t = (0,0)\right]$ for $n = 2$

By Eq. (7), Inequalities (8) and (9), and Equality (5), we obtain the following lower bound:

$$\begin{aligned}
&\mathbb{E}\left[\tilde{J}_t + \tilde{J}_{t+1} | f_t = (0,0)\right] \geq (1 + \epsilon_0 r^2 + 2\epsilon_0^2 r + \epsilon_0^2)\left(-\frac{1}{2}r^2 - 2\epsilon_0 r + \epsilon_0^2 r + \frac{1}{2}\epsilon_1^2 + \frac{(1-r)^2}{r}\right) \\
&+ (1 - \epsilon_0 r^2 - 2\epsilon_0^2 r - \epsilon_0^2)\left(-\frac{1}{2}r + \epsilon_1 r + \frac{1}{2}\epsilon_0(1-\epsilon_1)r + \frac{1}{2}\epsilon_1^2 r + \frac{1}{2}(1-r)^2 + \frac{1}{2}\epsilon_1^2 + \frac{(1-r)^2}{r}\right).
\end{aligned}$$

Using a computer algebra system, we find the following polynomial expression in ϵ_0 and ϵ_1:

$$\mathbb{E}\left[\tilde{J}_t + \tilde{J}_{t+1}|f_t = (0,0)\right] \geq -1 + 2\frac{(1-r)^2}{r}$$
$$+ \underbrace{\epsilon_0^6 + \frac{3}{2}\epsilon_0^5\epsilon_1}_{\geq 0} + \underbrace{\frac{7}{2}\epsilon_0^4}_{(1)} + \underbrace{6\epsilon_0^3\epsilon_1^2}_{(2)} + \underbrace{\frac{5}{2}\epsilon_0^2\epsilon_1^3}_{\geq 0} + \underbrace{4\epsilon_0^2\epsilon_1}_{(3)} + \underbrace{\frac{3}{2}\epsilon_0^2}_{(4)} + \underbrace{\frac{1}{2}\epsilon_0\epsilon_1^5}_{\geq 0} + \underbrace{\epsilon_0\epsilon_1^3 + \epsilon_0\epsilon_1^2}_{(5)} + \underbrace{\frac{5}{2}\epsilon_1}_{(6)}$$
$$- \left(\underbrace{\frac{7}{2}\epsilon_0^5}_{(1)} + \underbrace{\epsilon_0^4\epsilon_1^2}_{(2)} + \underbrace{\frac{3}{2}\epsilon_0^4\epsilon_1}_{(6)} + \underbrace{2\epsilon_0^3\epsilon_1^3}_{(2)} + \underbrace{4\epsilon_0^3\epsilon_1}_{(3)} + \underbrace{\frac{3}{2}\epsilon_0^3}_{(4)} + \frac{13}{2}\epsilon_0^2\epsilon_1^2 + \underbrace{\frac{3}{2}\epsilon_0\epsilon_1^4}_{(5)} + \underbrace{\frac{1}{2}\epsilon_0\epsilon_1}_{(6)} \right).$$

Now, we regroup terms of the form $c\epsilon_0^{\alpha_0}\epsilon_1^{\alpha_1}$ with terms of the form $-c\epsilon_0^{\beta_0}\epsilon_1^{\beta_1}$, with $\alpha_0 \leq \alpha_1$ and $\beta_0 \leq \beta_1$, in such a way that their sums are

$$c\epsilon_0^{\alpha_0}\epsilon_1^{\alpha_1}(1 - \epsilon_0^{\beta_0-\alpha_0}\epsilon_1^{\beta_1-\alpha_1}) \geq 0$$

for any $\epsilon_0, \epsilon_1 \in [0,1]$.

We then obtain

$$\mathbb{E}\left[\tilde{J}_t + \tilde{J}_{t+1}|f_t = (0,0)\right] \geq -1 + 2\frac{(1-r)^2}{r} - \frac{13}{2}\epsilon_0^2\epsilon_1^2$$
$$+ \underbrace{(6-1-2)\epsilon_0^3\epsilon_1^2}_{(2)} + \underbrace{\left(1 - \frac{1}{2}\right)\epsilon_0\epsilon_1^2}_{(5)} + \underbrace{\left(\frac{5}{2} - \frac{3}{2} - \frac{1}{2}\right)\epsilon_1}_{(6)}.$$

To conclude, remark that

$$\begin{aligned} 2\frac{(1-r)^2}{r} &= 2(1-r)^2 + 2\frac{(1-r)^3}{r} \\ &\geq 2(\epsilon_0 + \epsilon_1)^2 = 2\epsilon_0^2 + 4\epsilon_0\epsilon_1 + 2\epsilon_1^2. \end{aligned}$$

This is enough to compensate the last negative term $-\frac{13}{2}\epsilon_0^2\epsilon_1^2$.

6.2 Lower Bound of $\mathbb{E}\left[\tilde{J}_t + \tilde{J}_{t+1}|f_t = (1,0,0,0)\right]$ for $n = 3$

By Eqs. (14), (13), (12), (15) and (17), we obtain the following lower bound:

$$\begin{aligned} &\mathbb{E}\left[\tilde{J}_t + \tilde{J}_{t+1}|f_t = (1,0,0,0)\right] \\ &\geq \mathbb{E}\left[\tilde{J}_t|f_t = (1,0,0,0)\right] + \mathbb{P}\left(f_{t+1} \in S_1|f_t = (1,0,0,0)\right)\mathbb{E}\left[\tilde{J}_{t+1}|f_{t+1} \in S_1\right] \\ &+ \mathbb{P}\left(f_{t+1} = (1,0,0,0)|f_t = (1,0,0,0)\right)\mathbb{E}\left[\tilde{J}_{t+1}|f_{t+1} = (1,0,0,0)\right] \\ &+ \mathbb{P}\left(f_{t+1} = (0,0,0,0)|f_t = (1,0,0,0)\right) I_0. \end{aligned}$$

Now, replacing the value in ϵ_0 and ϵ_1 according to (13), (12), (15) and (17), and with the help of a computer algebra system, we obtain

$$\begin{aligned}
&\mathbb{E}\left[\tilde{J}_t + \tilde{J}_{t+1} | f_t = (1,0,0,0)\right] \geq -2 + 2\frac{(1-r)^3}{r} \\
&+ 3\epsilon_1 + \underbrace{4\epsilon_1^2}_{(1)} + \epsilon_1^4 + 2\epsilon_0\epsilon_1 + 3\epsilon_0\epsilon_1^2 + 5\epsilon_0\epsilon_1^3 + \underbrace{14\epsilon_0\epsilon_1^5}_{(2)} + \epsilon_0\epsilon_1^7 + 7\epsilon_0^2\epsilon_1 + \underbrace{13\epsilon_0^2\epsilon_1^3}_{(3)} \\
&+ 10\epsilon_0^2\epsilon_1^5 + \epsilon_0^2\epsilon_1^7 + 11\epsilon_0^3\epsilon_1 + \underbrace{26\epsilon_0^3\epsilon_1^3}_{(4)} + 2\epsilon_0^3\epsilon_1^5 + \underbrace{3\epsilon_0^4}_{(5)+(6)} + \underbrace{49\epsilon_0^4\epsilon_1^2}_{(7)} + 18\epsilon_0^4\epsilon_1^4 \\
&+ 12\epsilon_0^5\epsilon_1 + 11\epsilon_0^5\epsilon_1^3 + 2\epsilon_0^6\epsilon_1^2 + \underbrace{3\epsilon_0^7}_{(6)} + 3\epsilon_0^8\epsilon_1 + 2\epsilon_0^9 \\
&- \big(\underbrace{3\epsilon_1^3}_{(1)} + 15\epsilon_0\epsilon_1^4 + \underbrace{6\epsilon_0\epsilon_1^6}_{(2)} + 13\epsilon_0^2\epsilon_1^2 + \underbrace{12\epsilon_0^2\epsilon_1^4}_{(3)} + \underbrace{5\epsilon_0^2\epsilon_1^6}_{(2)} + 25\epsilon_0^3\epsilon_1^2 + \underbrace{12\epsilon_0^3\epsilon_1^4}_{(4)} + 24\epsilon_0^4\epsilon_1 \\
&+ \underbrace{43\epsilon_0^4\epsilon_1^3}_{(7)} + \underbrace{3\epsilon_0^4\epsilon_1^5}_{(4)} + \underbrace{\epsilon_0^5}_{(5)} + 19\epsilon_0^5\epsilon_1^2 + \underbrace{2\epsilon_0^5\epsilon_1^4}_{(5)} + \epsilon_0^6\epsilon_1 + \epsilon_0^6\epsilon_1^3 + 4\epsilon_0^7\epsilon_1 + \underbrace{5\epsilon_0^8}_{(6)}\big)
\end{aligned}$$

As in Appendix 6.1, we regroup terms of the form $c\epsilon_0^{\alpha_0}\epsilon_1^{\alpha_1}$ with terms of the form $-c\epsilon_0^{\beta_0}\epsilon_1^{\beta_1}$, with $\alpha_0 \leq \alpha_1$ and $\beta_0 \leq \beta_1$. The last negative terms are then compensated by terms in

$$\frac{(1-r)^3}{r} = (\epsilon_0 + \epsilon_1)^3 + \cdots + (\epsilon_0 + \epsilon_1)^8 + \frac{(1-r)^9}{r}.$$

Thus, $\mathbb{E}\left[\tilde{J}_t + \tilde{J}_{t+1} | f_t = (1,0,0,0)\right] > -2$.

6.3 Proof that $\mathbb{E}\left[\tilde{J}_t | f_t \in S_1\right] \geq I_0$ for $n = 3$

Equations (12) and (17) give that

$$\begin{aligned}
&\mathbb{E}\left[\tilde{J}_t | f_t \in S_1\right] - I_0 \\
=&\epsilon_0 + 2\epsilon_1 + \epsilon_0^2 + 3\epsilon_1^2 - 3\epsilon_1^3 + \epsilon_0\epsilon_1 - \epsilon_0^2\epsilon_1 + \epsilon_1^4 + \epsilon_0^3\epsilon_1 \\
&- \left(-\epsilon_0 + \epsilon_1 - \epsilon_0^2 + \epsilon_1^2 + 3\epsilon_0\epsilon_1 + 6\epsilon_0^3 + 2\epsilon_0^2\epsilon_1 - 3\epsilon_0^4 - 3\epsilon_0^3\epsilon_1\right) \\
=&2\epsilon_0 + \epsilon_1 + \underbrace{2\epsilon_0^2 + 2\epsilon_1^2} + \epsilon_1^4 + 4\epsilon_0^3\epsilon_1 + 3\epsilon_0^4 - (3\epsilon_1^3 + \underbrace{2\epsilon_0\epsilon_1} + 3\epsilon_0^2\epsilon_1 + 6\epsilon_0^3)
\end{aligned}$$

We use a remarkable identity to bound by below the underbraced terms. For the others negative terms, we use the fact that $0 \leq \epsilon_0, \epsilon_1 \leq 1/2$. Hence,

$$3\epsilon_1^3 \leq 3\left(\frac{1}{2}\right)^2 \epsilon_1, \; 3\epsilon_0^2\epsilon_1 \leq \frac{3}{4}\epsilon_0, \text{ and } 6\epsilon_0^3 = 4\epsilon_0^3 + 2\epsilon_0^3 \leq \epsilon_0 + \epsilon_0^2.$$

$$\begin{aligned}
&\mathbb{E}\left[\tilde{J}_t | f_t \in S_1\right] - I_0 \\
&\geq 2\epsilon_0 + \epsilon_1 + \underbrace{\epsilon_0^2 + \epsilon_1^2 + (\epsilon_0 - \epsilon_1)^2}_{} + \epsilon_1^4 + 4\epsilon_0^3\epsilon_1 + 3\epsilon_0^4 - \left(\frac{3}{4}\epsilon_1 + \frac{3}{4}\epsilon_0 + \epsilon_0 + \epsilon_0^2\right) \\
&= \frac{1}{4}\epsilon_0 + \frac{1}{4}\epsilon_1 + \epsilon_1^2 + (\epsilon_0 - \epsilon_1)^2 + \epsilon_1^4 + 4\epsilon_0^3\epsilon_1 + 3\epsilon_0^4 > 0.
\end{aligned}$$

6.4 Proof that $\mathbb{E}\left[\tilde{J}_t | f_t \in S_1\right] \geq \mathbb{E}\left[\tilde{J}_t | f_t = (1,0,0,0)\right]$ for $n = 3$

Equations (12) and (15) give that

$$\begin{aligned}
&\mathbb{E}\left[\tilde{J}_t | f_t \in S_1\right] - \mathbb{E}\left[\tilde{J}_t | f_t = (1,0,0,0)\right] \\
=&\epsilon_0 + 2\epsilon_1 + \epsilon_0^2 + 3\epsilon_1^2 - 3\epsilon_1^3 + \epsilon_0\epsilon_1 - \epsilon_0^2\epsilon_1 + \epsilon_1^4 + \epsilon_0^3\epsilon_1 \\
&- (-\epsilon_0 + \epsilon_1 + \epsilon_0^2 + \epsilon_1^2 + 2\epsilon_0\epsilon_1 + 2\epsilon_0^3 + 2\epsilon_0\epsilon_1^2 - \epsilon_0^4 - \epsilon_0\epsilon_1^3) \\
=&2\epsilon_0 + \epsilon_1 + 2\epsilon_1^2 + \epsilon_1^4 + \epsilon_0^3\epsilon_1 + \epsilon_0^4 + \epsilon_0\epsilon_1^3 \\
&- (3\epsilon_1^3 + \epsilon_0\epsilon_1 + \epsilon_0^2\epsilon_1 + 2\epsilon_0^3 + 2\epsilon_0\epsilon_1^2).
\end{aligned}$$

As in Appendix 6.3, the fact that $0 \leq \epsilon_0, \epsilon_1 \leq 1/2$ allows us to bound by below the negative terms.

$$\begin{aligned}
&\mathbb{E}\left[\tilde{J}_t | f_t \in S_1\right] - \mathbb{E}\left[\tilde{J}_t | f_t = (1,0,0,0)\right] \\
&\geq 2\epsilon_0 + \epsilon_1 + 2\epsilon_1^2 + \epsilon_1^4 + \epsilon_0^3\epsilon_1 + \epsilon_0^4 + \epsilon_0\epsilon_1^3 - \left(\frac{3}{4}\epsilon_1 + \frac{1}{2}\epsilon_0 + \frac{1}{4}\epsilon_1 + \frac{1}{2}\epsilon_0 + \frac{1}{2}\epsilon_0\right) \\
&= \frac{1}{2}\epsilon_0 + 2\epsilon_1^2 + \epsilon_1^4 + \epsilon_0^3\epsilon_1 + \epsilon_0^4 + \epsilon_0\epsilon_1^3 > 0.
\end{aligned}$$

6.5 Lower Bounds of $\mathbb{E}\left[\tilde{J}_t + \tilde{J}_{t+1} | f_t = (0,0,0,0)\right]$ for $n = 3$

When the Minimum is I_0: The lower bound of Eq. (19) becomes

$$\begin{aligned}
D_0 = I_0 &+ \mathbb{P}\left(f_{t+1} = (0,0,0,0) | f_t = (0,0,0,0)\right) I_0 \\
&+ \mathbb{P}\left(f_{t+1} \in S_1 | f_t = (0,0,0,0)\right) \mathbb{E}\left[\tilde{J}_{t+1} | f_{t+1} \in S_1\right] \\
&+ \mathbb{P}\left(f_{t+1} \in \{(1,0,0,0),(1,*,0,0)\} | f_t = (0,0,0,0)\right) \mathbb{E}\left[\tilde{J}_{t+1} | f_{t+1} = (1,0,0,0)\right] \\
&+ \mathbb{P}\left(f_{t+1} = (*,0,0,0) \cup E^* | f_t = (0,0,0,0)\right) I_0
\end{aligned}$$

Now, replace the terms of this equation by their values given in Eqs. (17), (12), (15) and deduced from Eq. (16). With the help of a computer algebra system, we obtain

$$
\begin{aligned}
D_0 &= -2 + 2\frac{(1-r)^3}{r} \\
&+ 3\epsilon_1 + 4\epsilon_1^2 + \epsilon_1^4 + 4\epsilon_0\epsilon_1 + 6\epsilon_0^2\epsilon_1^3 + 5\epsilon_0^2\epsilon_1^5 + 4\epsilon_0^3 + 2\epsilon_0^3\epsilon_1 + 14\epsilon_0^3\epsilon_1^3 + 5\epsilon_0^3\epsilon_1^5 + 15\epsilon_0^4\epsilon_1 \\
&+ \epsilon_0^4\epsilon_1^4 + 10\epsilon_0^5 + 15\epsilon_0^5\epsilon_1^2 + 2\epsilon_0^5\epsilon_1^4 + 6\epsilon_0^6\epsilon_1 + 6\epsilon_0^7 + 3\epsilon_0^7\epsilon_1^2 + 8\epsilon_0^8\epsilon_1 + 4\epsilon_0^9 \\
&- (3\epsilon_1^3 + 9\epsilon_0^2\epsilon_1^4 + \epsilon_0^2\epsilon_1^6 + 10\epsilon_0^3\epsilon_1^2 + 11\epsilon_0^3\epsilon_1^4 + \epsilon_0^3\epsilon_1^6 + 9\epsilon_0^4 + 7\epsilon_0^4\epsilon_1^2 + \epsilon_0^4\epsilon_1^3 + 18\epsilon_0^5\epsilon_1 \\
&+ 8\epsilon_0^5\epsilon_1^3 + 3\epsilon_0^6 + 4\epsilon_0^6\epsilon_1^2 + 11\epsilon_0^7\epsilon_1 + 10\epsilon_0^8)
\end{aligned}
$$

We conclude that it is greater than -2 as in Appendices 6.1 and 6.2, by grouping terms and developing $(1-r)^3/r$ as much as necessary.

This technique does not hold for the term in ϵ_0^4. Indeed, we obtain $6\epsilon_0^3 - 7\epsilon_0^4$ after that. To prove its positivity, we use the fact that $\epsilon_0 \leq 1/2$, and so $6\epsilon_0^3 - 7\epsilon_0^4 \geq (6 - 7/2)\epsilon_0^3 > 0$.

When the Minimum is $\mathbb{E}\left[\tilde{\boldsymbol{J}}\right]_{t+1} | \boldsymbol{f}_{t+1=(1,0,0,0)}$: The lower bound of Eq. (19) becomes

$$
\begin{aligned}
D_1 = I_0 &+ \mathbb{P}\left(f_{t+1} = (0,0,0,0) | f_t = (0,0,0,0)\right) I_0 \\
&+ \mathbb{P}\left(f_{t+1} \in S_1 | f_t = (0,0,0,0)\right) \mathbb{E}\left[\tilde{J}_{t+1} | f_{t+1} \in S_1\right] \\
&+ \mathbb{P}\left(f_{t+1} \in \{(1,0,0,0),(1,*,0,0)\} | f_t = (0,0,0,0)\right) \mathbb{E}\left[\tilde{J}_{t+1} | f_{t+1} = (1,0,0,0)\right] \\
&+ \mathbb{P}\left(f_{t+1} = (*,0,0,0) \cup E^* | f_t = (0,0,0,0)\right) \mathbb{E}\left[\tilde{J}_{t+1} | f_{t+1} = (1,0,0,0)\right]
\end{aligned}
$$

Now, replace the terms of this equation by their values given in Eqs. (17), (12), (15) and deduced from Eq. (16). With the help of a computer algebra system, we obtain

$$
\begin{aligned}
D_1 &= -2 + 2\frac{(1-r)^3}{r} \\
&+ 3\epsilon_1 + 4\epsilon_1^2 + \epsilon_1^4 + 4\epsilon_0\epsilon_1 + 6\epsilon_0^2\epsilon_1^3 + 5\epsilon_0^2\epsilon_1^5 + 4\epsilon_0^3 + \epsilon_0^3\epsilon_1 + 4\epsilon_0^3\epsilon_1^3 + 7\epsilon_0^4\epsilon_1 + 5\epsilon_0^4\epsilon_1^2 \\
&+ 3\epsilon_0^4\epsilon_1^4 + 6\epsilon_0^5 + 14\epsilon_0^5\epsilon_1^3 + 10\epsilon_0^6\epsilon_1 + 22\epsilon_0^7 + 12\epsilon_0^7\epsilon_1^2 + 20\epsilon_0^8\epsilon_1 + 8\epsilon_0^9 \\
&- (3\epsilon_1^3 + 9\epsilon_0^2\epsilon_1^4 + \epsilon_0^2\epsilon_1^6 + 5\epsilon_0^3\epsilon_1^2 + \epsilon_0^3\epsilon_1^4 + 7\epsilon_0^4 + 9\epsilon_0^4\epsilon_1^3 \\
&+ 15\epsilon_0^5\epsilon_1^2 + 4\epsilon_0^5\epsilon_1^4 + 7\epsilon_0^6 + 4\epsilon_0^6\epsilon_1^3 + 36\epsilon_0^7\epsilon_1 + 24\epsilon_0^8).
\end{aligned}
$$

We conclude that it is greater than -2 as in Appendices 6.1 and 6.2, by grouping terms and developing $(1-r)^3/r$ as much as necessary.

References

1. Bhasin, D., Karmakar, S., Podder, M., Roy, S.: On a class of PCA with size-3 neighborhood and their applications in percolation games. Electron. J. Probab. **28** (2023)

2. Bušić, A., Mairesse, J., Marcovici, I.: Probabilistic cellular automata, invariant measures, and perfect sampling. Adv. Appl. Probab. **45**(4), 960–980 (2013)
3. Casse, J.: Ergodicity of some probabilistic cellular automata with binary alphabet via random walks. Electron. J. Probab. **28**, 1–17 (2023)
4. Gács, P.: Reliable cellular automata with self-organization. J. Stat. Phys. **103**(1), 45–267 (2001)
5. Holroyd, A.E., Marcovici, I., Martin, J.B.: Percolation games, probabilistic cellular automata, and the hard-core model. Probab. Theor. Related Fields **174**(3–4), 1187–1217 (2019)
6. Mairesse, J., Marcovici, I.: Around probabilistic cellular automata. Theoret. Comput. Sci. **559**, 42–72 (2014)
7. Marcovici, I., Sablik, M., Taati, S.: Ergodicity of some classes of cellular automata subject to noise. Electron. J. Probab. **24** (2019)
8. Toom, A.L., Vasilyev, N.B., Stavskaya, O.N., Mityushin, L.G., Kuryumov, G.L., Pirogov, S.A.: Discrete local Markov systems. In: Dobrushin, R.L., Kryukov, V.I., Toom, A.L. (eds.) Stochastic Cellular Systems: Ergodicity, Memory, Morphogenesis. Manchester University Press (1990)

Author Index

Published by Springer Nature Switzerland AG 2026
S. Riva and A. Richard (Eds.): AUTOMATA 2025, LNCS 15831, p. 243, 2026.
https://doi.org/10.1007/978-3-032-01570-9

GPSR Compliance

The European Union's (EU) General Product Safety Regulation (GPSR) is a set of rules that requires consumer products to be safe and our obligations to ensure this.

If you have any concerns about our products, you can contact us on ProductSafety@springernature.com

In case Publisher is established outside the EU, the EU authorized representative is:

Springer Nature Customer Service Center GmbH
Europaplatz 3
69115 Heidelberg, Germany

Batch number: 09013048

Printed by Printforce, the Netherlands